THE WEALTH OF REFUGEES

THE WEALTH OF REFUGEES

HOW DISPLACED PEOPLE CAN BUILD ECONOMIES

ALEXANDER BETTS

OXFORD
UNIVERSITY PRESS

OXFORD

UNIVERSITY PRESS

Great Clarendon Street, Oxford, OX2 6DP,
United Kingdom

Oxford University Press is a department of the University of Oxford.
It furthers the University's objective of excellence in research, scholarship,
and education by publishing worldwide. Oxford is a registered trade mark of
Oxford University Press in the UK and in certain other countries

Published in the United States of America by Oxford University Press
198 Madison Avenue, New York, NY 10016, United States of America

British Library Cataloguing in Publication Data
Data available

Library of Congress Control Number: 2020943929

ISBN 978–0–19–887068–5

Printed and bound by
CPI Group (UK) Ltd, Croydon, CR0 4YY

In memory of Gil Loescher (1945–2020), who inspired me to believe that research can make a difference.

Acknowledgements

The title of this book borrows from Adam Smith's 1776 *The Wealth of Nations*, arguably the founding text of modern economics. It plays on the fact that throughout the intervening 250 years, economics has rarely considered the economic lives of some of those people who fall outside of the framework of the nation-state: refugees and other exiled populations.

Smith's treatise, like this book, was not just a work of economics. It was a political economy text, integrating reflections on ethics, economics, politics, and policy—the four main sections of this book. At its core, the *Wealth of Nations* posited a simple idea: that, generally, allowing people the autonomy to make their own choices and pursue their own interests leads to the best collective outcomes. And yet these ideas have seldom shaped refugee governance, a domain in which even basic socio-economic freedoms are frequently denied. At a more trivial level, my choice of title is intended to signal the book's focus on refugees' economic lives, to emphasize refugees' skills and capabilities, and to highlight the growing prevalence of displaced people around the world.

The numbers of displaced people and refugees are increasing due to a proliferation in the number of fragile states. And this problem is likely to be exacerbated by climate change and the economic legacy of coronavirus. The World Bank estimates that by 2050 some 140 million people may be displaced by climate change, and global economic recession threatens to amplify other drivers of displacement such as conflict and weak governance. And yet, rising populist nationalism is undermining the political willingness of rich and poor countries to admit migrants and refugees into their territories. Given these contradictory trends, I ask: how can we create sustainable refugee policies that can enable displaced people to live in safety and dignity, while still operating at scale?

My purpose in writing this book is to contribute towards practical solutions for refugees, and to do so based on social science research and evidence. In order to identify sustainable solutions, I focus predominantly on just three countries in East Africa: Ethiopia, Kenya, and Uganda. Between them, they host more refugees than the whole of the European Union. They have quite different approaches to refugees—Uganda lets them work, Kenya does not, and Ethiopia has gradually started to move towards giving refugees greater socio-economic freedoms. In different ways, though, all three countries have experimented with specific, innovative approaches to refugee assistance. They provide important lessons relevant for the rest of the world.

I examine these case studies through qualitative and quantitative research, and relate the findings to other refugee-hosting regions of the world in which I have also worked, including Latin America, the Middle East, and Europe. I explore four sets of questions. First, the ethics—what is right? Second, the economics—what works to achieve what is right? Third, the politics—how can we get governments to do the things that work and are right? Fourth, the policy—what specifically do governments and other actors need to do next?

The book's central argument is that, within this age of displacement, the key to sustainability lies in unlocking the potential contributions of refugees themselves. They bring skills, talents, and aspirations and can be a benefit rather than a burden to receiving societies. Realizing this potential relies upon moving beyond a purely humanitarian focus to fully include refugees in host-country economies, build economic opportunities in refugee-hosting regions, and navigate the ambiguous politics of refugee protection.

The scale of first-hand research involved in this book is vast, and I have not undertaken all of it alone. In particular, the work in Chapters 3–7 draws upon survey data collection that would have been impossible without the input of more than 200 refugee and host community research assistants, who worked with us across six main research sites in Ethiopia, Kenya, and Uganda. These chapters draw upon the analysis, guidance, and data collection of two senior researchers, Naohiko Omata and Olivier Sterck. They also relied upon the contribution of a number of research assistants and consultants, including Jordan Barnard, Raphael Bradenbrink, Imane Chaara, Antonia Delius, Eyoual Demeke, Leon Fryszer, Aregawi Gebremariam, Abis Getachew, Jonathan Greenland, Louise Guo, Helen Karanja, Jonas Kaufmann, Jana Kuhnt, Andonis Marden, Patrick Mutinda, Rashid Mwesigwa, Cory Rodgers, Jade Siu, Maria Flinder Stierna, and Clarissa Tumwine. Reflecting these contributons, Chapters 3–7 draw from work co-authored with several of these colleagues, originally published as part of the Refugee Economies

Programme policy papers series. Finally, that research also required significant coordination, for which I am grateful to Isabelle Aires and Madison Bakewell.

I am grateful to the UN Refugee Agency (UNHCR) for supporting my field research in Ethiopia, Kenya, and Uganda, including through the provision of transportation, accommodation, advice, and logistical support. I am especially appreciative of the contributions of Clementine Awu Nkweta-Salami, Raouf Mazou, Yonatan Araya, Tayyar Sukru Cansizoglu, Fathia Abdalla, Mohamed Shoman, Eva Lescrauwaet, Ann Encontre, Jaime Bourbon de Parme, Joel Boutroue, George Woode, Dejan Tanaskovic, Tapio Vahtola, Anna Korneeva, Christine Fu, and Ziad Ayoubi. At the World Food Programme (WFP), Zippy Mbati provided support for the Refugee Economies Programme's wider research in Kenya. I also thank the governments of Ethiopia, Kenya, and Uganda for granting me and my research teams permission to undertake first-hand research in cities and refugee camps within their countries.

A number of other people have facilitated research access in important ways. Heather Faulkner and Anna Haward were an invaluable source of guidance during my research in the UNHCR archives in Geneva. Felipe Muñoz and Vicente Echandia from the President's Office in Colombia, and John Patterson from the United States Agency for International Development (USAID) kindly invited me to Colombia to better understand the Venezuelan refugee crisis. The Forum of Young Global Leaders (YGLs) of the World Economic Forum (WEF) collaborated on two visits to Kakuma and Nairobi in 2018 and 2019, which provided useful access, and reflection space for some of the ideas in the book. I am grateful to Mariah Lavin, Mahmoud Jabari, Silje Ditlefsen, Adrian Monck, Ed Hough, and Peter Holmes à Court, as well as my fellow YGLs. Laura Hammond of the School of Oriental and African Studies (SOAS) convened a useful symposium in Addis Ababa for UKRI's Global Challenges Research Fund (GCRF) grantees, and generously shared contacts with policy-makers in Addis.

I am thankful to illustrator Sally Dunne for allowing me to use her award-winning sketch of the Kakuma refugee camps, as the basis for the front cover. Her illustration is part of a series entitled 'At Home in Kakuma Refugee Camp'. The image captures both the remoteness and vibrancy of the camps, a theme that is present throughout the book.

The research in this book would not have been possible without several research grants. The IKEA Foundation generously funded the research of the Refugee Economies Programme, which has informed Chapters 3–7. Within the Foundation, I am especially thankful to Per Heggenes, Annemieke De Jong, Annelies Withofs, Ly Nguyen, and Steven Chapman for their support. This research also benefited greatly from earlier support from Stephanie and Hunter Hunt, and the Danish Ministry of Foreign Affairs. The British Academy kindly awarded me a mid-career fellowship, which supported the research on which Chapters 8–11 are based. Research funded by an ESRC-AHRC (Economic and Social Research Council and Arts and Humanities Research Council) 'Global Challenges' grant contributed to some of the reflections on refugee-led organizations in Chapter 14. The research has also benefitted from the support of the WEF and WFP.

I am also grateful for the institutional support of the Refugee Studies Centre, Brasenose College, and the Department of International Development at the University of Oxford. And within Oxford numerous colleagues have supported research and writing for this book, whether directly or indirectly. They include John Bowers, Diego Ancochea-Sánchez, Graham Bray, Evan Easton-Calabria, Paul Collier, Cathryn Costello, Jeff Crisp, Stefan Dercon, Matthew Gibney, Andrew Hurrell, Kate Pincock, Eduardo Posada-Carbo, Isabel Ruiz, Carlos Vargas-Silva, and Sarah Whatmore. I am also grateful to my Oxford-based running buddies, who have talked over the work and kept me sane throughout the research process—Ed Brooks, Richard Burman, and Rahil Sachak-Patwa.

Beyond Oxford, I have benefited from the opportunity to present and receive feedback on sections of the book through a number of public lectures and invited presentations. I am especially glad to have had opportunities to give the Chr. Michelsen Annual Lecture in Bergen, the Ispahani-Bhutto Annual Lecture at La Verne University, the Fung Global Fellows opening lecture at Princeton University, and a keynote lecture as part of the 'Roots and Routes' series at the Kenan Institute for Global Ethics at Duke University. I thank Jeremy Adelman, Ian Lising, Ottar Maestad, and Suzanne Shanahan for these invitations, all of which led to valuable feedback. Other colleagues around the world who have shaped my thinking through their ideas and suggestions include Alex Aleinikoff, Emily Arnold-Fernandez, Sasha Chanoff, Helen Dempster, Elena Fiddian-Qasmiyeh, Robert Hakiza, Bob Keohane, Ulrike Krause, Lam Joar, Barbara Moser-Mercer, James Milner, and Emily Paddon Rhoads.

The bulk of the research and writing for the book took place before the coronavirus pandemic began in 2020. However, I have updated the book, notably through an additional chapter—Chapter 14. In that chapter, I make the case that the legacy of COVID-19 makes the book's research and argument even more urgent and relevant. I suggest that the economic recession created by COVID-19 will exacerbate the premise on which this book is built: that the world faces rising numbers of displaced people but declining political will to protect refugees, and that reconciling these conflicting imperatives depends upon recognizing and building upon the contribution of refugees themselves.

At Oxford University Press, I am grateful for the support, enthusiasm, and guidance of my editor, Dominic Byatt, and his colleague Olivia Wells.

Last but not least, this book would not have been possible without the love, support, and distraction of my wonderful family—Emily, Leo, Soxy, and Thea.

AB

October 2020, Oxford

Contents

List of figures and tables

Figures

Tables

Map of main research sites

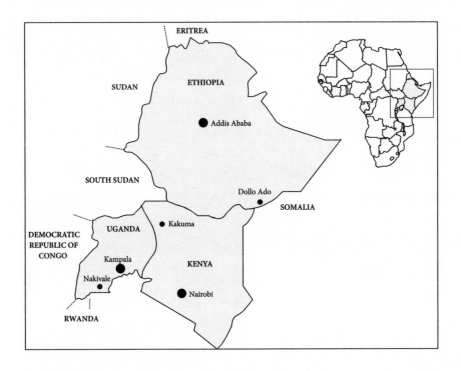

I

Introduction

Human displacement is one of the defining issues of the twenty-first century. Amid oppression, violence, and economic collapse, more people than ever are now forced to flee their homes. Most are quite literally running for their lives, abandoning villages and towns bombed, burned to the ground, or targeted by men with guns. For the first time in history, more than 80 million people are displaced, greater than 1 per cent of humanity.[1]

Most displaced people remain within their own country. But more than 25 million are refugees, compelled to leave their country in order to survive. From Syria to Venezuela, the main cause is governments that either attack their own people or fail to prevent other terrible things happening. Such governments are unwilling or unable to ensure the most basic conditions for a dignified life—a life that you or I would think worth living. Leaving behind familiar communities and cultures, refugees face an uncertain and sometimes unwelcoming response in the countries they reach. And the scale of the challenge will soon worsen as climate change makes vast areas of the planet uninhabitable, and exacerbates crisis and conflict.

Of course, the ideal solution would be to address the underlying causes. Ending wars, overthrowing authoritarian governments, and cutting greenhouse gas emissions would reduce displacement numbers. But the world has struggled to find solutions to these root causes, and the international community has proved deficient at replacing bad governments. Consequently, we are mostly left to address the human consequences of global insecurity; finding ways to temporarily accommodate or permanently integrate displaced people in other communities, and enabling them to live in dignity and with purpose.

This too is challenging because many receiving societies are reluctant to accept large numbers of refugees, and populist politicians in rich and poor countries often exploit public concerns for electoral gain. Rather than highlighting the contribution that refugees can make to receiving societies, or the moral obligation to host, politicians from the United States to Tanzania emphasize the threat to the economy, security, or identity. In this context, the question is: how can the world find ways to sustainably host growing numbers of refugees and displaced people?

This question matters for the rich world. In Europe, North America, and Australasia, upholding refugee rights is critical to maintaining liberal, democratic values.[2] To be regarded as liberal and legitimate, rich countries cannot simply turn their backs on people who flee for their lives. One important way to assist refugees is to allow them enter the country, either by letting them arrive spontaneously as asylum seekers, or through organized resettlement programmes.

Asylum and resettlement in the rich world have an indispensable role to play, but they are only ever likely to be for the minority of displaced people. The overwhelming majority of displaced people do not travel to rich countries. Although some refugees embark on long and dangerous journeys; most cross the nearest border to nearby camps and cities. The biggest challenge for refugee policy is how to create meaningful and dignified lives within these mainly poor countries that are close to warzones and tyranny.

This is a book about what works. And what can work. It aims to be practical, relevant, and solutions-oriented. Importantly, it is evidence-based. In a policy field—refugees and migration—in which narrative, claim, and counter-claim are often made without recourse to fact, this book uses a range of social science methods to explore the kinds of policies and practices that can actually provide sustainable sanctuary to refugees and other displaced populations. It does so mainly by learning from the experience of three countries in East Africa which, despite hosting more refugees than the whole of the European Union (EU) and more than five times as many as North America,[3] have each adopted innovative, and in some ways progressive, refugee policies aimed at mutually benefitting refugees and host-country citizens. The goal is not to romanticize these countries' experiences; they have been far from perfect. Nor is it to suggest they can simply be replicated elsewhere; context matters. Rather, the aim is to critically assess what has been effective, and under what conditions.

The search for sustainability

My starting point is three observations about trends in forced displacement and refugee movements, which are likely to endure, relating to geography, numbers, and politics.

First, contrary to popular belief, most refugees are not in Europe or North America. Some 85 per cent of the world's refugees are in low- and middle-income countries.[4] This is because such countries often neighbour crisis countries, and because they often have porous borders, meaning that the first country to which people flee is usually a neighbouring state. Most refugees do not have the means, aspiration, or freedom to travel further. They remain in camps or cities in the region they come from. And this may offer some advantages: sometimes a common language, a similar economy, and the ability to easily retain contact with the homeland. For example, Somalis fleeing to the so-called Somali region of southern Ethiopia are able to speak Somali with the host community, engage in similar income-generating activities as back home, and sometimes go back and forth to south-central Somalia to maintain farms or property.

However, both refugees in such countries and the low- and middle-income countries that host them frequently face significant challenges. Refugees are usually required to reside in camps, with restrictions on the right to work and their mobility. Their access to basic services such as education and healthcare may be inadequate. And, even close to home, they may face discrimination. It is unsurprising that a small, but probably growing,[5] number choose to move onwards in search of a better life. For the countries that host them, the inequitable distribution of refugees around the world means that it is the countries with the fewest resources that bear the greatest responsibility. Although refugees often make an economic contribution to the areas that host them and most host countries respect the right of refugees to remain on their territory, large numbers may also be perceived as a source of insecurity, economic competition, or environmental degradation. For decades, Tanzania, for example, has repeatedly argued that despite hosting hundreds of thousands of refugees, it has lacked adequate support from the international community, sometimes scaling back on refugee rights in protest.[6]

Second, numbers of forcibly displaced people and refugees are increasing, virtually year-on-year. The number of both displaced persons—including those displaced within their own country and across borders—and refugees, who represent a large proportion of that group, is higher than at any time since the Second World War. Most flee from chronically fragile or failed states, with over half of the world's recognized refugees from just Syria, South Sudan, and Afghanistan. But practically each year, the list of fragile, and hence refugee-producing, countries seems to expand. Venezuela and Yemen are among the countries that have recently gone from relative stability to societal collapse, and it will be many years before people can go home. Several factors underlie the trend in fragile states, but among them is the widening distribution of power in the international system, which is exacerbating big power rivalries between the United States, Russia, and China. These rivalries play out within small states of geo-strategic importance, and yet simultaneously paralyse the UN Security Council in its search for solutions. All the credible projections on the distribution of global power suggest that this trend is unlikely to abate unless China and the United States build a shared vision for responding to fragile states.

And a further trend is likely to further exacerbate displacement: climate change.[7] Anthropogenic climate change is an incontrovertible fact and it will affect many areas of social life, which in turn have implications for migration and displacement. In extreme cases, such as natural disasters, desertification, and sinking islands the effects on displacement will be direct. In other cases, the effect will be to amplify and exacerbate other sources of displacement such as food insecurity and conflict.[8] Where states are weak, climate change will have its greatest impact on displacement.[9] Already, we are seeing the effects on forced displacement. In the Northern Triangle of Central America, the surge in forced movement of people from rural communities in Honduras and Nicaragua to the US has been partly attributed to the effects of climate change on food security, and its interaction with weak governance.[10] Across the Sahel, resource competition attributable to climate change is exacerbating existing conflicts in ways that have led to displacement in Niger and the Central African Republic.[11] Although there is nothing inevitable about future forced displacement scenarios, current trends strongly suggest that numbers will grow, possibly significantly.

Third, the politics relating to refugees and migration is increasingly divisive. In Europe, North America, and Australasia, migration has steadily risen in its political salience to become one of the most important electoral issues.[12] In some countries and regions, it has become *the* most important political issue for voters. The so-called European refugee crisis of 2015–16 was opportunistically mobilized by populist politicians in a way that polarized societies, and ushered in electoral success for the far right.[13] In the absence of the crisis, and the way in which it was politically represented, it is arguable that Brexit in the UK,[14] as well as the rise of Alternative für Deutschland in Germany, would not have taken place.[15] In the US, the politics of immigration has shaped growing societal division and escalating xenophobia.[16] Across the Western world, immigration has become a scapegoat issue, serving as a proxy for other unrelated social problems such as the disappearance of labour-intensive manufacturing jobs and precarious financial markets.[17] Regardless of how disingenuous much of the political narrative has been, the political consensus in the rich world is for strict limits on mass migration.[18]

The politics is not much more auspicious in many parts of the Global South. Xenophobia and the politics of immigration are not simply rich-world phenomena. Some governments observed Europe's response to the refugee crisis and have mimicked the same restrictive policies towards refugees. In 2016, observing how Europe paid off Turkey to curtail the movement of Syrians across the Aegean Sea, Kenya threatened to immediately close the Dadaab refugee camps and expel all Somali refugees as a thinly veiled means to induce greater international support.[19] Only slightly less cynically, concern about refugee numbers has been a key part of election campaigns at both national and municipal levels from Colombia to Lebanon. Anti-immigration rhetoric has become a global vote-winner, and asylum for the displaced is caught up in the maelstrom. There is, however, one significant difference between the positions of high-income counties, on the one hand, and low- and middle-income countries, on the other, when it comes to refugees. Relatively rich countries are, at least, in a position to engage in responsibility-sharing with relatively poor countries that host refugees, in ways that may be mutually beneficial for the states, if not always for refugees themselves.

And, as we will discuss in Chapter 14, the global economic recession created by the COVID-19 pandemic will exacerbate each of these trends, increasing levels of displacement and creating the conditions in which xenophobia thrives.

Given these three starting observations about current and future trends, there is a need to identify approaches that can be sustainable. So, what does sustainability mean in the refugee context? I argue that it has three key elements.

First, for refugees, a sustainable response must deliver their basic needs and legal entitlements. In the language of refugee governance, it needs to deliver protection, assistance, and solutions. Protection implies access to all rights under refugee and human rights law, most notably the right not to be forcibly returned to a country in which there is a serious risk of harm. Assistance means access to basic services to ensure a guaranteed minimum standard of living. Solutions relate to ensuring long-term integration within a society, whether through return to the country of origin, or integration and naturalization in a new country.

Second, sustainability requires a model that can maintain political support at local, national, and international levels. In order to endure over time, and to avoid backlash, refugee policies need to be able to retain the backing of politicians, and to remain in power those politicians need to be able to retain the support of their electorates and constituencies. Political authorities in hosting regions, whether at municipal or provincial level, need to be able to credibly argue that the local host community benefits from the presence of refugees. National host governments need to be able to credibly argue that hosting refugees brings benefits that are in the national interest. And the wider world of donor governments needs to derive benefits that justify the allocation of scarce national resources towards supporting host countries in other parts of the world.

Third, a sustainable refugee model must be able to function at scale and endure over time. Given rising numbers, the growing number of chronically fragile and failed states in the world, and the spectre of climate change, the world needs to envisage models that can not only work for 25 million refugees today, but potentially also for significantly larger populations, perhaps even of 50 or 100 million people crossing borders because they cannot access the minimum conditions for living in safety and dignity. To deliver at scale, approaches will need to be as efficient as possible in terms of economic, social, and political costs.

Reconciling these competing criteria is one of the key global policy challenges of the twenty-first century. The goal of this book is to begin the search for models that can resolve the challenge of providing sustainable sanctuary.

The book is written from the tradition of political realism. My aim is for my research to be politically relevant. Of course, not all research on refugees and forced migration needs to be politically relevant, and critical perspectives that distance themselves from politics have an important role to play, not least in challenging power structures and questioning the way we think about the world.[20] My aim, though, is to engage policy-makers and practitioners. That does not mean that I am uncritical of dominant power structures, but that I am chiefly concerned with providing insights that are applicable to the contemporary world.[21]

Achieving relevance relies upon working from within a framework of political constraint, and being explicit about the assumptions that define those constraints. From an 'ideal-theory' perspective, one might hope that it is values that ultimately shape political decisions regarding refugees.[22] But my previous research and policy experience in the refugee field tells me that this is not always the case. And so, I work from a 'non-ideal theory' perspective, within which I regard national level politicians to be mainly concerned with preserving power and intergovernmental politics to be mainly shaped by the pursuit of interests and power. Of course, values and norms can and do play a role but their influence is mediated through political competition. When they are compatible with the interests of the powerful, they flourish; when they are not, they wither.[23]

This means that when I think about the refugee system, I am trying to find a model of sustainability that reconciles the moral obligation to ensure refugees' access to protection, assistance, and solutions, with the constraints of world politics. In that sense, my approach might be broadly characterized as 'migration realism'.[24]

Refugees and development

There is a growing consensus among policy-makers that the best way to achieve sustainability is to help refugees to help themselves. If refugees can be empowered to meet their basic needs independently of aid, and also contribute to the economy of the host society, this has the potential to benefit everyone. For refugees, it can support socio-economic inclusion and improve access to entitlements and opportunities. For host communities, it can allow them to share in the benefits of new job creation and the improvement of public services. For donor governments, it may provide a way to provide cost-effective refugee assistance at scale.

This idea is encapsulated in the concept of refugee 'self-reliance'—the notion that rather than having long-term dependence on humanitarian aid, refugees can instead be supported to gradually support themselves through external investment in the long-term economic development of the regions that host them. The UN Refugee Agency (UNHCR) defines self-reliance as 'the social and economic ability of an individual, a household, or a community to meet essential needs (including protection, food, water, shelter, personal safety, health, and education) in a sustainable manner and with dignity'.[25]

Self-reliance is often seen as closely related to the idea of moving 'from relief to development' or 'bridging the humanitarian-development gap'. The long-standing default model of closed refugee camps,[26] providing refugees with indefinite access to humanitarian aid—conventionally in-kind food assistance and basic shelter—but denying their access to employment, freedom of movement, and adequate education, is now widely understood as outdated and unsustainable. It has been characterized as 'refugee warehousing—a denial of rights and a waste of humanity',[27] and that characterization is apt.

Although humanitarian aid may be crucial during an emergency phase, or to address vulnerabilities, it becomes problematic if it endures indefinitely, sometimes for decades, and justifies the denial of rights and the curtailment of nurturing refugees' skills, talents, and aspirations. So-called protracted refugee situations, such as the nearly thirty-year-old Dadaab camps in north-eastern Kenya exemplify the misery of refugees being effectively ware-housed for decades without the prospect of going home or being properly socio-economically integrated in the host society.[28] Indeed, socio-economic rights make up most of the entire second half of the 1951 Convention on the Status of Refugees, and yet they have been systematically undermined for decades by dominant humanitarian practices.

Instead, development assistance that supports job creation, infrastructural expansion, and improvement in public services for *both* refugees and the host community is now widely regarded as a more sustainable pathway, offering refugees greater autonomy, dignity, and purpose, and enabling their presence to benefit surrounding communities in what are often remote and under-developed border regions.

Politically, refugee self-reliance is often framed as 'win-win'. The logic is that it can offer a basis for interest convergence between Northern donor states and Southern host states. Northern donors have an interest in redu-cing the need for onward migration by refugees and in creating more cost-effective models of refugee assistance. Southern host states have an interest in attracting additional development resources that can not only benefit refugees but also support programmes and projects that benefit their citizens. That interest convergence is, in turn, what unlocks greater opportunities for refugees.

This basic vision for sustainability is not new. In different forms, self-reliance has been around since the inter-war years of the 1920s when Greece, faced with large numbers of refugees arriving from former Ottoman Empire states, including what is now Syria, allocated plots of land to the new arrivals, and collaborated with the International Labour Organization (ILO) on the creation of agricultural work schemes that could benefit both refugees and communities in remote rural areas.[29] In much of East Africa, throughout the 1960s and 1970s, development programmes in border areas with spontaneously created rural settlements were the standard response in newly independent countries such as Uganda and Tanzania. During the 1980s and 1990s, the United Nations formalized the concept of 'Refugee Aid and Development', seeking to encourage donors to contribute 'additional' development assistance to share the 'burden' borne by refugee-hosting countries.[30] UNHCR organized three major regional conferences, built around the concept—the International Conferences on Refugees in Africa (ICARA I and II) of 1981 and 1984 and the International Conference on Refugees in Central America (CIREFCA) of 1989.[31]

From the start of the millennium, there was a revival of interest in 'targeted development assistance' as a means to achieve self-reliance, as European donor countries in particular became increasingly interested in managing growing levels of asylum seekers moving from 'regions of origin' to Europe. A string of global initiatives were launched with the same goals: to overcome 'the relief-to-development gap' and support refugee self-reliance through development assistance. From 2003 to 2005 the vehicle was UNHCR's Convention Plus initiative; from 2013 to 2015, it was the multi-stakeholder Solutions Alliance.[32]

Some of the ideas and language have evolved. Today, there is a much greater role for business and the private sector. Investment does not just have to come from donor states, but whether because of corporate social responsibility or, ideally, core business concerns, private investors have been recognized as a means to enhance development opportunities in refugee-hosting regions. Self-reliance has had previous incarnations such as 'self-sufficiency', 'self-supporting', and even 'free-livers'. The key development actors have also changed, from ILO in the early years, to the United Nations Development Programme (UNDP) during the 1980s and 1990s, to the World Bank today. But the basic concepts have shown significant continuity. And the same exemplars of the model—notably Uganda—have regularly been deployed by international organizations and donors to high-light the validity of the approach.[33]

Today, there is more consensus than ever that this 'self-reliance' vision is the key to sustainable refugee policy. It is arguably the central organizing concept behind the UN Global Compact on Refugees, launched as a process in 2016 and agreed at the UN General Assembly in 2018 as the international community's main collective response to the aftermath of the European refugee crisis of 2015–16. Although it is officially only one of four pillars, the the other pillars of the Compact each relate to the long-established 'durable solutions'—repatriation, local integration, and resettlement—, long elusive to the majority of refugees. And the World Bank is investing more in the approach than any development organization in history.

However, it is also an idea that has been increasingly critiqued by academics for its repeated failure to deliver on its promise, its connections to supposedly 'neo-liberal' ideas, and its political instrumentalization by self-interested governments.[34]

To be clear, the basic outline of the model is one that I support, and have done for two decades since witnessing the effects of denying refugees access to basic socio-economic rights. It is a model that potentially offers the best available outcomes for refugees, and meets the criteria for sustainability. It is, in a sense, the only game in town for the majority of the world's refugees.

But as intuitively persuasive as the approach has been, it has been equally elusive in terms of either its effective implementation or it extensive rollout across host countries. Both now and historically, very few low- and middle-income countries have adopted effective self-reliance models that offer refugees their full set of socio-economic rights. The right to work and choose a place of residence for refugees remain rare. And few donor countries have committed adequate resources to offer the promised benefits to host communities. Indeed, part of the reason why the model has been repeatedly revived by the international community using different acronyms and monikers is that it is an approach that is satisfyingly easy to articulate but elusively difficult to implement.

A big part of the gap, though, has been the absence of systematic learning. Initiatives have been tried, failed, forgotten, and then, after a brief interregnum, frequently revived. For example, at a global level, ICARA I and II, Convention Plus, and the Solutions Alliance have all fallen by the wayside with little legacy, and yet the ideas within them have been recycled and reframed, usually with minimal adaptation. At a national level, particular contexts such as Uganda and Zambia have been framed as self-reliance 'successes' but often based on limited empirical evidence. Whether in academia or the policy world, there has been scant quantitative or even qualitative evidence about what actually works, for whom, and under what conditions. There is therefore an urgent need for a more evidence-based approach to thinking about the relationship between refugees and development.

An evidence-based approach

My interest in researching the economic lives of refugees began more than two decades ago. One summer, while I was still a teenager and studying for an economics degree, I spent time doing voluntary work in a reception centre for asylum seekers and refugees in the Netherlands. I went not knowing a great deal about refugees. I had expected to experience a sense of pity for people who had had to flee war zones or tyrannical regimes around the world; but what I found was a sense of inspiration. I met people from as far afield as Iraq, Kosovo, and Liberia, and many had skills, talents, and aspirations. As I have recounted often, a Bosniak lawyer taught me the basics of public international law and an Iranian former Olympian tried to teach me table tennis.

But the tragedy was that these people were trapped in a bureaucratic process, unable to work, until it had been determined whether or not they were 'refugees'. Sometimes this process would take three or even five years, and at the end of that period many families simply faced deportation. A system that denied talented people the possibility to work seemed to me to be inherently unfair, but it also struck me as economically absurd to leave people reliant on assistance when most wanted to make a social and economic contribution. That experience sent me back to my undergraduate university determined to write a dissertation on the economics of refugees. And I did, but I was struck by how little literature and evidence there was on the economic lives of refugees, or even on the politics that shapes refugees' access to economic opportunity.

Given the absence of research on the economics of refugees, or indeed relevant datasets that could be the basis for such work, I pivoted the early part of my academic career towards looking at the politics of refugee assistance. But during that period, I wrote about the history and politics of 'refugees and development', and tried to understand the political conditions that made refugee self-reliance possible. Part of the motivation for this research was that, as I travelled across Africa for research, the same tragedy I had witnessed in the Netherlands a decade earlier was being repeated: refugees with skills and talents were being denied the right to work.

However, after spending a year as a post-doc at Stanford, surrounded by the start-ups and social enterprises of Silicon Valley, I realized that markets, as well as states, needed to be part of the solution for refugees. They were, after all, the source of jobs that so many refugees had told me they wanted. It was time to go back to economics. When I returned to Oxford in 2012, I set up the basis of what became the 'Refugee Economies Programme' at the university. We began with a pilot study in Uganda, a year later. We chose to focus on Uganda not because it was representative of refugee-hosting countries, but because it was exceptional, in having given refugees access to the right to work and choose their residence. And we wanted to try to quantify some of the effects of giving refugees basic socio-economic freedoms. What happens when refugees are economically included and given access to enabling environments? What are the consequences for both refugees and the host community?

The so-called European refugee crisis of 2015–16 created a huge upsurge in public interest in refugees. With it came greater interest in evidence-based solutions. Perhaps reflecting the general absence of quantitative or comparative research on refugees, there was huge interest in the few such studies available, our research in Uganda, which received extensive media coverage because it used a combination of data and human stories to highlight what policy-makers had known intuitively for a long time: one of the best ways to create sustainable refugee policies was to create enabling environments, including opportunities for economic inclusion, close to home. But our first findings were based on just one country, and not even a complete picture of that country, having focused just on the capital city and settlements in only one of the two major refugee-hosting regions of the country.

In that context, the IKEA Foundation—the largest private-sector contributor to the UN's refugee response—provided us with a grant to scale the research of the Refugee Economies Programme. This time we focused on urban and camp contexts in three countries: Uganda, Kenya, and Ethiopia. We chose these countries in order to have a meaningful regional focus and be able to compare outcomes for some of the same refugee populations, such as Congolese and Somali refugees, across different countries. Furthermore, these countries have long hosted significant numbers of refugees. In 2020, they hosted around 2.5 million refugees—about 10 per cent of the world's total number of refugees.

The countries also happen to be particularly interesting because they exhibit variation in terms of the institutional and structural environments they create for refugees' economic lives. Uganda has offered refugees the right to work and freedom of movement since independence. Kenya has a long-standing encampment policy towards refugees. Ethiopia has recently begun to transition from encampment towards offering the right to work.

Our overall research objective was to understand the economic lives of refugees and their impact on the nearby host communities. More specifically, though, three fundamental questions animated our work, all with a clear relationship to the question of sustainability. First, what explains *welfare outcomes* for refugees and host communities? Put simply, when do some people thrive and others merely survive? Second, what explains *social cohesion* between refugees and host communities? Put simply, when do refugees and hosts get along and when do they not? Third, what explains *onward migration*? Put simply, when do refugees remain in camps or settlements, and when do they move onwards to cities, other nearby countries, or even move onwards to rich countries?

Up to that point, academic research on refugees was, with a few notable exceptions,[35] generally qualitative and focused on single-country cases. Meanwhile, policy research often used quantitative methods but applied different methods in different countries, making meaningful comparison difficult. Our approach was a mixed-methods, participatory approach. We sequenced qualitative and quantitative research in each research site. Beginning with qualitative research allowed us to first understand and build relationships within communities before designing and implementing quantitative survey methods. A particular feature of our research has been training refugees and members of the host community as peer researchers and enumerators; through our research we have trained over 200 members of the communities in basic social science methods.

Through our survey data collection, we created one of the first-ever panel datasets—data that is both multi-country and recorded over time—relating to the economic lives of refugees. Between 2017 and 2020, we collected first-hand data on the economic lives of 16,000 refugees and nearby host community members in six main research sites: Kampala and Nakivale in Uganda; Nairobi and Kakuma in Kenya; and Addis Ababa and Dollo Ado in Ethiopia. The resulting Refugee Economies Dataset was unique in covering refugees and hosts, urban and camp contexts, and following some of our respondents over time. Our quantitative data was based on random sampling, allowing it to be representative of our populations of interest.

The Refugee Economies Dataset is wide-ranging. It covers areas as diverse as employment, income and assets, education, health, social participation, migration history, aspirations, and refugee–host community perceptions and interactions. It enables a range of patterns, correlations, and statistical relationships to be explored, whether through descriptive statistics or regression analysis. The data can be analysed for particular sites or populations, or comparatively across contexts and populations.

Overall, it can give us an insight into the factors that shape socio-economic outcomes for refugees and the nearby host communities. These insights can in turn shed light on the kinds of policies that might lead to normatively better socio-economic outcomes. And through comparison across contexts, it can also give us some insights into the impact that different institutional environments have on refugees' outcomes, behaviours, and choices. And we have also used the data to complement specific impact evaluations, examining, for example, the effects of innovative interventions such as cash-based assistance in the new Kalobeyei settlement in Kenya or the establishment of agricultural cooperatives in the Dollo Ado camps in Ethiopia.

In other words, our economic analysis can contribute towards an evidence-based understanding of what works, under what conditions, and for whom. But what it cannot do is tell us about the politics of how it can be made to work. There has been a long-standing gap in high-quality comparative political research relating to refugees. What configurations of interests, power, and ideas are necessary for progressive, or indeed sustainable, policies to be implemented? These questions matter because they can teach us about the incentives needed to facilitate self-reliance. I have tried to complement the refugee economies research with an additional focus on the politics of economic inclusion. Under what conditions do host governments give refugees access to socio-economic rights such as the right to work? When and why are self-reliance policies adopted in lieu of encampment policies?

I have therefore supplemented our economic analysis with political analysis. Between 2018 and 2019, I undertook British Academy-funded research in our three focus countries to explore the politics of self-reliance. What incentives are needed at the local and national levels to persuade host governments to socio-economically integrate refugees? And when are international donors willing to provide such incentives? Our three focus countries are of particular relevance for exploring these questions because Uganda has a long-standing commitment to self-reliance; Kenya insists refugees live in camps but in practice has begun to adopt elements of the Ugandan model in one particular part of the country; Ethiopia has recently passed legislation allowing refugees to work and move freely but has yet to implement that legislation. Understanding the politics of socio-economic rights within these countries can therefore offer insights into the carrots and sticks that are needed to persuade host governments to adopt better policies.

Focusing on the economics and politics of refugee self-reliance in just three countries cannot provide all the answers. The context in East Africa is not the same as in other parts of the continent, let alone the Middle East, Asia, or Latin America. Nevertheless, it provides a starting point for learning lessons about the political economy of self-reliance from three host countries that have, unlike most others, taken steps towards better integrating refugees.

This book and its argument

This is therefore a book with a practical focus on what works. Its approach might be characterized as 'global challenge-led'. Rather than starting with a particular academic debate, or trying to build incrementally on a body of knowledge, its point of departure is to frame a real-world challenge and then draw upon interdisciplinary social science to seek answers. In this case the practical question is: how can we create sustainable refugee policies that allow all refugees to live dignified and purposeful lives, while carrying political support at local, national, and international levels?

The underlying research draws upon theory and methods from a range of disciplines. The main two disciplinary approaches are economics and politics. However, I also draw upon ideas and methods from anthropology, sociology, and history. Across the chapters, the methods used are eclectic and include surveys, impact evaluations, intervention-based research, natural experiments, archival research, semi-structured interviews, participant observation, and focus groups. Some of the underlying research I did alone (notably Chapters 8–11), much of it (notably Chapters 3–7) relied upon building interdisciplinary research teams through the Refugee Economies Programme in order to collect data at scale.

I divide the book into four main parts, covering ethics, economics, politics, and policy. Each one asks a question that contributes towards building an evidence base for the design of sustainable refugee policies. Part I, covering *ethics*, asks 'what is right?'. What, from a normative perspective are the criteria for sustainable refugee policies? It outlines and defends the three main criteria, but also engages with possible normative critiques. Part II, on *economics*, asks 'what works?'. From the research that we have undertaken what can we learn about best practices for supporting the socio-economic inclusion of refugees? What specifically can innovative models like the Ugandan self-reliance model, the designed Kalobeyei settlement in Kenya, and the private-sector-funded Dollo Ado camps in Ethiopia teach us about the design of functioning refugee economies? Part III deals with *politics*, and asks 'what persuades?'. Under what conditions do host governments create the conditions for sustainable refugee economies to emerge? When do they provide refugees with socio-economic rights and opportunities? Finally, Part IV, *policy*, discusses what the research means for practice, explores its implications for other regions of the world, and unpacks how it relates to future trends in forced displacement.

I argue that in an age of displacement, we need to find principled but pragmatic ways to provide refugee protection at scale. All countries have an ethical obligation and strategic interest to admit refugees onto their own territory, but solutions for the majority will be found in the low- and middle-income countries that neighbour conflict and crisis. In these countries, the socio-economic inclusion of refugees has the potential to be mutually beneficial for refugees, host communities, and governments. The key is a development-based approach: to expand the socio-economic entitlements and capabilities of both refugees and the proximate host community, including through the right and opportunity to work, and through improved access to public services such as education and healthcare. Better socio-economic opportunities for refugees correlate with better welfare outcomes for refugees, improved social cohesion between refugees and hosts, and a reduced demand for onward migration.

In cities, empowering refugees is about ensuring inclusion within existing economies. But urbanization alone is not the answer. In Ethiopia, Kenya, and Uganda, only a small minority of registered refugees live in cities.[36] Many governments, including those in our three focus countries, are reluctant to tolerate urban refugees, and impose significant restrictions. I show that refugees earn more, own more, and work more in the city, but they are not necessarily happier, healthier, or better fed than those who live in rural areas. Host communities in rural areas also tend to be more welcoming of refugees than in big cities, where social cohesion appears more elusive. There is therefore also a need to consider rural solutions for refugees, but which go beyond traditional encampment.

In rural areas, the challenge is how to build viable economies in what are usually remote border regions. There are relatively few examples of attempts to systematically reimagine refugee camps in ways that are based on a development-based approach, or that offer integrated, market-based opportunities to both refugees and the host community. Kalobeyei in Kenya and Dollo Ado in Ethiopia are among the most striking examples anywhere in the world. Kalobeyei was designed as an integrated, market-based settlement for both refugees and hosts. Dollo Ado benefitted from the largest private-sector investment ever received by a refugee camp, and the rollout of a new model of 'cooperatives' to enable refugees and hosts to work alongside one another. In both cases, I show that outcomes have been far from perfect. But both have made progress and offer opportunities to learn. In such contexts, refugee self-reliance is likely to remain elusive unless policy-makers adapt their focus from small-scale 'livelihoods' interventions, towards recognizing the larger economic and political preconditions for building viable economies in remote border regions.

On a political level, a crucial dimension of self-reliance has been securing the support of host governments. The politics of self-reliance is interest-driven. Donor governments have generally been prepared to fund self-reliance insofar as it reduces long-term aid budgets or is believed to reduce onward migration. Host governments have been prepared to support the socio-economic inclusion of refugees insofar as it attracts development resources that benefit host citizens and support elite patronage networks at national and local levels. For example, Uganda has consistently supported self-reliance because its politicians benefit from doing so. Since independence, it has used refugee self-reliance to attract international development assistance. Successive regimes have channelled some of these resources through patronage networks into strategically important refugee-hosting regions such as West Nile and the south-west, reinforcing central government authority. Across each of our focus countries, socio-economic opportunity has opened up mainly insofar as potential gatekeepers and veto players at national and local levels have been effectively bought off with international resources. These ambiguous politics, I argue, are a reality of global refugee politics, and they need to be understood.

Above all, though, I suggest that the key to unlocking sustainable solutions for refugees is to recognize and build upon the capabilities of refugees themselves. Of course, many refugees have vulnerabilities, but like all human beings, most also have the potential to contribute economically, socially, and culturally if given the opportunity.

PART
I

Ethics—*what is right?*

2

The search for sustainability

Introduction

What does 'sustainability' mean in the refugee context? It is a term frequently used in development and environmental contexts. In the broadest sense, sustainability implies the ability to endure over time. Sustainable policies are those that can be maintained without unravelling due to resource constraints in the future, whether those constraints are environmental or political, for example.

The language of sustainability has been used in the broader migration context. A debate about 'sustainable migration' has arisen in the context of the political backlash against immigration in rich societies across Europe and North America. There are growing concerns about 'brain drain' from developing countries, and the erosion of migrant rights around the world including through the loss of life due to dangerous journeys and restrictive border practices.

Marta Erdal and her colleagues define 'sustainable migration' as 'migration that ensures a well-balanced distribution of costs and benefits for the individuals, societies and affected states, today and in the future'.[1] They highlight the multidimensional nature of the concept as requiring political, economic, social, and cultural sustainability across societies in countries of origin, transit, and destination. This offers a useful starting point but defers the question of what that 'well-balanced distribution' needs to look like in order to avoid significant political backlash. In response, I argued with Paul Collier that sustainable migration is inherently political and ethical; sustainable migration policies must 'have the democratic support of the receiving society, meet the long-term interests of the receiving state, sending society, and migrants themselves, and fulfil basic ethical obligations'.[2]

Sustainability, though, means something different in the distinctive context of refugee policy. The need to consider what sustainability means in relation to refugees was brought to the fore by the political response to the 'European refugee crisis' of 2015–16 when more than a million asylum seekers arrived in the European Union (EU). The combination of numbers, incoherent policy responses, and irresponsible political rhetoric contributed to political backlash. Asylum and immigration became the most salient political issue in the many EU countries. A backlash against open-door asylum policies took hold. In Germany, Chancellor Angela Merkel initially pronounced '*Wir Schaffen Das*' ('we can do it') in August 2015 but by early 2016, she had been forced to backtrack, close borders, and work with Turkey and the Balkan countries to reduce the onward movement of Syrian refugees.[3]

Tipping points were reached across Europe, as opportunistic and populist politicians used refugee and migration movements as a scapegoat for broader societal issues. The 'refugee crisis' offered a rallying call for populist politicians to mobilize voters affected by deeper socio-economic issues such as austerity and the loss of labour-intensive manufacturing jobs to automation and offshoring.[4] From Brexit in the UK to the rise of the far-right Alternative für Deutschland in Germany, the refugee crisis contributed to the unravelling of democratic institutions as populists across Europe made strikingly similar arguments about the impact of refugees and migrants on the economy, security, and identity. Far-right candidates were elected to national parliaments in practically every EU member state. Emboldened by seeing the electoral rewards of anti-asylum and immigration rhetoric, US politics soon followed.[5]

It is not just rich countries that face challenges of political sustainability. In 2016, Kenya threatened to close the Dadaab refugee camps and expel Somali refugees amid public backlash following a series of Somali-perpetrated terrorist attacks in the country. Since the start of the Syrian conflict, Lebanon has hosted the highest number of refugees per capita in the world, but with high numbers perceived to affect citizens' access to employment and public services, it closed its border with Syria in 2018 and has been accused of forcibly repatriating Syrian refugees.[6] Opinion polls across Latin America reveal that countries hosting large numbers of Venezuelan refugees—from Ecuador to Peru—have suffered a collapse in political support for open policies as numbers have risen and created competition for jobs and services.[7]

What does this mean in terms of how we think about sustainability? Under what conditions does backlash arise? Are there clear thresholds and tipping points that undermine public support? To what extent should we take into account the risk of backlash when designing refugee policies, or does doing so risk rewarding populist opportunism?

There are no hard and fast rules in terms of the relationship between numbers and backlash. Some societies can tolerate higher numbers than others—Germany, Uganda, and Jordan—have coped remarkably with hosting significant numbers of refugees. Others—Japan, the Gulf States, and the Visegrad countries (Czech Republic, Hungary, Slovakia, and Poland)—have a strikingly low acceptance of refugees on their territory. Others, such as Denmark[8] and Tanzania[9] for example, have transitioned from being historically tolerant societies towards having much more pervasive anti-refugee sentiment. And even within the same societies, degrees of tolerance may ebb and flow over time depending on the wider socio-economic and political context: the US showed remarkable tolerance towards immigration throughout the early twentieth century but then underwent a backlash in the late 1920s amid recession;[10] West Germany tolerated large numbers of guest workers throughout the 1960s and then abolished the scheme amid the economic consequences of the 1973 oil crisis.[11]

But despite geographical and temporal variation, there is, sadly, a pattern that occurs as societies receive high numbers of refugees. As numbers rise, opportunistic politicians tend to make the same three arguments relating to the economy, security, and identity. Refugees are portrayed as a source of competition, threat, or difference. And, over time, opinion polls often shift against support for refugees, leading towards policies that frequently include border closure or deportation. We see this pattern for Europe, for the Syrian influx in the Middle East, and for the Venezuelan crisis in Latin America, for example.

However, the relationship between numbers and public opinion is not a deterministic one; it is mediated by at least two sets of factors. First, whether there are potential sources of grievance between refugees and hosts, such as whether the economy can absorb a significant expansion in labour without displacing native jobs, whether there is a history of refugee-related violence or insecurity in hosting areas, and whether there is perceived cultural proximity or distance between hosts and refugees. Second, whether mitigating policies are introduced to enable host communities to share in the benefits of receiving refugees through, for example, additional investment in creating jobs and improving public services.[12]

In this context, what do normative criteria for sustainability look like? In other words, what would just or ethical principles for sustainability be?

My starting point is to ground this chapter in what moral philosophers call 'non-ideal theory' as opposed to 'ideal theory'. Ideal theory attempts to explore what a just world should look like. It assumes that if the moral argument is strong enough, there can be strict compliance with its implications.[13] The boundaries for what is ethical have to remain within the boundaries of what is possible under favourable circumstances. In contrast, proponents of non-ideal theory argue that knowing what an ideal society would look like is simply not helpful as a guide to action in the real world.[14] In the words of Matthew Gibney, 'criticality requires feasibility'.[15] Put simply, making claims about how the world should look requires us to know what options are actually available to us in the real world. And this entails engaging with the constraints of politics; the 'political' needs to be a central part of applied moral reasoning. Within political theory there are long-standing debates on how we should understand the political constraints of applied morality.[16] For the purposes of this chapter, I follow a tradition of political realism; sustainable refugee policies must be reconcilable with politics.[17]

But which political constraints are real, and which ones are merely the narratives and rhetoric of opportunistic political elites?[18] From this perspective, it may be worthwhile to distinguish between 'hard' and 'soft' constraints: those that we can change through argumentation or negotiation, and those that we cannot. Simply because we would like all countries to open their borders to refugees under all circumstances and accord a full set of civil, political, economic, social, and cultural rights does not mean it will happen. But it does not necessarily make those arguments redundant if, under certain conditions, they actually contribute to change.[19] Political realism does not therefore mean that arguments based on ethics, values, and norms cannot sometimes succeed in changing the attitudes of political elites towards refugees. But their degree of relevance is an empirical question. And to effect change in the real world, we need to take seriously the reality that many political elites perceive hosting large numbers of refugees as a cost. Against this backdrop, improving outcomes for refugees requires that we engage with the empirical reality of rising numbers, geographical concentration in low- and middle-income countries, and increasing political hostility on a global scale. It necessitates that we find creative ways to reconcile refugee policy with power and interests at global, national, and local levels.

Based on these premises, I outline three normative criteria for sustainability—rights, politics, and scale. First, sustainable policies must ensure that refugees have access to protection, assistance, and solutions. Second, they must be acceptable to political elites at the global, national, and local levels. Third, they must function at scale and endure as numbers increase. Put simply, the challenge is: how can we enable refugees to receive access to their full set of rights, while maintaining political support, and operating at the scale required in an age of displacement?

I argue that the only realistic way to meet these criteria is by creating a model based primarily on supporting refugees in neighbouring low- and middle-income countries close to home. But it requires significant investment in area-based development to create opportunities for both refugees and host communities to access meaningful employment and public services, ensuring that refugees can live with dignity and purpose until they can either go home or it becomes clear that they need to be integrated elsewhere. It also requires that such approaches are complemented by the availability of resettlement to rich countries around the world, albeit for a minority of refugees and for clearly defined reasons: as a route out of limbo when repatriation is not possible, as an alternative option for the most vulnerable, or for other reasons linked to family unity, employment, or educational opportunity. And it requires a supplementary role for spontaneous arrival asylum in the rich world as a 'check and balance' for refugees unable, for whatever reason, to access asylum in a neighbouring country.

I structure this chapter around three main parts. First, I derive and explain the normative criteria for sustainability in the refugee system. Second, I outline three archetypal models for allocating responsibility for refugees, suggesting that they have complementary but distinctive roles to play in achieving sustainability. Third, I engage with three possible objections to this vision of sustainability.

Normative criteria for sustainability

The three starting premises for my analysis are those I outlined in the Introduction, relating to geography, numbers, and politics. First, most refugees are located in low- and middle-income countries that neighbour areas of conflict and crisis, and this will remain the case. Specifically, 85 per cent of refugees come from such countries and although there has been variation in this figure over the past three decades, it has consistently been above 70 per cent. Second, the numbers of displaced people are going to grow over time in the context of fragile states and climate change. Specifically, numbers have risen year on year for the last five years, and are the highest since the Second World War, while the World Bank estimates 143 million people will be displaced by climate change by 2050.[20] Third, the political willingness of rich countries to accept large numbers of displaced people onto their territory will remain limited for the foreseeable future. Specifically, resettlement numbers for refugees have been consistently limited to 1–2 per cent of the world's total refugees, while public attitudes towards spontaneous arrival asylum in the US and Europe have generally been positive when numbers have remained low.[21] In general, attitudes to asylum and immigration in rich countries have been negatively affected by wider economic trends, including the collapse of labour-intensive manufacturing jobs in Europe and North America.[22]

These three trends are not necessarily inevitable but they are extremely likely to continue, and so they represent my starting assumptions for thinking about sustainability in a non-ideal world. Any realistic theory of sustainability has to work within these constraints. Based on these premises, I outline three criteria for sustainability: rights, politics, and scale.

Rights

Sustainable refugee policies must first and foremost fulfil the core purpose of refuge: to ensure that refugees receive access to their rights, as both refugees and human beings. States have individual and collective duties towards refugees. These can be derived from a number of ethical perspectives.

This starting point is the idea that all human beings, by virtue of their common humanity, have a right to have rights.[23] Some rights—such as basic security, basic subsistence, and basic liberty—are 'basic' insofar as, without them, it is impossible to enjoy any other rights.[24] It is the primary duty of an individual's country of citizenship to ensure those rights.[25] However, when that state is unable or unwilling to provide those rights (i.e. that person faces 'persecution' or serious harm) and they are outside their country of origin (i.e. the person is in a situation often described as 'alienage'), responsibility passes to the wider international community or whichever country that person is in.[26]

For political theorists, the moral basis for this transfer of responsibility is debated. For some, it is grounded in a humanitarian obligation—'a duty of rescue'—that human beings have towards strangers in extreme and urgent need.[27] For others, it is grounded in obligations that nation-states have simply in order to be regarded as legitimate actors within the international state system. If a premise of the international state system is that everyone should have a right to be a member of a state somewhere in the world, then legitimate states have an obligation to ensure membership is universally available.[28] In practice, these two perspectives are compatible and can be reconciled by distinguishing the particular circumstances of different groups of refugees. In the event that people flee a state that persecutes them because of who they are, there may be no prospect of re-establishing the assumed relationship between state and citizen, and so an alternative citizenship may be required.[29] In the event that people flee a state that persecutes them because of who they are, there may be no prospect of re-establishing the assumed relationship between state and citizen, and so an alternative citizenship may be required. In the event that people flee generalized violence or a temporary crisis, the forms of protection (and membership)[30] required may not necessarily entail citizenship.[31]

States should be collectively prepared to contribute, by providing access to territory or money towards ensuring these ethical obligations are fulfilled. The duty to protect the rights of people who flee, and to provide them with a pathway towards effective citizenship, are a shared responsibility between the country to which a refugee flees and the wider international community.[32] The responsibility should not exclusively lie with the immediate neighbouring 'first country of asylum' simply because of the 'accident of geography' of being next door to a crisis country.[33]

Philosophers disagree on the extent to which these duties are absolute or contingent. For Peter Singer and Renata Singer, given the extreme vulnerability of refugees, receiving countries and international donors should be willing to support refugees all the way up to the point at which the marginal benefit to the refugee is equivalent to the marginal cost to the receiving citizen.[34] For others, such as Matthew Gibney, this demand is too onerous; a more realistic standard would be for governments to be obliged to help insofar as the cost of doing so is relatively low.[35] Generally, when there is international cooperation and global responsibility-sharing, this is a moot point as the cost of providing refugee rights usually remains low. It is in the absence of international cooperation that particular states and their citizens are more likely to bear an unduly heavy cost by hosting refugees.

If we accept the premise that states have obligations towards refugees by virtue of our common humanity, then what, specifically, does a sustainable refugee system have to provide? Three things—protection, assistance, and solutions. Protection is a contested term but at a minimum, it implies ensuring that refugees are not forcibly sent back to a country in which they may face serious harm, and instead can live in safety, and receive access to their civil, political, economic, social, and cultural rights. Assistance implies having access to basic services such as in health, education, and basic welfare provision for the most vulnerable. But, like any functioning welfare system, assistance should encourage the attainment of autonomy over time. Solutions relate to the 'durable solutions' of repatriation, resettlement, or local integration—a pathway to reintegration within a state system and a route towards effective citizenship within a timely period, whether back home or elsewhere.

Put simply, any sustainable refugee system should be providing these three things to all refugees. However, there are other things that, although desirable insofar as they may improve welfare and are compatible with the other criteria of sustainability, are not core to the purpose of the refugee system. For example, giving refugees free choice in their final destination may be inherently worthwhile insofar as it increases wellbeing without jeopardizing sustainability. But it is neither a human right nor central to the ethical scope and purpose of a refugee system. It should therefore not be prioritized over and above creating a sustainable system that provides protection, assistance, and solutions for all refugees.

Politics

To be sustainable, a refugee system must retain political support at international, national, and local levels. However, around the world, asylum and immigration have become politically divisive issues. And there are common patterns to the politics of backlash.

As numbers rise, populist politicians mobilize based on an anti-immigration platform. Often public concern has little to do with refugees or migrants per se, but it frequently serves as a proxy issue for other underlying grievances such as the loss of labour intensive manufacturing jobs or cuts to public services. Across Europe, North America, and Australasia, the last decade has seen a rise in the political salience of asylum and immigration. And that rising salience has usually been associated with a populist backlash against 'progressive' asylum and immigration policies, which in turn has influenced mainstream government policies reducing the scope for welcoming and integrating refugees.

In the aftermath of the European refugee crisis of 2015–16, there was a seismic shift in the politics of immigration. Germany received the largest number of refugees, more than 1 million across the two years. Initially in late August 2015, Chancellor Angela Merkel proclaimed '*Wir Schaffen Das*'. She suspended implementation of Europe's Dublin regulations that assign responsibility for asylum claims to the first countries of arrival, allowing mainly Syrian refugees to cross into Germany from Austria and other neighbouring countries. The open-door policy was initially hailed as progressive.[36]

However, the approach did not last. By early 2016, the mood in the country had changed dramatically. The media and other politicians began to question the sustainability of the open-door policy. On New Year's Eve, a series of attacks that the media falsely alleged were carried out by Syrian men against German women exacerbated the shift in public opinion.[37] By late January, Merkel had back-tracked and was forced to work bilaterally with other EU member states to close the Balkans route to Europe. She also began talks with Turkish Prime Minister Erdoğan on a bilateral agreement, announced in March, to reduce onward movement by Syrian refugees and others coming mainly from Iraq and Afghanistan across the Aegean Sea.[38] Within Germany itself, the *Wir Schaffen Das* moment quickly came to an end, the far-right Alternative für Deutschland party grew rapidly in popularity and won ninety seats in the Bundestag with 12.6 per cent of the vote, based almost entirely on its campaigning around the impact of Merkel's briefly progressive refugee policies.[39] Merkel later expressed regret at decisions regarding Germany's refugee policies of late 2015.[40]

According to *Eurobarometer*, migration was the single most important political issue to voters in Germany, Austria, the UK, Sweden, and Denmark by 2016, and the second most important issue in Italy.[41] Across Europe as a whole it became the single most important issue. Opinion polls also revealed a combination of increasing polarization on attitudes to immigration and declining confidence in European governments' immigration policies. This rising political trend created political opportunities across Europe. Matteo Salvini's Northern League in Italy, Sebastian Kurz's People's Party in Austria, Nigel Farage's UK Independence Party, Marine Le Pen's Front National, Geert Wilders' Freedom Party in the Netherlands, for example, all mobilized primarily based on an anti-immigration platform that used the refugee crisis and the resulting increase in the political salience of migration as the basis for popular mobilization.[42] As these parties won votes, mainstream politics shifted to become ever more conservative in its asylum and immigration policies in order to combat the far right.

Across the continent, Europe effectively closed its doors to refugees. European government policies converged around a series of common approaches. The focus was on 'irregular migration', including reducing the onward movement of asylum seekers. Internally, this involved a series of deterrence measures, such as reduced welfare entitlements for asylum seekers and accelerated deportation for rejected claimants. Externally, this involved collaboration with Turkey and Libya to prevent the onward movement of asylum seekers across the Mediterranean.[43] The European Commission's New Pact on Migration and Asylum, launched in September 2020, reflected these priorities. Although broad and wide-ranging, it emphasized the management of irregular migration, the rapid assessment and deportation of failed asylum seekers, and collaboration with transit countries outside the EU.[44]

In the US, politicization took place even without rising immigration numbers. Donald Trump mobilized electoral support in 2016 based on anti-immigration rhetoric even at a time when US border patrol apprehensions along the southern border—a long-standing indicator of irregular migration levels—were at a twenty-year low.[45] Trump used the European refugee crisis as a basis for his 2016 presidential election campaign, connecting Syrian refugees to terrorism and threats to national security.[46] Within his first hour in office he was promising a border wall with Mexico and large-scale deportation of 'illegal aliens'. However, the political salience of immigration for US voters rose further only as the number of border apprehensions rose to record levels by 2019. In the year between September 2018 and September 2019, almost as many Central American asylum seekers tried to reach the US as had come to Europe in 2015.[47] A combination of violence, weak governance, and environmental stress led to a record number of asylum seekers heading north from the Northern Triangle countries of Honduras, Guatemala, and El Salvador.[48] As numbers rose, opinion polls turned against asylum seekers, and the Trump administration deployed increasingly restrictive policies, including incarcerating children and processing asylum applications in Mexico.[49]

The evidence suggests that underlying public grievances across the rich world have little to do with migration per se. For example, in the UK, Germany, and the US, there is a strikingly consistent geographical pattern to anti-immigration voting patterns and public opinion. The regions or voting districts with the greatest likelihood to vote for anti-immigration parties or to hold anti-immigration opinions tend to have two things in common. They have among the lowest levels of immigration, but they also tend to be the regions that have undergone industrial decline, losing labour-intensive manufacturing jobs to offshoring and automation.[50] The pattern applies to the highest Brexit-voting areas in the UK, hotbeds of Trump support in the US, and Alternative für Deutschland strongholds in Saxony, for example.

In this context, the political scope for welcoming or resettling large numbers of refugees in the rich world is extremely limited. And there seems little prospect of changing this in the short term, despite some indications of declining support for populist extremism in the US and elsewhere by 2020. This is because the politics of asylum and immigration in the rich world is being shaped by structural trends that are unlikely to lessen over time: automation, the movement of labour-intensive manufacturing jobs to South-East Asia, austerity, precarious financial markets, the rise of China, and recently COVID-19. Put simply, the West's relative economic decline has contributed to a populist politics with long-term implications for the viability of large-scale sanctuary in rich countries.

But there is also empirical evidence that an open borders policy would change the demographic composition of rich countries. Given the opportunity, hundreds of millions of people around the world would migrate from poor to rich countries. Gallup has created a Potential Net Migration Index, which explores how much the population of a particular country would change if everyone who wanted to move actually moved where they wanted to. It showed for instance that the population of the US would increase by 46 per cent, Canada by 147 per cent, the UK by 37 per cent, and Australia by 179 per cent, while Mexico's would decrease by 20 per cent and Ethiopia's by 27 per cent. Indeed, the polling organization found that 42 million Latin Americans would like to move to the US.[51] Of course, it is important to keep in mind the striking difference between people's 'wish' to migrate versus the numbers that actual 'plan' to migrate;[52] however, the data on aspirations nevertheless highlights that in a world of economic inequality, a growing global youth population, and rising aspirations, there is growing demand for South–North migration.

Against this backdrop, rich countries can and should take in refugees. But the numbers that can be politically sustained are likely to be small. The difficulty is that political tipping points can also be observed in other parts of the world. From Latin America to the Middle East and Africa, the pattern of backlash is broadly the same. Numbers rise, political opinion turns negative, populist groups mobilize, and rights are restricted. The pattern may be mediated by other factors: labour market capacity, cultural proximity between refugees and hosts, policy choices, ratification of international legal instruments, and centralized governments with the capacity to override localized concerns. However, from Peru to Lebanon, and Bangladesh to Tanzania, we have seen rising numbers of refugees gradually leading to backlash. And the main opportunity to mitigate this effect seems to have been significant external investment in employment and public services to the benefit of both refugees and host communities.

To take an example, by 2019, 4.2 million Venezuelans had fled the country, with predictions suggesting the numbers would continue to rise.[53] Across Latin America, initially generous and hospitable host-country policies have been eroded by the same pattern: numbers grow, jobs are displaced, stress is placed on public services, and communal tensions increase. This has turned opinion polls against refugees, and brought xenophobic narratives into politics, creating pressure on mainstream politicians to implement more restrictive policies.[54]

At first, for instance, Peru opened its borders, allowing Venezuelans to apply for short-term stays or for asylum, and from January 2017 until December 2018, offering Venezuelan migrants temporary access to work, education, and banking services. But by the end of 2018, Peru suspended that practice amid concerns that it was creating an incentive for more Venezuelans to come. In 2017, Brazil began offering Venezuelan migrants a two-year residency visa and gave all asylum seekers access to work permits and basic services. In 2018, however, the governor of Roraima State appealed to the Supreme Court to close the border until the conditions for 'humanitarian reception' were in place. The case was dismissed by the Federal Supreme Court on the grounds of international legal obligations and constitutional provisions, but it exemplified a changing immigration politics in the country with President Jair Bolsonaro withdrawing from the UN Compact for Safe, Orderly, and Regular Migration in January 2019. Brazil has also tried, with limited success, to carry out an internal relocation scheme, in which around 5,000 Venezuelans in the border area have been transferred to seventeen other states across the country. For its part, Ecuador initially welcomed fleeing Venezuelans, but eventually introduced stricter border controls in August 2018. In January, the country witnessed a xenophobic backlash after a Venezuelan killed his pregnant Ecuadorian girlfriend; in the face of the resulting anger and violence, many Venezuelans left Ecuador for Colombia.[55]

Opinion polls reveal that throughout the region, the pattern has been a consistent shift between 2017 and 2019 from support for Venezuelan refugees and migrants towards support for more restrictive policies.[56] Even Colombia, the most generous host country in the region, has followed the same pattern. Between 2017 and 2019, the country opened its doors to roughly 1.5 million Venezuelans and has granted them the right to work and to receive basic services through a registration and regularization programme known as the *Permiso Especial de Permanencia* (PEP). However, with Venezuelans comprising 2.65 per cent of the overall population, growing concern in border regions and cities about the displacement of Colombians from the informal economy, and huge stress on public health and education provision. Opinion polls shifted from 70 per cent to 49 per cent approval for the government's open-door policy in the lead-up to the November 2019 local elections.[57]

The main means to mitigate this type of backlash appears to be external investment in jobs and public services for both refugees and citizens. Colombia, for instance, has complained that as a middle-income country, it has received just \$300 million over two years for the refugee crisis, and this has mainly gone through international non-governmental organizations (NGOs) rather than the government or private sector. This, the government argues is well below 10 per cent per capita of what Middle East countries received during the Syria crisis, and, privately, Colombian Government officials highlight that the lack of investment increases the risk of political backlash because of the displacement effect on employment and public service provision.[58]

Lebanon, the largest per capita refugee host in the world, has also faced a growing political backlash against refugees. It has experienced immense pressure on public services, including more than 300,000 Syrians entering the Lebanese school system, leading to citizens' children only accessing half-day schooling. By 2019, Foreign Minister Gebran Bassil was using increasingly nationalistic language and mobilizing against Syrian refugees with protest slogans such as 'employ a Lebanese' and 'Syria get out'.[59] Accordingly, Lebanon's security forces, called General Security, began implementing legal restrictions that had previously not been enforced, including closing down Syrian-owned shops and demolishing 'permanent' refugee homes. Although the backlash was due to a combination of factors, such as austerity measures amid economic downturn and sectarian tensions, a major factor has been a sense of pressure on jobs, infrastructure, and public services for citizens, coupled with inadequate international assistance.[60]

Tanzania, host to 380,000 refugees mostly from Burundi and the Democratic Republic of Congo, has historically been one of the most generous refugee-hosting countries in the world despite being among the poorest thirty countries in the world. It pioneered rural self-reliance programmes for refugees under Julius Nyerere and offered naturalization to tens of thousands of Burundians under Jakaya Kikwete.[61] Since assuming power in 2015, though, President Magufuli has resorted to increasingly populist rhetoric on refugees, implementing a range of new restrictions such as further limiting refugees' mobility and accelerating their repatriation.

His justification has been the stress placed on infrastructure, the economy, and security in refugee-hosting regions such as Kigoma. He has further argued that, despite Tanzania's long-time commitment to hosting refugees, it has received limited international support. And members of the Tanzanian Government can easily recite a catalogue of what they see as failures of international responsibility-sharing. Indeed, during the anti-colonial liberation wars of the 1960s and 1970s, President Nyerere offered an 'open door' policy to hundreds of thousands fleeing southern African neighbours. Refugees were given access to land, and it was one of the most progressive refugee-hosting countries in the world. But when Tanzania finally approached international donors for support to make this approach sustainable at the International Conferences on Assistance to Refugees in Africa in 1981 and 1984, pledges were made by major donor countries that were not delivered. In the mid-1990s, when Tanzania received mass influxes from Burundi in 1993 and then over 250,000 Rwandans in just three days in 1994, it faced criticism for its forced repatriation of many Rwandans but received only limited support. In 2008, it announced that it would naturalize 162,000 Burundian refugees who had arrived in 1972. Once again, commitments of international support went unfulfilled. By February 2018, Magufuli explained that against this historical backdrop, his government would withdraw from the UN Refugee Agency (UNHCR)'s Comprehensive Refugee Response Framework (CRRF), a key element of the Global Compact on Refugees.[62]

Bangladesh has been hosting growing numbers of Rohingya refugees fleeing crimes against humanity and accusations of genocide in neighbouring Myanmar since the 1990s but the numbers have grown rapidly since 2017 to around 1 million. Almost all have settled in sprawling camps in the country's Cox's Bazar District. In some districts, refugees have outnumbered the local host population. The population increase has been identified as placing considerable pressure on the local employment market, infrastructure, and public services.[63] The political mobilization of a minority of Rohingya within the camps through armed organizations engaged in cross-border incursions,[64] such as the Arakan Rohingya Salvation Army (ARSA), have been viewed by the government as a security threat. Over time, there has been a growing political backlash, and politicians have responded with a clampdown. By 2019, the government imposed restrictions on movement, internet access in the camps, and began building barbed-wire fences around the camps. It was also implicated in extra-judicial killings of refugees, and has been pushing strongly for the repatriation of the Rohingya even though UNHCR and others have insisted that it would be premature and unsafe for people to return home.[65]

These examples show that the commitment of neighbouring states to host refugees cannot be taken for granted. Maintaining host-government support is critical to sustainability, and requires significant investment in jobs, infrastructure, and public services.

The capacity to maintain political support at international, national, and local levels has to be a key normative criterion for sustainability. Advocating for 'ideal' policies that ignore political reality will simply lead to backlash and result in worse outcomes for refugee rights. However, in thinking about tipping points at which rising numbers lead to political backlash, it is also worthwhile to distinguish between 'hard' and 'soft' constraints. Simply because a 'populist' politician represents a constraint as immovable does not mean this cannot be changed. But equally, just because a 'liberal' politician represents a constraint as infinitely changeable does not mean that it can be ignored without consequence. The analytical challenge is to identify where and how politics can be changed, and where and how policy must adapt to the underlying politics. In some areas, appeal to values, changing narratives, and using ethical arguments may be persuasive over the long term. In other areas, the only means to achieve sustainability will be to work with prevailing power structures and interests, and seek to reconcile refugee policy with realpolitik.

Scale

The third criterion for sustainability is that refugee policies must be capable of enduring over time, and functioning at scale. This is because all of the trends suggest displacement numbers will continue to rise. The twenty-first century will become an age of displacement. Of course, there are things that can be done to address the underlying causes: ending wars, rebuilding fragile states, combatting climate change, strengthening human rights, and addressing global inequality would all significantly reduce future levels of displacement. But these are areas that the world is struggling with. Concerted collective action is proving elusive and displacement is a symptom of a wider failure of international cooperation. We cannot know the future, but we can build scenarios based on current trends.

Displacement numbers are rising year on year, and the biggest current driver is fragile states. A small number of chronically fragile countries—such as Syria, Afghanistan, and South Sudan—are a major source of displacement. However, new fragile states such as Venezuela, Yemen, and Libya increase displacement numbers each year. Refugee numbers are a sub-set of those displaced; rising internal displacement leads many of those who can, to cross international borders. A polarized UN Security Council thwarts international cooperation to address the underlying causes of state collapse. And the shift towards a multi-polar world, which is likely to continue for the next fifty years or beyond, predicts continued polarization within the multilateral system, as well as violent proxy conflicts involving the world's great powers.

Climate change is probably the biggest reason why an age of displacement looms on the horizon. Precise predictions about the impact on displacement are difficult, and a range of extrapolations have been made from 200 million by 2050 by the International Organization for Migration (IOM)[66] to 143 million by 2050 by the World Bank.[67] As one academic put it, some of these types of predictions rely upon 'heroic extrapolations'.[68] Although we know it will be severe, we do not know exactly what the scientific impact of anthropogenic climate change will be for displacement. There are a range of scenarios, but all involve rising sea levels, extreme weather events, desertification, flooding, and the transformation of habitats. We know that this will have social consequences in areas ranging from food security to livelihoods, albeit that the impact will vary with context and adaptation strategy. These social consequences will lead to impacts on mobility, migration, and displacement. From disappearing islands to natural disasters, people will be forced to flee. Furthermore, a significant impact of climate change will be its multiplier effects, exacerbating other drivers of displacement such as fragility and conflict. None of this is certain, because climate change and its relationship to displacement are mediated by social and political choices,[69] but it is likely.

At the moment, the world is struggling to make sense of the changing drivers of displacement. Restrictive politics around the world has left little appetite on either the right or left to expand the categories of people with a human rights-based entitlement to migrate beyond existing legal definitions. As a result, the traditional refugee / economic migrant dichotomy dominates politics and policy-making around the world, even though current drivers of displacement often defy simple categorization. The 1951 Convention definition of a refugee as someone fleeing based on 'a well-founded fear of persecution' remains the primary standard. And although it is often interpreted in light of contemporary circumstances to include groups such as those fleeing 'generalized violence', bureaucratic and judicial interpretations adapt slowly and inconsistently, leaving significant gaps.

I have used the term 'survival migration' to describe people fleeing complex drivers of displacement in fragile states, who do not neatly fit the definition of being either a refugee or an economic migrant. Their predicament is characterized by the interaction of weak governance, generalized violence, and food insecurity, for example. From Somalia to Afghanistan, an increasing proportion of the world's displaced fall into this category. Conditions make it impossible for many people to sustain the minimum conditions of human dignity without crossing a border, and yet many would not fit the 1951 Refugee Convention definition.

I first used the term 'survival migration' in the context of the exodus of Zimbabweans from Robert Mugabe's regime in the early 2000s.[70] Between 2003 and 2010, around 2 million Zimbabweans fled across to South Africa and other neighbouring states. Like Venezuelans today, for example, most were fleeing the economic consequences of the underlying political situation, rather than political persecution per se. Basic services were no longer available; poor governance and hyperinflation had ravaged the economy; people fleeing were faced with crime banditry in the border regions. In southern Africa, host states such as South Africa and Botswana could have invoked the 1969 Organization of African Unity (OAU) refugee convention definition of a 'refugee' as someone fleeing 'a serious disturbance to public order in whole or in part of the country'. But politics and sheer numbers pushed against that. And, as in Latin America today, UNHCR lacked the capacity and resources to countenance a large-scale refugee response. It was only from 2010, after deporting literally hundreds of thousands of Zimbabweans back to Mugabe's regime that a moratorium on deportation was put in place—but with virtually no additional assistance.

Today, it is a trend we see elsewhere in the world. In the Central American context, what we have witnessed at the US's south-western border is an archetypal example of survival migration. In 2019, an average of nearly 100,000 people per month are estimated to have left the Northern Triangle region of Central America for the US. This represented more than double the number of the each of the previous five years. Although 52 per cent of those moving identified 'economic opportunity' as their primary motive and 18 per cent cited 'insecurity and violence' as the main driver.[71] However, institutionally trying to distinguish between 'refugees' and 'economic migrants' does not do justice to the changing drivers of movement in the Northern Triangle.

Driving displacement has been the interaction of state fragility, generalized insecurity, extreme socio-economic deprivation, and environmental degradation. As the Centre for American Progress has written,

> there is no single, dominant factor—such as a war or a natural catastrophe—driving recent migration patterns in the Americas. Rather, the countries producing the largest share of migrants are all afflicted, to varying degrees, by an interlocking set of political, economic, and social challenges that have given rise to pervasive insecurity and desperation.[72]

Poverty levels are high across the Northern Triangle. Drought has contributed to large-scale crop failure, undermining livelihoods and food security in predominantly agricultural societies. And there are suggestions that climate change is making this worse. Meanwhile, weak governance contributes to pervasive levels of corruption, violence, and the absence of public services.

In the context of the Venezuelan crisis, policy-makers were utterly unsure how to label the crisis. Like the Zimbabwean situation in the early 2000s, people fled the economic consequences of the underlying political situation, rather than political persecution per se. The country was characterized by political mismanagement and socio-economic collapse from late 2015. Maduro armed up to half a million people and the country has close to the highest murder rate in the world. By late 2018 there was 500,000 per cent hyperinflation, 90 per cent poverty, and lack of access to food and basic services, and the numbers fleeing the country have gradually increased since 2017. In 2015, 22,000 Colombians were expelled and the borders closed as wealthier Venezuelans with family networks in the US and elsewhere began to leave. The mass exodus really only began, though, from 2017 as the full economic crisis took hold. Since then over 4 million Venezuelans, around 7–12 per cent of the population, have left the country. This is an unprecedented migration crisis for the region, comparable to the Central American crisis of the 1980s, when 15 per cent of El Salvador's population fled. Reflecting the uncertainty of how to label the crisis, policy responses diverge from country to country. International organizations have struggled to define the crisis. Until May 2019, UNHCR avoided describing fleeing Venezuelans as 'refugees' and then, under pressure from human rights activists, released a statement suggesting that 'most' Venezuelans actually are refugees in need of international protection.[73] The World Bank has characterized the drivers of migration as 'mainly based on economic reasons but with the characteristics of a refugee situation in terms of the speed of influx and levels of vulnerability'.[74]

From a political perspective, there has been a widespread reluctance to describe individuals like these Zimbabwean and Venezuelan, let alone Central American, migrants as 'refugees', even though it has been incontrovertible that they were fleeing failed states and were in need of international protection. The spectre of climate change will further accentuate the gap between dominant legal policy categories, on the one hand, and the realities of an age of displacement, on the other hand. In order to create sustainable refugee policies for an age of displacement, policy-makers will have to recognize and confront this gap between past categories and future realities. Once this change is recognized, it will be even more necessary to design operational models that can function at scale and endure over time.

Three allocation mechanisms for refugees

The question then is how best to fulfil and reconcile these three criteria for sustainability. What type of refugee system is likely to be effective? An international institutional framework for responding to refugees has to be able to fulfil a number of functions. It needs to provide a common definition of 'refugees', outline shared standards of response to refugees, and offer a basis for assigning governmental responsibility for refugees. The existing refugee system has historically been strong in outlining the first two of these—defining refugees and the rights to which they are entitled. However, the third element has been more ambiguous. Implicitly, it has assigned responsibility to whichever state's territory or jurisdiction a refugee happens to be in, and then left it to other states' discretion how to share responsibility with a host state. But if we hope to strive for sustainability, we need to identify a principle-based mechanism for allocating responsibility for refugees.

Once we recognize that all states have obligations towards refugees and that all states should engage in responsibility-sharing to support refugees, three archetypal allocation mechanisms stand out for allocating primary responsibility for particular refugees which we might describe as: free choice, equitable quotas, and neighbouring countries. In practice, all three co-exist. Here, though, I outline the archetypes and argue that while each one has a specific role to play—and all must be preserved and strengthened—a model based predominantly on the third approach is the only viable avenue for achieving sustainability.

Free choice

Allowing refugees to select their destination themselves is one possible allocation mechanism. The existing system is ambiguous about allowing this. Existing legal rules give some leeway for refugee choice. Countries are obliged under international refugee and human rights law to refrain from sending refugees back to countries in which they may face persecution or, by extension, serious harm. Refugee law is silent on how states collaborate to relocate refugees between 'safe countries'.[75] This leaves discretion for groups of states to create what are called 'safe third country' policies, such as the so-called Dublin system in the EU, to allocate primary responsibility to the first safe country a refugee reaches.[76] In practice, people fleeing, with a well-founded fear of persecution, can usually claim refugee status in the country whose territory or jurisdiction they reach without then being relocated to another 'safe' country, whether it is one that they have passed through or one to which responsibility is contracted.

However, the reality is that most countries around the world that do not neighbour conflict or crisis countries create significant barriers to what is called 'spontaneous arrival asylum'. Whether through visa requirements, border controls, or migration partnerships with third countries, most rich countries deploy a range of deterrence measures to prevent refugees moving across continents to seek asylum in, for example, Europe, the United States, or Australia. The result is that in order to claim asylum in a destination country of her choice, a refugee will usually require access to resources or networks in order to facilitate access to territory, whether through smuggling networks or legal routes of entry.

But to what extent should free choice be the primary allocation mechanism within the refugee system? Some liberal political theorists argue that freedom of movement is a human right. Kieran Oberman argues that movement, including across borders, is a crucial freedom like the right to speak, move, worship, or marry.[77] It is an integral part of a person's capacity to pursue her own life goals, and she should have a right to make mobility decisions without infringement. Chris Bertram suggests that any constraints on freedom must be based on the consent of all those whom they affect.[78] Within a state, consent would be an accepted principle for democratic rule, and he suggested this should equally apply to the transnational exercise of state authority. Would-be migrants and actual migrants should therefore have to consent to any structures based on coercion that affect their free choice. Meanwhile, Lea Ypi claims that the right to freedom of movement is especially important in a world in which the privileged position of people in rich countries is based on past and present injustice,[79] through the role of colonialism and global inequality in shaping access to a range of privileges including access to mobility rights.

Indeed, the choice of refugees to move freely from one 'safe' state to another is ethically analogous to the context of other forms of international freedom of movement.

All things being equal, promoting freedom of choice is a good thing. If the welfare of one person can be increased, without reducing the welfare of someone else then it is ethically incontrovertible to support the action. However, in practice, rights and claims relating to migration frequently clash. A range of political theorists offer reasons why it may be justifiable for states to limit international migration. From a communitarian perspective, Michael Walzer famously likened states to neighbourhoods, clubs, and families to argue that states and their citizens have the right to choose rules on membership.[80] Others have grounded citizens' rights to control entry to territory on different normative foundations. David Miller argues that states have a right to restrict immigration, save for a few exceptions.[81] These rights are based on a more nuanced interpretation of membership, grounded in democratic institutions, community, and history. And, for him, the exceptions exist only when someone faces a threat to their right to life or serious harm in the absence of access to territory. Matthew Gibney grounds the right to restrict immigration in the argument that human beings distinguish between special obligations to family, friends, and fellow citizens, from general obligations towards distant strangers.[82] Based on this distinction, any refugee policy within a liberal democratic state can only be effective insofar as the costs to citizens remain relatively low. Meanwhile, even from a liberal perspective, Joseph Carens recognizes the need for liberal theories of immigration to be reconciled with real-world constraints, and be viable options for democratically elected politicians.[83] Indeed, the strongest argument against open-door immigration policies in rich countries is probably a consequentialist argument based on the real-world implications in terms of political backlash and the knock-on effects for the liberal institutions that protect basic freedoms.

Given their flight from serious harm, refugees can be argued to have stronger moral claims to enter the territory of another state than other migrants not fleeing serious harm. Refugees' distinctive right to migrate is based on the circumstances necessitating border crossing in order to access fundamental rights. Migration matters insofar as it leads to access to the rights associated with being a refugee—notably protection, assistance, and solutions. However, insofar as these rights are met in any one particular country, the grounds for privileging refugees' free choice of destination over and above other groups of migrants are weak. The right of refugees (as refugees) to migrate is therefore a qualified right, which matters as a means to access other rights, rather than as an absolute entitlement.

In response to this, one might argue that refugees have a greater ethical claim to total freedom of movement than other people, simply because of their past ordeal. Refugees have already faced traumatic circumstances; migration control is inherently coercive, and using coercion against already vulnerable people could be considered additionally problematic. But the idea that past experience necessarily creates exemption from a rules-based framework is not something we would tend to accept in other areas. Instead, any distinction would need to be based on some specific characteristic of a particular refugee's predicament that required discretionary onward movement. Such a claim might, for example, be based on specific vulnerabilities for which discretionary migration provided a necessary part of the solution, or characteristics that are not specific to being a refugee per se such as family reunification or access to education.

The problem is that existing mechanisms of self-selection are ethically arbitrary. Empirically, refugees able to use spontaneous arrival asylum to claim refugee status in rich countries tend to be among the more socio-economically privileged. For example, survey data shows that Syrian refugees arriving spontaneously in Europe in 2015–16 were disproportionately likely to be male, young, and educated compared to those who remained in neighbouring host states such as Turkey, Lebanon, and Jordan.[84] Furthermore, having a seemingly inequitable basis for selecting refugees to travel to rich countries has consistently undermined political confidence in asylum and immigration policies in Europe and Australia, for example.[85] Given that asylum in rich countries is a politically finite commodity—albeit one that can be expanded based on progressive political change—scarce resources to support refugees need to be allocated in a principled and consistent manner in order to retain public confidence.

If numbers were low relative to political context, then allowing all refugees the free choice to move to rich countries might be ethically desirable. In accordance with liberal principles, it would allow enhanced freedom without creating costs or harm for others. But as we saw earlier, with higher numbers relative to political context, free choice for all becomes more challenging. It is something that is unnecessary in order to meet the core aims and purpose of the refugee system, but may risk jeopardizing political support for a system that fulfils its core functions for all refugees.

In terms of thresholds and backlash, high-, low-, and middle-income countries may all be affected. However, there are three distinctions between rich and poor host countries, which somewhat counterintuitively mean that the latter will generally have greater capacity to admit refugees onto their territory. First, the Potential Net Migration Index (PNMI) is lower for low- and middle-income countries, meaning that, other things being equal, immigration will be less politicized than in richer countries. The second stems from comparative advantage. Rich countries are in a position to transfer resources to support jobs, infrastructure, and public services in poor countries, potentially expanding political willingness to host refugees, in a way that is less available for rich countries.[86] The third is that the greater cultural and economic proximity between neighbouring host countries and countries of origin is likely to reduce the challenges, and hence political costs, of temporary integration. For these reasons, it may be generally more feasible—given significant investment from rich countries—for immediate neighbours to host larger numbers of refugees than to offer a free choice of final destination.

Nevertheless, an element of free choice is needed. The right to engage in spontaneous arrival asylum provides an important 'check and balance' in case people cannot find 'effective' protection closer to home or have other specific moral claims to move onwards. The reality today is that too few of the world's refugees receive adequate protection in exile, let alone timely access to long-term solutions, and so spontaneous movement becomes necessary to compensate for the failings of the wider refugee system in the countries that neighbour conflict and crisis. Spontaneous arrival asylum also offers a means to ensure a symbolic commitment by rich countries to accept refugees, which is necessary to sustain the willingness to host by neighbouring countries. However, leaving a door ajar for some self-selection relies upon two things: identifying the conditions under which free choice is ethically desirable, and creating mechanisms that make it operationally feasible and politically sustainable. In relation to the former, onward movement may be necessary for people who have been in limbo beyond a reasonable duration without prospect of a durable solution. It may also be necessary for people with specific vulnerabilities or needs that can only be met through onward movement such as family reunification or access to educational and even career opportunities that are unavailable in a neighbouring country.

However, given these criteria, there may be more effective ways to allow some choice-based onward movement than relying upon spontaneous movement, which often means using smugglers to bypass border controls. Such mechanisms include rich countries providing resettlement places based on specific criteria or providing humanitarian or other visas that allow people to travel safely rather than resorting to smuggling networks that place their lives at risk, allocate the right to migrate in morally arbitrary ways, and undercut public confidence in the wider refugee system.

Overall, therefore, it is not sustainable to rely upon free choice as the primary allocation mechanism for refugees when faced with the challenges of geography, numbers, and politics presented by an age of displacement. However, some element of choice needs to be retained as a check and balance for the most vulnerable, those who cannot access their rights close to home, and those who have other strong destination-specific claims unrelated to their refugee status. Specific mechanisms need to be created for refugees in particular circumstances to have wider migration options— including through resettlement, and humanitarian and other visas. And in some cases, such as when a migrant's circumstances back home suddenly change and she becomes a refugee (known as *sur place* refugees) or when effective protection and timely access to solutions are unavailable close to home, being able to spontaneously seek asylum anywhere in the world represents an important mechanism of last resort.

Equitable quotas

On the face of it, one means of allocating responsibility for refugees would be to establish quotas for the numbers of refugees each country should accept and then distribute them around the world accordingly. Indeed, the principle of 'responsibility-sharing' is widely acknowledged within the refugee system. The Preamble to the 1951 Convention notes that 'considering that the grant of asylum may place unduly heavy burdens on certain countries, and that a satisfactory solution of a problem which the United Nations has recognized the international scope and nature cannot therefore be achieved without international co-operation'.[87] Meanwhile the Global Compact on Refugees, agreed at the UN General Assembly in 2018 reasserts the principle.[88] However, the refugee system has historically lacked clearly defined mechanisms to ensure responsibility is actually shared on a fair and justifiable basis. Consequently, given strong norms of asylum (obligations that states have towards refugees who reach their territory) and weak norms of responsibility-sharing, geography has been the primary determinant of how refugees are distributed around the world.

A number of authors, most notably James Hathaway and Alexander Neve have argued that the most obvious way to ensure equitable responsibility-sharing would be by establishing resettlement quotas.[89] Indeed, Astri Suhrke has noted, based on the assumption that refugee protection is a global public good, that the temptation of states to free-ride on other states' provision of refugee protection means that to achieve an optimal provision of refugee protection requires the creation of binding quotas.[90] The allocation of quotas might, for example, be based on states' relative capacities to accept refugees, determined by factors such as their gross domestic product (GDP), popula-tion, or unemployment rate.[91] A quota-based approach has been applied in other international institutions, whether as a positive obligation to contrib-ute to global public goods or as a negative duty to refrain from creating global public bads.[92] Contributions quotas have been applied in areas of global economic governance, such as the management of the World Bank and International Monetary Fund (IMF)[93] or contributions to North Atlantic Treaty Organization (NATO).[94] Restrictive quotas have been used in international environmental agreements in areas such as the man-agement of fisheries or other common resources.[95]

James Hathaway has been one of the most consistent advocates for such a scheme in the refugee system, suggesting that a resettlement quota system represents the most effective means to fulfil to underlying purpose of the refugee regime. He has further argued that such schemes do not have to be based on a rigid approach to quotas but might include the notion of 'common-but-differentiated responsibility-sharing', allowing some states to specialize in providing money and others resettlement or asylum places. Hathaway argued that the creation of quotas for resettlement should have been a primary focus of the UN's Global Compact on Refugees.[96]

The argument for quotas is that they enable all states to be collectively better off than they would be acting in isolation. By cooperating rather than competing, quotas can overcome collective action failures, leading to higher net provision of a particular global public good. International agreement on quotas can be based on either fixed or market-based quota systems.

In other policy fields some quota systems have been designed to include market-based mechanisms that further improve efficiency by allowing states to trade their quotas. For example, the 1997 Kyoto Protocol to the 1992 UN Framework Convention on Climate Change (UNFCCC) included a so-called 'cap and trade' system whereby industries would be allocated allowances—either based on their past pollution levels or on an initial auction—limiting their annual greenhouse gas emissions. But rather than necessarily having to meet the obligations themselves, they could compensate another actor to meet the target on their behalf. The benefit of such an approach is that it enables a given quota to be met at a lower net cost.

The idea of tradeable quotas has been explored in relation to the global refugee system.[97] States would be allocated an obligation to accept a given percentage of the world's refugees based, for example, on their GDP/capita or other capacity-related criteria. However, they could then compensate another state to meet that quota on their behalf through a mutually agreed level of compensation. Those who favour such an approach have argued that it would ensure both an equitable and efficient distribution of the world's refugees, and increase the resources available to poorer countries were they to accept a disproportionately higher number of refugees.

Jesús Moraga and Hillel Rapoport, for instance, propose a Tradeable Refugee-Admission Quota System (TRAQS) model for allocating respon- sibility for refugees within the EU.[98] Stage one involves assigning quotas based on a 'distribution key' for a fair allocation of refugees based on popu- lation size, GDP, unemployment rate, and the number of spontaneous arrival asylum applications and resettlement places during the immediate past. Stage two involves making the initial quotas 'tradeable' by creating a market for admissions quotas. Furthermore. Moraga and Rapoport suggest that an additional third stage could even be added to allow refugees to have some choice in their final destination: a 'matching mechanism' to allow refugees to rank their preferred destination, allowing them to be assigned to their preference countries until the quotas for any particular country are filled.

Tradeable admissions quota schemes have the advantage of meeting overall refugee needs in a way that is collectively more efficient because it allows states to decide on their relative comparative advantage in either 'hosting' or 'funding' refugee protection. As Moraga and Rapoport put it, 'the market for admissions will allocate refugees so that they marginal cost of hosting them is equalised across destinations. The solution is efficient in that it minimises the total cost (or, for a given total costs, allows for the accommodation of more refugees)'.[99]

The application of tradeable quotas to the refugee context has been criticized from a variety of angles. Deborah Anker and colleagues, for example, argue that refugee quota trading risks commodifying refugees.[100] Mollie Gerver argues that such schemes potentially create rewards for action that states ought to follow anyway out of ethical and legal obligation; as she puts it 'the final country to receive refugees would be rewarded for not breaking what is currently the law, rather than rewarded for receiving more refugees than is required under the law'.[101] On the other hand, Jaakko Kuosmanen examines three common objections to such schemes: that they fail to take into account refugees' destination preferences (the 'preference objection'), that they demean refugees by commodifying their experiences (the 'dignity objection'), and that they risk exploiting weak countries by allowing them to be paid to host refugees (the 'exploitation objection').[102] He argues that all of these objections can be rejected or addressed through thoughtful institutional design. Indeed, his argument is that none of these objections outweighs the importance of ensuring that the core purpose of the refugee system—to provide protection, assistance, and solutions—can be met efficiently, and in ways that are an improvement on the status quo.

Indeed, Gerver and Kuosmanen both rightly highlight that Anker et al.'s commodification critique does not stack up. Tradeable quotas arguably commodify 'refugee protection' rather than refugees per se. But more importantly, if a particular form of institutional design improves access to protection, assistance, and solutions compared to the status quo, then that is surely the main standard by which it should be judged. Will Jones and Alex Teytelboym show how such schemes could be designed in ways that include far greater respect for the preferences, agency, and autonomy of refugees.[103] Moreover, Gerver's objection that the scheme would actually lead to worse outcomes than the status quo is based on a presumption of full legal compliance with international refugee law under the status quo, which, in the contemporary world is very far from the case.

The main objection to quotas, whether tradeable or not, comes from whether they are politically viable in practice. While they offer a means to fulfil our first normative criterion for sustainability, offering protection, assistance, and solutions, can they meet the other two criteria, of being reconcilable with politics and functional at scale? Proponents would argue that, yes, they can because they can collectively make all states better off than they otherwise would be. At best, quotas could lead to equity, efficiency, predictability, and hence better outcomes for both refugees and states. However, if this really is the case, why have states been so reluctant to consider quota schemes for refugees?

The glib answer is politics. Not all states come to the refugee system as equals. The most salient analytical feature of the international refugee system is power asymmetry.[104] In game theoretical terms, quotas work well to address Prisoner's Dilemma situations: they enable states with symmetrical interests and power relations to reach mutually beneficial outcome. But the refugee system is better characterized by the analogy of games such as the Suasion Game (also known as the Rambo Game), in which there is a power asymmetry between the main actors. The main asymmetry in the refugee system is between 'host states' proximate to crisis and conflict and 'donor state' far away from conflict. While the former would have strong incentives to accept binding quotas, the latter have strong incentives to preserve the status quo, whereby geography is the primary determinant of how responsibility for hosting refugees is allocated.

This type of power asymmetry between proximate and distant countries was present in the EU's failed attempt to create relocation quotas for refugees during the European refugee crisis. In September 2015, the European Council agreed to implement a relatively small regional relocation system for 160,000 refugees to be relocated from Greece and Italy across the EU. The European Commission's proposal was only passed because it was subject to qualified majority voting, meaning that the strong objections of several member states could be overridden. Even in a regional context in which there were relatively lower levels of power asymmetry compared to a global scale, relatively distant countries refused to accept the obligation to accept refugees from the EU's frontline countries. A year after the agreement, only 6,000 refugees had been relocated, and targets were revised downwards, as states refused to voluntarily participate.[105] Even when the Moria refugee camp on the Greek island of Lesbos burned to the ground in September 2020, EU member states struggled to relocate the 13,000 people who were made homeless and destitute as a result.

Quota schemes might be a component part of a sustainable refugee system. They can allow refugee resettlement to be undertaken on a more collaborative, equitable, and efficient basis. However, at inception they rely upon relatively more powerful actors giving up discretionary authority relating to resettlement, reducing some of the scope to take into account citizen preferences. And while they may be willing to do this for clearly defined cohorts of refugees and during particular situations, such schemes are likely to be vetoed by powerful states at large-scale or on an open-ended basis. The only way in which large-scale resettlement quota schemes could be created would be if citizens were persuaded on a large-scale that it was the morally right thing to do; and, while not impossible, everything we know about contemporary refugee politics suggests this is unlikely. Furthermore, there is a risk that attempting to impose binding quotas might reduce the willingness of electorates to support other elements of a sustainable refugee system such as a commitment to provide development and humanitarian assistance.

And it is also worth noting that, on a practical level, not all refugees need to be geographically relocated around the world. Many refugees have a preference to ultimately return home and so, rather than being assimilated in rich countries, it makes more sense for most to receive protection, assistance, and even solutions in a country that neighbours their homeland.

A more promising route is to encourage states to voluntarily contribute towards resettlement schemes, on the basis that it represents an important component of a sustainable refugee system. However, realistically, it will only be for relatively small numbers of refugees, and it should be used to target refugees for whom resettlement is a necessary part of their ability to access protection, assistance, and solutions. More specifically, resettlement should be applied to support people with specific needs that cannot be met closer to home or to enable those indefinitely trapped in limbo to access durable solutions.

Neighbouring countries

The only viable way to ensure protection, assistance, and solutions for all refugees, in a way that can be reconciled with both politics and the increasing scale of displacement over time, is to focus primarily on the countries that immediately neighbour areas of conflict and crisis.

These are the countries where most refugees are and will continue to be for the foreseeable future. And yet, the models we currently adopt in 'first countries of asylum' are often unfit for purpose. Across the countries that host 85 per cent of the world's refugees, the default solutions are usually the long-term encampment of refugees, often without the right to work or free-dom of movement, or urban self-settlement with limited access to assistance. These default responses are often sub-optimal for everyone involved. For refugees, they lead to restrictions on socio-economic rights and opportun-ities. For host countries, they do not maximize the potential to attract inter-national investment or for refugees to use their skills and talents to benefit the economy. For international donors, they lead to the inefficient use of scarce aid resources and risk an increased demand for onward migration.

The alternative approach is to reimagine refugee protection within neighbouring countries. Is it possible to create a model that meets our cri-teria for sustainability—one in which refugees have access to their full set of civil, political, economic, social, and cultural rights in the neighbouring countries and receive timely access to a durable solution, which can all be provided at scale while maintaining global, national, and local support?

The best means to achieve this is through what might be described as a development-based approach.

What might such an approach look like in practice? It has to involve transforming refugee-hosting regions into spaces of socio-economic oppor-tunity for both refugees and the nearby host communities. This requires significant external investment in job creation, infrastructure, and public services in refugee-hosting regions, whether rural or urban, and allowing refugees and citizens to share the benefits. Rather than an 'encampment' approach to refugee protection, it can involve opportunities for 'self-reliance', empowering refugees to help themselves and, in turn, to contribute to the host economy. Rather than a focus on just providing humanitarian aid, through food, clothing, and shelter, it would also involve development assistance to build local economies. Rather than perpetuating a narrative of

THE SEARCH FOR SUSTAINABILITY

refugees as an inevitable 'burden', it would seek to identify ways in which they can be a 'benefit' to the host economy and society. Rather than being based on closed camps that are just for refugees, it would strive to create opportunities for integrated settlements, shared by refugees and hosts, that can endure even after refugees have gone home. Rather than simply focusing on a particular population, it relies upon an area-based approach to development.

Underpinning this is a logic of 'common but differentiated responsibility-sharing' between states. Rather than all states in the refugee system contributing to refugee protection in identical ways, there is scope for a high degree of specialization. Distant, high-income countries contribute investment through development assistance (and resettlement places), while proximate, low- and middle-income countries provide the territory for the model. To be workable, the level of investment in development assistance has to be sufficient to enable refugees to access all their rights in exile while benefitting host citizens sufficiently to maintain local and national political support. It is precisely because of the potential convergence in interests between 'donors' and 'hosts' that the approach has the possibility to be sustainable, even in an age of displacement.

This vision is not new, even if it has recently been branded 'The New Way of Working' by UNHCR and others. The need to 'bridge the humanitarian-development gap' has long been highlighted in refugee policy circles. In many ways, it is as old as the modern refugee regime. From rural integration programmes for Assyrian refugees arriving in Greece in the 1920s to Tanzania's integrated rural settlements of the 1960s and 1970s to the integration of Guatemalan refugees in Mexico's Yucatan Peninsula in the 1990s, ideas relating to 'refugees and development' or 'self-reliance' have been tried, with sporadic success.

Despite these examples, however, the model has proved elusive in most parts of the world. And, at various historical junctures, the United Nations' attempts to scale the model—through initiatives with various acronyms and labels, from RAD and Convention Plus to the CRRF—have had a relatively modest legacy. This, however, has not necessarily been because the model is the wrong one; indeed, it is perhaps the only one that potentially meets our sustainability criteria. Rather, it is because there has been an absence of systematic learning about the economic and political conditions needed to make it a reality.

To further clarify, the development-based approach has three main elements, all closely inter-related: capabilities, autonomy, and markets.

First, it is based on recognizing that refugees have capabilities as well as vulnerabilities. Although many displaced people are vulnerable and in need of humanitarian assistance, this is only part of the story. Despite their common experience of fleeing awful circumstances, refugees are diverse and have a range of skills, talents, and aspirations. This means many have the potential capacity to study, work, and build businesses. But to make this possible, opportunities are needed that are all too often unavailable in refugee-hosting contexts. Creating viable, enabling environments relies upon significant investment in employment and livelihoods, infrastructure such as roads, electricity, water, and internet connectivity, and public services such as health and education.

Second, it aims to support refugees' autonomy. Rather than creating long-term dependency on humanitarian aid, it seeks to empower refugees to help themselves, and to contribute to the host societies. This approach has often been described as self-reliance—supporting refugees to meet their basic needs independently of aid. And while self-reliance has often been seen in purely economic terms, it also has important social and political dimensions, requiring a shift wherever possible towards allowing refugees opportunities for political representation and self-governance. Achieving this, however, relies upon changing how refugees are usually governed, giving them socio-economic rights and freedoms, and ensuring they can participate actively in the decision-making of humanitarian organizations.

Third, it is built upon the creation of functioning markets, in which both refugees and proximate citizens have an equal right to participate. Participation in functioning markets is crucial for the achievement of autonomy and for host communities to benefit economically from the presence of refugees. It enables refugees to engage in all aspects of economic life: as buyers, sellers, employees, employers, borrowers, lenders, producers, and consumers. But this relies upon creating an environment that is conducive to private-sector investment, business development, and entrepreneurship. And this in turn, relies upon the government and international community investing in the public goods needed for private-sector-led development to take hold, whether in agriculture, manufacturing, services, or the digital economy; moving towards cash-based assistance models; and improving access to capital among refugee and host communities.

A development-based approach has the potential to lead to sustainability because it can meet the requirements relating to rights, politics, and scale. It can enhance rights by ensuring refugees are accorded not only civil and political rights but also, their often neglected, socio-economic rights. It can also support durable solutions by ensuring that refugees can develop and maintain the human capital needed to contribute to either the reconstruction of their country of origin or a third country following resettlement. It can maintain political support because it is built upon interest convergence at global, national, and local levels, provided there is significant external investment that enables citizens to share in the benefits, preventing or mitigating the type of backlash described earlier in this chapter. And, unlike the other two archetypal allocation models, it has the potential to operate at scale and endure over time. Integrated settlements in neighbouring countries may potentially host hundreds of thousands of refugees in regions which often have similar economic and cultural characteristics to their country of origin.

However, the specific characteristics of sustainable refugee settlements nevertheless remain vague. Even if we accept that most refugees will need to receive protection in neighbouring countries and the best way to achieve this is a 'development-based approach', this still leaves a lot that is open-ended. Identifying effective models, and the conditions which will lead to sustainability is an empirical question that requires evidence.

In 2014, UNHCR published its *Policy on Alternatives to Camps*. It recognizes that while camps can be essential during an emergency, they 'can have significant negative effects over the long-term'. It suggests that camps can lead to 'dependency and weaken the ability of refugees to manage their own lives, which perpetuates the trauma of displacement and creates barriers to solutions'. On that basis, it suggests that camps should be the exception, highlighting the need to explore alternative, diverse forms of context-specific alternatives.[106] Such alternatives might include urban living in major cities, integration within progressive small towns in border regions, creating new integrated settlements, or transforming existing camps into sustainable settlements. However, what has been missing is a compelling evidence base relating to the conditions under which particular forms of sustainable alternatives to encampment can be created or emerge over time in particular contexts. What models are available in terms of design, and what incentives are needed to induce national and local actors to adopt them?

Before turning to the evidence on the economics and politics of creating sustainable refugee settlements, however, it is first worth considering possible critiques of a development-based approach that focuses predominantly on the neighbouring countries. By doing so we might be able to mitigate the potential hazards that come from such an approach, including the risk that such an approach may be applied disingenuously by politicians or policy-makers.

Critiques of development-based approaches

There are at least three possible objections to focusing primarily on a development-based approaches in neighbouring countries which are worth discussing because they have implications for the kinds of ethical principles that need to underlie their design and implementation.

Containment?

Many detractors of a development-based approach are concerned that an approach that focuses on 'first countries of asylum' risks 'containing' refugees in their regions of origin, whether directly or through the policies that it legitimates.[107] It is undeniable that a lot of the political motivation for the economic inclusion of refugees in neighbouring countries comes from a desire to reduce onward movement to Europe and the rich world. Ever since the early 2000s, a core group of European states, notably Denmark, the Netherlands, and the UK have pushed for an approach called 'protection in the region of origin', premised upon strengthening assistance close to home as a means to reduce the need for 'irregular secondary movement'. And these ideas run through the contemporary push by Europeans states to support development-based approaches to refugee assistance, including 'self-reliance'. For example, the 4.6 billion euro EU Emergency Trust Fund for stability and addressing root causes of irregular migration and displacement in Africa (EUTF for Africa), which supports refugee self-reliance in Africa, was created in 2015 with an explicit goal of reducing onward refugee migration to Europe.[108]

However, there are a whole series of arguments as to why, even if this is a significant part of the motive, focusing on regions of origin is normatively justifiable from the perspective of non-ideal theory, especially in an age of displacement. There is a debate within the ethics of asylum literature on whether liberal democratic states have greater obligations towards proximate or far-away refugees. Walzer argues, based on an 'acts versus omissions' distinction, that states have greater obligations towards those who are proximate because the act of using coercion against a nearby refugee is worse than the omission of failing to support distant refugees.[109] But this acts versus omissions distinction is morally untenable. We have a shared, global responsibility to ensure protection, assistance, and solutions for *all* refugees. And, as Gibney points out, it is valid to collectively work towards a shared global response that better meets the needs of all refugees and does so at lower collective cost to states.[110]

There are other reasons why the 'containment' argument does not stand up well against a development-based approach. 1) Given that most refugees are already in low- and middle-income countries, that is where we should focus our support. 2) The desire to manage migration is a central part of the motivation that underlies rich countries' willingness to pay to fund development opportunities for the majority of the world's refugees. From a consequentialist perspective, it is therefore a key element of what enables interest-based support for a development-based approach. 3) The purpose of the refugee system is not migration. And, although one might argue that all people have a right to migrate, open borders is not something that is feasible from a non-ideal perspective. It is simply not realistic or sustainable to move everyone to rich countries; but rich countries can pay to create better lives for refugees closer to their countries of origin. 4) The future reconstruction and development of countries of origin relies upon their citizens ultimately going home, and they are empirically more likely to do so if they stay close to home. 5) It is likely to be easier to create opportunities for people in countries with similar economies and cultural contexts than to absorb and assimilate them to very different societies. 6) If we recognize that rich countries in today's world have a strong incentive to limit migration, then surely it is better for them to create models that build anchors rather than walls; offering refugees better lives closer to home instead of relying on coercion to limit onward movement.[111] 7) If we believe that migration, relocation, or resettlement are important for some groups of refugees, then, in a non-ideal world, it is imperative to ensure that those scarce opportunities are allocated on a principled basis—both because it is inherently desirable to justly allocate scarce resources and because it is may be the only means to sustain political support for such opportunities.

However, the critique does draw our attention to the need to ensure that the rhetoric of development-based approaches 'in regions of origin' is not used to legitimate a restrictive agenda that simply leaves refugees indefinitely in intractable limbo in camps, with few rights and opportunities. In this context, resettlement has a key role to play as a complement to the focus on neighbouring countries. It is important on a practical level to protect people who have specific vulnerabilities or needs that cannot be met in camps, such as family unity, education, or particular forms of work. It is important as a means to ensure that people who cannot eventually return home or be naturalized in the host country have a pathway to integration and citizenship somewhere. And it also matters on a symbolic level to demonstrate that hosting refugees is a shared, global responsibility.

Neo-liberalism?

Another common criticism of this vision of development-based approaches relates to the ethics of a market-based approach to refugees. The 'neo-liberalism' charge is that that we risk exposing vulnerable refugees to exploitative competition.[112] Indeed, there are ethical issues at stake. What do markets do to create winners and losers among refugees? To what extent is inequality, or even the occurrence of 'refugee millionaires', in refugee camps or settlements morally acceptable? What are the risks of harm from multinational corporations investing in refugee settlements or employing refugees, and can they be mitigated?

Indeed, there is a literature on the ethics of capitalism, which provides a range of common critiques. First, there is the standard Marxist critique that capitalism leads to the extraction of surplus value from labour by the owners of capital. However, we do generally accept that profit is a justifiable reward to capitalists for investing capital, taking on risk, and providing expertise and organizational oversight.[113] Second, there is Arjun Appadurai's 'commodification' argument that capitalism too often objectifies human beings by regarding them as a means to an end rather than a moral end in their own right.[114] Third, there is the argument that capitalism shapes culture. By reducing everything to commodity and property, markets have effects on character and community, potentially undermining other sources of reciprocity.[115]

However, markets can also offer significant benefits. First, they enable individuals to have autonomy to freely choose what they consume and produce subject to the constraints of the market. Second, they allow groups of people to attain better overall outcomes than they otherwise would attain—Pareto improvement—by exchanging with others until marginal benefits are equalized across all goods and all market participants. Third, participation in markets can promote dignity and reduce dependency by enabling people to self-identify as self-sufficient. For example, being able to work is generally associated with better psychosocial outcomes than dependency on social security or humanitarian assistance.

From a liberal perspective, the standard we would generally use to assess the validity of extending markets is whether it enhances agency for individuals and communities. Following Amartya Sen's notion of 'development as freedom',[116] this could be conceived as comprising both the entitlement to choose and the capability to choose. Autonomy underpins the history of Western political thought. John Stuart Mill argued in *On Liberty* that mature rational individuals should be permitted to choose any course of action (the 'liberty principle'), with two provisos: that there be no harmful consequences to another person (the 'harm condition'), and that people not be allowed to indefinitely relinquish their own freedom (the 'slavery condition').[117] Applied to a refugee context, this suggests we should be designing 'the surrogate state' of refugee protection in such a way that maximizes autonomy in all areas, social, political, and economic, with two conditions: first, that we may limit freedom in areas in which harms are conferred upon others, whether the wider refugee community or the host society, for example; second, that any trade-off of freedom for other entitlements such as assistance should be a) consensual and b) lead to the long-term enhancement of autonomy.

In the refugee context, there are specific reasons to believe that the freedom to engage in market-based exchange can have positive benefits, compared to the alternative of long-term dependency on humanitarian aid. Refugees in camps around the world consistently say they want jobs and the chance to support their families, and so, from this perspective, expanding their autonomy and choice through work and opportunity is a good thing. It is what many refugees claim to want. Furthermore, a number of psychological studies reveal that work contributes to better psychosocial outcomes for refugees.[118]

It is also worth noting that there is nothing incompatible with empowering refugees through access to markets and also ensuring protection for the most vulnerable. Indeed, the starting point is that most refugee camps have historically been run based on a de facto socialist assumption—everyone should get the same, and attain the same welfare outcome. The shift I am advocating is not towards a libertarian extreme; it is more equivalent to a move from a socialist status quo towards the analogue of a social democratic model, in which both assistance and markets co-exist.

There is a general acceptance that for most of the world, functioning market economies are the best available resource allocation system, despite their imperfections. And so, if the neo-liberal charge is going to stand up, we need to ask whether there is anything specific about refugees that means they require additional levels of protection from markets. How different or distinctive are refugees as market-based actors? Are any of these differences ethically salient? Three possible distinctions stand out.

First, regulation. Refugee generally face different institutional constraints compared to citizens, in areas that may include the right to work, business registration, the enforcement of contracts, and property rights. This shapes the terms on which they enter markets, including the labour market. Whether they face de facto or de jure differences in regulatory constraints, compared to hosts, any additional constraints—such as higher levels of police harassment or 'taxation'—undermine the assumption that refugees come to markets as equals. In particular, where refugees face limitations relating to their mobility, this undermines the premise of the Heckscher-Ohlin model that labour can simply relocate to where it receives the greatest return. This restriction is especially likely in a refugee camp environment, and if refugees have limited mobility but capital does not, the risk is to create contexts analogous to the 'Bantustans' of Apartheid South Africa, in which mobile capital thrived by extracting labour from immobile workers.[119] This contrasts with cities, in which refugees are more likely to be de facto integrated but where the evidence suggests refugees nevertheless still usually face a degree of regulatory asymmetry.

The best way to overcome this is therefore to reduce the regulatory asymmetry between refugees and citizens. But even if there is some degree of asymmetry, refugees may still be better off being able to engage in markets than excluded from them. The key to preventing exploitation (in the liberal rather than the Marxist sense) is to ensure that refugees have a meaningful capacity to withhold consent by, for example, withdrawing their labour without risking poverty or destitution.

Second, protection. Refugees are, by definition, in need of international protection. Does this mean that we have an additional duty of care relating to their interaction with markets? From an international law perspective, economic and social rights are a central aspect of international refugee law. It requires that refugees enjoy an equivalent standard to the wider national context. But from an ethical perspective does the fact refugees are in need of international protection really mean they need protecting from markets? Probably not. The purpose of international protection is to ensure that, when people flee persecution, they do not face forced return to persecution and that they have access to their basic rights. The goal is to restore normality; it is not to infantilize. But are there additional protection needs for specific vulnerabilities, and might any of these vulnerabilities be exacerbated by access to markets?

Clearly there are some duties of care that need to be extended to all refugees, such as *non-refoulement*. Others—notably protection from socio-economic vulnerabilities—are likely to be needed by different refugees to different degrees. Insofar as international actors are in a surrogate governance role, by running camps or settlements, they are playing a custodianship role. This does not rule out a role for markets at all. But it implies two conditions for markets playing a role: it should be in the interest of refugees, individually and collectively, and there should be the possibility to opt out of work without being penalized. In other words, there must still be a social protection safety net available to all refugees.

Third, community. Another plausibly salient ethical distinction between refugees and citizens is their different structures of community. Particularly in camps, but possibly also in some urban contexts, refugees may have cultures that manage exchange, reciprocity, or finance, for example, in ways that are distinctive from a free market logic. For example, among Somali refugee communities, Islamic finance or trust-based social insurance mechanisms often play a key role in structuring economic life. Is there a risk that embracing a market-based logic within refugee settings risks displacing or 'crowding out' community structures? Here again, I would argue that it is not the place of international protection actors to protect refugees from cultural change. The key is to ensure that it is possible for refugees to collectively and individually maintain non-market based cultural practices alongside being able to participate in a market-based economy.

Imperialism?

Another possible objection to development-based approaches is that it that they impose a solution on refugees or on host countries. However, this does not need to be the case. My vision for sustainable refugee protection is one in which refugees can gradually achieve greater opportunities for self-governance. One of the long-standing presumptions within refugee studies is that a feature of the refugee experience is that people are rendered as what Hannah Arendt and Giorgio Agamben call 'bare life', denuded of their political identity.[120] This could not be further from the truth. Even in exile, refugees frequently engage in political activity, whether oriented towards the host country, country of origin, or transnationally.[121] And yet there remains a pervasive assumption that refugee camps and settlements should primarily be governed by international organizations in collaboration with the host-country government. While this may be necessary during an emergency phase, over time, refugees should have opportunities to participate in self-governance in order to shape the rules and regulations that define their social worlds.

In work with Kate Pincock and Evan Easton-Calabria, I explore the ways in which refugees already mobilize to create a range of refugee-led organizations (RLOs) within refugee camps and cities.[122] Despite a lack of international funding or recognition, RLOs frequently provide a crucial source of social protection in areas including social insurance, education, and livelihood. In order to do so, they usually have to bypass the formal humanitarian system and seek other sources of funding through their own transnational networks. In Kampala, for instance, at least three RLOs have raised over $100,000 and assisted more than 1,000 people each, but none has been able to achieve any formal status as an implementing or operational partner of UNHCR. The wide-ranging practices and success of some of those organizations highlight the potential for refugees to play a greater role in the provision of protection and assistance, as well as for more participatory forms of refugee governance.

Felix Bender examines the ethics of self-governance in refugee camps from the perspective of 'non-ideal theory'.[123] He begins from two sets of premises. First, refugee camps constitute a political unit. They are a territorially bounded unit and they are subject to rules and governance structures. Second, people have a right to public autonomy. This is because people have a right to control the external conditions that shape their lives. Public autonomy is the only way to collectively define a 'legitimate' regulation or an infringement of personal autonomy. And only by being publicly autonomous can we inform decisions about those conditions and rules.

Indeed, one of the challenges of providing refugees with opportunities for self-governance is that the host state exercises authority on its territory, and that in practice refugee communities are often not hermetically sealed but interact with and are interdependent with the surrounding host communities. However, there is an easy solution to this. One could envisage hybrid governance models that take into account complex social systems.

While there may be overlaps between refugee communities and the host society, this is a challenge that exists in a variety of multi-layered authority structure, such as cities.

From this perspective, a sustainable approach can be an opportunity to create integrated settlement structures that do not impose governance, but gradually shift towards models of self-governance, which enable both refugees and host communities to exert public autonomy in shaping their own lives in exile. As well as being inherently valuable in promoting autonomy, it may even represent another means to achieve sustainability by reducing potential costs and sources of conflict for the host society.

A variant of the imperialism argument is that the approach imposes a solution on host countries.[124] Certainly, the necessity and possibility for focusing mainly on neighbouring countries is a reflection of power asymmetry in world politics. Host states are predominantly in the Global South and donor states are predominantly in the Global North. The former have little choice but to admit refugees; the latter have discretion in the degree to which they engage in responsibility-sharing. Roger Zetter argues that the elements of a development-based approach—which he describes as 'the humanitarian-development nexus'—reflect North–South power asymmetries in the international political economy.[125] This is analytically correct and important as a critique of power. But it need not, as Zetter suggests, imply 'imperialism' or 'empire'. It implies that states, who come to the international system with different degrees of bargaining power, negotiate based on their relative status and interests. And without the means to immediately overcome power imbalances in the global system, international cooperation—based on interest convergence—offers the best available means to improve outcomes for both refugees and the citizens of host countries *given* the existing structures of world politics.

Conclusion

We live in an age of displacement. Fragile states, armed conflict, food insecurity, climate change, and global pandemics are among the factors that will increasingly interact to drive people from their homes. However, the paradox is that as refugee numbers rise, societies are becoming ever less welcoming to migrants in general. It is this tension that makes sustainability an important concept in relation to refugee assistance. How can we ensure that refugees have access to protection, assistance, and solutions in a way that retains political support, and can endure at scale and over time? Reconciling rights, politics, and scale will be an ongoing challenge for the global refugee system. But if that system is going to survive, it will have to meet that challenge head on.

In thinking about models for sustainability, I have been guided by political realism, adopting what philosophers call a non-ideal theory approach of considering ethical and normative questions within the constraints of contemporary world politics. Based on an assumption that the underlying drivers of restrictive migration politics, particularly but not only in rich countries, are likely to worsen rather than improve, I have looked for ways in which sustainability might be achieved despite those limitations.

Over the long term, we might hope for a better world in general. Persuasion and appeal to the values of the next generation may well lead to a more just global order, it may well end wars and combat climate change, and it might even lead more societies to welcome refugees and migrants in general by recognizing the contributions they can make. In the short term, however, world politics—including refugee politics—is largely shaped by power and interests. And that is the reality that our analysis and our policies need to adapt to. Multi-polarity, the reduced legitimacy of international liberal order, and the relative economic decline of the 'West' are among the factors that will bedevil the world's capacity to combat the root causes of displacement and its willingness to absorb large numbers of refugees.

In this context, I have outlined three archetypal models for allocating responsibility for refugees: free choice, equitable quotas, and neighbouring countries. Elements of all three are seen in the existing refugee system and aspects of all three should be preserved. But only the third model can ensure refugee rights in a way that is compatible with politics and scale. For the overwhelming majority of the world's refugees, an approach that focuses on creating enabling environments for both refugees and host communities in the countries that neighbour conflict and crisis is the best available option. But our current, dominant responses in these countries are not fit for purpose; we should strive to do far better. With a focus on capabilities, autonomy, and markets, a development-based approach should offer opportunities for refugees and the proximate host communities to flourish, until refugees are able to go home or be integrated elsewhere. And it should be complemented by the principled use of resettlement for people who would otherwise end up in indefinite limbo or who simply cannot attain access to their rights in a neighbouring country, and spontaneous arrival asylum as a safety net for those who cannot otherwise access their entitlements.

Preserving—and expanding—refugee protection is possible. But it requires us to adapt our old analytical lenses and be strategic in how we pursue it. It requires knowledge, evidence, and ongoing learning about what actually works, and under what conditions, within a changing world. In the next chapters, we move from the normative to the empirical. We examine the conditions under which we can create sustainable refugee policies in practice. Focusing on East Africa, we look at the economics to understand what works, and at the politics to understand how it can be made to work.

PART
II

Economics—*what works?*

3

Refugee economies

Introduction

Refugees, being human beings, have economic lives. This may seem like an obvious, even banal, claim. But it is one that has often been marginal to how policy-makers have responded to refugees. They have more commonly been viewed primarily as passive victims in need of humanitarian assistance, or as a threat to security. And yet in cities and camps everywhere, refugees engage in all aspects of economic life—consumption, production, exchange, saving, borrowing, and lending. In doing so they often make significant contributions to receiving societies.

The popular image of a refugee camp is endless lines of tents with UN trucks delivering food aid. In practice, though, many are often a hive of economic activity. The Nakivale settlement in Uganda has three formal markets—Juru, Rubondo, and Base Camp—and each one has market stalls run by both refugees and Ugandans, buying and selling everything from sorghum to meat, mobile phones, textiles, and alcoholic beverages. The shops that line the streets of its New Congo, Little Kigali, and Somali Village areas include a Somali bus company, a Congolese-run cinema, Ethiopian restaurants, a computer gaming shop where young people use the internet or play FIFA. The telecommunications companies Orange and MTN have vendors spread across the settlement, selling handsets, sim cards, and airtime.

In some ways, Nakivale is unusual—it is Africa's oldest refugee settlement and Uganda allows refugees to work. But even in the countries with tighter regulatory restrictions, informal market-based activity is usually widespread. The Kakuma refugee camps in Kenya have over 2,000 registered small businesses, nearly half the total for the entire region,[1] which is geographically larger than Switzerland.[2] Most are small in scale, employing no more than one or two people, usually other family members. The majority are food retailers but art-work, jewellery, sports equipment, and services such as hairdressing and child care can all be purchased. Exceptionally, larger businesses emerge. Mesfin Getahun, an Ethiopian refugee known as 'the millionaire of Kakuma', runs one of the largest food wholesalers in the region, even supplying World Food Programme (WFP) programmes.[3]

The scale of markets in camps should not be exaggerated or romanticized. The International Finance Corporation estimated Kakuma's economy to be worth $56 million, but that is just $300 a year in per capita expenditure.[4] Nevertheless, refugee camps are economies. Market-based activity can be seen in practically every refugee camp in the world—from the Shams Elysée boulevard running through the middle of the Za'atari camp in Jordan to the Lamba Chiya Bazar in the Kutupalong Camp in Bangladesh. Only rarely have I visited camps that did not have recognized markets—earlier incarnations of the Ali Addeh camp in Djibouti and the Azraq camp in Jordan—and, even in those, informal economic activity took place below the radar and supply chains and networks connected the camps regionally, nationally, and globally.

In cities across the developing world—from Amman to Bogotá—refugees are usually further integrated into existing economies than they are in camps, albeit that they may face far greater obstacles to gaining full participation than citizens. The larger market opportunities are illustrated by refugees' generally much higher incomes in cities than camps—around a 300 per cent difference across our research sites. In other words, by moving to cities, refugees might give up humanitarian aid, but they are likely to earn higher incomes. However, when compared to citizens, refugees often face greater discrimination, police harassment, language barriers, lack of access to finance, and legal restrictions on employment and entrepreneurship. These impediments do not extinguish economic activity but they raise transaction costs, reflected in an urban 'income gap' between citizens and refugees living in the same neighbourhoods.

Many refugees participate in existing urban markets, despite regulatory restrictions. Kampala's Owino market, the largest market in East Africa, offers a space for many refugee businesses to buy and sell. Congolese fabrics and jewellery, Rwandan dairy produce, and Eritrean-run internet cafes can be found in or on the margins of the market. Elsewhere, many ethnic suburbs (sometimes called 'ethnoburbs') create their own localized markets, attracting visitors from across the city. Perhaps most famously, Eastleigh in Nairobi has become known as 'Little Mogadishu', with up to 100,000

Somali refugees and migrants living alongside Kenyan Somalis. Among Kenyans, Eastleigh has become renowned as a dynamic and affordable market in which to purchase clothing, food, and jewellery imported from Mogadishu and the Middle East.[5] The suburb is estimated to contribute up to a quarter of Nairobi's entire tax revenue. 'Somali areas' such as Kisenyi in Kampala and Bole Michael in Addis Ababa play a similar role, albeit on a smaller scale.

These dynamics are not unique to low- and middle-income countries. In the aftermath of the 2015–16 European refugee crisis, stories of refugee entrepreneurship have been promoted across Europe's cities. Some Syrian businesses have thrived. In Berlin, Hiba and Khaled Albassir run Khashabna ('Our Wood' in Arabic) which sells hand-made garden furniture imported from Damascus.[6] Salma Al Armarchi runs Jasmin Catering, which provides meals for corporate events.[7] Refugee entrepreneurship in Europe has been supported by a range of accelerators and incubators, from the Migration Hub in Berlin to the Entrepreneurial Refugee Network in London. Meanwhile, multinational corporations from Ben & Jerry's to Deloitte have tried to support 'refugee entrepreneurs'. The evidence, however, suggests that Syrian refugees in Europe still face major barriers to both employment and entrepreneurship. Nevertheless, with government and private investment in training, employment rates for Syrians in Germany increased from 20 per cent in 2015 to 35 per cent three years later,[8] offering a means to fill some of a country with an ageing population's present and future labour shortages.

Why does it matter that we recognize and study the economic lives of refugees?

First, it matters in terms of rights. Refugees have socio-economic rights under both international refugee and human rights law.[9] And these often go unmet and sometimes fall well below the standards enjoyed by the host community. Creating an effective right to an adequate standard of living is about both entitlements and capabilities. It is about both law and economic opportunity.[10] Enjoying socio-economic opportunities is also causally connected to people's sense of dignity, purpose, and wellbeing. Indeed, a number of psychological studies show how access to employment for instance is correlated with a range of positive mental health outcomes, both in general and for refugees in particular.[11] Understanding the conditions under which refugees can and cannot access socio-economic rights is therefore of fundamental concern for their human rights.

Second, it matters for policy. Understanding the economic lives and behaviour of refugees offers a means to identify the policy levers that may lead to particular outcomes in terms of welfare, social cohesion, and migration. For example, knowing that a particular 'X' percentage increase in education, access to land, or employment is associated with a 'Y' percentage increase in income or expenditure, controlling for a particular set of variables, can help to identify effective and efficient ways to improve the lives of refugees. That enables public and private actors to design evidence-based programmes that improve outcomes for refugees and host communities, while also ensuring that such programmes make best use of scarce resources. Explaining variation in observed outcomes is therefore crucial for evidence-based policy-making.

Third, it matters for politics. Recognizing refugees' skills, talents, and aspirations offers an opportunity to reshape public narrative. It enables changes in framing, from burden to benefit, from vulnerability to capacity, and from passivity to agency. Existing research on public attitudes across Europe reveals that the public, regardless of age, income, education, or political ideology are more likely to be supportive of refugees who are perceived to make an economic contribution. Kirk Bansak and his colleagues use data from fifteen EU states to show that 'the expected economic contribution or potential economic burden of asylum seekers play an important role in structuring asylum preferences', with refugees' employment background explaining up to 13 percentage points of difference in public support.[12] Meanwhile, in Kenya, there is some evidence that the public supports refugees being allowed to contribute to the national economy; only 7 per cent of Kenyans believe refugees actually contribute to the economy but 72 per cent believe the government should enable them to do so by offering the right to work.[13] Highlighting the economic lives of refugees—using a combination of data and human stories—therefore offers a means for influencing public attitudes and sustaining democratic support for progressive refugee policies.

There are, of course, critiques of focusing too narrowly on the economic lives of refugees.[14] We should not romanticize or exaggerate the economic capacities of refugees. Many refugees have vulnerabilities and may not be able to support themselves or their families. In practice, most refugee entrepreneurship is small-scale 'necessity entrepreneurship' and the majority of the world's refugees are poor and struggling. Some refugees are at risk of exploitation and abuse within a market-based economy, especially when they lack effective recourse to law. There is a further risk that governments abuse a focus on refugees' economic activities to disingenuously justify the premature withdrawal of humanitarian assistance or to erode human rights obligations. Any focus on refugees' contribution to economic development, the critics argue, must not lead to a hierarchy in which refugees become conditionally valued for their economic contributions. All refugees should have a core basket of entitlements—international protection— irrespective of their economic status.

But these very valid critiques should not, however, be interpreted as arguments against research on the economic lives of refugees. They are arguments for more accurately describing, understanding, and explaining the diversity of refugees' economic lives, and then using this knowledge to build on the latent and obvious potential that exists to strengthen opportunities for all.

In this chapter, I outline some of the most interesting insights developed by the Refugee Economies Programme based at the University of Oxford. I discuss some of the theory, methodology, and empirical findings of the work. First, I outline the concept of 'refugee economies'. Second, I explain the origins of the Refugee Economies Dataset. Third, I outline some of the insights offered by the data in three areas: welfare, social cohesion, and mobility. I explain why these insights matter for the design of sustainable refugee policies.

Refugee economies concept

'Refugee economies' can be defined as the resource allocations systems in which refugees participate.[15] One possible critique of this concept is the idea that it creates a sense of 'separateness' between refugees and the wider economy. To avoid this connotation, it has been suggested that it may be more appropriate to talk about 'economies in which refugees participate' rather than 'refugee economies'. It is generally true that refugees do participate in wider global, national, and local economic systems, even when they reside in remote refugee camps. For example, in camps across East Africa, Somali shops sell tins of tuna fish, a fish that cannot be found in local waters and is imported from as far afield as Thailand, via Saudi Arabia and ports such a Mombasa or Djibouti. From supply chain to remittances, refugees' economic lives are interconnected with wider economic systems, including transnationally.

The concept of 'refugee economies' is therefore not intended to imply geographical isolation; it is intended to signal analytical distinctiveness. Are there particular characteristics that make refugees' economic lives different from other populations, such as citizens or other migrants? Despite their within-group diversity, do refugees face different sets of opportunities and constraints as a result of being refugees? And, if so, what are these distinctive features? Are these differences inherent to the experience of being a refugee or contingent on other factors?

Other than geography, there are at least two ways in which 'economies' can be distinguished from one another. The first, which is consistent with the assumptions of neo-classical economics, is based on *institutions*.[16] For example, a national economy, a household,[17] a prison economy,[18] or the Kibbutzim[19] have been conceived as distinctive economies because of their institutional separateness. They have particular regulatory systems, which lead to specific incentive structures for individual behaviour. The second, derived from behavioural economics, is based on *identity*.[20] Behavioural economics suggests that particular groups of people may make economic decisions differently because of variation in a range of psychological, emotional, cultural, and social factors.

Some of these ideas have been influential in development economics. In relation to institutions, the so-called 'new institutional economics of development', for example, has shown how institutions affect development outcomes.[21] This work, developed notably by economist Douglass North, highlights two main mechanisms: transaction costs and information. Institutions—such as property rights, contract guarantees, and bankruptcy laws—affect the costs of market transactions. This is because they change the ability of people in negotiation, monitoring, and enforcement of contracts. Weak or restrictive institutions impose higher costs on people, which in turn undermines performance. Institutions also shape available information which influences economic decision-making. For example, in agrarian economies, imperfect information relating to climate, technology, or the supply of credit can adversely affect capital, insurance, or futures markets, and undermine performance.[22]

There has been a growing focus on the role of identity in development economics. George Akerlof and Rachel Kranton have shown that people's social identities shape their choices and actions. They look, for example, at the role of gender and race in shaping behaviour and decision-making relating to areas as diverse as consumption, work, and education.[23]

The identity economics literature has rarely been applied to rethink development economics.[24]

A related change has been to ask what is distinctive about the 'the poor', not just in terms of outcomes but also their distinctive economic behaviour and decision-making. Although they do not draw upon identity economics, Abhijit Banerjee and Esther Duflo have tried to understand the economic lives of the poor.[25] They examine a series of behavioural observations that cannot be adequately explained from a neo-classical economic perspective. Through a series of surveys around the world, they examine how 'the extremely poor', those living on less than \$1 per day, and 'the poor', those living on less than \$2 per day, survive. Their analysis gives rise to a series of empirical puzzles for which existing economic theory struggles to provide answers, such as low levels of specialization, high numbers of entrepreneurs, relatively low food consumption levels, relatively low savings rates, and low levels of investment in education.

So, what is distinctive about the economic lives of refugees? Is there a need to look to analytically distinguish the economic lives of refugees in a similar way to how Banerjee and Duflo focus on 'the economic lives of the poor'? And, if so, what are the analytically salient features of being a refugee that might justify thinking about refugee economies? What makes them worthy of independent study, as opposed to just applying development economics as usual? Are refugees economically different from citizens or other migrants, for example?

The earliest, pioneering literature on the economic lives of refugees is mainly qualitative and descriptive,[26] or identifies specific features of refugee camp economies but without exploring whether these features are actually unique to refugee economies.[27] Subsequent literature on the economics of refugees is mainly focused on measuring the impact of refugees on host societies.[28] Does the presence of refugees have a positive or negative impact on, for example, labour markets, crime, and social cohesion, and under what conditions? Other fruitful avenues of enquiry have included research on repatriation decision-making,[29] and the impact of displacement on refugees' social status.[30] There have also been a growing number of impact evaluations on interventions such as cash assistance.[31] This growing body of work is ground-breaking in the application of economics to Refugee Studies.

However, what has not been systematically examined, either deductively or inductively, is the broader theoretical question of what, if anything, is economically distinctive about the economic lives of refugees. And this is the question I address below.

In terms of *institutions*, refugees are likely to face a different set of extrinsic constraints and enabling factors compared to non-refugees. This is because they will usually have different sets of rights and duties compared to citizens or other migrants. On the one hand, they may face greater legal and regulatory constraints in areas such as rights relating to employment, mobility, banking, and property ownership.[32] These differences may increase the relative transaction costs of economic activity. On the other hand, they may also have access to different forms of entitlements such as access to assistance or protection.

In terms of *identity*, refugees may have different intrinsic characteristics that constitute them as economic actors, and hence influence their behaviour and decision-making. The most salient of these that is specific to being a refugee is likely to be the impact of transitional or traumatic events resulting from the experiences of persecution, flight, and reception within the host country. There is evidence that previous exposure to traumatic events may influence economic behaviour by, for example, shortening time horizons or changing perceptions of time.[33] Economists have shown the importance of time horizons for decision-making in areas such as credit, debt, savings, investment, entrepreneurship, and employment.[34] Refugees' identities will also be distinctive from host nationals—although not necessarily from other migrants—by the fact of being outside their country of origin. Indeed, a different set of norms and social networks may influence refugees' economic behaviour compared to that of host-country citizens.[35]

These hypotheses about the sources of distinctiveness of refugee economies could be tested empirically. This could be done by using randomized control trial (RCT) or experimental methods, assessing the impact of particular interventions—relating to institutions or identity—on a 'treatment group' and a 'control group'. Alternatively, and this has been our main approach, these hypotheses might be explored through survey methods that compare refugees' economic lives with proximate members of the host community. For example, we have found evidence that, controlling for other sources of variation, refugees are different from proximate host community members in each of the categories listed here.[36]

In terms of institutions, regulatory restrictions on socio-economic rights mean that refugees generally pay higher transaction costs for economic activity than host communities. These costs are incurred through higher levels of police bribes, greater risk of arrest, higher 'business taxes', and reduced access to financial services. We find this pattern consistently across urban and camp contexts, for all nationalities, and across all of our three focus countries. For example, compared to the local host population, Somali refugees in the Kakuma refugee camps are three times more likely to pay business tax, nearly five times more likely to have to pay police bribes.

In terms of identity, refugees appear to generally have worse mental health scores compared to nearby host communities, possibly due to being displaced. On the other hand, refugees, because they have migrated, receive positive benefits from their stronger transnational networks compared to the host community, which lead to higher levels of remittances (in some contexts these are ten times greater among refugee populations than nearby host communities), while social networks based on ethnicity often enable access to additional sources of social protection. Indeed, we consistently find across all of our research sites and focus populations that refugees are more likely to participate in community associations than the host communty.[37]

The Refugee Economies Dataset

There has historically been very little data on the economic lives of refugees. Policy-makers and practitioners have, until recently, not prioritized the systematic collection of socio-economic data relating to forcibly displaced persons, whether they are refugees or internally displaced persons (IDPs). And academics have rarely had the capacity to collect large-scale first-hand data based on comparable methods across countries, populations, and contexts. The literature on the economic lives of refugees reflects this, generally focusing on single country contexts and making creative use of whatever secondary data is available.

As an economics undergraduate, I had been inspired by my experience of doing voluntary work with refugees in the Netherlands to write a dissertation on the economics of forced migration. At that time, however, at the turn of the millennium, there was quite literally no relevant literature or data to work with.

It would be over a decade later that philanthropic research funding enabled me to finally build an original dataset on the economic lives of refugees, focusing on camps and cities in Uganda. The findings of that research were published as *Refugee Economies: Forced Displacement and Development.*[38] That research used first-hand qualitative and quantitative data collection to showcase the range of ways in which refugees engage in economic activity, and contribute to host economies. However, it also has a series of limitations: it focused on refugees but not host communities; it focused only on a single country; and it only focused on the south-west region of Uganda—which for many reasons offers an almost uniquely auspicious context for refugees' economic activities.

In order to address some of these limitations, my team and I created the Refugee Economies Programme. The aim was to create one of the first ever panel datasets (i.e. data that was both multi-country and time-series) on the economic lives of refugees. It would include refugees and host communities, cities and camps, and follow people over time.

The research team was deliberately interdisciplinary, comprising economists and anthropologists, to ensure a balance of qualitative and quantitative methods. Integral to the team were two senior researchers, Naohiko Omata led much of the qualitative research and Olivier Sterck led the quantitative research. The aim was to collect a wide range of socio-economic date that could enable us to answer a whole series of questions, including explaining variation in three main areas: 1) welfare outcomes, 2) social cohesion, and 3) mobility. These are the questions that matter for policy and practice because they potentially tell us how to design more sustainable refugee policies.

In an ideal world, a panel dataset would be global in scale, and track all refugees over time. But with finite resources, we needed to start somewhere. East Africa is the region I know best, and where the team had already built relevant networks. It was also a region that hosted a significant proportion of the world's refugees—21 per cent by the end of 2018 from a range of countries of origin, including Somalia, South Sudan, the Democratic Republic of Congo, Eritrea, and Burundi.[39] From the region, we selected three countries on the basis of their contrasting policies towards refugees: Uganda, Kenya, and Ethiopia.

At the time that we embarked on our research, Uganda, Kenya, and Ethiopia hosted more refugees than the whole of the European Union (EU) combined, some 2.9 million. Even more relevantly, they had contrasting refugee policies and legislation, and yet hosted at least some of the same nationality groups (notably, Somali refugees). At one end of the spectrum,

Uganda allowed refugees the right to work and enjoy a significant degree of freedom of movement. At the other end of the spectrum, Kenya denied refugees the right to work and move freely. And, in the middle, Ethiopia was gradually embarking on a transition from an approach similar to Kenya's towards one potentially more similar to Uganda. This enabled us to select the countries based on variation in at least one independent variable of interest—the institutional and regulatory context that shapes refugees' socio-economic entitlements and opportunities. Within the countries, we focused on the capital city and at least one group of camps or settlements— Nakivale, Kakuma, Dollo Ado—intended to be illustrative rather than representative of other camps across the focus countries.

Across all sites, we adopted a mixed-methods, participatory approach. All of our research began with qualitative research, including a range of focus groups and semi-structured interviews with refugees, members of the host community, as well as UN, governmental, and non-governmental policy-makers and practitioners. We then used quantitative surveys, which included a range of common questions across all sites in order to allow for meaningful comparative analysis across the panel dataset, as well as a number of context specific questions derived from our qualitative research.

We trained refugees and members of the host community as research assistants and enumerators. In total, approximately 200 researchers were recruited from each of the different nationality groups with which we worked across both waves of data collection. All of our community researchers received basic training in social science research methods. The benefits of recruiting community members as researchers was significant in terms of enhancing access and building community-level trust, as well as leaving a positive training legacy. We have subsequently followed the career progression of the researchers, many of whom have gone onto higher education, employment with other research institutions, non-governmental organizations (NGOs), the United Nations, or led community organizations, for example.

The survey questionnaire was intentionally wide-ranging in order to enable us to explore a range of correlations. It included modules covering demographic information, economic activities, income, expenditure, assets, education, health and wellbeing, food security, financial inclusion, networks, mobility, social cohesion, sport, and community participation, for example. The survey was translated into a range of languages, and then back-translated in order to check accuracy. In Uganda, for example, the survey questionnaire was translated into Somali, Kiswahili, Luganda, and Runyankole.

Our sampling strategy varied with context. Our aim was to use random sampling, proportionate to the overall size of each population of interest, while achieving a sufficiently large overall sample size to enable meaningful analysis. In practice, achieving random sampling in densely populated urban areas and refugee camps is no easy feat.

Where we were able to obtain full and accurate contact details for the entire population of interest, we were able to use *simple random sampling*. In Addis Ababa, for example, the UN Refugee Agency (UNHCR) shared names and contact details from their database of urban refugee households, for both registered Somali and Eritrean refugees. We then decided to limit our study to the main host areas: Bole Michael for Somalis and Gofa Mebrat for Eritreans, targeting enough households to ensure a large enough sample to identify statistical relationships.

Within each household we interviewed the head of household, the primary food preparer (when this person was different from the head of household), and up to three other members of the household. In order to sample the proximate host community, we then delineated a certain geographical radius around our main refugee-hosting areas and then selected fifteen households for every fifty mapped out, derived from an overall sample target based on power calculations.

In most of our contexts, however, simple random sampling was not a viable option because we could not obtain complete and accurate contact information for the populations of interest. And so, we instead used a technique called *two-stage cluster sampling*. The first stage involved building a map of the population of interest as a means to identify and randomly select 'enumeration areas' (whether blocks, households, or buildings). In some cases, we could do this using existing government or United Nations census data. In other cases, such as the Congolese communities in Nairobi, and the host communities around Dollo Ado, Kakuma, and Nakivale, we needed to create our own maps in consultation with community leaders in combination with satellite images. The second stage involved randomly and proportionately selecting respondent households from these maps up to the overall sample size needed to ensure adequate statistical power. Across the waves of data collection, we would usually interview the household head, main food preparer, and a designated maximum number of additional household members.

For example, in Kakuma, we used existing UNHCR data to map out the distribution of different nationalities across the sub-camps and blocks. We then randomly selected blocks proportionate to the number of individuals of each nationality living within the blocks. The selected blocks were mapped by enumerators. Each household and their nationality was documented on the map. Random sampling was then used to select households on the map. For each nationality, we interviewed eight households in twenty selected blocks, in order to give a sample size of 480 households—160 households for each of the target nationalities, Somalis, Congolese, and Kenyans. Data collection was carried out by our community research assistants, and checked by field-based supervisors as it was uploaded.

It took more than three years to build the dataset, with data collection taking place between October 2016 and December 2019. The total sample size for all three countries is 16,710, comprising 9,020 refugees and 7,680 members of the proximate host community (Table 3.1).

In addition to this, we also undertook a second wave of data collection with the same cohort of refugees and host community members in Kenya. For Nairobi, we collected the second wave two years after the first, and for Kakuma, it was exactly three years after the first wave. This was made possible because following the conclusion of the first wave, we recorded contact phone numbers, documented addresses, and requested consent to follow-up later. Out of the first wave sample of 4,354, 3,096 people consented to participate in the second wave and could be identified (Table 3.2). The purpose of this second wave of data collection for Kenya was two-fold—to explore what, if anything, had changed during the elapsed time, and, most importantly, to assess the sample attrition rate during the intervening period, as a means to explore patterns of migration, mobility, and residency. This time series data collection was only undertaken for Kenya.

In the following sections, I illustrate some of the insights that emerge from initial analysis of our dataset in relation to three main questions, all central to the search for sustainable refugee policies: welfare outcomes, social cohesion, and migration. These are just some of the questions that can be explored using the Refugee Economies Dataset.[40] But they are the questions that matter most for thinking about 'what works'. This is because they help us to identify the policies and practices that can make refugees better off, more welcome, and less likely to resort to onward migration.

Table 3.1. Sample size from first wave of data collection

Country	City/Camp	Somali	Congolese	Eritrean	S. Sudanese	Host	Total
Kenya	Nairobi	566	712	–	–	1,191	2,469
	Kakuma	459	445	–	463	605	1,509
Uganda	Kampala	459	473	–	–	955	1,887
	Nakivale	823	804	–	–	667	2,294
Ethiopia	Addis Ababa	417	–	693	–	1,331	2,441
	Dollo Ado	2,712	–	–	–	2,931	5,643
Total		5,436	2,434	693	463	7,680	16,710

Table 3.2. Sample size from second wave of data collection in Kenya

	Refugees	Hosts	Total
Nairobi	850	589	1,439
Kakuma	1,189	468	1,657
Total	2,039	1,057	3,096

Welfare outcomes

What determines welfare outcomes for refugees, and also for nearby members of the host community? When do some people thrive rather than merely survive? What determines, for example, variation in refugees' income, assets, consumption, employment levels, subjective wellbeing, food security, and physical and mental health outcomes? Astoundingly, these are questions that have almost never been asked by academics or policy-makers.

There is practically no literature *explaining* variation in refugees' welfare levels. This is a particularly striking gap given that there is a refugee system that ostensibly exists to improve outcomes for refugees. And yet humanitarian organizations have historically operated with a very limited evidence base for knowing which policy interventions will make people better off. What are the specific policy levers that will lead refugees to have higher income, employment, and asset levels? Organizations working with refugees have seldom asked.

This deficiency is partly due to the absence of quantitative academic research within Refugee and Forced Migration Studies. However, it is also because refugees have tended to be viewed through a humanitarian rather than a development lens and the international humanitarian system privileges particular types of data, focused mainly on indicators relating to minimum standards. These indicators have usually been designed to assess organizational performance in areas such as health, nutrition, emergency shelter, and water and sanitation, against industry standards (for example, the so-called Sphere Standards). This data is important, especially for humanitarian accountability. But a purely humanitarian focus risks marginalizing the broader question of what explains variation in socio-economic outcomes for refugees and host communities.

Data explaining variation in socio-economic outcomes for refugees matters because it can support the design of programmes that move beyond humanitarian minimalism, and instead support human flourishing. This in turn is a key part of the move towards creating more sustainable refugee settlements, in which individuals, households, and communities can live more autonomous and dignified lives. It moves beyond the presumption that refugee communities should only live in a state of Soviet *kolkhoz*-like minimalism and not aspire to a progressive expansion of entitlements and capabilities. Thankfully, there is now a growing recognition by both UNHCR and the World Bank that this type of data is important,[41] and the nature and scope of 'humanitarian data' is ever-expanding,[42] but data on the socio-economic lives of refugees and nearby host communities nevertheless remain scarce.

In development economics, there is a relatively large amount of literature on the microeconomic determinants of individual and household welfare, especially in Africa. It explores the determinants of income and poverty,[43] food security,[44] health,[45] and subjective wellbeing.[46] However, this research agenda has not been applied to refugees in developing countries; the little research that explains variation in refugees' welfare outcomes almost exclusively focuses on refugees in the US and Europe,[47] and on mental health outcomes.[48] We are able to use our dataset to partly address this chasm in the literature.

The first thing we learn from our descriptive statistics is that there is a systematic *'development gap' between refugees and host communities*. This gap appears to hold across countries and across both urban and camp contexts (see Table 3.3). It applies across indicators—income, assets, subjective wellbeing, food security, and physical health and mental health, for example. Put simply, refugees are worse off than the host community. The only statistically significant exception to this pattern is Kakuma camp in the Turkana County in Kenya, where the host community are worse off than refugees in a number of key indicators. The exceptionalism of Kakuma, though, is linked to the extreme levels of poverty among the local Turkana population.

To elaborate, refugees are about half as likely to have a job (a remunerated economic activity) as the nearby host community. About 28 per cent of camp refugees and 38 per cent of urban refugees have a job, compared to 55 per cent and 66 per cent of the host community. Among those with a job, refugees earn nearly half as much: about $80 per month compared to $150 per month, with earnings for both communities being, on average, three times higher in cities than camp locations. There is, however, some variation. Both hosts and refugees are more likely to have work in Uganda, followed

Table 3.3. The 'Refugee–Host Development Gap'—summary of estimated median welfare indicators for refugee and proximate host populations across all six sites

Country	Context	Population	Income (US$/ month for those employed)[a]	Employment (%)[b]	Subjective Wellbeing (/5)[c]	Food Security (%)[d]	Health Score (higher is worse)[e]	Mental Health Score (higher is worse)[f]
Kenya	Camp	Refugees	68★	24★	1.5	26	6.2★	6.5★
		Hosts	42★	48★	2	14	3.8★	4.5★
	Urban	Refugees	151	49★	1.6	57★	4.8★	5.5
		Hosts	208	72★	1.8	79★	1.2★	3.9
Uganda	Camp	Refugees	32	40★	0.8★	23	6.4★	8.6★
		Hosts	15	90★	1.8★	38	4.9★	5.4★
	Urban	Refugees	94	40★	1.4★	43★	5.9★	7.7★
		Hosts	113	71★	2.2★	70★	3.3★	5.1★
Ethiopia	Camp	Refugees	47★	21★	1.8★	15★	3.4★	4.5★
		Hosts	121★	29★	3.4★	52★	2.6★	2.8★
	Urban	Refugees	66★	20★	1★	56★	6.4★	8.7★
		Hosts	225★	55★	2.8★	93★	2.7★	4★

Notes: ★ Statistically significant differences (at a 95% confidence interval) between refugees and hosts.

[a] Median monthly income for remunerated economic activity among those with a remunerated economic activity (winsorized for outer 5% to remove spurious outliers). Note these figures are nominal dollar amounts, and not adjusted for purchasing power parity.

[b] Percentage with a remunerated economic activity (employed or self-employed).

[c] Median subjective wellbeing score based on a Likert Scale used to express how much people agree or disagree with a particular statement.

[d] Percentage measured to be 'food secure' based on Household Food Insecurity Access Scale (HFIAS).

[e] Median health score, based on WHS-DAS scoring system. Higher score indicated worse health.

[f] Median mental health score, based on Public Health Questionnaire, PHQ-9. Higher score indicated worse mental health.

by Kenya, and then Ethiopia. The sources of employment also vary: in the cities (and Uganda's Nakivale settlement) whatever employment is available tends to come from the market; in the Dollo Ado and Kakuma refugee camps, it mainly comes from NGOs and international organizations. For all our sites, it is only in Kampala and Nairobi that the median earned income across the entire adult refugee population is more than $1 per day.

In terms of assets, we compiled an asset index based on a series of questions about different types of asset ownership. The general pattern we found was that urban hosts had the greatest asset ownership, followed by urban refugees, followed by rural hosts, followed by rural or camp-based refugees. Refugees in Kakuma were the only group with higher asset ownership than the proximate host community. In terms of food security, a significantly greater percentage of refugees are food insecure than hosts everywhere except Kakuma. Across all the sites, the average 'gap' in the proportion that are food secure is about 29 percentage points in cities (81 per cent for hosts versus 52 per cent for refugees) and 15 percentage points in the camps (36 per cent versus 21 per cent).

In terms of subjective wellbeing, we also found that for every one of our sites, refugees had lower subjective wellbeing than host communities, with refugees tending to be 'rather unsatisfied' and proximate host community members tending to be 'neutral' or even 'satisfied'. Strikingly, refugees and hosts are no more satisfied in the cities than in camp contexts. Relatedly, across all contexts, refugees have worse mental and physical health scores than the host community. Camp refugees have an average WHO-DAS 'health score' of 5.3 and urban refugees of 5.7, compared to 3.8 and 2.4 for the nearby host communities (where a higher score indicates worse health). They have a PHQ-9 'mental health score' of 6.5 for refugees in camps and 7.3 for refugees in cities, compared to 4.2 and 4.3 for the respective host communities (where a higher score indicates worse mental health).

This data indicates that welfare outcomes for refugees in cities are greater than for refugees in rural contexts on some but not all key indicators. Although refugees may earn more, own more, and work more in the city, they are not necessarily happier, healthier, or better fed than those who live in camps. Put simply, *urbanization is not a panacea for improving refugees' welfare.*

The next question, though, is what explains variation in these welfare indicators? And hence what levers need to be pulled in order to change these outcomes? To take an example, our regression analysis shows that variation in income (among those who work) is significantly influenced by several variables. The more years of education a refugee has, the higher their earnings.

The better their health score, the higher their earnings. In other words, core public services matter. Identity also matters: men and older refugees tend to earn more, and so do Somalis, even controlling for other variables such as transnational networks. This give rise to the need to take into account factors such as gender and nationality when designing livelihoods programmes. Finally, geography matters: living in a city or in a country that allows refugees to work, for example, are associated with higher incomes.

The implication is that if we want refugees to earn more, there is a need to provide them with the right to work, access to education, and healthcare, but also ensure that livelihoods programmes are sensitive to gender and nationality.

However, the other aspect of improving incomes is increasing access to work, given the relatively low proportion of refugees who have a remunerated economic activity. Regression analysis highlights a series of factors that are associated with a greater likelihood of having a job. Some of these factors are similar to those that explain income: health, gender, and age. However, others are different. Vocational training is statistically significant and positively correlated with employment but academic education is not. Strikingly, we found that remittances are negatively associated with having a job. In other words, receiving money transfers from abroad may actually serve as a deterrent to work, perhaps because it offers an alternative source of income. We observed this relationship by using 'having siblings in the West' as a proxy for access to remittances, and found it to be statistically significant and negatively correlated with work.

Finally, it was also interesting to observe that, controlling for other variables, living in Uganda—ironically the country with the strongest right to work—correlates negatively with having a job. However, this is likely to only be because, in contrast to camps in Kenya and Ethiopia, NGOs and international organizations are not employing large numbers of refugees. When we disaggregate sources of employment in Uganda, we find that a higher proportion are employed by host-country citizens or other refugees than in the other two countries.

Social cohesion

What explains the quality of the relationship between refugees and the nearby host community? When are hosts likely to have positive opinions about refugees, and vice versa? And under what conditions is the host community likely to have particular concerns about the impact of refugees on identity, security, or the economy? What role does refugee–host interaction play in shaping these attitudes?

Social cohesion between refugees and hosts matters for creating sustainable refugee policies. If host communities have positive attitudes towards refugees, then it seems likely that host governments will be more willing and able to adopt and maintain progressive and inclusive refugee policies. However, there has, until now, been relatively little research on the determinants of social cohesion between refugees and host communities, particularly in relation to developing countries.

There is a political science literature on (what it calls) 'native' attitudes towards immigration.[49] It focuses in particular on the impact of inter-group interaction on host community attitudes towards migrants. However, this literature mainly focused on Europe and North America, only rarely focuses specifically on refugees, and usually examines the national level rather than the sub-national level. There is practically no research, for example, that explores the impact of inter-group interaction on host community attitudes towards refugees in a developing world context.

The literature on public opinion and immigration usually tries to explain dependent variables such as attitudes, policy preferences, and voting preferences. Its main methodological challenge has generally been to isolate variables, especially in the absence of panel datasets or experimental methods. Nevertheless, the European and North American-focused research identifies two main sets of explanations underlying 'native' (i.e. host community) attitudes.[50]

First, *economic explanations*. From this perspective, host communities are concerned with the effects of immigration on labour market competition, i.e. increased supply of low-skilled workers leads to a decrease in wages;[51] or the fiscal implications, i.e. immigrants pay less taxes and claim more benefits.[52] However, empirical evidence for these hypotheses is limited. In terms of the labour market competition hypothesis, opposition to immigrants is not focused on immigrants with similar skills to the host community. In terms of the fiscal burden hypothesis, higher income people are no more likely to oppose low-skilled labour.[53]

Second, *cultural explanations*. From this perspective, 'natives' are more likely to favour immigrants with common identities such as nationality, ethnicity, and race.[54] However, the mechanisms that underlie this have often been hard to identify. There is a consensus in the literature that what matters is the 'sociotropic' role of culture—i.e. perceptions of difference—and that the relationship between cultural difference and exclusionary attitudes is not inevitable but contingent upon contextual mediating factors such as the media and elite discourse.[55]

The most influential hypothesis relating to the sociotropic role of culture is that inter-group contact plays an important role in shaping attitudes. Gordon Allport's seminal work on 'contact theory' suggests that, under certain conditions, inter-group contact can reduce prejudice between majority and minority groups. The conditions he identified include socio-economic equality, shared norms, cooperation, and institutional support.[56] The ideas have been widely applied to examine attitudes and prejudice relating to, for example, race, sexual orientation, religion, and immigration.

The evidence on the impact of inter-group contact on receiving community attitudes to immigrants is mixed. Lincoln Quillian finds a positive relationship;[57] Daniel Hopkins finds that it may be negative if it relates to a sudden influx or if national rhetoric reinforces a sense of threat to security.[58] Research on the impact of contact on attitudes to refugees is generally focused on single country cases, only focuses on Europe, mainly uses support for right-wing parties as a proxy for attitudes, and faces the methodological problem of focusing on areas in which refugees can select their location (which may be based partly on the welcome they receive, creating an 'endogeneity problem'). Andreas Steinmayr[59] and Christian Dustmann and colleagues,[60] for example, look at Austria and Denmark respectively and find that contact has a negative effect on support for right-wing parties. However, Elias Dinas and colleagues find the opposite; looking at the European refugee crisis in Greece, they show how exposure leads to an increase in right-wing support on the Greek islands.[61] They use the natural experiment of focusing on previously unaffected islands during a mass influx. The mechanisms they identify are sociotropic and relate to the perceived negative impact of sudden mass influx on culture.

However, there are grounds to believe that the determinants of host community attitudes to refugees in developing countries may be quite different. Most refugees will be from immediate neighbouring countries, suggesting the possibility for greater cultural proximity. Economies will be generally weaker, potentially introducing competition for scarce resources. Political systems may be quite different in Africa compared to Europe, for instance. Furthermore, in low- and middle-income countries, refugees frequently do not have free choice to move to the most welcoming area but often have to reside in 'designated areas'. The sources of social cohesion between refugees and host communities in Africa may therefore be quite different from the factors highlighted by existing research in Europe. One of very few studies to examine host community perceptions of the impact of refugee presence is the World Bank's *Yes, in My Backyard?* study highlighting the positive impact of refugees on host communities around the Kakuma camps.[62]

Within our Refugee Economies Dataset, we collected data relating to host community perceptions of refugees, refugees' perceptions of the host community, and the type (sharing a conversation, meal, or business exchange, for example) and frequency of interactions between refugees and the host community. This data on perceptions and interactions offers an opportunity to systematically explore the determinants of social cohesion. Our descriptive statistics reveal several interesting patterns.

First, there are notable *differences between camps and cities*. Across all three countries, host communities proximate to camps nearly all agree (or strongly agree) that refugees bring increased economic opportunities for the host communities and that they generate employment. This is most strongly the case for Kakuma (3.5 out of 4 on a Likert scale in which 1 is 'strongly disagree', 2 is 'disagree', 3 is 'agree', and 4 is 'strongly agree' for creating economic opportunity) and Dollo Ado (3.7), and only moderately the case in Nakivale (2.8).

In contrast, host communities in urban areas consistently tend to disagree that there is a positive impact on the economy or employment. This may reflect that in camp environments, the presence of humanitarian assistance creates a range of employment opportunities and new markets. Indeed, among host communities near Kakuma and Dollo Ado, humanitarian aid agencies were the single biggest employer for host communities. In Nakivale, in contrast, the self-reliance model in Uganda means the humanitarian assistance model is smaller in scale and so the positive economic impact on the host community is likely to be less. Indeed, allocation of plots of land is generally seen as a source of resentment in Nakivale (with a 2.9 out of 4 on a similar Likert scale for agreement with the statement 'refugees are taking over our land'), reinforcing the idea that the specific type of aid model matters.

Second, *economic issues are more important than security issues*. Host communities across all sites are generally neutral on whether refugees contribute to insecurity or not. The only exception to this is Kakuma, where the

Turkana host community generally agree that refugees cause insecurity. Interestingly, this is not because security around Kakuma is any worse than elsewhere: 84 per cent of the Turkana and 62 per cent of refugees claim that the security level is generally good, which is much higher than other, particularly urban, contexts like Nairobi where 51 per cent of hosts and 39 per cent of refugees think that the security level is good, or Addis Ababa, where it is 74 per cent and 33 per cent respectively. Instead, our data suggests it may be related to other factors; the Turkana host community is more likely to regard refugees as 'competitors' than in any of the other sites (3.5 out of 4 on a Likert scale). Furthermore, our qualitative research reveals that there have been a number of violent clashes between refugees and the host Turkana, sometimes relating to claims of cattle rustling or isolated individual disputes that escalate rapidly to communal violence.

Third, *cultural proximity may support positive attitudes.* Across all three countries, Ethiopian hosts have the most inclusive attitudes towards refugees. This is especially the case in the Dollo Ado camps, where both refugees and the host community are predominantly ethnically Somali and share a common language. However, a similar logic holds for Addis Ababa, where Somalis are generally living in areas such as Bole Michael, alongside Somali Ethiopians, and many Eritreans are living alongside Tigrayans in areas like Gofa Mebrat. Hosts' relatively more positive attitudes towards refugees are generally reciprocated in Ethiopia: refugees in Ethiopia are more positive about their hosts than refugees in Kenya and Uganda. Indeed, Ethiopian hosts are more open to offering refugees greater rights than in the other two countries. Ethiopians in Addis and Dollo Ado tend to agree that refugees should have the right to both work and live where they want in Ethiopia. In contrast, Ugandans and Kenyans tend to agree that refugees should have the right to work but not the right to live where they want to.

In terms of regression analysis, we explored the impact of inter-group interaction on host community attitudes towards refugees. For Uganda only, we measured the frequency of interaction by asking members of the host community how often they have a conversation, engage in a business exchange, or share a meal with refugees. We found that the level of *inter-group interaction is positively correlated with host community perceptions of refugees as economic contributors* and creators of employment opportunities. This relationship applies to both the urban and rural context. However, interestingly, there was no statistically significant correlation between inter-group interaction and the perception of refugees as either 'a threat to security' or as 'competitors'.

This suggests that Allport's 'contact theory' has a role to play in understanding social cohesion in refugee-hosting regions. Our findings imply that promoting inter-group interaction in camp and urban contexts may be a means to improve host community attitudes towards refugees. However, it suggests that economic and security-related perceptions may emerge from different sources. In other words, economic perceptions may result from people's own experiences, whereas security-related perceptions may emerge independently of people's own interactions with refugees. These claims are complemented by some of our impact evaluation findings in Dollo Ado (in Chapter 7), which show that 'cooperative' livelihood programmes that encourage greater interaction between refugees and host communities may lead to improved refugee–host community relations.

Our qualitative research further suggests some of the mechanisms for how particular forms of inter-group interaction may influence host community attitudes towards refugees. In particular, consumption and employment relationships tend to be related to positive host community perceptions of the economic contribution of refugees. Meanwhile, competition over resources, particularly within the informal economy and in relation to land disputes, seems to be related to the perception of refugees as an economic burden. Experiences of these different types of interaction also seem to be related to socio-economic status, with more affluent members of the host community generally more likely to recognize refugees' contribution, and less affluent groups more likely to be concerned about resource competition. Put simply, individual host community perceptions tend to be shaped by whether or not that person regards themselves to be a 'winner' or a 'loser' from the presence of refugees.

To take the example of Nakivale in Uganda, the host community and refugees have high levels of economic interaction, partly because the settlement lacks defined boundaries, with some Ugandan villages actually located inside the settlement. On the one hand, Ugandans value refugees as consumers and employees. Refugees buy from Ugandan shops. One Ugandan trader explained, 'I am selling farming tools like hoes, household items (water, soda), and stationary. Customers are both refugees and hosts. I receive ten to fifteen customers per day—and half of them are refugees.'

One community leader explained, 'We have been selling bananas to refugees…We know refugees economically contribute…Our economy is connected with Nakivale.' This translates into positive perceptions; the chairperson of Kabatumba village claimed, 'The presence of refugees is positive for local villages. Refugees have money and buy our crops from us…If the camp disappeared, locals would suffer a lot. We cannot survive here without the camp.' A government official confirmed, 'We are very positive…Markets inside the camp are crucial for locals because they buy and sell items.' Ugandan farmers also employ refugees as casual farmworkers. A Ugandan banana plantation owner explained, 'I employ two to three refugees as seasonal agricultural labour. I usually pay them in bananas but sometimes I give them wage. They are good workers.'

On the other hand, however, competition for resources relating to land sometimes contributes to negative perceptions. Increases in the refugee population have created more competition for land, and this has led to inter-group tension. One Congolese cattle-owner explained,

> Whenever I carry cattle near Ugandan villages, they chase me out. They sometimes even attack the cattle. They have their own cattle and they don't want us to invade their glazing area. But Ugandans bring their cattle inside the camp area and they graze there…The fundamental issue is simply land shortage.

A Ugandan church leader explained 'Refugees are good people. As long as refugees stay inside the settlement area, we have no problem. But when they come to our land, it is a problem.' Consequently, how natives perceive refugees appears to vary depending upon whether a particular host community member runs a business that employs or sells to refugees, or experiences competition for scarce resources such as land. One Congolese refugee leader acknowledged this Janus-faced relationship: 'There are two types of locals in Rubondo. Good ones are those hiring refugees as farm workers. Usually for their banana plantation. Bad ones are cattle keepers. They destroy our crops and damage our farming.'

To take another example, Kenyans living in the areas of Nairobi that host Congolese refugees—such as Kayole and Kasarani—especially value refugees' contribution as consumers and employees. Edwin, a shop owner of electronic items in Kayole, explained: 'Many Congolese refugees are buying items from my shop. They buy TVs and other gadgets. They are good customers for me…I receive about thirty customers per day and four to six of them are refugees. They are friendly and can speak Swahili.' And Congolese refugees are also viewed as an important source of casual labour. One

Kenyan security company we found in Kasarani employed about forty Congolese refugees among its 300 staff, although when we spoke to one, he complained about low pay and poor conditions, saying he worked twelve hour shifts, seven days a week, for half the salary of Kenyan staff. Nancy, a Kenyan hair salon owner in Kayole explained why she appreciates being able to employ Congolese refugees: 'I employ six people; two of them are Congolese refugees...They came to my salon and asked for a job. I interviewed them and discovered they are qualified...I really like them...I prefer refugees to Kenyans.'

But beyond consumption and employment benefits for local businesses, we also found sources of tension among the general population related to competition for informal sector work. This was especially evident in the suburb of Kitingela, where roughly 2,000 Congolese refugees live. Many are casual labourers in the informal sector; they work as barbers, security guards, waiters, and porters, for example. One refugee explained 'Now the tension between refugees and locals is mounting. Some nationals are getting concerned as if refugees take away their employment.' In March 2017, this led to communal violence. One Kenyan witness explained,

> Most of these protestors were Kenyan manual workers who also engaged in lower paid jobs such as hawkers, security guards, factory workers. They have no special skills and only limited levels of education. They claimed the number of Congolese refugees has become too big in Kitengela and were taking away our jobs...It is understandable some Kenyans see them as economic threat or competitors.

On the other hand, Kenyan business owners in Kitengela took the opposite view. The owner of an M-Pesa and phone shop dismissed the grievances as 'nonsense', claiming 'the Kenyan protestors made no sense to me. Simply Congolese refugees are better workers and they deserve employment...The employers should be able to decide who to hire. This is business not charity...I definitely prefer to hire refugees.' This example demonstrates that host community attitudes towards refugees are shaped by their specific economic interactions with refugees, and also their position in society. Business owners who employ or sell to refugees appear to have positive perceptions, while people of lower socio-economic status felt more threatened by competition for informal sector work. Put simply, the economic 'winners' of refugees' presence appear to have more positive attitudes; the economic 'losers' appear to have more negative attitudes.

Migration, mobility, and residency

What explains refugees' migration, mobility, and residency choices? When they flee, nearly all refugees first enter a country that neighbours their homeland. But where do they go next, and what determines their choices? Why do some refugees choose to live in camps and others in cities? How and why do they select between particular camps and cities? When do they relocate within a given camp or city? When do they choose to stay in the country of first asylum, to go home to their country of origin, or emigrate to another country? If and when they emigrate, what determines whether they move within their region of origin or further afield?

Some of these questions—such as those relating to internal and international movement—have been widely explored for migration in general,[63] but there is limited evidence specifically relating to refugees' mobility and residency choices. Nevertheless, there is some discussion within both policy and academia relating to the determinants of refugees' international migration choices. This focuses mainly on the conditions under which refugees move from first countries of asylum to other countries as asylum seekers, how destinations and routes are selected, and what impact government policies have in influencing those choices.[64]

Within policy circles, there is a predominant interest in whether development opportunities lead to higher or lower levels of onward migration from refugees from poor host countries to rich countries. The presumption in many government-funded initiatives is that increasing income, employment, and wealth levels for refugees in first countries of asylum will reduce the need and aspiration of displaced populations to resort to what has been called irregular secondary movement. This has been especially the case in European Union policy with, for the example, the EU Emergency Trust Fund for Africa making explicit the goal of using development-based interventions to reduce the number of asylum seekers coming to Europe. But will making refugees richer make them less likely to emigrate to Europe?

Within academic circles, there has been significant push-back against the assumption that development can reduce refugee migration to rich countries. During the European refugee crisis, Hein de Haas and others highlighted that increasing development often increases emigration.[65] For labour migration, there is indeed an established 'migration hump' relationship (Figure 3.1), which describes an inverted U-shape relationship between

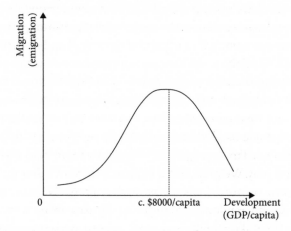

Figure 3.1. Conventional understanding of the 'migration hump' relationship

development and migration whereby at lower levels of gross domestic product (GDP)/capita—up to around $8,000[66]—rising income leads to a rising aspiration and ability to emigrate.[67] A variety of mechanisms have been identified for this relationship, including overcoming credit constraints, improving access to information, and reducing barriers to immigration.

However, there is little evidence either way on whether the migration hump relationship actually applies to refugees in first countries of asylum. Data in support of the migration hump mostly relates to labour migration. It is based on a combination of macroeconomic data from the twentieth century showing how, as countries get richer emigrant numbers initially increase, and microeconomic data focusing mainly on Mexican and Central American emigration to the US revealing how individuals, households, and communities are more likely to emigrate as they get richer.[68] There are grounds for considering that refugees' migration decisions may deviate from the standard migration hump relationship in cases where individuals were originally forced to flee and did not choose to migrate.[69]

Methodologically, it is challenging to collect representative data relating to refugees' migration, mobility, and residency choices. Where data has been collected it tends to be based on post-hoc interviews or surveys with those who have already migrated, asking them to explain or retrospectively recall their choices. This leads to a selection bias by only including those who have claimed asylum in rich countries, and undermining meaningful comparison with those who have not emigrated.[70] This 'receiving country bias' (i.e. that data collection mainly takes place in destination countries in Europe and North America) is common in migration research,[71] and reflects the practical and technical challenges of creating representative baseline data before people move and then tracking the same people over time.

We have addressed this methodological gap by surveying refugee households and then going back later to re-interview the same household, and—where people had left their original home—undertaking a follow-up survey with other family members or neighbours to find out where they had gone, and why. We piloted this approach in Kenya. In our first wave of data collection in 2016 in Kakuma and 2017 in Nairobi, we collected representative and randomly sampled survey data from 2,730 refugees in Nairobi and the Kakuma refugee camps. In 2019, we returned at exactly the same time of year as the earlier surveys, to undertake a second wave of data collection with the same respondents in both Kenyan contexts. Kenya was the only one of our three focus countries in which we undertook two waves of data collection with the same respondent population.

Out of 2,087 identifiable refugees, 404 had moved on from their original household (167 in Nairobi and 237 in Kakuma), giving an 'attrition rate' of 17 per cent for Nairobi during the two years and 21 per cent in Kakuma over the three years. Our follow-up 'attrition survey' revealed where these 404 refugees had moved to, while our baseline data enabled us to systematically examine whether particular types of movement are associated with particular socio-economic characteristics, while controlling for other variables. We complemented this method with further quantitative data on refugees' migration aspirations, collected in both waves of data collection, and in-depth qualitative interviews, including with some of the surveyed households.

The first thing we found was that refugees' movements are complex and diverse. They cannot be reduced to a simplistic focus on onward migration to rich countries. Of those who moved during the survey period, 1 per cent undertook irregular migration to Europe—which is less than 0.1 per cent of the overall refugee population per year. The number moving onwards to neighbouring states in the region—notably Uganda—was almost eight times greater. From Kakuma most international movement was repatriation; equivalent to about 2.7 per cent of the total Kakuma refugee population per year. From Nairobi, most international movement was for regular migration,

Table 3.4. Approximate percentage of overall refugee population moving each year

Type of Movement	Nairobi (city)	Kakuma (camp)
Repatriation	0.3%	2.7%
Resettlement, Student Visa, or Family Reunification	1.4%	0.5%
Migration to Europe	0.1%	0.1%
Migration to Other African Countries	0.8%	0.5%
Internal Migration within Kenya	1.9%	1.6%
Intra-Urban/Intra Camp	4.2%	1.7%
Total Annual Attrition	**8.7%**	**7.1%**

through for example resettlement, student visas, or family reunification, equivalent to about 1.4 per cent of the overall Nairobi refugee population per year (Table 3.4).

However, by far the largest category of movement was internal migration within Kenya. In Nairobi, a significant number of refugees—around 4.2 per cent per year—relocate within the city. This is mainly the result of evictions, demolitions, or rent increases forcing people from their homes. Without secure property rights or real estate contracts, refugees appear especially vulnerable to eviction. Meanwhile, around 1.9 per cent of refugees in Nairobi choose to leave the city each year, some to other secondary cities and a minority—mainly those who were without jobs, older, and female—back to refugee camps. In the case of Kakuma, around 1.6 per cent per year relocate to other cities within Kenya, mainly to Nairobi but also to secondary cities such as Kitale, Eldoret, and Kisumu. Around 1.7 per cent per year also relocate within the camps.

We found that having a job (or some form of remunerated economic activity) reduces the likelihood of going abroad by about 3 per cent, controlling for other variables. We also saw that younger and single refugees are more likely to have moved abroad. This provides some suggestion that, rather than the 'migration hump' relationship applying to refugees, it may be the case that development indicators such as access to employment may actually reduce the likelihood of onward migration. This finding needs to be qualified, however, by the fact that it is based on aggregating all forms of international movement (whether irregular migration, regular migration, resettlement, or repatriation, for example)—due to the small size of our attrition sample who undertake international migration (198 of the 404 people).[72]

Nevertheless, we complemented this attrition study by also examining migration aspiration data from the full second wave sample of 2,039 refugee respondents in Kenya. And this further strengthened the evidence against the applicability of the migration hump relationship to refugee movements from Kenya. We found that, controlling for other variables, asset holdings—as an indicator of wealth—are negatively associated with having an aspiration to emigrate outside of the African region, and positively associated with having an aspiration to move within Africa and within Kenya (excluding intra-urban and intra-camp movements). Put simply, this implies that socio-economically better off refugees are less likely to aspire to move outside Africa, and more likely to aspire to move within the country of first asylum or within Africa. The implications of this are potentially important because they suggest that making refugees better off may reduce their aspiration to move from first countries of asylum to Europe or North America.

Our qualitative research, which also included longitudinally following the trajectory of individuals and households between 2016 and 2019, highlights further complexities. In particular it reveals how the ways in which policy-makers think about dominant refugee mobility categories such as 'onward migration', 'repatriation', and 'resettlement' may sometimes misrepresent the reality of those movement.

First, we found relatively few examples of refugees in Kenya planning 'onward migration' to Europe, but relatively frequent discussions among economically vulnerable refugees about moving to Uganda in search of better economic prospects. Uganda is an especially important migration option for Somali refugees. Dek, a young Somali, who came to Kakuma in 2008 and with his mother and siblings explained how his uncle moved to Kampala for better economic opportunities:

> In 2017, my uncle went to Uganda to search for jobs. But soon he came back to Kakuma camp [for a registration exercise]. In 2019, he went back to Uganda again. We have relatives (also Somali refugees) in Uganda and they encouraged him to come and join them in Uganda. They have a grocery shop in Kampala. My uncle stays with them and helps their business there…I didn't go to Uganda with him because I am now in school in the camp. I didn't want to cut off my education.

Meanwhile, Bashir, a Somali refugee, explained:

> Now I am thinking of moving to Uganda. Uganda is cheaper than here and safer. I had more freedom of movement there. It is easy to get travel document

to Uganda. My plan is to leave my wife and five children in Nakivale settlement to access a free home, education, and work. In the meantime, I will stay in Kampala to work and make money. I have many Somali relatives living in Kampala.

Second, 'repatriation' was identified not only as a means to go home but sometime a stepping stone towards onward migration. For example, in Kakuma UNHCR has been providing a repatriation package, with a $350 incentive to return home ($150 in Kakuma and $200 allocated upon arrival). A long-time researcher of this phenomenon, Rahul Oka explained, 'According to our study, yes, Somali refugees are returning via UNHCR repatriation programme but once they go back, [some] move again and use the stipend as capital to restart their life, often in Uganda.'

Repatriation is sometimes also motived by economic desperation, and may be short-lived. Samson, a 23-year-old male came to Kakuma in 2002. He returned to South Sudan in 2010, 2015, and 2019 each time after he completed his education in Kakuma camp:

> Between 2017 and 2018, I worked as an incentive worker [someone who works for an NGO for a low wage] in Kakuma but this did not give me enough to help my family. I have six younger siblings. I had to look for better jobs but there are no such jobs in Kakuma. So I went to South Sudan in 2019 April. I spent two months searching for jobs and higher education opportunities. I didn't see any success. I did apply for jobs at NGOs but no success... I searched for scholarships for pursuing higher education but did not get one. So I came back to Kakuma in August 2019...[Life in the camp is] tedious, no excitement, no prospects, no hope. No sign of changes. Same food, same friends...I often discuss with my friends: 'How can we move out of this camp? How can we change our life?' I don't see any progress in this camp.

Repatriation is also not always permanent. John, a 30-year-old South Sudanese refugee, who lives with his wife and three children in the camp, explained how he went back and forth without informing UNHCR: 'In 2015, I returned to South Sudan to see my mother...I stayed only two weeks...In 2017, I again went to South Sudan. My mother was ill so I needed to see her. I spent one and a half months there and then came back to Kakuma'. Natalia, another South Sudanese refugee moved back and forth between Kakuma and South Sudan: 'In 2013, I went to South Sudan to check the security situation in Juba. I went alone and stayed there for three months.'

Third, 'resettlement' is frequently interconnected with individual and household decisions relating to other forms of migration. For example, several refugees commented that they selected to live in Kakuma, or relocated to the camps, in the hope that it would increase their access to resettlement opportunities. For example, Yaku, a Somali community representative in Kakuma, returned from Mombasa but came back to the camp even though he had work in Mombasa, because of a belief that it might lead to resettlement: 'I went to Mombasa between August 2018 and April 2019 to search for a job. I had no external help from abroad, and incentive work paid too little; so I searched for opportunities outside the camp ...I got tailoring work from my friend but I came back to Kakuma camp because I was called for a resettlement interview.'

For others, the prospect of accessing resettlement has implications for how they consider alternative migration options such as repatriation. Issa, a school teacher, whose parents and siblings repatriated to Somalia in 2017, explained 'I decided to remain in Kakuma to seek a chance of resettlement. If resettled, I will assist my family from abroad. Also, it did not make sense to me to go back to Somalia now. The situation is very precarious. There are not many employment opportunities there. If resettlement happens, I will go and support my family from abroad. Alternatively, if Somalia becomes peaceful, I may go back there. Now, I am waiting to see what options emerge.' Recognizing this interdependency of different migration and mobility options is especially important in a context in which resettlement options are being foreclosed; one Somali refugee explained '[The closure of resettlement is creating] significant impact on our lives. There are many suspended resettlement cases. There are psychological effects on them as they are left in limbo.'

These qualitative observations reinforce the view that refugees' mobility choices are complex and diverse, and sometimes transcend dominant policy categories. Furthermore, the choice made between competing mobility and residency options are often highly strategic, but based on imperfect information, uncertainty, and the use of split-family strategies as a form of risk management. They also reinforce the view that seeking to move abroad— by whatever means—may be driven by a lack of economic opportunity within Kenya.

Overall, the findings from our research in Kenya cannot be generalized beyond Nairobi and Kakuma, and they are specific to the time period between 2017 and 2019. Nevertheless, they reveal the complexity of refugees' migration, mobility, and residency choices. They show that refugees in Kenya are highly mobile even after their initial flight, but not necessarily in the ways anticipated by dominant policy categories and discourse. During our three-year period of study, irregular migration to rich countries made up a tiny proportion of refugees' overall movements. Most international movement was regular migration, based on resettlement or repatriation, for example, or intra-African movement. More common than international migration—and often neglected by policy-makers—were forms of internal migration within the country of asylum, intra-urban, intra-camp, and between cities and camps. Nevertheless, our qualitative and quantitative data suggest that creating development opportunities may actually reduce the aspiration to emigrate to rich countries outside Africa, indicating that the 'migration hump' relationship may not apply to refugees in the way it does to labour migrants.

Conclusion

The Refugee Economies Dataset represents one of the first multi-country panel datasets on the economic lives of refugees. It covers urban and camp contexts, refugees and hosts, three countries, and provides time series data for one of the countries. The comprehensive nature of the questions asked within the survey creates the opportunity to explore a range of correlations. In this chapter, I have examined three main questions, each relevant for the design of sustainable refugee policies. The analysis cannot be considered generalizable beyond our research contexts and populations of interest. However, the underlying data is based on random sampling and can be considered representative of the target populations. And it generates hypotheses that have relevance beyond the region and populations of focus.

The hypotheses it generates include the following. First, there is a 'development gap' between refugees and hosts. Refugees generally have worse welfare outcomes than the proximate host community. Second, refugees' income levels are shaped by a range of factors, including employment and living in a country that provides the right to work. Third, social cohesion is influenced by the perceived economic contribution of refugees. Fourth, onward migration to rich countries is small but the aspiration to migrate internationally may be negatively correlated with development indicators such as asset levels.

Overall, our analysis suggests that enhancing socio-economic entitlements— and particularly the right to work—for refugees may lead to improved welfare outcomes for refugees and host communities, improved social cohesion, and reduced onward migration. Put simply, the evidence strengthens the case for a development-based approach to refugee assistance.

What exactly could such an approach look like in practice? In the next chapters (4-7), I further sharpen the focus on what works by examining country-specific case studies in more depth. I combine insights from our dataset with lessons from a series of our own impact evaluations. The aim is to assess some of the supposedly most innovative policies and practices from across the region, and answer some key questions. What role can cities play? What difference does the right to work make? Can market-based settlements be designed from scratch? Can the private sector play a role in borderland development? By exploring these themes, I hope to gradually build up a more granular picture of what works, for whom, and under what conditions.

4

The limits of urbanization

Introduction

Around the world, more refugees—around 61 per cent—now live in cities than rural areas. Urban refugee numbers are estimated to have surpassed camp numbers for the first time in 2006. This reflects the wider global trend towards urbanization. However, there is also significant regional variation. In Africa, urbanization in general is lower,[1] and there are relatively fewer urban refugees. Within Sub-Saharan Africa, the exception to this is South Africa. In East Africa, the overwhelming majority of registered refugees live in camps and settlements. According to the UN Refugee Agency (UNHCR), 16 per cent of Kenya's refugees live in Nairobi, less than 6 per cent of Uganda's refugees live in Kampala, and less than 4 per cent of Ethiopia's refugees live in Addis Ababa. Of course, some live in secondary cities but this is generally not documented, and the estimates are small.[2] The urban–rural distribution of refugees reflects government restrictions, the relative availability of assistance versus employment, and the preferences of refugees.

The composition of urban and camp cohorts is generally different. Those in cities tend to be older and male, and those in camps tend to be younger and female. Sometimes, refugee households divide their families, with those able to work moving to the city and those with assistance needs or care responsibilities remaining in camps. The relative advantages of cities include greater autonomy and the availability of employment and economic opportunity. The disadvantages usually result from government controls, and include limited assistance and elevated risks of labour market exploitation.[3] With a lack of humanitarian assistance, urban refugees usually rely upon a combination of informal employment and their own networks as sources of subsistence and social protection.[4]

Our East Africa-specific dataset offered three key insights. First, refugees earn more, own more, and work more in the city, but they are not necessarily happier, healthier, or better fed than those who live in rural areas. Second, host communities are generally more positive towards refugees in rural than urban settings. Third, there is temporary and permanent movement by refugees between camps and cities in both directions. Collectively, these insights suggest that neither urban nor rural residency is inherently better for refugees than the other. Each option represents a constrained choice that offers relative pros and cons.

Creating a sustainable refugee system requires expanding entitlements and opportunities for refugees and host communities in both urban and rural contexts. In subsequent chapters, I focus my attention on the rural context. In this chapter, I explore what we can learn from the experience of refugees in three capital cities: Addis Ababa, Kampala, and Nairobi. Each of the host governments imposes at least some restrictions on urban refugees. Uganda generally lets refugees live in cities but has sometimes imposed limitations when numbers rise; Kenya legally obliges most refugees to live in camps but makes some exceptions and broadly tolerates refugees in Nairobi; Ethiopia has historically limited urban refugee numbers but has a small-scale 'Out-of-Camp Policy' (OCP), mainly available to Eritrean refugees.

I show that, despite differences, refugees in all three cities share some common experiences. They face severe and specific constraints on their economic activities. Most rely upon the informal economy and their own networks, and are extremely precarious. Much can be done to improve the sustainability of urban refugee policies. However, I suggest that this will require major change in the willingness of host governments to economically include refugees and a rethink of urban refugee assistance models. Urbanization alone is not, as is sometimes implied, a panacea for refugee protection.

Addis Ababa

The story of urban refuge in Addis is bleak. It is generally one of unemployment, dependency on remittances, and hopelessness. In a city with 23 per cent unemployment, and serious restrictions on refugees' economic activities, most young refugees regard irregular migration to Europe as their only source of aspiration.[5]

The number of registered refugees living in the capital city is small at just 22,000 people, although there may be several thousand more unregistered refugees.[6] The registered refugees divide into two populations who are ostensibly there for very different reasons. Some 17,000 Eritrean refugees reside in Addis under the OCP through which they claim to be sufficiently autonomous to live without aid. In addition, 5,000 Somali refugees live there under the 'urban assistance programme' on the grounds that they have vulnerabilities that cannot be met in camps. The latter group receives a small amount of financial assistance; the former group does not. And yet, despite these different starting points, both communities face extreme precarity.

Both groups reside mainly in particular suburbs alongside their co-nationals. For Somali refugees this is usually the Bole Michael area, the city's 'Little Mogadishu', also inhabited by large numbers of ethnic Somali Ethiopians. For Eritreans, this is a range of neighbourhoods, such as Gofa Mebrat, which are often also populated by ethnic Tigrayan Ethiopians. Focus group discussions revealed that both populations regarded life in the city to be challenging but a better alternative than the camps. One Eritrean man who arrived from the northern camps explained, 'Camp life was hard. It is very remote and there is very hot weather. There is a high incidence of malaria, and limited access to education. The living conditions were so poor.' A Somali refugee man who moved with his family from the camps in the south-east similarly said, 'Camp conditions are not good. There is poor security, bad sanitation, and few health and medical facilities. Addis is better in general. In particular, here we have better access to health services'.

Government regulations have long limited the numbers of refugees allowed to reside in the city, and prohibited their right to work or register businesses. New legislation in 2019 promised to gradually change this, but it has yet to be implemented, and in practice the old restrictions remain. Economic opportunities for refugees are rare. Across the country, the unemployment rate is 14.5 per cent, and around 2 million more young people enter the employment market each year. Addis has the highest unemployment in the country. Reflecting this, we found that 79 per cent of Eritrean refugees and 93 per cent of Somalis are unemployed. Among the small minority who work, employment is limited to informal sector work, and average income levels are significantly lower than for the proximate host community. As we saw in Chapter 3, the median monthly income for the few who do work is just $65 for Somali refugees and $67 for Eritreans, compared with $225 for the nearby host communities.

The little work that is available is in low-paid informal sector roles such as cleaners, waiters, beauticians, mechanics, or street vendors. One Eritrean man, who works informally in a laundry, explained:

> I work eight hours per day and seven days a week. My salary is 1500 ETB [$40] per month...I am not happy with this salary but I never negotiated. I don't want to lose my work...Life is very expensive. I am always under pressure to pay rent and other costs.

Somali families are generally unable to cover living costs with the stipends they receive from UNHCR. One household head in Bole Michael explained, 'Our family receives cash support of 3350 ETB [$88] per month for our entire family but this is too small to cover all expenses.' Where refugee businesses do exist, they are usually unregistered, do not pay tax, were created without significant start-up capital, and rarely employ staff.

Both refugee communities tend to rely upon three sets of social networks: with hosts, other refugees, and transnationally. Links to the host community are the main source of both employment and self-employment opportunities. Jobs are found by word of mouth. A 22-year-old Eritrean explained how he got informal work: 'I am working at a metal workshop...The owner is Ethiopian. I got connected to him through my Eritrean refugee friend...There are five employees at this workshop and all of them are Eritrean refugees.' The few Somali refugees who have found work have usually done so through the Somali Ethiopian community in Bole Michael. One Somali woman who works at a grocery shop owned by a Somali Ethiopian: 'The owner lives in my neighbourhood...I knew he had a business so I asked him to give me a job'. Refugees also rely on the host community to register businesses on their behalf. One Eritrean, explained

> I run a bar...I secured the initial capital [through remittances] from my relatives in the US...I don't have a business license. The license belongs to an Ethiopian but I am the one running this bar. I paid him to register the business on my behalf...I give him 16,000 ETB [$420] every month but I will keep the rest of the income as profit.

Eritreans also require an Ethiopian 'guarantor' simply in order to obtain OCP status and be allowed to live in the city. The majority of these are based on friendships or family connection, but some are through agents who provide the service for a fee. The guarantor relationship sometimes extends into other areas. For example, 10 per cent of Eritrean refugees live with their guarantor, 9 per cent receive support from their guarantor, and a majority meet with their guarantor at least once a month. One OCP refugee told us: 'I used my brother's cousin's wife as a guarantor...Their family is from Eritrea but she was born in Ethiopia and has citizenship.'

Refugees in Addis depend mainly on remittances. According to one Eritrean refugee, 'those who have access to good amount of remittances don't need to work. Working is only for those who don't have access to remittances or receive only small amounts of money.' Thirty-two per cent of Somali refugees and 69 per cent of Eritrean refugees receive access to remittances with an average monthly level of $73 for Eritreans and $157 for Somalis. A 24-year-old Somali refugee who lives in Bole Michael with his mother, is one of those who benefit from regular remittances from her sister in the US: 'From family in the US, we get about $200 per month. This is the only source of income for us because we do not have work here.' Since his arrival in Addis Ababa in 2014, he and his mother have been living exclusively on remittances for more than four years. An Ethiopian researcher at Addis Ababa University: 'In Ethiopia, access to remittances is essential because refugees are not allowed to work here. Their lifestyle is remittance reliant.' Indeed, numerous refugees, both from Eritrea and Somalia, highlighted the significance of remittances as their 'lifeline'. Access to remittances is an important factor differentiating socio-economic status of refugees; one community leader explained, 'In the Somali community, the rich people are remittance recipients but not all refugees can access remittances. I know some refugees receive $50–100 every month...Poor refugees try to survive by doing casual labour like washing clothing, hawking, or working as porters.'

Refugees report feeling a sense of boredom, idleness, and hopelessness. Without work and dependent on remittances, few refugees in Addis see a future in the city. Our data reveals a striking 'mental health gap' between refugees and the host community. Most of the refugees saw no future in Ethiopia, and over 90 per cent of refugees aspire to move onwards to Europe, North America, or Australia, although only 60 per cent believe this is realistic, and an overwhelming majority would prefer to take legal rather than illegal migration routes.

Young refugees reported being unable to either work or pursue their education. One Eritrean in his early 20s explained, 'Here, life is boring. We stay at home, sleeping, chatting, drinking coffee, doing sports like volley-ball and football. We are all young but we are killing time every day. We want to move out of dependency but there's no way out'. A Somali of a similar age said:

> We have to kill time here. We see movies, DVD, watch TV, play football, do the PlayStation, and read. I had hope before to move to the US where I would

have access to education, freedom, betterment. But hope is diminishing. I cannot go back to Somalia yet. I feel hopeless.

The only way out for many young refugees is to contemplate onward migration. One Ethiopian academic explained 'This [onward migration] is really a big issue. So many refugees seek secondary movement for betterment... There are many smugglers and traffickers here. They are an established business here.' An Eritrean refugee leader explained that the route to Europe is a treacherous one:

> Many youth try to make a travel plan to get to Europe, but the cost is prohibitive as the whole trip costs around $6,000. The usual route is from Ethiopia to Sudan and then Libya. Smugglers take them to Libya and there ask for more money to cross the sea. If refugees cannot pay, they will be put them in jail. They have to work as slaves in order to be released by the smugglers. I know at least two Eritrean refugees who worked in Libya for eight months and then moved to Europe.

Nairobi

The refugee experience in Nairobi differs in important ways from Addis. In terms of the right to work, refugees are not legally allowed to work. However, work in the informal sector is broadly tolerated by the government, albeit that refugees face the constant threat of police stopping them and soliciting bribes. In terms of the opportunity to work, Nairobi's much larger markets offer opportunity to those with capital to start businesses. As a result, some Somalis with strong transnational connections thrive, but other refugees rely on precarious low-wage employment.

Legislation formally requires that refugees in Kenya live in camps. The legal exceptions to this 'encampment' policy are refugees in the resettlement process, and those with particular needs relating to health, education, or security that cannot be met in the camps. The number of 'movement passes' granted, though, is far lower than the number of registered refugees—81,000—actually living in Nairobi, most of whom are there illicitly. In practice, though, once refugees are in the city, they are broadly tolerated by the government, and only rarely sent back to the camps.

Occasionally, there are government crackdowns in Eastleigh, in particular. But these are rare, and usually coincide with a major terrorist incident associated with Somali Islamic terrorism. For example, the 2013 Westgate shopping mall attacks, the 2015 Garissa University attacks, and the 2019 Riverside Hotel attacks, after which the government threatened to round up Somali refugees in Eastleigh and either return them to Dadaab or forcibly repatriate them.

Generally, refugees in Nairobi are tolerated by the government, but face daily harassment by police eager to extract bribes from people who are in a precarious legal situation. Somali refugees in particular are easily identifiable and report regularly being stopped by police and instructed to pay bribes or risk deportation. And refugees' ambiguous legal status in Nairobi brings other sources of precarity, such as the constant risk of eviction given their lack of rights relating to property and tenancy.

Despite, these constraints, the attraction of Nairobi is its vast market opportunities. It has the biggest economy in East Africa. About half of all refugees in Nairobi have paid work, more than in any of our other research contexts. But it is also highly competitive, with 43 per cent youth unemployment and most employment being in the informal sector. And, as in Uganda and Ethiopia, urban refugees give up practically all access to humanitarian assistance. As a result, some refugees thrive, but others struggle to survive. On average, refugees earn far more than in the camps or elsewhere and have higher levels of employment. But, there is considerable variation income among refugees, and being a refugee in Nairobi is associated with poor wellbeing outcomes in other areas such as mental health.

Refugees who are able to access remittances and capital to start business, usually registered by Kenyan nationals, sometimes do well. Those without access to capital are often left to struggle in low-wage, informal sector jobs. This difference is reflected in the contrast between the experience of the Somali and Congolese refugee communities in the city, as well as inequalities within those communities.

Nairobi's refugees generally live in specific neighbourhoods. The city's more than 30,000 registered Somali refugees tend to reside in the now famous Eastleigh estate, known as the 'Little Mogadishu' of Nairobi, because of its large Somali and Kenyan Somali population. Eastleigh is a thriving commercial centre, full of shopping centres, street markets, and money transfer businesses. People travel from all across the city to buy and sell fabrics, textiles, and food items, for example. Anthropologist Neil Carrier describes the Eastleigh estate as characterized by mobility, exchange, and interconnectivity.[7] Far from being the nucleus for money laundering or Islamic terrorism often imagined, Carrier shows how Eastleigh represents a historical market hub, with transnational connections, to which many refugees make important contributions despite the daily struggle.

But there is also vast inequality among Somali refugees in Eastleigh. One of the distinguishing factors among refugees is whether or not they have access to remittances as the basis for start-up capital. Mohamed, a Somali community leader, explained the inequality that sometimes exists:

> There is economic disparity among Somali refugees. Some are doing well. They are running big businesses and many of them are also receiving remittances from abroad. But this wealthy group is very small in number. The vast majority of refugees are poor. They are mostly hawkers. Others are employed by Somali Kenyans as shopkeepers, porters, or security guards. They make tiny incomes from casual labour.[8]

This observation is supported by the data. Some 52 per cent of Somalis with paid work are self-employed. They can be found running garment shops, restaurants, cafes, bakeries, grocery stores, hotels, forex bureaus, mini-supermarkets, and real estate businesses, albeit that they usually require a Kenyan Somali to register the business on their behalf. And the larger business owners frequently report earning in excess of $200 per month. In contrast, those who are employed tend to earn less. As employees, they work as shop keepers, restaurant staff, clerks, or security guards, for example, sometimes earning $50–100 per month in higher-status jobs. However, Somalis in precarious informal sector employment such as casual domestic labour or hawking sometimes earned as little as $15–20 per month.

For Somalis in particular, transnational networks are also crucial to success in the city. Katra came to Eastleigh in 2006 and runs a clothing business. The company is co-owned with a cousin who has been resettled from Kenya to the United States. They each put in $5,000: '$10,000 is a big amount of money. In Eastleigh, to start this kind of business requires such an amount. In addition to buying clothing, we need to pay rent and license fees, for example'. Some Somali businesses in Eastleigh have also formed links with Chinese traders in order to acquire textiles. One refugee who runs a clothing business explained: 'Initially, the items were from various places but now most of goods are from China...We were introduced by other Somalis...Now we order items via email and WhatsApp. My business partner goes to China twice a year.' Eastleigh is indeed part of the global economy, connected to supply chains around the world.

Poorer Somalis also rely upon their own networks, but as a source of social protection. Links to Kenyan Somalis were especially important for employment. Omar, who had been living in Nairobi since 2005, and worked as a driver for a Somali transportation company, explained, 'I drive trucks to carry oil... I know the owner of this transportation company. I used to work for him as a mechanic and driver... He is from the same clan in Somalia but I met him in Kenya'. Meanwhile, Anap, a female Somali in her thirties is among the many refugees to jointly own a business in Nairobi with a Somali Kenyan collaborator:

> I co-own this shoe shop with a Somali Kenyan partner... It is much easier and safe to involve Kenyans in business. It is easier to get documents. The city council make it difficult for refugees to request a business license. They also ask for bribes from us.

The city's more than 30,000 Congolese refugees are more dispersed and live in Nairobi's more peripheral suburbs such as Kasarani, Kayole, and Githurai.[9] Unlike Somalis, Congolese refugees tend to speak Swahili, are generally Christian, and are often considered difficult to ethnically distinguish from nationals. They therefore tend to assimilate more easily within predominantly host community suburbs. One non-governmental organization (NGO) worker suggested that 'Compared to Somali, Congolese refugees are much easier to be integrated in Kenyan society... they can speak Swahili... and their features are a kind of similar to Kenyan people'. Nevertheless, these are generally poor neighbourhoods, with large immigrant populations, sometimes characterized by competition for scarce resources, including employment.

The experience of Congolese refugees is generally quite different from that of Somalis. A smaller proportion—around 38 per cent—of Congolese workers are self-employed, often as hawkers or street vendors. Although they are generally valued by Kenyan entrepreneurs as a source of customers and cheap labour, they more likely to be in low-wage, casual employment, in sectors such as hair and beauty, construction, cleaning, or security, for example. Among those with income-generating activities, the median income is less than half that of Somali refugees in Eastleigh. And competition for scarce informal sector jobs has occasionally sparked tension and even violence between Kenyans and Congolese refugees in suburbs such as Kasarani.

Kampala

Uganda's capital city offers a more optimistic insight into the economic contributions refugees can make to cities if given greater freedoms. The city's diverse refugee communities—Rwandans, Ethiopians, Somalis, Congolese, and South Sudanese, for example—all bring something unique to the city's dynamic and diverse economy. While many struggle, almost half of refugees have an income-generating activity of some kind, and their economic contribution is widely recognized by Ugandans. Nevertheless, refugees' economic lives in the city should not be romanticized; most rely upon small scale self-employment or low-wage labour, and the average earned income among refugees (when removing outliers) is barely $1 per day.

Kampala provides significantly more freedom to its 85,000 refugees than other capital cities across the region. Under the 2006 Refugee Act, as we will see in more detail in Chapter 5, they are legally allowed to reside in the city and to work, albeit that in doing so they implicitly declare themselves to be capable of living independently of aid.

However, despite these legislative freedoms, Uganda's urban refugees still face different restrictions compared to citizens. These include rules on accessing banking and financial services, the process for business registration, and limitations on property ownership. For those who struggle, a handful of NGOs offer counselling programmes or basic vocational training and livelihoods programmes in areas such as hairdressing, tailoring, and textile design; however, these are small-scale and serve only a limited number of refugees.

Occasionally, the government also backtracks on its putatively progressive policies; for example, in 2019, amid rising urban numbers, the government announced that refugees could henceforth only register in the country's designated refugee settlements; in 2020, meanwhile, the government publicly announced that refugees in cities would not be eligible for COVID-19-related food assistance.

Many of Kampala's refugees live within specific suburbs. Nearly all Somalis live in the geographically contiguous Kisenyi area, while most Congolese refugees co-reside with Ugandans in the Nsambya and Katwe areas. Other nationalities are more are dispersed across the city. Refugees are considerably worse off than the nearby host communities. Our research shows that Somali and Congolese refugees are almost half as likely as nearby hosts to have an income-generating activity (44 per cent versus 71 per cent), and those that do earn less than the host community ($94 versus $113, excluding outliers). In some communities, notably among the Somalis, the shortfall is partly subsidized by remittances; with about half of Somalis in Kisenyi receiving at least some remittances.

Suburbs such as Kisenyi, Nsambya, and Katwe are close to Kampala's thriving downtown markets. The Owino market, for instance, is the largest market in East Africa. And, reflecting this, self-employment is the biggest source of work in the city, accounting for 62 per cent of Congolese and 52 per cent of Somali jobs. Remittances are an important enabling factor for entrepreneurship, especially within the Somali community, within which average household remittances were reported as over $700 in Kisenyi, compared to around $100 within the Congolese communities.

Some refugees are able to thrive by building businesses that make use of Owino's transnational trade links. For example, in the wide range of Somali shops in Kisenyi, products can be found from across the Islamic world. These often arrive through Somali-controlled supply chains and trade networks, linking Kampala to Kenya, UAE, Saudi Arabia, Pakistan, and elsewhere. Basmati rice, spaghetti, canned camel milk, tinned tuna fish, and some favoured Somali cosmetics will frequently arrive from the Middle East, via Nairobi's Eastleigh markets, before coming to Owino. Muhammed, for example, showed us around his shop in Kisenyi, explaining, 'I have contacts in Eastleigh in Nairobi. They can get the products that people here want to buy.'

And Kampala's markets also create opportunities for small-scale entrepreneurship, sometimes based on ethnic specialization. Many Congolese refugees, for example, buy and sell brightly coloured ceremonial fabric called 'bitenge' (or 'kitenge') and jewellery. In many cases, Congolese refugees buy these materials from Ugandan wholesalers and then sell them on a small scale as street vendors. One Ugandan wholesaler explained, 'Congolese people are the most important customers for me. I receive about a hundred retail buyers per day. Seventy of them are Congolese refugees'. A Ugandan merchant explained how she travels to buy the products in Busia in Kenya, and then sells them on to Congolese 'hawkers' to retail on the streets of Kampala. And some Ugandans have even created similar wholesale businesses because of the demand from refugees. One said, 'There are so many Congolese refugees and I knew they like bitenge so I started this business. I buy in the Cooper complex [one of the large Kampala markets] and sell to ... refugee hawkers'.

Other forms of 'ethnic' economic specialization are evident. Ethiopians, especially the Oromo, are active in the foreign exchange and money transfer industries. Eritreans run many of the city's internet cafes. Rwandans are associated with the trade in second-hand clothing and shoes. Meanwhile,

Somalis thrive in retail commerce, but also frequently benefit from their close connections ethnic Somali-Ugandans. For example, several large-scale Somali-Ugandan businesses prioritize offering employment to Somali refugees. One Somali-Ugandan-owned oil company alone, City Oil, employs nearly sixty Somali refugees as shop-keepers, cashiers, security guards, and clerks at just one of its more than twenty franchises across the greater Kampala area. One Somali refugee working for the company explained, 'There are many Somali refugees working for City Oil. We have a language in common. We have cultural and religious bonds. So, it is easy to work together.'[10]

For Ugandan business owners, refugees often represent a welcome source of cheap labour. One supermarket located near a suburb with a large number of Congolese refugees has employed Congolese refugees as porters and checkout staff for more than a decade. The owner explained, 'At my shop, I employ some Congolese refugees... I hire them because they are cheaper than Ugandan labour. This is seasonal recruitment so there is no contract. Whenever I need people, I call these Congolese refugees'.

However, the wage differential compared to nationals is a source of resentment for some refugees. One Congolese employee in a clothing shop explained 'This monthly salary of 250,000 UGX [$66] is not enough. I cannot cover all [my] costs. At the end of the month nothing remains. So no saving and no investment. Especially when I get ill, it is hard to cover medical bills.'

Generally, refugees are valued by the host community as employees, customers, and tenants. And sometimes they are even job creators for Ugandan nationals. In Kisenyi, for instance, it was common to find Ugandan casual labourers working in Somali restaurants and shops. In an early study, we estimated that 21 per cent of refugees in Kampala run a business that employs at least one other person, and of those they employ 40 per cent are Ugandans. Reflecting these contributions, our dataset revealed that about half of nearby host community members agreed that refugees make an economic contribution. And host community members with higher levels of interaction with refugees, including business interactions, were more likely to have positive perceptions of refugees' economic contribution, provided they too had an income-generating activity.

Nevertheless, many refugees in Kampala are extremely vulnerable. They rely on the informal economy. One UNHCR protection officer reminded us, 'Most refugees [in Kampala] are just surviving. Their daily life is full of uncertainty, instability, and unpredictability. In my view, only a few refugees are self-reliant. Kampala is not easy. Education is not free. The same for hospitals.' With limited access to public services and practically no international assistance, many refugees turn to refugee-led organizations (RLOs) as a source of social protection. The leader of one RLO, which provides psychosocial support and livelihoods training to other refugees told me 'Kampala really is a struggle for most refugees. They cannot make enough money to live. The international organizations are not really present, and so we try as best as we can to fill some of the gaps.'

Conclusion

This chapter has offered a brief window into the economic lives of refugees in three African cities. Addis is perhaps the most challenging, with close to zero employment, almost total dependency on remittances, and a pervasive sense of hopelessness among young people who regard emigration as their only viable option. Nairobi provides the largest market for jobs and entrepreneurship, and a small number of refugees thrive, but most refugees face precarity and are heavily penalized for their economic activities by government restrictions. Kampala offers the greatest freedom, enabling refugees to engage in entrepreneurial activity, but most of that activity is small-scale and usually does not provide an adequate source of income to meet living costs.

Despite these differences, the three contexts exhibit similarities. In each city, the combination of government restrictions and the absence of international assistance makes urban survival challenging for refugees, and most refugees are dependent upon the informal economy and their social networks. Across all the cities, refugees generally earn more and work more than they would in the camps but they earn significantly less than host citizens because of the greater restrictions they face. Furthermore, although refugees are often appreciated by local businesses for their economic contributions as employees and customers, they are also sometimes viewed as a source of competition for scarce resources. And in each case, we also see the significant gendered implications of urbanization: for example, the majority in cities are men and the majority in camps and settlements are women.

Offering urban refuge is a central part of creating a sustainable refugee system. But urban sanctuary is currently far from sustainable. For refugees in

East Africa, moving to cities can offer the opportunity to work and earn more, but it often leads to worse welfare outcomes in areas such as health, mental health, and food security compared even to camps. For host communities, it can offer entrepreneurs a ready supply of workers and consumers, but can also lead to tension over competition for informal sector work. For the international community, there may be a risk that without prospects in the city, refugees may have even greater aspirations to migrate elsewhere.

Making urban sanctuary sustainable will rely upon a number of policy changes. Above all, host governments—both central governments and municipal authorities—will need to reduce barriers to urban refugees' socio-economic participation, including by ensuring rights to work, register businesses, own property, and open bank accounts. This in turn will require incentives from the international community, something we explore further in Chapter 8. In addition, though, international organizations will need to redesign their urban assistance programmes. Our research suggests that the kinds of tasks that are needed include spatially targeted additional public services and job creation for both refugees and hosts in relevant neighbourhoods; investment in urban job creation; youth engagement and training programmes for both refugees and host communities; support for legal aid services that can ensure refugees' recourse to the rule of law; the design of inclusive spaces for increased refugee–host interaction; and greater financial inclusion to support refugee entrepreneurship.[11]

Urban assistance models can be improved. However, our analysis also suggests that not all of the world's refugees can be sustainably integrated in cities. Most governments, including those in East Africa, are reluctant to integrate all refugees into cities. They are likely to continue to place restrictions on urban refugees. Furthermore, refugees in cities are not necessarily unambiguously better off than refugees in rural areas, even if they generally work and earn more.

Put simply, urbanization will not, by itself, be an adequate solution for refugee protection. Sustainable sanctuary will need to be both urban and rural.

5

Uganda

The right to work and freedom of movement

Introduction

In the search for models of sustainable refugee assistance, it makes sense to begin by examining 'success stories'. Uganda's refugee policies have been widely recognized as among the most progressive in the world. The BBC described Uganda as 'one of the best places to be a refugee'.[1] Despite currently hosting more refugees than any country in Africa, it allows refugees the right to work and significant freedom of movement. The Ugandan self-reliance model contrasts with many other refugee-hosting countries in the region, which often require refugees to live in camps and deny them access to labour markets.

Uganda's model has three core elements that distinguish it from most other refugee-hosting countries. First, its regulatory framework: it lets refugees work and choose their place of residence. Second, its assistance model: it allocates plots of land for refugees to cultivate within its rural settlements. Third, its model of refugee–host interaction: it encourages integrated social service provision and market access.

Ever since the Nakivale settlement, Africa's oldest refugee camp, opened in 1958, Uganda has provided refugees with plots of land in rural settlements, allowing them to engage in subsistence farming. Vibrant and entrepreneurial markets have emerged in many of the refugee settlements in both the south-west, originally host to Rwandan refugees, and the northern West Nile region of the country, mainly host to South Sudanese refugees. Refugees who wish to live in cities like Kampala are able to do so, albeit that they give up access to nearly all assistance. And the government has persevered with the model despite refugee numbers more than tripling to over a million, following crisis and conflict in South Sudan and the Democratic Republic of Congo between 2015 and 2017.

Uganda's self-reliance model has existed in different forms virtually since the country's independence in 1962. It was formalized in policy through the Self-Reliance Strategy (SRS), established with donor support, in 1999. The right to work and to choose a place of residence were incorporated within legislation in the 2006 Refugee Act. However, the model really captured international attention during the European refugee crisis of 2015–16, when the European and North American public became interested in finding more sustainable models of refugee assistance. The approach received widespread popular acclaim. The *New York Times* described Uganda as 'a global model for how it treats refugees', the *Washington Post* proclaimed 'Uganda treats refugees better than the United States', and the *Economist* declared 'Uganda is a model for dealing with refugees'.[2]

With recognition has come increased opportunities for funding. The United Nations Refugee Agency (UNHCR) created a succession of new acronyms to package the Ugandan model for international donors. Updating the SRS model, it unveiled the Refugee and Host Population Empowerment Strategic Framework (ReHoPE) in 2016, replacing it with the Comprehensive Refugee Response Framework (CRRF) for Uganda in 2018. Both had in common the goal of supporting socio-economic opportunities for both refugees and the nearby host communities. Although policy labels have changed over time, there has been significant continuity in the underlying model.

However, some commentators have pushed back against the romanticization of the Ugandan model. The Uganda-based non-governmental organization (NGO) the International Refugee Rights Initiative (IRRI), in particular, published a report in 2018 that posed important but challenging questions for the model. It pointed to questions about refugees' political freedoms, the absence of pathways to citizenship for refugees, and the limitations of Uganda's assistance model. It noted that 'with so few success stories in the context of global displacement, there has been a tendency to idealize Uganda's refugee response'. It rightly argued 'for a debate over what is and is not working in the Ugandan context based on a strong evidence-base'.[3]

So, what difference does Uganda's self-reliance model make in practice? Which aspects work, under what conditions, and for whom? In this chapter, I empirically explore the strengths and weaknesses of the Ugandan model. The Ugandan model provides a unique opportunity to understand what difference the right to work and freedom of movement make for refugees and the host community. And this has implications for advocacy, programming, and policy elsewhere. As the *Economist* put it, 'the successes and failures of Uganda's liberal refugee policy have lessons for elsewhere'.[4]

Of course, providing rigorous quantitative evidence on the impact of Uganda's self-reliance model is methodologically challenging. It relies upon some kind of counterfactual; we need to be able to compare outcomes for refugees and hosts *within* the model to those for refugees and hosts *outside* the model. As a starting point for this, I therefore compare outcomes for refugees and hosts in Uganda with those in neighbouring Kenya. The comparison is valuable because, although the countries are in the same region and receive some of the same refugee populations, they have contrasting regulatory and policy frameworks relating to refugees. While Uganda allows the right to work and freedom of movement, Kenya imposes significant restrictions on both of these rights. Kenya's legislation formally requires refugees to reside in designated camps in which work permits are unavailable. While Uganda has a self-reliance policy, Kenya has an 'encampment' policy.

Using comparable survey methods, the Refugee Economies Programme collected data in 2017 and 2018 in urban and camps contexts in Uganda (Kampala and Nakivale) and Kenya (Nairobi and Kakuma).[5] The comparison is of course imperfect: other factors beyond law and policy are likely to explain variation in outcomes for refugees and host communities across the two countries. Meanwhile, although the data is representative for refugees and hosts within these contexts, these sites are not necessarily representative of all refugees in the two countries. Nevertheless, the comparison at least allows us to hold constant some sources of variation; for example, we are able to focus on outcomes for the same nationality groups (Congolese and Somali refugees) in both countries.

In this chapter, I examine three Uganda-specific questions which are brought to life through comparison with Kenya. Each question focuses on different aspects of what is ostensibly unique about the Ugandan model. First, on the regulatory framework: what difference do the right to work and the right to move make? Second, on the assistance model: do self-reliance policies lead to self-reliance outcomes? Third, on refugee–host interactions: does Uganda's integrated service approach lead to improved community relations? Within each section, I outline what is distinctive about the Ugandan model and explore its relationship to a range of welfare outcomes.

The analysis reveals the difference the Ugandan model makes. Drawing upon the research of the Refugee Economies Programme,[6] it highlights four major advantages to Uganda's regulatory framework: greater mobility, lower transaction costs for economic activity, higher incomes when adjusted for purchasing power, and more sustainable sources of employment. Nevertheless, it also highlights some limitations to Uganda's assistance model, notably in relation to the viability of its land allocation model in rural settlements, the inadequacy of access to education in the settlements, and the ineffectiveness of urban assistance. Overall, the research offers a strong endorsement of the value of allowing refugees the right to work and freedom of movement, but calls for a more nuanced view of the strengths and weaknesses of refugee assistance in Uganda.

The key takeaway is that, while the Ugandan model is by no means perfect, it shows that a regulatory framework that provides basic socio-economic freedoms, such as the right to work and freedom of movement, leads to a series of better socio-economic outcomes than would be the case in the absence of those entitlements.

Comparing Uganda and Kenya

Assessing the impact of the self-reliance model relies upon being able to compare outcomes for refugees within the model to those outside the model. The ideal method for doing that would be a 'randomized control trial', introducing the model for a 'treatment' but not for an otherwise similar 'control' group and assessing impact over time. The challenge with doing that for a variable such as 'right to work' is that it would be very difficult to persuade a government to gradually introduce the right to work as part of such a study. Consequently, the next best, albeit imperfect, option is to compare outcomes within two pre-existing and contrasting models, within which as many other variables as possible can be held constant.

In order to do that, we compared welfare outcomes for refugees and host communities in Uganda with those in neighbouring Kenya. We chose this comparison because the countries have contrasting legal and policy frameworks relating to refugees but both are in the same region and host refugee populations from the same countries.

Case selection is based on Uganda and Kenya's contrasting regulatory frameworks and assistance models. Uganda's 'self-reliance model' and

Kenya's 'encampment policy' have commonly been identified as occupying contrasting ends of the refugee policy spectrum. And yet, as neighbouring countries, both hosting Congolese, Somali, and South Sudanese refugees, they have enough in common to make comparison meaningful. Within each country, we selected an urban and rural comparator. We compared Kampala and Nairobi, as refugee-hosting capital cities, and we compared the Nakivale settlement in Uganda with the Kakuma camps in Kenya. While Nakivale is one of thirteen designated settlements in Uganda, Kakuma is one of two sets of camps in Kenya. We select them partly because they have a number of things in common: they are both widely regarded as the most progressive and economically dynamic camps or settlements in their respective country, they both have a long history (Nakivale was created in 1958 and Kakuma in 1992), and they both host Congolese and Somali refugees in sufficient numbers to enable meaningful comparison.

As we saw in Chapter 4, Kampala hosts nearly 100,000 refugees. Most Somalis live in the highly entrepreneurial Kisenyi area, while most Congolese refugees co-reside with Ugandans in the Nsambya and Katwe areas. Nairobi is similar with around 100,000 refugees, with Somalis also living collectively in the Eastleigh area while Congolese are more widely dispersed across areas such as Kasarani and Githurai.

In Uganda, the vast majority of refugees live in one of the country's designated settlements, which are jointly managed by the Office of the Prime Minister (OPM) and UNHCR. Nakivale settlement is home to approximately 105,000 refugees. Until recently, it was Uganda's largest settlement. Its biggest populations are Congolese, Somali, and Burundian. An hour's drive from the district capital of Mbarara, the settlement area is divided geographically into three administrative zones: Base camp, Juru, and Rubondo. Meanwhile, Kakuma is slightly larger with 180,000 refugees of mainly Congolese, Somali, and South Sudanese origin, and divides into four main camps, Kakuma 1 to 4, and a new settlement called Kalobeyei. Although close to Kakuma Town and Lokichoggio, it is more remote from large-scale market activity than Nakivale.

Although they are neighbours, there are three major contrasts between Uganda and Kenya's refugee policy models (summarized in Table 5.1). First, in terms of regulation, while Uganda's 'self-reliance model' allows refugees to work and move freely, Kenya's 'encampment policy' does not. Second, in terms of assistance, Uganda generally adopts an open settlements model in

Table 5.1. Comparing Uganda's and Kenya's refugee policy models

Dimension of the Model	Uganda 'Self-reliance Model'	Kenya 'Encampment Policy'
Regulatory Framework	Right to work and move freely	No right to work or move freely
Assistance Model	Self-reliance in settlements and cities	International aid in camps, and precarity in cities
Refugee–Host Interaction	Refugees within national service provision	Nationals within international service provision

which refugees are offered access to land for cultivation; Kenya has a camp model premised upon international aid delivery. In cities, Uganda allows refugees to have economic freedom; in Kenya, they are generally prohibited from living outside camps. Third, in terms of refugee–host interaction, in Uganda refugees are integrated into national service provision; in Kenya, refugees more often receive access to parallel services provided by the international community, which nationals can usually also access. We are interested in exploring what difference these three contrasting features make.

The research draws upon the dataset described in Chapter 3, including data for over 8,000 refugees and host community members in urban (Kampala and Nairobi) and camp contexts (Nakivale and Kakuma), which is based on random sampling.[7] We focus in this chapter only on outcomes for Congolese and Somali refugees, because these nationality groups are common across all four contexts. The quantitative data is representative of our focus populations and selected sites but cannot be considered representative of all refugees or host communities in Uganda and Kenya. It does not include the West Nile region of Uganda or the Dadaab camps in Kenya, which both host significant numbers of refugees, for example.

We recognize that the Ugandan and Kenyan contexts vary in a range of ways beyond the legal and policy variables we are interested in, and that a range of other factors are likely to contribute to our observed outcomes. We therefore used qualitative research as a means to interpret our quantitative observations, and to elaborate on the causal mechanisms that may underpin quantitative patterns and correlations.

Regulatory framework

On the surface, Uganda and Kenya's refugee policies could not be more different. They occupy opposite ends of the regulatory spectrum when it comes to refugees' socio-economic rights. Uganda allows refugees to work and select their place of residence. Kenya requires refugees to live in designated camps where they are unable to apply for work permits.

Uganda's Refugee Act of 2006 represents its main source of legislation relating to refugees. Described as 'a model for Africa' by UNHCR, it provides refugees with the right to work, move around the country, and live in community. Section 29(e) explains that refugees shall enjoy 'the same treatment accorded to aliens generally in similar situations', including the right to (iv) 'establish commercial and industrial companies in accordance with applicable laws' and (vi) 'the right to have access to employment opportunities and engage in gainful employment'. Meanwhile, Section 30 provides that 'a recognised refugee is entitled to free movement in Uganda', albeit subject to national security and public order provisions.[8]

The Act came into force in 2009 at a time when Uganda hosted just 140,000 refugees. It replaced the Control of Aliens Refugee Act (1960), known as CARA. Although CARA required refugees to reside in settlements and marginalized imported elements of international refugee law, it also included the right to work. Section 15 stated: 'Arrangements shall be made for offering employment to refugees who shall be paid at the appropriate rate of wages prevailing in Uganda for the performance of similar work'. While advocacy organizations such as the Refugee Law Project (RLP) described the 2006 Act as having 'some deficiencies, loopholes, inadequacies, room for excesses, and glaring omissions', notably in areas like the prohibition of refugees' political activities and its ambiguous definition of protection, the Act has more widely been viewed as highly progressive in terms of creating legislation that recognizes refugees' socio-economic rights.[9]

In contrast, Kenya's refugee legislation is often viewed as highly restrictive. James Milner has described Kenyan policy as being characterized by 'encampment and abdication' since the early 1990s.[10] Although Kenya tolerated the self-settlement of refugees until the late 1980s, the large-scale influx of Somali refugees led to a policy change towards requiring refugees to reside in the Dadaab or Kakuma camps from 1992 onwards. This de facto policy framework was enshrined in legislation through the Kenyan Refugee

Act of 2006, which restricts refugees' freedom of movement, and indirectly limits their right to work.

Section 16(2) of the Refugee Act explains that 'the Minister may, by notice of the Gazette, in consultation with the host community, designate places and areas in Kenya to live—a)... transit centres; b) refugee camps'. Section 16(4) appears to offer refugees the right to work:'every refugee and member of his family in Kenya shall, in respect of wage-earning employment, be subject to the same restrictions as are imposed on persons who are not citizens of Kenya'.[11] Indeed, Section 40 of the 2011 Kenyan Citizenship and Immigration Act creates a category of work permits for refugees known as Class M Permits. However, in practice, these permits, issued by the director of immigration services are only available in Nairobi. While legislation was brought to parliament in 2017 that proposed to give refugees in Kenya the right to work and access to land, similar to Ugandan legislation, the proposed Bill was rejected by the president on the grounds that it was not based on adequate consultation in accordance with the requirements of the Constitution. When a new Refugee Bill was brought to parliament in 2019, all references to the right to work or freedom of movement had been removed.[12]

The contrasting state of refugee legislation between the two countries has been widely recognized. The real question, though, is: what does the contrasting regulatory framework mean in practice? To what extent do differences in law and policy relating to work and mobility rights actually translate into different outcomes in terms of employment and mobility? While, intuitively, we might predict that the Ugandan model would inevitably lead to more progressive outcomes, the reality is more nuanced.

The Refugee Economies Programme's research shows that the right to work and freedom of movement do make a difference in four key areas: mobility, transaction costs for economic activity, income, and employment (summarized in Table 5.2).

Greater mobility

One would expect the right to move freely and choose a place of residence to correlate with greater mobility, and it does. This is revealed by comparing mobility patterns between refugees in Uganda's Nakivale settlement with those in Kenya's Kakuma camps. The key data point is that refugees in Uganda's Nakivale settlement are 70 per cent more likely to have travelled

Table 5.2. Summary of the main positive findings relating to the impact of Uganda's
regulatory framework, when comparatively benchmarked against Kenya

Greater Mobility	70% more likely to travel from camps
Lower Transaction Costs for Economic Activity	Somalis 20 times lower arrest and bribe rates in Kampala
Higher Incomes	16% higher income at purchasing power parity, controlling for other variables
More Sustainable Employment	Most refugee employment in Uganda by other refugees (compared to NGOs or nationals in Kenya)

to a major city in the last year than refugees in Kenya's Kakuma camp. Of
course, other factors such as geography and transportation will also impact
mobility, but the evidence indicates that the right to move is probably
associated with greater movement. To break down the data, 22 per cent of
Congolese and 29 per cent of Somalis in Nakivale reported leaving the
settlement during the previous year, compared with 13 per cent of Congolese
and 17 per cent of Somalis in Kakuma. This is a gap of around 70 per cent
for both communities.

Greater mobility rights are valued because they enable refugees to adopt
economic strategies than might otherwise be unavailable or expensive. This
seems to be especially important to Somali refugees because Somali refugees
run businesses that rely upon managing supply chains that go beyond the
boundaries of the camps.

In the Nakivale settlement, commerce is the most common income-generating
activity among Somalis. This contrasts with the mainly agricultural focus of
the Congolese. Even a cursory glance at the inventory of Somali-run retail
shops shows how many of the products have come from outside Uganda.
Tuna fish imported from Thailand via Saudi Arabia, Mombasa, and Kampala
comes in through Somali-operated, transnational supply chains. Many of
the soft plastic toys carry 'made in Mogadishu' labels.

Being able to personally leave the settlements is an important part of
accessing these supply chains. Fatuma, a Somali refugee who runs an eclectic
retail shop in the Somali-dominated zone 3 of Nakivale, selling food, spices,
shoes, cosmetics, and perfume, explained the importance of mobility for her
business:

> I go to Kampala every two months to purchase my stuff. I usually buy in
> Owino and Chikubu markets in Kampala...When I go there, I stay at my
> friend's place in Kisenyi...I initially started this business with my Somali

refugee friend who moved from Nakivale to Kampala. She started sending items to me to sell in the camp and we were sharing profits…Later she got resettled to Sweden. But I continued this business.

And even if Somali entrepreneurs do not own their own transport, another Somali business in the 'Little Mogadishu' (zone 3) area of the settlement provides a daily bus service to Kampala, something that would be restricted under Kenya's regulatory framework.

Some Somali families even divide their living arrangements between Kampala and Nakivale in order to maximize household income. Many Somalis who are registered in Nakivale in order to ensure their families access assistance actually live and work in Kampala. For example, in our data collection, only 40 per cent of Somali refugees in Kampala were actually registered as living in the city; the rest were registered in one of the settlements but living in the city for business purposes. For example, Osman runs a brokerage business and a small food stand in Kisenyi, the Somali area of Kampala, while his wife and six children remain in Nakivale.

Furthermore, Uganda's regulatory framework is more attractive to refugees than Kenya's regulatory framework. A large proportion of refugees actually choose their host country based on the regulatory environment. Over 80 per cent of our Somali refugee sample in Uganda have moved from Kenya to Uganda, many after spending a number of years in Kenya. Of those who moved, around 30 per cent cited the absence of freedom to work and move as the primary reason for onward movement.

Lower transaction costs for economic activity

Restrictive regulation does not stop refugees from engaging in economic activities. But it pushes it into the informal economy, making it much more difficult and expensive. Refugees in Kenya are working and moving but they are moving less and paying far higher transaction costs for doing so.

The comparison between Kampala and Nairobi shows the impact of the right to work. We found that Somali refugees in Kampala face more than twenty times lower rates of arrest and police bribery than Somali refugees in Nairobi. Because police in Nairobi are relatively poorly paid by the government they rely upon eliciting bribes as a key part of their income-generating strategy. And Somali refugees are an easy target, usually living in one area and being ethnically and linguistically recognizable. Twenty-nine per cent of Somalis reported being arrested in the last three months and, as a community, they report paying an average of $23 in police bribes over that time. This compares to negligible levels of arrest and bribe solicitation in Kampala. One Somali refugee, who moved from Nairobi to Kampala, explained: 'Kenya is tough. Police harass refugees. We cannot move freely. We have to carry our ID all the time in Kenya. Nairobi is also dangerous and has so much crime…Uganda is safer and more peaceful. When we are walking, no one harasses us. It is much easier to live here.'

Unlike Kenya, only a few respondents in Uganda mentioned experiencing harassment from police or other national authorities. One of our Congolese research assistants in Nakivale, William, explained 'I have been living in Nakivale since 2008. I have never experienced any police harassment. I don't think this is an issue for other refugees in Nakivale. In the first place, there is very little presence of police inside the settlement.' Abdinasir, a Somali refugee who has been selling construction materials like cement, iron sheet, nails, and wood stock in Nakivale since 2014, often visits the nearby city of Mbarara to buy construction materials. When asked if he ever experiences police harassment, he said 'Never. Nobody has ever stopped me.' Another Congolese refugee, Rogers, explained that he is able to operate as a mobile trader, selling fabric and jewellery anywhere he chooses. He explained that his experience is representative of others settling the ceremonial fabric bitenge: 'Many [Congolese refugee] hawkers now travel and explore other markets for bitenge. They are reaching distant areas from Kampala like Hoima, Paidha, and Mbarara. Some even go beyond border and reach Tanzania, Kenya.' One observable difference between Somali refugees in Kampala and those in Nairobi is the number of businesses that are jointly owned with ethnic Somali Kenyans. In Kenya, joint business ventures with Somali Kenyans are a common strategy to overcome regulatory barriers relating to business registration. In Uganda, there are fewer businesses set up on the basis of shared ownership with host nationals.

Higher incomes

Meaningfully comparing refugees' incomes across countries is challenging. Even assuming people accurately reveal their true incomes, it relies upon controlling for both differences between the populations (e.g. in terms of nationality, education, and gender) and differences between the countries (e.g. in terms of the cost of living). In Chapter 3, we saw how in nominal terms, refugees in Kenya appear to earn more in dollars than those in Uganda

($68 versus $32 in camps, and $151 versus $94 in cities). However, the picture begins to change when we control for population and cost of living.

In terms of descriptive statistics, the first thing we can do is compare the same nationality groups with one another (Congolese and Somalis across the two countries), and to convert median income levels to what is called 'purchasing power parity' (PPP), a way of controlling for differences in price levels across the countries. The former is important because our data in Kenya, for instance, includes relatively poorer South Sudanese refugees. The latter is important because the cost of living is, according to the World Bank, around 50 per cent greater in Kenya than Uganda.[13]

When we adjusted for the cost of living, we found that the median income of refugees in Uganda engaged in some form of remunerated economic activity is generally higher than for those in Kenya. This is especially striking because Kenya is almost twice as rich as Uganda in GDP/capita PPP terms,[14] and because the opposite pattern that we observe for refugees is true for the host communities. Proximate host communities in Uganda have around half the median income (even at PPP) of those in Kenya. This presents a paradox of relatively richer refugees in Uganda compared to Kenya, alongside relatively poorer host communities.

The only notable exception to this pattern is working Congolese refugees in Nakivale ($60/month at PPP) who earn about half as much as working Congolese in Kakuma ($100/month at PPP), and this contrasts with the pattern for Somalis, for whom the pattern is the other way around ($120 in Kakuma compared to $190 in Nakivale at PPP).[15] This exception reflects that Congolese and Somalis are doing fundamentally different things in Nakivale. The Congolese, like the neighbouring Ugandan hosts, are engaged in subsistence agriculture, growing maize, beans, sorghum, and vegetables for their own consumption and commercial sales. Meanwhile, Somalis are engaged in commerce, and choose not to do agricultural work. In Kampala, refugees also earn more at PPP than in Nairobi, despite the general assumption that Nairobi offers a bigger market. Working Somali refugees in Kampala earn more than those in Nairobi ($450 compared to $320 at PPP), and a similar pattern can be found for working Congolese refugees ($200 compared to $140 at PPP).

The finding that employed refugees in Uganda have greater purchasing power than employed refuges in Kenya is reinforced through regression analysis. We found that being a refugee with an income-generating activity in Uganda is associated with having a 16 per cent higher income (at PPP) than being a refugee with an income-generating activity in Kenya, controlling for other variables such as education, gender, and nationality.[16] More specifically, regression analysis also tells us that the statistically significant determinants of variation in income for refugees across our two-country dataset are: public goods (education and health), identity (gender, age, being Somali), and regulation (being in city rather than a camp, and being in Uganda rather than Kenya).

Within our regression analysis, we specifically found that, controlling for other variables, the (dummy) variable 'being in Uganda' is statistically significant[17] and is positively correlated with higher income at PPP. This is likely to be because of the type of income-generating activities that Uganda's regulatory framework allows refugees to undertake. Businesses face fewer restrictions and so levels of self-employment and legal employment at a market-based salary are far greater. Meanwhile, refugees in Kenya are restricted in terms of the types of activities they can undertake, with low-wage 'incentive work' for international organizations and NGOs being far more common than in Uganda.

In summary, our data shows that refugees who work in Uganda have greater purchasing power than those in Kenya, despite residing in a much poorer country and within relatively poorer communities, and part of this difference is correlated simply with residing in Uganda. One possible interpretation is that Uganda's regulatory framework may make a quite striking difference to the income of its refugees, enabling them to do better than refugees elsewhere even while residing within relatively poorer communities.

More sustainable sources of employment

One of the most striking findings in our data is that the sources of employment for refugees in Uganda are different from those in Kenya. In particular, employed refugees in Uganda are on average more than five times as likely to be employed by other refugees of the same nationality than are employed refugees in Kenya.

Surprisingly given the regulatory context, overall employment rates for Somali and Congolese refugees in Kenya are actually higher than for those in Uganda. In the camp and settlement context, this is mainly because Kakuma offers low-paid 'incentive work' to refugees. In the urban context, it may be because Nairobi represents a larger labour market, even though refugees are required to work in the informal economy.

To be more specific, in Kakuma, 66 per cent of Congolese and 34 per cent of Somalis have some form of employment,[18] compared to 47 per cent of Congolese and 23 per cent of Somalis in Nakivale. This observation, however, requires nuance. In Kakuma, refugees have greater access to 'incentive work' for international organizations and NGOs in a variety of positions, from cleaners to electricians, while Nakivale refugees rely more on market-based sources of employment. For example, in Kakuma, over 80 per cent of employed Congolese are incentive workers compared with less than 5 per cent of employed Congolese in Nakivale.[19] In contrast, most jobs in Nakivale come from businesses run by refugees or Ugandans.

In the urban context, refugee employment levels are also slightly higher in Nairobi than Kampala: 55 per cent of Congolese and 44 per cent of Somalis have a job in Nairobi compared to 47 per cent of Congolese and 24 per cent of Somalis in Kampala. Indeed, this may be partly due to Nairobi having a larger market. One Somali refugee who had moved from Nairobi to Kampala explained:

> Nairobi has more economic opportunities for us [compared to Kampala]. Nairobi also has a much larger Somali community. A lot of Somali investment goes to Nairobi. There are many active businesses owned by Somali people…Also life is cheaper in Nairobi than Kampala…[because] almost all items in Kampala such as milk, rice and clothing are imported through Kenya.

However, the sources of employment in Uganda appear to be more sustainable. In particular, refugees in Uganda are far more likely to be employed by other co-national refugees, while refugees in Kenya are more likely to be employed by NGOs and international organizations in camps, and illicitly by members of the host community in cities.

In Kampala, practically all Somali employment and a third of Congolese employment is reported to be by co-nationals, compared to just 2 per cent for Somalis and 4 per cent for Congolese in Nairobi. Indeed, throughout Kisenyi, many refugees end up working within the businesses created by other refugees. Shops, restaurants, and cafes set up with start-up capital often derived from remittances create jobs for family and community members. And Uganda's regulatory framework, unlike Kenya's allows refugees to register these businesses and to be employers.

In summary, Somali and Congolese refugees are surprisingly more likely to have remunerated work in Kenya than in Uganda, However, the sources of employment are very different. In Uganda, refugees are creating jobs for other refugees. In Kenya, refugees in the city are more likely to rely upon being employed by Kenyans in informal sector jobs, and those in rural areas are more likely to rely upon low-paid 'incentive work' with NGOs. In the long-term refugees creating jobs for other refugees may well be a more sustainable option, but it is largely precluded by Kenya's regulatory framework.

Assistance model

There are similarities between the assistance models for refugees in Uganda and Kenya. However, a distinguishing feature of the Ugandan model is the longstanding allocation of plots of land for cultivation to refugees living in the settlements. In theory, this enables them to grow crops for subsistence and for sale, supplementing food rations and any other sources of income.

As we will see in Chapter 9, the basis of Uganda's settlement model has been present since the late 1950s. As refugees fled colonial liberation wars, Cold War proxy conflicts, and ethnic conflict across the Great Lakes and Horn of Africa, Uganda encouraged spontaneous self-settlement in its underpopulated areas. With low numbers, there was sufficient arable land across south-western Uganda to create sustainable opportunities. With an increase in refugee numbers during the 1990s, notably (South) Sudanese refugees arriving in the West Nile region in northern Uganda, the country received increasing international attention and humanitarian assistance.

Reflecting an increased international interest in Ugandan refugee policy, and the government's desire to attract more resources and recognition, Uganda and UNHCR jointly launched the SRS in 1999, formalizing its longstanding rural self-settlement policy and extending self-reliance's application to the more arid West Nile region. Its aim was 'to improve the standard of living of the people of refugee-hosting districts, including the refugees', for example by empowering refugees to help themselves, and by creating a model of integrated service provision for refugees and host communities. The SRS attracted additional donor assistance, although it received some early criticism for being linked to cuts in food assistance. Within the 2016 ReHoPE strategy, the centrality of the settlements model was recognized, and supported through additional World Bank loans under International Development Association (IDA18) funding.

Within Nakivale and the other south-western settlements, refugees are offered plots of land for both shelter and cultivation. In Nakivale today, shelter plots are generally 15 × 20m and cultivation plots are generally 20 × 50m. Refugees receive user rights but do not receive the freehold to the land. One of the challenges is that, over time, the size of the plots has been reduced due to declining availability of the land. Meanwhile, the quality, fertility, and proximity to market of available land has generally worsened with increasing refugee numbers. Nevertheless, the option to receive and cultivate land on this scale represents a unique feature of refugee assistance in Uganda. The new Kalobeyei settlement near Kakuma is experimenting with the distribution of plots of land for cultivation but on a much smaller scale.

Beyond that, assistance models for refugees in Kenya and Uganda have striking similarities. In both Kakuma and Nakivale, refugees receive in-kind food assistance (during our research period just 5 per cent was provided in a cash equivalent in the main Kakuma camps) from the World Food Programme (WFP) and access to a core set of 'non-food items', including firewood. Despite the self-reliance model, food assistance is available equally to all refugees in the Ugandan settlements and there is no means-testing or graduation model. There are a range of services available through NGO implementing partners to support limited vocational training, sports and community participation, and access to technology, for example.

Meanwhile, assistance in Nairobi and Kampala is similarly limited. In Uganda, by moving to the city, refugees make the decision that they are able to be self-sufficient and are willing to forego the food and material assistance available within the settlements. UNHCR's only implementing partner in Kampala, Interaid, provides some limited support, through livelihoods training and psychosocial support to a small proportion of the most vulnerable refugees. In Kenya, refugees similarly give up any formal support for shelter or material needs, and only some limited support is available through NGO implementing partners and community-based organizations.

Access to public services across the two countries has some important differences. Uganda has an integrated service provision model for refugees and host community members. Refugees and hosts access the same health and education facilities, provided by the Government of Uganda. Even when international donor assistance contributes to the creation of a school or hospital in the settlements, it is a government school or hospital. For example, the Nakivale Secondary School, opened in 2010, has 1,100 refugee students and 400 Ugandan students. In Kenya, by contrast, the refugee camps have some parallel services, provided by the international community mainly for refugees, even though, in practice, these are frequently also open to the host community. To oversimplify, Uganda's model integrates refugees into national provision; Kenya's model integrates nationals into refugee provision.

In addition to differences in regulation, Uganda's approach therefore implies some key differences in its assistance model, notably the allocation of plots of land in settlements and the fully integrated provision of public services. But to what extent do these 'self-reliance policies' actually lead to 'self-reliance outcomes'? Here we compare outcomes relating to a series of welfare indicators. Overall, we find that Uganda's assistance model has strengths and weaknesses when compared with Kenya.

Inadequate land for rural self-reliance

The provision of plots of land to refugees within settlements is one of the most celebrated features of the Ugandan assistance model. But its impact has rarely been assessed. We found that having access to plots of land positively correlates with better dietary diversity, food security, and calorie intake. The larger the plot, the better people do. In principle, a functioning land allocation system can be an effective means to support refugees from agricultural backgrounds. However, our data suggests two important caveats to this in the Ugandan context.

First, Uganda's current land allocation model is not working effectively. Due to growing refugee numbers, the quantity and quality of land available to new arrivals is inadequate. Strikingly, 80 per cent of Congolese households who arrived in Nakivale before 2012 have access to land, compared with 17 per cent of Congolese households who arrived after 2012. Land scarcity is in turn contributing to land disputes. The implication is that if refugee numbers continue to remain high, a rethink may be needed in terms of how finite land is allocated and cultivated. Second, the land allocation model should only be considered an option for some groups of refugees. Somali refugees do not engage in subsistence agriculture, and refugees who engage in agriculture generally have lower incomes and welfare outcomes than refugees who work in other sectors such as commerce.

One way of interpreting this is that agriculture is not a good route to improved welfare. However, refugees who are from agricultural backgrounds do have better outcomes if they have access to land. This suggests that the issue with Uganda's land allocation model is more related to context and implementation. Our qualitative research substantiates this.

Many refugees have experienced reductions in the size of the plots provided by the OPM, which is responsible for settlement management. As Jean-Pierre, a Congolese refugee who has lived in the Rubondo area of the settlement since late 2006 explained:

> Initially I got a plot of 50m × 100m = 5000m². I started farming using the plot. But later my land was reduced due to influxes of new refugees. I experienced

this twice. In 2013, first reduction due to Congolese refugee influxes. In 2013, I had to give up 20m × 60m = 1200m². In 2015, second reduction due to Burundian refugee influxes. In 2015, I gave up 20m × 60m taken off = 1200m²...Of course, my crop production was significantly reduced. I did not have enough land for same production...OPM said 'you have to help each other. You are given large land so please share with your fellow refugees.' So I accepted it.

Both UNHCR and the Ugandan Government are aware of the challenge posed by land scarcity. Monica, the OPM commander of the Nakivale settlement stated that 'In Nakivale, self-reliance support is land-based...New arrivals find it hard to become self-reliant due to reduced land size. They need external support.' A senior official at UNHCR Uganda highlighted the impact on living conditions in Nakivale:

> General conditions in Nakivale are worsening. There is environmental degradation, and no graduation away from food assistance, with many refugees remaining reliant on food rations...Furthermore, not all refugees are given access to productive and arable agricultural land.

There is a strong consensus, particularly amongst Congolese refugees, that it is increasingly difficult to become self-reliant by doing farming alone in Nakivale. When we followed up with informants from our 2013 research, they frequently referenced deteriorating living conditions in Nakivale; one of our former research assistants noted:

> In Nakivale, things have been getting worse. The major change from the last time is that there are even more refugees in Nakivale. This means that everyone has less land with more people.

Limited access to education

One area in which Kenya systematically outperforms Uganda relates to refugees' access to education. In regression analysis based on our pooled data from Uganda and Kenya, and controlling for other variables, being in Uganda is associated with two years less education for refugees who arrived before the age of 16. Disaggregating this data suggests that while there is no significant difference between Kampala and Nairobi, the difference increases to three years for Nakivale and Kakuma. To put this very simply, our research shows that refugees who arrived in Nakivale before the age of 16 have on average three years' less education than refugees who arrived in Kakuma before the age of 16. This finding is corroborated by UNHCR data, which shows that overall primary school enrolment rates for refugees are 54 per cent in Nakivale compared to 92 per cent in Kakuma.

Our qualitative research suggests two possible reasons for the contrast. First, Congolese and Somali refugees report greater practical challenges relating to education in Uganda, including issues relating to distance, language, and cost. Second, the international community has a greater role in education provision in Kakuma than in Nakivale. Indeed, in Kakuma, schools are mainly run by UNHCR and its implementing partners, while in Nakivale they are mainly run by the national government. The implication is that Uganda's integrated service provision model may need greater international support, particularly in relation to overcoming practical barriers to access.

Our qualitative research revealed some of the challenges refugees face in accessing education in Uganda. In Kampala, refugees are supposed to enjoy equal access to social services as Ugandan nationals. However, in practice, this means that refugees usually have to pay to access services that Ugandan nationals also have to pay for. One Congolese refugee told us:

> For some minor diseases, seeing doctors can be free but most cases we have to pay…Also, there is a good number of Congolese refugees who are out of school. Many parents fail to pay school fees. At a primary level, one term at public school costs about 200,000 UGX [$54] and there are three terms per year. Imagine if you have multiple children. At secondary school, each term costs 400,000 UGX [$108].

Meanwhile, refugees in Nakivale complained about lack of access to education. Participants in a focus group discussion in Rubondo zone observed:

> We have only two public primary schools and three private primary schools in Rubondo. Class rooms are packed with more than 100 students in one class…There is only 1 secondary school for all of Nakivale but it is far away, 20km from the camp.

UNHCR staff members in Nakivale were certainly aware of this limited access to education in Nakivale.

> In the entire Nakivale settlement, there is only one secondary school in Base camp zone. There are 23km apart from Rubondo…Although it is a public school, it requires tuition—200,000 UGX [$54] per term and there are three terms per year.

In all contexts, Somalis receive significantly less years of formal education than Congolese refugees, and less than the host community everywhere except Kakuma, where the Turkana receive virtually no education. Somalis' lower access to formal education is likely to be for cultural reasons. Somali refugees often run and attend Madrassa schools, which meet a demand for Quranic education and offer lower tuition fees. For example, Hassan, a Somali refugee who came to Kampala in 2012, established a madrassa school in 2015 with donations from Somali refugee parents in Kampala. At the time of the research, his school had about 120 students who were all Somali refugees. At his school, in order to offer educational opportunities to wider refugee populations, the tuition is set according to ability-to-pay:

> The tuition depends on students' circumstances. We have no fixed fee. From poor and orphans, we don't take any fees. But normally, each student should pay 30,000 UGX [$8] per month.

According to Hassan, there are around thirty to forty Madrassa schools in Kampala. These aim to fill in gaps in educational access amongst refugees, and are also viewed as important for building religious and cultural identity.

Weak urban assistance

Urban refugees have, on average, higher incomes and better socio-economic outcomes than those in camps and settlements. However, having given up access to most formal assistance, many struggle to access basic services, including health and education. In particular, the urban Congolese population has worse outcomes than the urban Somali population. Social protection and economic opportunity tend to come from within the community or are underwritten by remittances.

Just one implementing partner, Interaid, has had responsibility for UNHCR's urban programmes since 1995. Its programmes are only for the most vulnerable, and focus on psychosocial support and some limited vocational training opportunities. Refugees repeatedly raise questions about the quality of its services. One Kampala-based refugee leader explained:

> What Interaid does is fight refugee-led organisations because they see us as competition. UNHCR is working with four local organisations and they are all national organisations. In Kampala, it is just Interaid, and they have been the only urban IP for 25 years. The UN audit on the corruption scandal said one of the organisations was involved in corruption. It wasn't named but all of the refugees know who it was.[20]

Meanwhile, dozens of refugee-led organizations (RLOs) fill the gap in urban assistance but are largely excluded from the formal humanitarian system.[21] Some RLOs such as Bondeko, Hope of Children and Women Victims of Violence (HOCW), and Young African Refugees for Integral Development (YARID) have managed to bypass the international humanitarian system and access grants that total over $100,000 across a number of years.

Other sources of assistance are through networks rather than registered organizations. In Somali refugee communities in Kampala, for example, *ayutos*—a form of informal rotating savings and credit scheme—represent an important source of collective savings and social insurance, especially amongst female refugees. One *ayuto* organizer explained why there are so many *ayutos*: 'In Kampala, having an independent business is our lifeline for survival. We have to take care of ourselves...We are not familiar with banks. I don't even have a bank account.' Other similar systems exist in the Somali community. Hajab, a Somali sub-clan leader of the Dir clan, explained that his clan operates an insurance system for clan members, named Qaran:

> Qaran means 'help each other' in Somali. Every month, we collect 10,000 UGX [$2.50] from all 60 members. We put this money into a bank account. Any diaspora members of our clan must contribute at least 50 when they come to Uganda. If any members fall into trouble or face major disasters such as severe illness, arrests or the death of someone, we give the saved money to them.

For Congolese refugees, rotating savings and credit associations (ROSCAs) are also frequently used. These member-only groups have credit and savings functions, and some have expanded to provide skills and business management training. It can give loans even to non-members as long as they carry collateral and guarantors. The manager of one such scheme, Hope Development, based in Kampala, explained how the group has evolved over time:

> Initially we started as a saving group. We just put money together and gave it to someone...In 2016 we got formally registered as a saving and credit cooperative and started credit services. There are 132 current members in total (mainly from the DRC [Democratic Republic of Congo], Rwanda, and Uganda, and also some South Sudanese and Burundians), but we provide services to non-members.

Refugee–host interaction

Uganda's self-reliance model has an emphasis on integrated service provision. Its combination of rural settlements and the right to reside freely in cities mean that, in theory, refugees and host community members can interact freely. Furthermore, public services like health and education are generally provided by the national government and available to both refugees and hosts.

As a settlement, Nakivale has porous borders. Refugees come and go freely, and many Ugandan nationals come to the settlement to buy and sell goods and services. Some even run businesses in the settlement. Meanwhile the main Nakivale schools and hospitals serve both refugee and host populations. As a camp, Kakuma operates on a different basis. While Kenyan nationals do come to the camp for business, entry is more controlled and it is more challenging for refugees to venture out to towns and cities without applying for a movement pass. Furthermore, Kakuma operates a system of parallel service provision, in which UN agencies and NGO implementing partners provide health and education services, albeit while allowing Kenyan nationals to also use those services. Put crudely, in Nakivale refugees are integrated into national services; in Kakuma citizens are integrated into international services.

The two contexts are also different in terms of the degree of economic inequality between refugees and host nationals. In Kakuma, both Somali and Congolese refugees have higher levels of income, expenditure, assets, and food security than the local Turkana, albeit that the Turkana have higher employment rates than the Somalis. In Nakivale, Ugandan nationals have far higher rates of employment (90 per cent) than refugees (47 per cent for Congolese and 23 per cent for Somalis), and comparable levels of income, assets, and food security to Congolese refugees, albeit with generally worse outcomes compared to Somalis. Although the host community in Nakivale are generally subsistence farmers with low incomes, there is less inequality between refugees and hosts in Nakivale than in Kakuma.

Put simply, Nakivale is characterized by greater opportunities for interaction and lower levels of refugee–host inequality than Kakuma. These observations lead to the question: what different outcomes can we obverse in terms of refugee–host perceptions?

Generally, relations between refugees and hosts are cordial around both Nakivale and Kakuma. But there is a striking contrast. Relations on an economic level appear better in Kakuma but relations on a security level appear better in Nakivale.

First, in terms of economic interdependence, when responding to questions of mutual perception, the Turkana around Kakuma have a more positive perception of the economic contribution of refugees to the host economy than Ugandans living close to Nakivale. Our qualitative research suggests that one reason for the more positive refugee–host perceptions in Kakuma compared to Nakivale may be that the skills and activities of refugees and hosts are complementary in Kakuma, whereas refugees and hosts in Nakivale often undertake the same economic activities, leading to a greater perception of competition. In Kakuma, for example, the local Turkana tend to specialize in areas such a livestock, charcoal, and firewood, which are prohibited areas of activity for refugees. In Nakivale, the host community is growing the same set of crops as the many refugees involved in agricultural work. However, Ugandan traders are likely to identify the presence of refugees as a significant economic benefit. This observation has wider implications: it suggests that refugees may be more likely to be perceived as a boon for the economy when they bring different sets of skills and activities than those already available within the host community.

For some people in Nakivale, land competition has recently become a source of tension. The number of refugees living in Nakivale has increased more than 60 per cent in the last five years but the size of the settlement has remained the same. Among the refugee and Ugandan households that have access to land for cultivation about 32 per cent have experienced a land dispute at least once. The main reasons for land disputes are conflicting claims relating to land ownership and land boundaries. The increased number of refugees in Uganda is clearly affecting their relationship with host populations. In 2017, for example, there was a demonstration led by Ugandans against refugees in Nakivale relating to land disputes. Local protesters demanded a clear boundary between camp and non-camp areas. According to refugees in Nakivale, this demonstration lasted about two weeks, making some refugees feel threatened. As one Congolese refugee commented: 'During the demo, we all stayed at home and did not send children to school. We stopped farming.'

However, some Ugandan villagers nearby Nakivale felt that responsibility for the tensions lay with OPM, rather than refugees themselves. On condition of anonymity, one Ugandan trader who lives in Nyarugusu village which is located in the Base camp of the Nakivale settlement, critiqued OPM as a source of the land conflict with refugees:

> We have problems with OPM, not with refugees. OPM don't have any clear planning about land allocation to refugees...Our village has contested the boundary issue with OPM. As far as I know, at least there are 3 different boundaries...Locals are marginalised by the increasing number of refugees.

While some conflicts are emerging, most Ugandans seem aware of the economic interdependence with the settlement and the surrounding areas. As one Ugandan local said 'Now refugees are too many, taking too much space from Ugandans. But at the same time refugees are our main customers.'

Second, in relation to security, refugees and the host community are much more likely to perceive the other as a source of insecurity in Kakuma than Nakivale. Indeed, this is likely to be related to the wider security context of the region. In Turkana County, which hosts Kakuma, there are large numbers of guns, and the wider context of local insecurity often translates into violence. Around Nakivale, violence is rare and even land disputes have generally been dealt with peacefully.

Conclusion

Uganda's self-reliance model offers an opportunity to learn about some of the elements needed to create a better assistance model for refugees. Perhaps its most important evidence-based contribution is to show the importance of government regulation for refugee welfare. We learn from Uganda that the right to work and freedom of movement make a difference to refugees' socio-economic outcomes in four areas: greater mobility, lower transaction costs for economic activity, higher incomes, and more sustainable sources of employment. Although we have only assessed the impact of the regulatory framework on refugees' socio-economic outcomes, each of these impacts has the potential to benefit the national economy by increasing aggregate levels of production and consumption.

However, our research also reveals the need for a more nuanced view of Uganda's self-reliance model, based on an evidence-based understanding of what works, for whom, and under what conditions. On the one hand, we should not overly romanticize 'success stories'. On the other hand, we should not dismiss successes because of imperfections. For example, although Uganda's land allocation model has the potential to lead to better food security outcomes, in practice there is insufficient land and the land allocation model within the settlements is becoming dysfunctional. Access to education in the Uganda settlements is weaker than in Kenya's refugee camps. And urban assistance in Kampala is inadequate. These observations caution against an overly romanticized view of the Uganda model. It is also important to recognize that the same self-reliance policies frequently have different implications for particular refugee populations.

The main takeaway is that providing refugees with the right to work and freedom of movement makes a difference. Uganda deserves praise and international support for continuing to embrace a self-reliance model. Although it retains notable legal restrictions on refugee rights, the country's approach to socio-economic rights can be regarded as relatively positive in terms of its impact on refugees, and conceivably also the host community. However, some aspects of the Ugandan model—such as urban assistance and land allocation—have weaknesses. And, as we will see in Chapter 9, Ugandan refugee policy emerged within a very particular historical and political context. This suggests that creating sustainable refugee policies is not simply about replicating all aspects of the Ugandan approach. We also need to look elsewhere for sources of insight and inspiration.

6

Kalobeyei

A market-based settlement model

Introduction

In Chapter 5, we learned about the strengths and weaknesses of the Ugandan self-reliance model. Despite its limitations, it offers the most sustainable model of refugee assistance in Africa, and probably also globally. But is it possible to replicate elements of the Ugandan self-reliance model elsewhere? What relevance does it have to the majority of countries that have historically had more restrictive approaches towards refugees? Could parts of the Ugandan model be introduced into a country that does not allow refugees to work or move freely?

Kenya is not known for its progressive refugee policies. In a remote north-western region of the country, however, a new approach is emerging. Turkana County, located near the border with South Sudan and home to the Kakuma refugee camps,[1] has chosen to support the socio-economic inclusion of refugees. Despite being one of the poorest regions of Kenya, its approach contrasts markedly with policies in other refugee-hosting parts of the country. The governor of Turkana County, Josphat Nanok, recognized that refugees represent a potential benefit rather than a burden to the county. Having previously worked for humanitarian organizations, he understood that the presence of refugees and aid agencies offers a unique opportunity to attract development assistance and investment and thereby benefit the host community.

That alternative vision has become known as the Kalobeyei Integrated Socio-Economic Development Plan (KISEDP), a fifteen-year strategy for the sub-county of Turkana West, where the Kakuma camps are based.[2] It has funding from the European Union and a range of bilateral donors.

It is based upon two core elements: a new settlement and a regional development plan.

First, the new Kalobeyei settlement, built just 3.5km from the old Kakuma refugee camps, and opened in 2016. Unlike the Kakuma camps, in existence since 1992 and home to over 150,000 refugees, it was created as an integrated settlement, intended to be for both refugees and members of the host community. Its goal is to create opportunities for refugees' self-reliance, while also improving socio-economic outcomes for the indigenous Turkana host community through a range of market-based opportunities. Once particular ideas are piloted in Kalobeyei, the intention is that they could be scaled across Kakuma.

Second, a regional development plan for the whole of the sub-county of Turkana West, including the refugee camps, the new settlement, and the surrounding areas. Rather than just focusing on the camps, the KISEDP aims to improve outcomes for the entire population of the sub-county. It is an area-based development plan. Because of the emphasis on integrated development for both refugees and hosts, the UN Refugee Agency (UNHCR) has described Kalobeyei as 'our new approach that is going global'.[3]

Kalobeyei was designed from scratch by the United Nations in consultation with the county government as a 'hybrid' settlement for refugees and the surrounding Turkana community. And it has introduced a range of innovative market-based mechanisms to promote refugee self-reliance, which diverge from the types of assistance used in Kakuma. These include cash-based programmes to meet housing, nutritional, and other material needs; specific training to support refugees and host community entrepreneurship; and programmes to support dryland agriculture including through household 'kitchen gardens'. In that sense, Kalobeyei emulates many of the settlements designed in Uganda between the 1950s and 1980s, but includes a more conscious focus on market-based interventions and on supporting an area-based development model for the wider region.

The first time I learned about Kalobeyei was when I saw plans in early 2016, drawn with the refugee community living on one side, the host community living on the other, and a market and shared services like health and education located in between. At that stage, there was nothing on the land, just open semi-arid plains on the road from Kakuma towards the small Kalobeyei Town en route to Lokichoggio. The initial plan was to relocate refugees from the overcrowded Kakuma camps. But their reluctance to relocate, coupled with the sudden arrival of large number of new South Sudanese, meant that at first Kalobeyei simply offered temporary shelter and emergency relief to new arrivals.

Gradually, though, new market-based initiatives were rolled out. While aid agencies in Kakuma mainly offered in-kind food assistance, Kalobeyei provided 95 per cent of assistance in the form of an artificial currency called Bamba Chakula ('get your food' in Swahili). The electronically distributed currency—sent to refugees every month via SMS—could be spent on food in specially licensed Bamba Chakula shops, all run by either refugees or members of the host community. Homes in Kalobeyei were supported to create dryland 'kitchen gardens', engaging in small-scale subsistence agriculture on their own designated plots, something not previously encouraged in Kakuma. And rather than having to accept the traditional one-size-fits-all housing design rolled out across Kakuma, 800 refugees in Kalobeyei participated in the world's first ever 'cash-for-shelter' programme in a refugee camp. They were allocated a grant of around $1,400 per household and allowed to select between different shelter designs, commission local builders to construct the property, and then retain any surplus.

By 2019, around 38,000 refugees, mainly from South Sudan, were living in Kalobeyei and, although few local Turkana had moved in, a community was in residence. Unrestricted cash assistance was gradually replacing Bamba Chakula in the settlement.[4] There were also plans to build the best sports facilities in the county in the settlement. Aspiring Refugee Olympic Team athletes from across Kakuma could be found training every morning on the playing fields of Kalobeyei.[5] The long-term goal was not to retain a stark separation between the Kalobeyei and Kakuma models, but to pilot a new approach in Kalobeyei that could ultimately be scaled across Kakuma.

The Kalobeyei 'experiment' matters far beyond Turkana County or even Kenya. It has wider, global implications for our understanding of refugee self-reliance. It offers a rare opportunity to learn about whether it is actually possible to build settlements that support self-reliance, even in remote border locations. Kalobeyei aspires to test an innovative model of refugee assistance, one based on integration with the host community and a series of market-based opportunities for self-reliance. In contrast, the nearby Kakuma camps have initially preserved the main features of a traditional assistance model: in-kind food assistance, limited integration with the host community, and greater restrictions on market-based activities.

Between 2017 and 2020, our Oxford-based research team collaborated with the World Food Programme (WFP) to understand the impact of Kalobeyei's design on refugee self-reliance. Has the overall model led to better outcomes than those previously available in Kakuma? What impact have Kalobeyei's market-based interventions had on households and businesses in the settlement? In this chapter, I provide an overview of our main findings. I show that, despite being extremely innovative, Kalobeyei's embryonic market-based settlement model has not led to significantly higher levels of self-reliance for refugees compared to the traditional aid model in the nearby Kakuma camps. Furthermore, although the settlement's market-based interventions, such as cash-based assistance, have had generally positive outcomes for households and business, they have also had limitations. The argument I make is that the Kalobeyei model is a step in the right direction, but that in order to be effective self-reliance and market-based approaches need to be accompanied by regional-level macroeconomic development.

Measuring self-reliance in Kalobeyei

The original aims of the Kalobeyei settlement were twofold: to create an integrated settlement for both refugees and the host community; and to support refugee self-reliance. Gradually, the first aim dissipated as relatively few Turkana moved to the settlement. But the latter has endured. The push for self-reliance is seen by the international community as better for refugees' welfare but also a means to gradually reduce the size of the overall humanitarian assistance budget. If refugees can help themselves, it is likely to be better for refugees, hosts, and donors.

The way in which new arrivals were allocated between Kakuma and Kalobeyei made it methodologically feasible to compare outcomes for newly arrived refugees allocated to two contrasting aid models. This is because, since 2016, refugees fleeing from war-torn South Sudan into Turkana County have been sent to either the new Kalobeyei settlement or the old Kakuma camps, depending almost exclusively on their dates of arrival rather than based on characteristics that might influence socio-economic outcomes.

The creation of Kalobeyei therefore offered an opportunity for what social scientists call a 'natural experiment'—an empirical study in which people are exposed to control conditions based on random assignment, even though these are determined by factors outside of the control of the researchers.[6] The quasi-random allocation of new South Sudanese arrivals into two contrasting assistance models provided an opportunity to follow a random sample of each cohort over time, to observe whether they experience different outcomes, and for this to be plausibly attributable to the characteristics of the contrasting assistance models.

Our team therefore tracked the progress of a random sample of recently arrived (post-March 2016) South Sudanese refugees integrated into the two contrasting assistance models, in order to assess what difference Kalobeyei's model actually makes. Given Kalobeyei's explicit goal of promoting self-reliance, we decided to measure change over time in a series of self-reliance indicators, following our representative sample of recently arrived South Sudanese refugees (and a control group of other nationalities) within each of the two models. The data is based on two waves of data collection in August and September 2017, and July and August 2018 following over 2,500 adults from nearly 1,400 households with an 'attrition rate' of about 25 per cent between the waves of data collection.[7]

Would self-reliance outcomes and enabling factors actually be any better for refugees in Kalobeyei than for those in Kakuma, and does self-reliance in Kalobeyei show signs of improvement over time?

The starting point was to establish a way to measure self-reliance,[8] and measuring self-reliance requires a clear definition.[9] UNHCR's definition of self-reliance is 'the social and economic ability of an individual, a household, or a community to meet essential needs in a sustainable matter and with dignity'.[10] Put simply, self-reliance is a process through which people become able to achieve a certain threshold of socio-economic outcomes independently of aid.

Although international humanitarian organizations and governments now routinely identify self-reliance as an objective of their programmes, the subsequent attainment of self-reliance has rarely been measured. The risk is that without measurement, organizations and governments remain unaccountable for whether 'self-reliance' programmes actually make a difference. Only recently, a handful of non-governmental organizations (NGOs) and academics have begun to explore ways to measure self-reliance in the refugee context. The NGOs RefugePoint and the Women's Refugee Commission have been especially proactive in building a coalition to develop self-reliance indicators. However, on the rare occasions that indicators have been designed, they have mainly focused on a set of general indicators of wellbeing rather than measures that necessarily indicate the ability of individuals, households, or communities to meet basic needs independently of aid.[11]

Here I identify a set of factors that measure progress based on self-reliance. They cover people's basic needs (food security, health and wellbeing, and social participation), whether they feel able to meet these independently of aid (autonomy), and how well adapted the settlement is to support self-reliance (markets, public goods, and legal and social environment). For each of the factors, we created measurable indicators that enable us to identify the proportion of the population who have achieved self-reliance in relation to a particular factor, and to compare these across time and space. These indicators are not the only way to measure self-reliance but they provide a starting point.

I summarize our findings in Table 6.1. Each of the main self-reliance factors can be translated into indicators. For each indicator, we highlight whether South Sudanese refugees in Kalobeyei were doing (statistically) significantly better or worse in 2018 than 2017, and whether they are (statistically) significantly better or worse in Kalobeyei than recently arrived South Sudanese in Kakuma in 2018.

In the final column of Table 6.1, we estimate the proportion of people in Kalobeyei who have attained a given threshold for self-reliance in relation to each indicator. Each self-reliance percentage is calculated based on the construction of what statisticians call a 'dummy variable'. For example, for 'food security', we used the Household Food Insecurity Access Scale (HFIAS), which categorizes households into four levels of food insecurity: secure (1), mild (2), moderate (3), and severe (4). Our indicator is based on whether the household is in 4 or 1–3. We did not try to create a single composite indicator of overall self-reliance because weighting the different indicators would be extremely subjective.

Comparing self-reliance in Kalobeyei and Kakuma

It is clear that very few recently arrived South Sudanese refugees in Kalobeyei, or indeed Kakuma, can be considered to be self-reliant. In Kalobeyei, perhaps most strikingly, 6 per cent of South Sudanese refugees

Table 6.1. Summary of self-reliance indicators

Factor	Indicator	Trend (2017–18)	Comparison (vs Kakuma)	Self-reliance in Kalobeyei
Food Security	Food security index	Worse	Better	17%
Health and Wellbeing	Physical health score	Better	Worse	64%
	Mental health score	Better	Worse	93%
Social Participation	Sports participation	Better	Worse	25%
	Community association membership	Better	Similar	10%
Autonomy	Perceived independence from aid	Worse	Worse	2%
Legal and Social Environment	Business interactions with hosts (monthly)	Better	Better	54%
Markets	Employment rate	Stable	Similar	6%
	Bank account	Better	Similar	2%
Public Goods	Water access (reliable)	Better	Better	60%
	Security (adequate)	Better	Similar	65%
	Education (more than 6 years)	Better	Similar	59%
	Electricity access (reliable)	Stable	Similar	1%

Note: Indicators are based on the percentage of South Sudanese refugees in Kalobeyei attaining a given threshold of self-reliance, and comparison is with recently arrived South Sudanese in Kakuma in 2018.

had an income-generating activity and less than 2 per cent regarded themselves as being independent from aid two years after the settlement opened.

However, there is evidence that at least some aspects of the Kalobeyei model are working better than the alternative of the 'old' encampment model in Kakuma, and that there is gradual improvement over time. For example, Kalobeyei residents have achieved higher levels of food security, dietary diversity, food consumption, and calorie intake. These outcomes correlate with possessing a (harvested) kitchen garden. Kalobeyei also has higher levels of interaction between the refugee and host communities, suggesting that even though relatively few members of the host community have moved to the Kalobeyei settlement, the attempt to create an 'integrated' model is at least leading to more business transactions, conversations, and shared meals, for instance, between the communities. Encouragingly, our analysis also shows gradual improvement. Between 2017 and 2018, refugees in Kalobeyei witnessed improvements in reported access to public goods, financial inclusion, and health outcomes, for example, all of which can be connected to Kalobeyei-specific interventions.

In terms of *food security*, diets in Kalobeyei are relatively better than those in Kakuma. Dietary diversity, food consumption, daily calorie intake, and food security levels are all better.[12] For example, the average daily calorie intake in 2018 was around 2,900 for South Sudanese in Kalobeyei compared with 2,500 for recently arrived South Sudanese in Kakuma. The reason for the relatively better nutritional outcomes in Kalobeyei appears to be directly related to two of the innovative external interventions.

The first one is the 'kitchen garden' programmes supported by international organizations in Kalobeyei. Turkana West is arid, daytime temperatures often reach as high as 40°C, and mean annual rainfall is only 18cm, and so farming has been relatively rare. One of Kalobeyei's key innovations has been to encourage refugee households in Kalobeyei to engage in dryland agriculture. By providing new arrivals with plots of land, seeds, tools, and access to training, including through dryland agriculture classes to children in the primary schools of Kalobeyei, there has been an uptake of agricultural activity.

The kitchen garden scheme began in early 2017. A meeting was called requesting expressions of interests in farming, and those interested were allocated kitchen garden plots. Some 790 farmers (60 per cent refugees and 40 per cent host community) participated, with farming taking place mostly on the northern side of the settlement. Quarter-acre plots were provided, and farmers were given access to basic training and equipment such as tools and seeds. Because the first harvest was impressive, many more households expressed an interest in the kitchen garden scheme. While South Sudanese participation in agriculture in Kakuma declined between 2017 and 2018 (from 24 per cent to 19 per cent), it increased in Kalobeyei (from 36 per cent to 46 per cent). Meanwhile engagement in subsistence agriculture is improving diets: in regression analysis, we found that having a (harvested) kitchen garden was associated with significantly better food security and dietary diversity outcomes.

Farming in Turkana West is extremely challenging. It is unreliable, hard to scale, and the scope for agriculture to support self-reliance is likely to remain limited. Efforts to drill boreholes in Kalobeyei have generally failed, and much of the water for the settlement is instead piped directly from the Tarach River. Refugees reported that the lack of water is the greatest constraint on agriculture. As one Burundian resident of Kalobeyei explained: 'The problem of agriculture is first of all water. Truly, the soil is fertile but the problem is water. There is no rain, and the difficulties of watering the crops limits you from cultivating over a large area.' Harvests, too, are susceptible to climatic variation. For example, between 2017 and 2018, food security outcomes worsened in both Kalobeyei and Kakuma because reduced rainfall led to crop failure across the region. Recognizing this, international organizations have gradually tried to introduce new technologies such as hydroponics to improve water storage and transportation.

The second intervention that may also have a positive effect on diet is Bamba Chakula. The scheme has increased the choice available to refugees in Kalobeyei compared to refugees in Kakuma. Because refugees in Kalobeyei receive 95 per cent of food assistance as Bamba Chakula compared to just 30 per cent of assistance in Kakuma, refugees in Kalobeyei are able to exercise greater choice in how they select between particular products. This is reflected in the significantly greater dietary diversity of South Sudanese refugees in Kalobeyei compared with that of recently arrived South Sudanese in Kakuma (a 5.9 compared with a 4.8 Household Dietary Diversity Score). Despite this, some refugees in Kalobeyei report that even under Bamba Chakula there were still restrictions compared to having simple cash assistance; one Dinka refugee told us, 'What is missing in Bamba Chakula is meat. You know, we love meat.'

However, despite relative progress in Kalobeyei, food security outcomes in both Kalobeyei and Kakuma remain poor in absolute terms. A total of 88 per cent of South Sudanese recent arrivals in Kakuma and 83 per cent of South Sudanese recent arrivals in Kalobeyei are severely food insecure. Meanwhile a Food Consumption Score (FCS), a composite score calculated based on the frequency of consuming particular food groups in the previous seven days, of 39 for South Sudanese in Kalobeyei compares with 36.3 in Kakuma, which barely meets the minimum standard for an adequate diet.

In terms of *health and wellbeing*, it remains relatively early to assess the impact of the Kalobeyei model on health outcomes, not least given that health outcomes will continue to be heavily influenced by pre-arrival circumstances. Nevertheless, health and wellbeing are an important part of assessing the extent to which individuals and households can be regarded as self-reliant. In terms of physical health, we used a recognized World Health Organization (WHO) scale to create a composite health score based on using six survey questions from the so-called WHO's 'Disability Assessment Schedule' (DAS) scale.

Our findings show a significant improvement in health for South Sudanese in Kalobeyei between 2017 and 2018, going from slightly worse outcomes than for newly arrived South Sudanese in Kakuma to slightly better. This may be a reflection of improvements in health infrastructure made within Kalobeyei between 2017 and 2018, which have included the construction of new clinics. Based on using the WHO's so-called PHQ-9 (Patient Health Questionnaire-9) mental health questionnaire, we also found that mental health outcomes for South Sudanese refugees have improved in both contexts, especially in Kalobeyei. In Table 6.1 we draw on this data to construct a dummy variable for one indicator of adequate physical health, based on physical mobility, and one indicator of mental health, based on depression, and find that 64 per cent and 93 per cent of South Sudanese in Kalobeyei meet the threshold of adequate physical and mental health.

In terms of overall subjective wellbeing, though, most refugees in Kalobeyei are dissatisfied with their lives. Subjective wellbeing has improved significantly in Kalobeyei and Kakuma between 2017 and 2018 for all surveyed groups. However, most perspectives remain towards the negative end of the spectrum. It is worth noting that the most vehement complaints during qualitative interviews came from those refugees who had been transferred from the Dadaab camps, many of whom described Kalobeyei as a dramatically worse place to live:

> When I was living in Dadaab I worked in a butchery. I used to buy goats from the market to slaughter to feed my children…We had cheaper milk, cheaper sugar, cheaper vegetables and cheaper clothes. I was getting every-thing cheaper…The Somali people who are there were also helping me. Here [in Kalobeyei] there is no income. There is hunger because the food provided is little. We don't even have shoes. Life is difficult for us. Before [in Dadaab] we had a better life. My husband used to work in the market selling livestock.

In terms of *social participation*, involvement in community-based associ-ations remains low in both Kakuma and Kalobeyei (around 11 per cent for South Sudanese, 4 per cent for Ethiopians, and 2 per cent for Burundians in

Kalobeyei compared to 12 per cent for recently arrived South Sudanese in Kakuma in 2018). Participation in sports activities is stable and remains much higher in Kakuma than Kalobeyei (42 per cent for recently arrived South Sudanese in Kakuma compared to 21 per cent for South Sudanese, 5 per cent for Burundians, and 19 per cent for Ethiopians in Kalobeyei). Indeed, while the NGO Lutheran World Federation (LWF) actively promotes sports participation and provides facilities and equipment across Kakuma, extra-curricular sports activities in Kalobeyei remain mainly focused on basic physical education within schools. The differences in these levels of participation are likely to be due to the established social networks and infrastructure in an older camp environment compared to those of a new settlement. Even though our data for South Sudanese in Kakuma relates to new arrivals, by moving into an established community, they are able to draw upon pre-existing community structures.

In terms of *autonomy*, most refugees in Kalobeyei and Kakuma still perceive themselves to be mainly dependent upon aid. Asked to rank themselves on a scale between 'independent' and 'completely dependent', the overwhelming majority of South Sudanese in Kalobeyei perceive themselves to be completely dependent, as do most South Sudanese recent arrivals in Kakuma, although Ethiopian and Burundian refugees in Kalobeyei are most likely to see themselves as 'mildly dependent'. When translated into a quantitative variable, we found that less than 2 per cent of South Sudanese in Kalobeyei perceive themselves to be independent of aid.

Anne, a South Sudanese woman living in Kalobeyei, told us that she has lost communication with her husband who had remained in South Sudan. She now lives with her six children and her late brother's five children. When asked how she provides for such a large household, she responded, 'I have no job. It is only by Bamba Chakula that I am living with my children. When that finishes, I go to the shop to take goods on credit.'

Many refugees expressed a desire to live in a more self-sufficient way, even if they had doubts about the prospects for self-reliance in Kalobeyei. In the words of a Burundian man living in Kalobeyei:

I eat, I sleep, but I don't see any future for tomorrow. I don't see the future of my children. What will my situation be tomorrow? What I ask, if I may, is that I may be in a place where I can do a job, where I can earn money. If possible, I would like to be in a place where the children that I will produce will have access to school, so that they can prepare for their own futures.

The lack of livelihood opportunities in Kalobeyei has left many feeling dependent and disempowered. As another South Sudanese woman said: 'A beggar has no choice. If the UN increases the amount of Bamba Chakula...that will be well and good with me. But there is nothing much we can say.'

In terms of the overall *legal and social environment*, Turkana West is located in an inauspicious geographical region of Kenya. It is arid and remote with poor infrastructure. Furthermore, despite being conceived as an integrated settlement, refugees in Kalobeyei face the same regulatory restrictions as those in Kakuma. The Refugee Act requires that refugees live within designated areas. And although, legally, refugees have the same employment rights as other non-citizens, in practice they have to obtain a special 'Class M' permit in order to be allowed to work. These permits, issued by the director of immigration services, are usually only available in Nairobi and are difficult for refugees to obtain. Consequently, refugees in both Kalobeyei and Kakuma continue to face important mobility and employment restrictions.

However, one area in which there are signs of progress in Kalobeyei relates to refugee–host community interaction. Refugees in Kalobeyei are significantly more likely to have had a business exchange or conversation with a member of the host community during the previous month than recent arrivals in Kakuma. Furthermore, levels of interaction improved between 2017 and 2018. For example, in 2018, 58 per cent of South Sudanese in Kalobeyei reported having regular business interactions with the host Turkana compared to 16 per cent of recent South Sudanese arrivals in Kakuma. These greater levels of interaction are likely to be attributable to the 'hybrid community' aspiration of Kalobeyei and the resulting encouragement and incentives for local Turkana to own businesses, and to work and reside in Kalobeyei. Indeed, the local host community receives integrated access to services such as healthcare, education, and water within Kalobeyei regardless of whether or not they live there.

Despite this greater and growing level of interaction, there is little indication that increased interaction is leading to higher levels of trust or social cohesion between the two communities. Across both Kakuma and Kalobeyei, when asked, refugees tended to disagree with statements about whether the Turkana are 'friendly and good people', 'trustworthy', or that 'refugees are well integrated with the Turkana'. Our qualitative research reveals that the greatest sources of tension relate to security issues and conflict over resources. As one South Sudanese woman explained, 'Things are not good. When you go out from here, just outside [the settlement], looking for firewood in the bush, you will be chased. You fear that you could even be raped.' The collection of firewood by refugees has been a persistent basis of conflict with the host community, who complain of both environmental degradation and the loss of economic opportunities. Many Turkana locals derive a substantial proportion of their income from the sale of firewood to refugees. In order to reduce the collection of firewood by refugees, UNHCR has contracted the local NGO, Lokado, to purchase firewood from Turkana villages to distribute to refugees, to create income-generating opportunities for the host community.

In terms of *markets*, market-based approaches to service delivery are at the core of the Kalobeyei settlement model. This includes provision of food via retail traders under the Bamba Chakula programme, the construction of houses via local contractors under the cash-for-shelter programme, and cash-based provision of hygiene and sanitation goods. Due to the location of the settlement and the absence of existing markets, these programmes rely on the gradual emergence of new markets. While this presents a development opportunity to the Turkana County Government, the absence of strong markets creates constraints on people's ability to achieve independence from aid.

There are at least three kinds of markets that are especially important in this regard: markets for goods and services; markets for jobs; and markets for credit and financial services. And yet all three remain extremely limited in Kalobeyei. First, as of 2019, there was no designated market area in Kalobeyei. And although some retail shops have emerged, a significant proportion exist because of the indirect subsidy of Bamba Chakula food assistance. For example, out of around 150 food retail shops in Kalobeyei, around forty-five are Bamba Chakula shops, distributing food based mainly on WFP food rations, and these (almost fully subsidized) shops account for around 37 per cent of the overall food retail market in Kalobeyei. Second, unemployment levels remained similarly high in both Kalobeyei and Kakuma for recent South Sudanese arrivals at around 94 per cent (compared to 75 per cent for Burundians and 86 per cent for Ethiopians in Kalobeyei). Even when there are job opportunities, they come from the aid economy. For South Sudanese recent arrivals, the main opportunities in Kalobeyei and Kakuma come from 'incentive work' with international organizations and NGOs. Burundian and Ethiopian refugees in Kalobeyei are more likely to be engaged in entrepreneurial activity.

And even for the few recent arrivals who have an income-generating activity, the median income is roughly equal to the World Bank's extreme poverty line: $60 per month for South Sudanese new arrivals in both Kalobeyei and Kakuma, compared to the World Bank poverty level of $1.90 per day, or $58 per month. Third, a lack of financial inclusion creates major barriers to entrepreneurship. Despite significant improvement between 2017 and 2018 across both sites, only 2.5 per cent of South Sudanese in Kalobeyei (and 14 per cent of Ethiopians and 10 per cent of Burundians) had a bank account, compared to just 4 per cent of recent South Sudanese arrivals in Kakuma. And while 800 additional households in Kalobeyei were given access to bank accounts by UNHCR in 2018 and 2019 as part of the cash-for-shelter scheme, this still leaves a gap in financial inclusion.

One of the biggest barriers to self-reliance therefore relates to lack of economic opportunity. Where signs of emerging markets do exist in Kalobeyei, they largely depend upon the aid economy through, for example, 'incentive work' as the primary source of employment, the creation of Bamba Chakula as the main driver of new retail outlets, and cash-for-shelter as the main source of financial inclusion. Put simply, while these markets may help meet some basic needs, they would not exist at their current scale in the absence of aid.

In terms of *public goods*, our data suggests gradual improvement across the board in both Kakuma and Kalobeyei, probably linked to increased investment. For South Sudanese in Kalobeyei, we find that 60 per cent report having access to reliable water, 65 per cent report having adequate security, and 59 per cent of adults have received more than six years of education. While these are imperfect, Kalobeyei in particular is gradually benefiting from the KISEDP. For example, in relation to healthcare, new clinics have continued to be built in Kalobeyei since our data collection.

Perhaps the biggest gap relates to electricity. Less than 1 per cent of South Sudanese households in Kalobeyei report having reliable access to electricity, with no agency providing electricity to camp residents. Some refugees have purchased gas- and kerosene-fuelled generators, or solar panels, which they use to sell electricity to their neighbours. A Burundian trader in Kakuma Two explained how this affects his business: 'We need electric power here. There are things that we are not selling because of lack of power. We cannot operate refrigerators.'

On the other hand, education, is relatively strong. Between them, Kakuma and Kalobeyei have has the highest concentration of primary and secondary schools in Turkana County, which has been renowned for having disproportionately low rates of enrolment and retention in childhood education. The proportion of households with at least one adult who completed at least six years of education is larger for South Sudanese in Kakuma (82 per cent) compared to South Sudanese in Kalobeyei (55 per cent). This, however, is probably a reflection of the demographic background of the cohorts rather than differences in programmes.

Overall, it is clear that refugees in Kakuma and Kalobeyei remain a long way from achieving self-reliance because most refugees are unable to meet their basic socio-economic needs independently of aid. And the reason for this is simple: the economies of both Kakuma and Kalobeyei remain based almost entirely on international assistance. These findings are sobering for the concept of self-reliance.

If refugees in Kalobeyei and Kakuma are to achieve self-reliance, then it will need the entire sub-county of Turkana West to begin 'exporting' to other parts of Kenya, the region, and the world. Economic growth and the possibility for self-reliance will, ultimately, have to come from growth in the economy of Turkana County. And this will depend upon a shift from the dominant microeconomic view of self-reliance towards situating self-reliance within a broader macroeconomic strategy.

Evaluating cash-based assistance in Kalobeyei

Cash assistance has been widely praised for improving the effectiveness and efficiency of development and humanitarian assistance. But it has rarely been applied in refugee contexts, in which the norm continues to be the delivery of in-kind assistance based on food rations. And while there is a strong body of evidence recognising the relative benefits of cash assistance, in terms of improving choice, efficiency, and the impact on local markets, little such research exists that is specific to refugee communities.[13]

One distinctive feature of Kalobeyei's market-based approach has been the adoption of cash-based assistance. The settlement has gradually shifted from: first, in-kind assistance; to, second, restricted cash assistance; to, third, unrestricted cash assistance. In the early phase of Kalobeyei's existence, humanitarian organizations provided in-kind food aid directly to refugees arriving from South Sudan, along similar lines to the type of in-kind assistance that had generally been provided in the Kakuma camps, with trucks gathering on a monthly basis to disburse sacks of cereal, pulses, and oil, distributed to families presenting with a ration card.

However, soon after opening in 2016, it began to roll-out a form of restricted cash assistance called Bamba Chakula. The approach is innovative in providing a transitional arrangement between in-kind and unrestricted cash assistance, and in having the dual aim of efficient aid delivery and private-sector development. The scheme provided refugees with mobile currency supplied through Safaricom, allowing them to choose their food items, with some restrictions on commodities like tobacco and alcohol. The amount allocated was 1,400 KES ($14) per month per person. The Bamba Chakula currency could be spent only at designated refugee and host community traders, identified and contracted through a competitive process. The contracted traders also received supplementary business training. By 2018, Bamba Chakula comprised 95 per cent of food assistance in Kalobeyei but only 30 per cent of assistance in Kakuma, with the remainder made up of in-kind assistance.

In the next phase, from mid-2019, unrestricted cash assistance was finally rolled-out to a group of just over 1,000 households living in one of Kalobeyei's three villages while the rest of the settlement's households initially continued to receive Bamba Chakula. The amount allocated remained 1,400 KES ($14) per month per person but was instead sent directly to an Equity bank account, set up for every recipient. The sequencing of these assistance models, and the way in which they have been applied to some but not all of the overall population, has offered a unique opportunity to learn.

As part of our research, we evaluated the impact of Kalobeyei's cash assistance models on both households and businesses.[14] What can Kalobeyei's experience teach us about the relative effectiveness of different types of cash-based assistance for refugees?

From in-kind to restricted cash assistance

At a household level, we drew upon the wider data collected to explore differences in outcomes for recently arrived South Sudanese refugees allocated to Kakuma or Kalobeyei. As we have already discussed, the fact that South Sudanese arriving in the region were allocated between the two contexts based purely on the date of their arrival offered an opportunity to explore and explain differences in economic outcomes between the two populations. Those arriving before 14th May 2016 were allocated to Kakuma, and those arriving between that date and 24th August 2017 were allocated to Kalobeyei. In September and October 2017, we collected representative data from over 2,500 South Sudanese allocated between the two models.

The initial challenge for our research team was to attribute these observed outcomes to differences between Kakuma and Kalobeyei. To do that, our team used a specific statistical technique called 'regression discontinuity', which is used to identify the causal impact of an intervention assigned (or not) based on a particular cut-off (such as a date of arrival) and based on the assumption that the 'treatment' and 'non-treatment' groups are otherwise similar.[15]

We found that there is a 'Kalobeyei effect': the refugees assigned to Kalobeyei had significantly better diets: greater dietary diversity, higher calorie intake, and better food security. They also identified as happier and more independent from humanitarian aid. However, there were no significant differences in non-food consumption or other key indicators such as employment.

The next challenge was to attribute these effects to specific differences between Kakuma and Kalobeyei. To do that we identified the range of factors ('mediators') that potentially explain the 'Kalobeyei effect'; for example, involvement in productive activities, health, education, finance, remittances, and—crucially for our purposes—the type of food assistance model. We found that most of the effect can be attributed to the different mode of food assistance: in-kind versus Bamba Chakula. The mechanism underlying this was revealed through our qualitative research: in Kakuma, refugees were reselling some of their food rations at much lower-than-cost prices in order to purchase preferred food or non-food items; in Kalobeyei, refugees were able to buy the food they preferred without incurring this additional transaction cost.[16]

To assess Bamba Chakula's impact on business, we undertook an additional survey of 730 food retail businesses, including Bamba Chakula contract holders, unsuccessful Bamba Chakula applicants, and businesses that did not apply for a contract. The survey took place in October 2018 and was based on a representative sample across the three groups of interest in both Kalobeyei and Kakuma, using existing international organization lists. We found that having a Bamba Chakula license provided a huge advantage, with such shops have better outcomes in terms of profits and sales.[17] In both Kalobeyei and Kakuma, Bamba Chakula shops have profits around four times greater and sales around twice as large as non-Bamba-Chakula shops. Kalobeyei-based Bamba Chakula traders also perform better than Kakuma-based Bamba Chakula traders, with around 15 per cent higher profit and sales levels.

These findings are, however, unsurprising given that Bamba Chakula traders were given a protected market worth $1 million per month. Because Bamba Chakula recipients were only allowed to spend this part of their assistance in the designated shops, contracted traders faced no competition from shops outside the scheme for a large proportion of refugees' overall food-related purchasing power. The size of the protected market was significant, giving fewer than 20 per cent of food retailers in Kakuma and Kalobeyei exclusive access to around one third of the camps and settlements' estimated $3 million per month food industry. It is equally unsurprising that the Bamba Chakula shops in Kalobeyei performed better than those in Kakuma given that the subsidy per shop was effectively greater, with $500,000 allocated in Bamba Chakula to each of Kakuma and Kalobeyei despite the former having nearly four times more contracted shops.[18]

In that sense, Bamba Chakula has played an important role in subsidizing the development of the food retail sector within Kalobeyei and Kakuma. There is evidence that the Bamba Chakula contracted shops are adopting more efficient business practices. They have higher margins than non-Bamba-Chakula shops, and are more likely to adopt particular business practices such as book keeping, market research, and giving special offers or bulk discounts. However, it is difficult to attribute these more efficient practices to Bamba Chakula, as the contracting process competitively selected contracted shops based on a range of pre-existing characteristics, including previous experience and training.

The Bamba Chakula experience also highlighted some of the challenges of subsidizing private-sector development, relating particularly to market structure and competition. There is a particularly high concentration of market power on the wholesale side. Five wholesalers, four of which are Kenyan and one of which is run by an Ethiopian refugee called Mesfin Getahun, dominate supply chains. Sixty-nine per cent of traders source exclusively from one of these five wholesalers. Refugee traders are often forced for form buying groups in order to balance the wholesalers' market dominance. And rather than selecting on price or quality, consumers frequently select retailers based on ethnicity, loyalty, and long-term credit relationships. One Somali refugee explained how customers often become tied to a particular retailer, 'Customers just say "record for me" and the trader cannot refuse. There is no way they can refuse, because they are very aware of the limited income we are receiving and the needs we have'.

Overall, Bamba Chakula represents a highly innovative means to stimulate business development. However, the experience also reveals the challenges of creating sustainable food markets in a context in which oligopolistic supply chains and long-term dependence upon aid inhibit the emergence of open competition at either the wholesale or retail levels.

From restricted to unrestricted cash

What about the subsequent move to unrestricted cash? Our research shows that it has been a qualified success. The initial roll out to 1,050 households in one geographically bounded part of the settlement, but not to the other households in the settlement, provided the opportunity to assess the relative impact of unrestricted cash compared to the restricted Bamba Chakula model. In order to construct a 'natural experiment', we randomly selected a 'treatment group' of unrestricted cash recipients and a 'control group' of Bamba Chakula recipients, collecting first hand data from a total of nearly 900 refugee households living in the settlement.[19]

We found that the move to unrestricted cash generally had a small positive impact by increasing the choice available to beneficiaries. Those who reported a preference for unrestricted cash did so on the basis that it enabled them to have more choice, in terms of what they buy and from whom they buy, enabling them to purchase non-food items such as shoes, clothing, utensils, and wood or charcoal. As a result, the transition from restricted to unrestricted cash is associated with making people happier, with people owning more, and reducing the inefficient practice of reselling food.

It has, however, also had some limitations. It has had no effect on food security or food expenditure, and although a third of people report preferring the unrestricted option, the majority are indifferent to the change because they have not experienced any discernible change. And the biggest reason for the majority of people not benefiting from increased choice relates to household debt.

Household debt is endemic in Kalobeyei because food assistance, whether in-kind or cash-based, is often the only available livelihood source. Within the settlement, there is a 6 per cent employment rate, only 8 per cent of households receive remittances, and savings are virtually non-existent. This means that when people experience shocks such as robbery, illness, or delays in food assistance, they are forced to take food on credit. We found that

89 per cent of households were in debt, with an average debt level of 15,000 KES ($144), equivalent to more than two months of assistance for a household of five people. This usually occurs by food retailers noting the debt and keeping either the Bamba Chakula SIM card or the ATM card as collateral. This has the effect of tying refugees indefinitely to one particular retailer. The consequence is to undermine competition and consumer choice, the main intended benefits of cash-based assistance. As a result of the vicious cycle, 89 per cent of households under the unrestricted cash scheme report never having withdrawn any of the allocated cash.

One South Sudanese man explained that how his family's debt cycle began with Bamba Chakula and has continued with unrestricted cash:

> [Under Bamba Chakula] I would sell part of the food for cash…Because of [this], I continued taking food on credit…On the day Bamba Chakula was changed to [unrestricted cash], the shop owner immediately received my money. My ATM card remains with the shop owner because I had credit with him…I cannot change the shop because the shop owner…has my ATM card.

The transition to cash has also had some implications for intra-household dynamics, and potentially also gender. Unlike with Bamba Chakula, unrestricted cash allows households to spend their assistance on alcohol and tobacco. Access to unrestricted cash assistance is associated with an increase in both alcohol and tobacco consumption: 14 per cent of households receiving unrestricted cash consumed alcohol, compared to 10 per cent of households receiving Bamba Chakula. For tobacco, 6 per cent of households receiving unrestricted cash and 4 per cent of households receiving Bamba Chakula are consumers.[20] However, the households consuming alcohol and tobacco were generally only spending a small proportion—an average of 4 per cent—of their overall budget on these commodities. Furthermore, 89 per cent of households reported having no internal disagreements on spending choices, which may in part be due to the fact that only a quarter of households in Kalobeyei have both a husband and wife living together.[21]

In sum, cash-based assistance offers a range of potential benefits including greater choice, efficiency, and improvements in wellbeing. However, in Kalobeyei some of the intended benefits have not been realized due to significant levels of household debt. The broader implication is that cash-based approaches can work, but there may be prerequisites for cash to be effective. People need to be able to make free and informed choices between alternative providers, and this requires that they have the capacity to absorb shocks without being forced into a vicious cycle of debt and dependency. Put simply: cash alone will not create a viable and inclusive market economy; it needs to be accompanied by broader and deeper market-based development.

The limitations of self-reliance

On the one hand, much of what is happening in Kalobeyei in the name of refugee 'self-reliance' is innovative. It is one of the only recent examples of an integrated settlement, designed from scratch, intended to offer markets and shared services to both refugees and the host community. And it is piloting a range of market-based approaches, many of which appear to be making a positive difference to refugees' welfare. The first ever cash-for-shelter scheme in a refugee context, although more expensive than standard humanitarian shelters, received praise from refugees for giving them choice and dignity, and enabled UNHCR to register 800 households for bank accounts with Equity Bank. One South Sudanese refugee told me: 'cash-for-shelter turns our shelter into a home. It has given us choice, and with the savings, we have been able to buy curtains, flooring, and even a lock. When you can lock the door, you feel you can invest. And we could not do that with the old shelters.' Kalobeyei's kitchen garden scheme can be shown to directly correlate with better food security outcomes for refugees.

The rollout of Bamba Chakula in Kalobeyei, as a transitional step between in-kind food assistance and unrestricted cash assistance, gave refugees greater choice while also helping to incubate and support the emergence of food retail businesses. Furthermore, the subsequent transition to unrestricted cash assistance has increased choice, leading to generally better outcomes for refugees. Kalobeyei demonstrates some of the promise of market-based approaches.

On the other hand, however, refugees in both Kalobeyei and Kakuma are a long way from self-reliance. And some of the cash-based interventions have struggled to fulfil their promise. Although our data was collected very early in the KISEDP process, even as early as 2019 Kalobeyei's main donors were demanding results and requesting a clear 'exit strategy' before committing additional resources. One international organization staff member explained in summer 2019, 'Donors like the EU and DFID [Department for

International Development] are already asking when they can leave. For them self-reliance is synonymous with exit.'[22]

Very few refugees living in Kalobeyei can be characterized as self-reliant, despite the explicit aspirations of the model. And our analysis suggests that self-reliance is unlikely to be achieved in the near future. Most refugees in Kalobeyei and Kakuma cannot meet their basic socio-economic needs, let alone manage independently of aid. Even in the rare cases where some refugees are able to meet their own basic socio-economic needs, it is largely because of the international aid economy. Sources of employment are coming from NGOs, sources of financial inclusion are mainly the result of programmes like cash-for-shelter, and a large proportion of Kalobeyei's retail expansion comes from Bamba Chakula. If international agencies withdrew assistance tomorrow, most of the apparent market-based activity and businesses in Kalobeyei and Kakuma would simply collapse.

This slightly grim picture should not, however, be interpreted as a criticism of the work of international organizations and NGOs. Rather, it reflects many of the inherent challenges of refugee self-reliance. The goal of enabling refugees to meet their socio-economic needs independently of aid is extremely ambitious. And it requires a series of enabling conditions to be present. Creating these conditions should be expected to take time and up-front investment, especially in a context such as Kalobeyei, in which a settlement has been built from scratch in a geographically remote and arid environment, with limited infrastructure and low levels of pre-existing economic development.

The only means to ensure long-term self-reliance will be to enable the region to 'export' to the wider Kenyan, regional, and global economy. According to UNHCR, refugee entrepreneurship in Kakuma and Kalobeyei is growing and the approximately 2,700 businesses in the camp and settlement make up more than 30 per cent of all businesses in Turkana County. However, given that Turkana County is remote (increasing transportation costs), arid (increasing production costs), and has very little infrastructure, significant investment would be needed in physical and human capital in order to create sustainable opportunities for businesses.

The long-term objective of self-reliance is the right one because it can improve refugees' and host communities' welfare. But aid agencies and donor governments need to understand quite how much investment is needed, especially in remote contexts like Turkana County, in order to make it possible. In the short-term, aid cannot be withdrawn early in the process but should instead be redirected towards activities that are based either on enhancing self-reliance enabling factors, or iteratively encouraging refugees' own investment in self-reliance enabling factors, including strengthening access to public goods, markets, networks, and enhancing the regulatory and social environment.

The Kalobeyei context reveals that the conceptual shift that needs to take place is from looking at self-reliance from a microeconomic perspective towards also seeing it as a macroeconomic concept. The microeconomic indicators of self-reliance that we are interested in—food security, health, employment, access to public goods—are embedded in the macroeconomic success of the entire region within which refugees are hosted. Consequently, the mindset shift that needs to take place is to go from a population-specific focus to an area-development focus. It is a move from 'small economy' to 'big economy'.

With that in mind, several steps are needed to work towards self-reliance in Kalobeyei and Kakuma: first, to not cut overall assistance in the short term; second, to gradually redirect assistance towards market-based activities such as unrestricted cash assistance, alongside providing the necessary incentive structures and training opportunities to encourage the development of markets and investment in productive activities; third, to invest significantly in public goods and physical infrastructure that enhance self-reliance enabling factors; fourth, to work with the regional and national governments to reduce regulatory barriers to refugees' economic activities, including those relating to mobility and the right to work; fifth, to invest in refugees and host communities' human capital and entrepreneurial skills; and sixth, in alignment with the regional and national development plans, to create a development plan for Kalobeyei and Kakuma which can offer sustainable 'export' opportunities to the wider economy, in sectors such as agriculture, manufacturing, or the digital economy.

In many ways, the Government of Turkana County and the international agencies in Kakuma have recognized this. The KISEDP was updated in late 2018 to reflect an overall shift in focus away from just the Kalobeyei settlement towards outlining an integrated development plan for the whole of the sub-county of Turkana West. But even beyond Turkana West, our data on the early years of the Kalobeyei 'experiment' provide a sobering reminder that 'self-reliance' cannot be a short-term panacea, but that empowering refugees to meet their socio-economic needs independently of aid represents a major long-term development project.

Conclusion

The early years of the Kalobeyei settlement have offered a unique possibility to learn about the viability and trajectory of refugee self-reliance. The opportunity to consider Kalobeyei as a 'natural experiment' stems from a particular configuration of circumstances: the new settlement was built immediately next to the old Kakuma camps, the settlement and camps initially had distinctively different assistance models, and newly arrived South Sudanese refugees were quasi-randomly allocated between the two models.

We have seen that creating refugee self-reliance in remote border locations is extremely challenging. Turkana West is arid, remote, and lacks infrastructure. In order to be able to assess self-reliance in Kalobeyei, we created a series of indicators for self-reliance. Two years after Kalobeyei opened to refugees, indicators for self-reliance were extremely poor and little better than for recent arrivals in Kakuma. Most refugees reported being dependent on aid, nearly all lacked an income-generating activity, and food insecurity was endemic. Even for the minority of Kalobeyei residents with an acceptable standard of living, their opportunities were mainly based on the aid economy, whether from opportunities created directly by NGOs and international organizations or indirectly from the circulation of aid money. These findings offer a sobering insight into how difficult it is to enable refugees to achieve autonomy.

Nevertheless, there are indications that Kalobeyei represents a step in the right direction. Kalobeyei residents have achieved slightly higher levels of dietary diversity, food consumption, calorie intake, and food security. This 'Kalobeyei effect' correlates with particular programmes, notably Bamba Chakula and the kitchen gardens available to Kalobeyei residents. The model offers higher levels of interaction between the refugee and host communities. Kalobeyei is also piloting and learning from a series of pioneering, market-based interventions such as cash-for-shelter and cash-based food assistance. Furthermore, there are signs of gradual improvement. Between 2017 and 2018, there was improvement in nearly all self-reliance indicators in Kalobeyei. Furthermore, the update to the KISEDP in 2018 to make it a development plan for the entire sub-county represents a recognition of the wider economic transformation needed to make self-reliance viable.

My argument is that Kalobeyei represents a step in the right direction. The evidence shows several better outcomes than those that were previously available in Kakuma. But there are three important caveats. First, donors and investors need to support the model for the long haul if it is to be successful. Self-reliance cannot be understood as a justification for a short-term donor exit strategy. Second, cash-based assistance programmes, although potentially effective, rely upon broader market development in order to have the greatest positive impact. Third, we need to shift the lens from just focusing on microeconomics towards also taking into account the macroeconomic preconditions for self-reliance. At a community level, self-reliance will only be viable if an entire region that hosts refugees makes the leap from simply circulating aid money to giving refugees the productive capacity to 'export' goods and services to the global economy.

Overall, Kalobeyei teaches us that designing settlements from scratch in remote border regions is challenging but not impossible. If the creation of new integrated settlements is to lead to sustainable economic opportunities for both refugees and host communities it requires political commitment, strategic and evidence-based planning, and significant long-term investment.

7

Dollo Ado

The private sector and border development

Introduction

What role can the private sector play in creating sustainable economies in remote refugee-hosting regions? Can the money, ideas, and networks it offers achieve things that might not otherwise be possible? The five Dollo Ado refugee camps were designed from scratch in the remote Somali region of Ethiopia between 2009 and 2011. Built in an arid area with limited infrastructure or economic opportunity, the camps faced significant initial challenges. Over a seven-year period from 2012, the IKEA Foundation invested nearly $100 million in the camps, initially to fund emergency relief but, increasingly, to support economic development and livelihood opportunities. The outlay is the largest private-sector investment ever made in a refugee setting. From a research perspective, it represents an unprecedented opportunity to explore the difference private-sector investment can make in creating sustainable opportunities for the 220,000 refugees and nearby host communities.

When the IKEA Foundation formed in 2009, it decided a major focus would be refugees. Seeking to rethink traditional models for refugee camps, it originally committed $65 million to support the design of the new Kambios camp adjacent to the Dadaab camps in Kenya. But with an influx of new Somali refugees and declining security in Dadaab, the Kenyan Government stopped plans for the new camp. In response, the UN Refugee Agency (UNHCR) asked the Foundation if it would be willing to move the investment to support a series of new camps being created for Somalis fleeing war, famine, and drought into Ethiopia.

They could hardly have picked a more challenging context. Sandwiched between a warzone in south-central Somalia, rumbling internal armed conflict between the Somali region and Oromia to the north, and with little infrastructure, no obvious natural resources, and a host community primarily engaged in nomadic pastoralism, building an economy on the Somalia–Ethiopia border appeared a remote prospect. Three-quarters of the refugees were women and children, and most were from rural backgrounds. Nevertheless, when the Foundation's CEO, Per Heggenes, visited for the first time in 2011, he decided that something needed to be done to improve the plight of people still arriving in large numbers.

As an independent charitable entity that owns most of IKEA's retail stores,[1] the IKEA Foundation's main motivation was philanthropic, driven by the Foundation's and company's shared mission statement 'to create a better everyday life for the many people'. While the company aims to provide this for people who can afford its consumer products, the Foundation directs its investment towards improving the lives of people in poverty. Its initial focus in Dollo Ado was providing resources for the emergency response, stabilization, and basic infrastructure. But, gradually, it shifted towards supporting livelihoods and self-reliance. Its goal was to create jobs and entrepreneurship where virtually none existed, and pilot a model that could be scaled elsewhere.

During the decade since, the Dollo Ado camps have changed beyond recognition. Around 29km of irrigation canals provide 1,000 hectares of agricultural land for 2,000 farming cooperative members. Livestock has been commercialized, with opportunities for hundreds of people across the entire value chain from trading cattle, to managing slaughterhouses and running milk cooperatives. Entrepreneurship has been promoted through the creation of a microfinance initiative serving over 500 borrowers and based on the principles of Islamic finance. Sources of renewable energy such as solar panels and fuel briquettes made from waste products have been supplied to the camps, in ways that have created income-generating activities for refugees and host community members. Many of the programmes have been implemented in participatory and culturally appropriate ways.

One of the main innovations in Dollo Ado has been the creation of new 'cooperatives' as the basis for organizing economic activity at the community level. These cooperatives are membership-based groups comprising both refugees and host community members, working in areas such as agriculture, livestock, and energy. The groups have initially been supported and subsidized by funded national and local non-governmental organization

(NGO) partners, but in each case the aspiration has been for the cooperatives to become autonomous and economically sustainable over time.

However, it has not all been plain sailing. Complex collaborations with local authorities and international organizations have been navigated, some initiatives have failed, and long-term sustainability remains precarious. The decade of investment offers an incredible opportunity to learn about how to build sustainable economies in remote areas, and the role of the private sector within that. In this chapter, I draw upon a combination of survey data, qualitative interviews, and data from an impact evaluation that our team conducted on the IKEA Foundation's livelihoods programmes in Dollo Ado to explore the extent to which private-sector investment can contribute to the creation of sustainable refugee settlements, even in the least auspicious environments.[2] I outline the story behind the IKEA Foundation's work in the Dollo Ado camps and examine its successes, failures, and what it can teach us about refugee economies.

Several of the IKEA Foundation interventions have made a considerable difference to their beneficiaries. They have also had some positive indirect impact on the wider communities. However, the experience also reveals quite how challenging it is to create sustainable economies in the most remote border locations. The camps and wider region are far from being self-sufficient, and most refugees remain poor and dependent upon food aid. Only 21 per cent of refugees have an income-generating activity at all, compared with just 29 per cent of the host community, and the largest source of employment for both communities is with humanitarian organizations. Even for refugees with a job, the median income is around $1 per day which, without food rations, would leave them below the World Bank's global poverty line. And less than 10 per cent of refugee households derive their primary income source from the three main areas on which the international community has focused its livelihoods development strategy—agriculture, livestock, and commerce. Most refugees and host community members still rely upon a combination of aid and the cross-border economy with Somalia as the basis of their survival strategies.

Overall, the Dollo Ado experiment has been a qualified success. It is innovative and the private sector's role and willingness to try things differently has changed lives and transformed traditional refugee assistance models for the better. It has also positively influenced government refugee policy at the national level and influenced thinking on a global scale.

However, the experience also reveals that there are major challenges for private-sector-led development to succeed in remote refugee-hosting regions. In practice, most of the investment in Dollo Ado has come from a combination of traditional aid money and philanthropic donations, rather than for-profit business. To create sustainable economic change across an entire region requires a deeper understanding of how to iteratively build an economy at both a micro- and a macroeconomic level. Dollo Ado's limitations partly stem from the absence of such a conceptual roadmap at the outset. But its greatest success may yet lie in what it can teach us, with hindsight, about how to conceptualize and sequence the future design of sustainable refugee economies.

Getting up and running

There are five Dollo Ado camps: Bokolmanyo, Melkadida, Kobe, Hilaweyn, and Buramino. The Ethiopian Government and UNHCR opened Bokolmanyo in 2009 and Melkadida in 2010 as a response to refugees fleeing from violence and insecurity. A severe drought in 2011 led to a new influx and the creation of three more camps: Kobe, Hilaweyn, and Buramino. The camps are geographically sequenced in age order, with the oldest, Bokolmanyo, being the furthest from the border with Somalia, and the newest, Buramino, being the nearest. A single dirt road, running parallel to the Genale River, connects the camps and leads to Dollo Ado town at the border. To the north of Bogol, the small market town next to Bokolmanyo, the road leads to the Oromia–Somali region border, which is beset by internal armed conflict.

In CEO Per Heggenes' words, the IKEA Foundation's involvement in Dollo Ado was initially 'coincidental'. The Foundation set out with a particular goal: 'The whole idea was to say let's take a camp and question the way everything was done and use this as a pilot to see how things could be done differently—use it as a research lab basically.' But the original plan was to do this in Kenya, through a new Dadaab refugee camp. Only when the Kenyan Government blocked the plan did the Foundation look for alternative options. And with famine and drought contributing to exodus from south-west Somalia into Ethiopia, UNHCR needed to create new camps in a region lacking infrastructure and with only around 120,000 mainly ethnic Somali inhabitants. The first two camps were already established, and the Foundation initially agreed to support building two further camps—Kobe and Hilaweyn.

But Dollo Ado at least offered one possibility that attracted Heggenes, the Genale River running close to the border; 'the significant reason we chose Dollo Ado was the river and the opportunity for agriculture. That was always, from the very start, the opportunity, the real asset we could use in our thinking about livelihoods and self-reliance'. There was no clear strategic plan at the outset; 'we wanted to learn as we went along' explained Heggenes, but 'the objective was to create a different approach to protracted refugee situations and use this as a laboratory to explore how responses could be done differently'.

Over a seven-year period, the Foundation has funded programmes through UNHCR, working in collaboration with ARRA (Ethiopia's Agency for Refugee and Returnee Affairs). The aim has been to support economic and social integration for both refugees and the host community. It represents the largest ever private-sector intervention to assist and protect refugees. The initial focus was on meeting basic needs and then building infrastructure, including shelter and a compound for UN staff. Then from 2015, Heggenes explained, the focus shifted towards self-reliance and sustainable livelihoods:

> Very early we decided we wanted to focus on self-reliance, acknowledging that when you are through with the crisis phase, it makes no sense to have people sitting around doing nothing and does not provide any purpose in people's lives, and is also a lost opportunity to create value and therefore reduce the costs for UNHCR.

A notable feature of the Foundation's approach was that it aspired to be participatory from the outset. To achieve this, the Foundation contracted consultants to set up a network of refugee and host community committees across the five camps. As Heggenes explained, 'coming from a business background, interacting with our customers [was] an obvious thing to do first and on an ongoing basis.'[3] At the time, this type of consultative approach was not always common within humanitarian organizations.

The first phase (2012–14) focused on infrastructure. Schools, health centres, and boreholes, for example, were financed, initially in Kobe and Hilaweyn and then across all the camps. The joint UNHCR–IKEA Foundation Programmes provided solar energy, through street lighting and solar lanterns for homes. And it piloted a largely failed shelter project implemented by the Norwegian Refugee Council (NRC), in which 10,000 shelters were constructed using bamboo, mud, and corrugated steel rooves, following a design competition. During this phase, the largest part of the grant focused on 'emergency relief' (10.5 million euros out of a total grant of 37.5 million euros).

The second phase (2015–18) shifted towards a major focus on building markets, mainly through livelihoods development—'anything to encourage livelihood development and trade, partly in agriculture and partly any other area that could work for the community.' To inform this work, the Foundation commissioned an inventory of skills and skills gaps through consultancy companies Transtec and FHI-360, which identified agriculture, livelihoods, and retail commerce as the most viable sectors for development. This phase also had a complementary focus on education and renewable energy. During this phase, 65 per cent of the 37.3 million euro grant was focused on either livelihoods (10.7 million euros) or education (13.6 million euros).

From 2019, a third phase is planned to support sustainability; in Heggenes' words,

> how can we replace aid money with private sector money. For example, how can we create an ecosystem that enables us to replace all the diesel generators with privately owned solar generators?... The more we can change this from a refugee assistance model to a self-sustaining community, that is the third phase for me... It is a real challenge to move businesses into Dollo Ado because it is so far away.

The process has been stop-start. In Heggenes' words, 'It has taken more time and more money than we imagined. Because we were naïve and didn't have a realistic plan around it.' The Foundation needed to build effective partnerships with both UNHCR and the government, and this took time. The first thing the Foundation learned was that it needed the right staff within UNHCR: 'risk is not necessarily something that is incentivized in an organization like UNHCR. And you need the right personalities—people who are excited by taking risk and not doing things the way they have always done them'. Early on, UNHCR tried to manage the relationship with IKEA through headquarters, keeping the Foundation's input at arm's length. This contributed to failures and repeated frustrations.

UNHCR had initially insisted on working through its existing country-level implementing partners. And this led to repeated failure. The NRC's implementation of the shelter design for 10,000 homes was literally eaten away by termites. An NRC-led youth empowerment programme (YEP) trained young people but in ways that had little relevance to local markets. And the initial delegation of the agricultural irrigation construction work to NRC and the Danish Refugee Council contributed to a failed gravity-based pumping system, which one UNHCR staff member called 'a crater on a hill' left both the IKEA Foundation and UNHCR's senior management frustrated. The existing implementing partners were agreeing to take on work for which they did not have the relevant expertise.

The turning point was May 2015, when then high commissioner António Guterres gave clear instructions to prioritize the IKEA projects. Clementine Nkweta-Salami arrived as UNHCR's new country representative in Addis Ababa. She used her authority to overcome bureaucratic obstacles. For example, when the IKEA Foundation favoured a Tigrayan NGO with significant expertise in agricultural engineering, the Relief Society of Tigray (ReST), as the implementing partner for the irrigation projects, the incoming representative found a way to gain approval for ReST's recognition as an official UNHCR implementing partner. She also gained senior colleagues' support to appoint a young and effective staff member, George Woode, as head of field office in Dollo Ado, despite another part of the organization being desperate to keep him. Failing staff, consultants, and implementing partners were replaced.

The culture began to change. One UNHCR staff member explained: 'Per was beginning to despair... We faced a lot of challenges in terms of the execution. We got rid of people who were just here to further their existence... We created a basis of transparency and trust.' Heggenes later explained,

> Without the push from people like Clementine who really wanted to make things work and really wanted do things right, we wouldn't have got there... and with George, leadership on the ground is extremely important. We had worked our way through several heads of field office. It was really when he came on board that things took off on a different way, and that has to do with his personality, his leadership skills, his ability to get things done.

Until the change in UNHCR staff, the relationship with the government had been poor. ARRA was extremely suspicious of the IKEA Foundation work. One UNHCR observer explained,

> ARRA asked, 'why here?' and 'why this?'... there was huge early suspicion, and in the early days we were not as transparent with ARRA as we could have

been. They wanted us to keep a lid on any activities that would undermine the relationship of refugees with the government which feeds into how society is managed in Ethiopia.

Likewise, technical incompetence did not help: 'Ethiopian agronomists in Dollo were watching us do this knowing it wouldn't work.' But George Woode found a new way to work with the government and local authorities to build trust. He put time into building relationships of trust with the local and customary officials. For example, in 2016 Woode was the first UNHCR staff member to engage in a dialogue with the regional king (*waber*) and his council. One national staff member explained, 'They have had a system in place for hundreds of years that is respected and understood. UNHCR hadn't talked to them before… The inclusion of a customary institution was the most critical thing—it helped minimize conflicts and created peaceful co-existence, removing the notion of share croppers, for example.' Trust was established with the local community.

And from April 2016, the relationship with the government was further improved when the outgoing head (deputy director) of ARRA, Ato Ayalew, was replaced by Ato Zeynu. Ayalew had been in the role for two decades and had a traditional and security-focused approach to refugees. Although Zeynu also had strong security credentials, his early career had been working with refugees, he was committed to human rights, and wanted to make a difference. Ato Zeynu came in with a new approach and built up a strong collaborative relationship with the new UNHCR team and with Per Heggenes. And, gradually, political and bureaucratic barriers began to fall. For example, UNHCR, ARRA, the Regional Government, and the Woreda were finally able to negotiate land access to proceed with viable agricultural irrigation. A UNHCR staff member explained, 'we agreed to access the land for a peppercorn rent ($1). We leased it for 30 years after which it would go back to them. We negotiated hard for an agreement [on the ratio of refugees and host community members involved in the share-cropping cooperatives]; it would be 50:50.' Having the right people in place, it seemed, was a precondition for effective implementation.

One UNHCR national staff member summarized the degree of change that took place from 2016:

I began here in July 2011. But I feel like I really joined UNHCR in 2016… Before that, the whole strategy was messed up. I don't blame anyone, because the environment was just not conducive for running livelihood programmes without interference...The first few years from 2012 to 2014 we were just negotiating and wasting the resources of the IPs [implementing partners], trying to get things in place...Until 2016...there were no written strategies, we had to learn from mistakes and failures.

Since 2016, however, a whole series of programmes designed to create economic sustainability have been implemented. The Foundation's programmes have had several implicit features in its approach to sustainability. It has tried to use *value-chain analysis* (e.g. maximizing opportunities across wholesale, production, and consumption); *multi-sectoral integration* (e.g. integrating livelihoods, energy, and the environment); *graduation* (i.e. providing initial subsidy through assets and training before gradually withdrawing these); *localization* (e.g. working with local partners wherever possible); and *cultural adaptation* (e.g. adapting to existing cultural opportunities). At the heart of its core livelihood programmes, though, has been a model of 'cooperatives', through which refugees and the host community jointly manage a livelihoods and training initiative, and share profits.

The IKEA Foundation-funded programmes that have emerged include irrigation and agricultural cooperatives; firewood cooperatives; meat-selling cooperatives and other livestock-related interventions; microfinance loans; energy cooperatives; solar home systems; a secondary school and teacher training college; a youth empowerment project; as well as ongoing support for infrastructure and emergency relief items. It is now impossible to walk through any of the camps without being struck by jointly branded UNHCR–ARRA–IKEA Foundation funding signs identifying pockets of productive activity.

Assessing impact

So what impact have these programmes had? One of the challenges in evaluating them is that no viable baseline data was collected prior to programme implementation. We therefore had to rely upon retrospective evaluation techniques to judge impact on both direct beneficiaries and the wider community. These techniques included key informant interviews, focus group discussions, and quantitative surveys comparing beneficiaries with comparable non-beneficiary control groups.

Agricultural cooperatives

The most visible manifestation of the Foundation's investment is 29km of irrigation canals that now weave around the outside of all but one of the camps. The raised, mainly concrete structures stand some 2m above the ground, transporting water from the Genale River to 1,000ha of designated agricultural land, leased for thirty years from the Regional Government. Building only began in 2017 and yet today visitors are invited to walk along the canals, with one foot on each of the canal walls, overlooking lush green fields harvesting everything from onions to corn, watermelons, and papayas. The irrigation system represents the first of its kind in a refugee camp context.

A series of farmers' cooperatives have been established to enable refugees and host communities to exploit the land within the command area. Across the camps, the basis model is similar. Cooperatives are made up of a 50:50 membership split between refugees and locals. Each member is given half a hectare of land to cultivate, and members were selected based mainly on their previous background in agriculture and their vulnerability. Of the profit they receive, members are expected to contribute a small proportion to cooperative savings—either 20 per cent of profits or a fixed amount of around 500 ETB [$10][4] per harvest depending on the cooperative's own bylaws. Savings are used to collectively purchase and finance the upkeep of inputs. However, tools, seeds, fertilizers, and pesticides are still provided by the main Ethiopian 'implementing partners', ReST, and the local NGO, the Women and Pastoralist Youth Development Organization (WaPYDO), which also offer basic technical and business training. One cooperative member explained how members were recruited:

> I was previously a share-cropper [a farmer given land tenancy by a landowner in exchange for a share of what is produced]. The Refugee Central Committee (RCC) sent us a message. We were known as farmers. So they wanted us. They asked, 'who needs to join this farm?'. They selected people who didn't have a good income. They took the microphone and walked through zones shouting this message. Everyone who came was accommodated. I came here because it was open land here—it was previously used as agricultural land and so had already been cleared...ARRA brought the refugees to the land to see it, one month after they were selected to be members...Many of us were share-croppers; others were daily labourers in agriculture or construction.

By mid-2019, there were over 1,000 cooperative members, split roughly equally between refugees and hosts across nine functioning cooperatives, with a plan to expand to 2,000 members. To assess impact, we surveyed 230 refugee cooperative members across four irrigation sites, and compared them with 335 refugee non-cooperative agricultural workers in nearby areas. What was striking was that the cooperatives made members better off than they previously were; however, they were not earning any more than other refugee and host community agricultural workers working in and around the camps.

Some 77 per cent of refugee cooperative members claimed to be financially 'better off' than before joining the cooperative and only 3 per cent 'worse off'. Over 70 per cent also claimed that the cooperatives improved relations between refugees and the host community. However, we found that refugee cooperative members actually had lower household income and consumption levels than comparable non-cooperative agricultural workers, controlling for other sources of difference such as soil quality and access to water.[5]

The reasons underlying this were interesting, and mainly seemed to relate to crop selection. Cooperatives were often selecting different and less successful crops than non-cooperative farmers such as maize rather than onions. For example, 43 per cent of cooperative members were selling onions, which had a market price of $0.53/kg compared with 71 per cent of non-cooperative members. Meanwhile, 31 per cent of cooperative members were growing maize for human consumption compared to 14 per cent of non-cooperative members, which had a much lower market price of $0.20/kg.[6] One of the important dynamics behind this appears to be that refugee cooperative members felt constrained in what they could grow because of their reliance on seed distribution by either NGO implementing partners or by the executive leaders of the cooperatives.

We also found that the cooperatives have varying degrees of success, based particularly on environmental factors such as soil quality, flood risk, and drought. On the one hand, flooding during 2018 negatively affected the completion of canals as well as destroying harvest yields. One cooperative member told us 'during the rainy season, most plots will be flooded, which can destroy the crops, as there is no protection'. One the other hand, during dry seasons, water management has proved challenging. And there is variation across sites. A UNHCR agricultural officer explained that the Melkadida 2 soil is affected by salt, for instance, and some areas of Kole (a host community village between Kobe and Hilaweyn) are not suitable for onions, while Kobe is known for its excellent soil. Even within irrigation sites, beneficiaries mentioned that the quality of the soil differs across plots. One member in the relatively successful Kobe coop told us that 'an issue is that the land is not the same for everyone, since it was provided randomly, so one person might get a "worse" plot than another person, where the salt content might be too high, or the water cannot reach'.

Members have to work hard to achieve harvestable crops; the vice chairman of the Kole cooperative explained, 'A lot of farmers stay on the land for long stretches of day. Sometimes I don't even remember my family! I'm an old man and I stay here on my plot.' Nevertheless, most cooperative members reported a rise in income and an improvement in their economic situation, especially in relation to their children's access to education and nutrition due to their cooperative membership, and that incomes were more 'stable' compared to their previous work as share-croppers or daily labourers. More specifically, we found that, on average, cooperative members reported a 20 per cent higher household income than refugee farmers that are currently working as crop sharers or daily labourers in host community farms. One female refugee farmer in Buramino explained that gradually she has been able to move from dependency towards self-reliance:

> We're working together for a common dream. Now we're very happy . . . My half hectare of land was bushland, experiencing the help of others, refugees and host, in clearing that land—pulling out stones and roots together—and now seeing crops growing, gives me confidence that I can help others now. Before I was only receiving, receiving all the time, I did not believe that I can be of help to anyone. Now I think I can be of help.

And there are also some reported benefits to the wider community. In a focus group discussion with the Kobe cooperative, one participant suggested that

> the impact is not only on us as beneficiaries, but also indirect beneficiaries. For example, we will share with our neighbours or some people that are not in the coop, so they are indirectly benefitting. Also, some of the goods are cheaper in the market than before [because there are more and they travel shorter distances].

Other members point to improvements in the relationship between refugees and the host community; one elaborated:

> You can even see the relationship between hosts and refugees in how the land has been provided. Half is for refugees; half is for locals. There is close integration by dividing the land like this (alternating plots). After joining the

coop, the relationship has become much closer. Before the cooperative most of us did not know any people in the host community, but now we know them.

Local host community land owners have also experienced benefits. One Ethiopian agriculture cooperative member in Hilaweyn owns 5ha of cropland next to the river. He has nine brothers and in total the wider family owns 30ha of farmland in the region. He chose to include all of his 5ha in the Hilaweyn 2 irrigation scheme and he is part of the cooperative in order to benefit from inputs and to maximize yield. He retains 2ha for his own cultivation, and has divided the rest into six 0.5ha plots for refugee cooperative members. He explained, 'I am still the owner of the land . . . When the refugees are back in Somalia, I will be the sole owner of the land again. Without the refugees, we would not be able to cultivate all of the land.'

Challenges remain in terms of sustainability. The main NGO-implementing partners still provide significant subsidy in terms of inputs, training, and technical support. Most beneficiaries said that they would 'keep going' without external support, but expressed doubts about their ability to do so at current levels. An irrigation engineer from one of the international NGOs explained his concerns about the transition to self-sufficiency:

> Two years from now, everything will be handed over. The plan is to upskill farm coop members—within one year is the plan. The job is not difficult, it's just a matter of making sure the cooperatives adopt the responsibility. But I'm afraid they won't do the job. For example, when there are minor problems right now, they call an IP or UNHCR to fix it.

Livestock value chain

Before the arrival of Somali refugees, the Dollo Ado area was mainly characterized by nomadic pastoralism, and livestock was one of few potential livelihood opportunities. Our research showed the market potential: 71 per cent of the host population and 45 per cent of refugee regularly eat meat, and 55 per cent of hosts and 30 per cent of refugees regularly consume milk.[7] However, for the most part, it was not commercialized. The community was rearing goats, sheep, and camels for a combination of household consumption and as a saving mechanisms. When the Somali refugees arrived, many also started to own livestock on a similar basis. The

IKEA Foundation and UNHCR recognized the potential to develop the livestock sector across the entire value chain. Since 2016, they have supported three cooperative types—livestock trading, meat-selling, and milk-selling—and two kinds of business group—the community-based animal health workers (CAHWs) and slaughterhouses in each of the camps. The most innovative aspect of this is the attempt to build opportunity across an entire value chain.

First, the livestock trading cooperatives (effectively the 'wholesalers'), supported locally by WaPYDO through subsidized licensing and infrastructure, vary in size between seventeen and sixty-two members each, with relatively low representation of host community members and few women. Most cooperative members had experience in livestock trading or agriculture before they joined the cooperative. Members pay a monthly contribution to the cooperative, in exchange for which they are fully licensed and able to participate in collective bargaining with both wholesalers and retailers within the livestock markets that exist across the camps. Although members report having difficulty paying the monthly contributions, participation has positioned members within the broader supply chain allowing them to supply animals for slaughter to the meat cooperatives, and improving collective access to facilities such as the slaughterhouse and veterinary services. In focus groups and interviews, most report earning higher incomes than they could earn without the cooperatives. One refugee member in Kobe explained, 'we joined the coop because we have no other opportunities, but it is not enough.' An Ethiopian member of the same cooperative explained how the cooperative functions:

> We buy the animals from inside the camp. We don't breed our own animals. But we have small herds. Normally we resell an animal after three to four days. In the rainy season, we sell more animals than in the dry season. The price is also higher now than in the dry season. In the rainy season, the price is 2,000–3,000 ETB [$40–60] for one goat on average; it is 900–1,500 ETB [$18–30] in the dry season but the price can go down to 400 ETB [$8] per goat. We work as groups. We have two groups in the cooperative: one group for refugees; one group for hosts—each group consists of twenty-eight people. Each group is divided in two teams of fourteen people. Each day, one refugee and one host team is coming to work—we operate shifts. We keep the revenue to buy the next goat but share the profit among the team. We save some of the profit in an account.

The main challenge is that incomes appear to be low. In the Kobe cooperative, for instance, most members own a handful of goats but make very little profit from buying and selling. The chairman of the Buramino cooperative, which has thirty members, explained the business model:

> We [divide into two groups and] work in shifts. Our [total] daily income is about 1,000 ETB [about $1 per member] which we divide as follows: coop savings of around 200–300 ETB/day (30 per cent) and daily life expenses of about 700 ETB (70 per cent). Everything is divided equally among members…If a new person joins, they have to bring some money to put in a percentage of what we already have in the account…We buy animals from Bokolmanyo, Filtu, Charity, and Hargella. We travel there to buy them. We take a vehicle from here to there. After buying them, we walk back. Sometimes we may be away for twenty to twenty-five days at a time. Sometimes up to thirty days. It takes longer sometimes if we are waiting for livestock in the other markets to arrive. The schedule is not always dependable. We buy goats and sheep, sometimes camels but they are expensive. Savings are held in order to protect members in case the market price drops and an individual loses money, or in case an animal dies. We even sometimes save to buy a camel… The biggest challenge is that we don't have enough capital to strengthen our business. Where we sell depends on the market—if it's not good, we hold on to them. [In addition to selling in the camps], we can travel to Dollo to sell. If it's bad there, have to cross into Mandera.

Members question whether they could continue to survive without NGO subsidies. Across the camps for instance there was excitement that WaPYDO had recently built a structure where the cooperatives can secure the animals, enabling them to 'buy thin animals and then fatten them to increase profit'. But the downside of this support is ongoing dependency. One member explained, 'It's true that we have been dependent on them. If they withdraw support, it will collapse—because we wouldn't be able to continue saving and supporting ourselves independently.' Another was more optimistic: 'If it were right now it would be difficult; we need to be stronger before we can be independent. Maybe in four years… We would continue on our own, one way or another, even if the donors left us—just like we did before.' The vice chairman of the Kobe cooperative was more optimistic about the prospects for self-reliance, comparing the coop structure to prior dependence on World Food Programme (WFP) food distribution:

> Before we were relying on WFP food distribution. We were very weak because we couldn't cover our own costs. After we created [the coop], we reached self-dependence…In the future, we expect to be better than this. We have recognition from WaPYDO. We want to get a loan in the near future—we haven't been able to get one from MFI [a microfinance initiative]. But because we're

recognized, we have been told that we'll get a loan. WaPYDO told us to submit our names to the 21st Century Pastoralist Development Association (CPDA) [the NGO loan provider]. The entire coop would receive the loan.

He also suggested that the wider investment by the IKEA Foundation has helped improve the market for livestock within the camps: 'The market became large. Life changed for refugees and hosts. Many people opened shops. More people were earning more money and the demand for goats increased significantly. Goats have become more expensive than before. There were no goats that came to the market before.'

Second, the meat-selling cooperatives (effectively, the 'retailers') sell goat, sheep, chicken, and camel meats from stalls in designated places in the refugee and host community markets. Five meat-selling cooperatives have been registered across the Dollo Ado camps since 2017, and formalized smaller pre-existing groups of butchers. The Foundation funding has supported new infrastructure, including five shaded meat-selling marketplaces, meat cages for individual sellers, and refrigerators have even been piloted in Kobe camp. The cooperatives vary in size from twenty to 106 members and also vary slightly in the meats in which they primarily specialize. For example, Kobe sells a higher proportion of camel meat.

In Melkadida, for instance, we visited the local meat-selling cooperative, in which mainly women sold sliced goat meat from a square, wooden, shaded structure. Each one sat in front of a metal storage cage, offering some protection from direct sunlight and flies. The women explained to us how much they have benefitted from the cooperatives and the supporting infrastructure. Immediately across the road, the IKEA Foundation has also built a livestock market, complete with facilities for selling, washing, and tax collection. And around the corner, cooperatives could benefit from the presence of one of the IKEA Foundation-funded slaughterhouses. Most cooperative members reported an increase in income compared to their previous situation, which in turn improved access to education and food at the household level. They also reported being able to afford private education for their children and having increased food diversity.

The chairman of the Hilaweyn meat-selling cooperative explained how the business model works:

> The cooperative struggles sometimes, which is why some only join for a month then drop out when they realise it can be difficult... We're divided into two functional groups. We alternate days at the market so everyone has a turn

to work and earn income [three days per week each]. We have 11 stalls at the market, and one window for selling camel. The stalls for goats, sheep operate 6 days a week. The window for camel is open 3 days/week. There's a slaughterhouse in the camp with butchers—some distance away from the market...We built a committee to select the butcher, vet, cleaner, and transporter...We buy the camels, goats, and sheep from the livestock market in Hilaweyn, and camel sometimes come from Dollo. Purchases are made with a collective pot of money. Profit is split evenly among those who are working that day.

But he also explained that they face challenges. Without fridges, the meat spoils after one day. They also spend a significant part of their revenue on four specialist employees—the butcher, vet, cleaner, and transporter. Furthermore, the chairman also argued that the cooperatives do not receive much ongoing support from WaPYDO or other implementing partners. Although they received a camel cart, he suggested that most of the investment has been in infrastructure, such as the slaughterhouse, market, and portable stalls. He suggested that they would also like more training in business skills.

Despite the challenges, our survey of 191 refugee meat-selling cooperative members shows that these cooperatives are associated with a range of positive outcomes. Members reported a doubling of median income (from an average of $20 per month to over $40) compared to before membership. They also had an average 61 per cent higher food consumption levels compared to the general refugee population in the camps and 75 per cent reported improved relations between refugees and the host community as a result of participation in the cooperative. However, one of the biggest challenges related to low income, and the relatively limited work available for each member. In Kobe, for example, the relatively high ratio of members to available work meant that each member worked an average of just three days per month earning an average of around $20 per month for its ninety-eight members, compared to fifteen days per month in Buramino yielding a median income of $85 per month for its twenty-six members.[8]

Third, the milk-selling cooperatives (effectively, a 'complementary retail opportunity') were formed from existing loosely structured business groups of milk sellers. They were created in all five camps from 2017, and made up of approximately ten to twenty members, who are predominantly women, selling goat, cow, and camel milk from a shared shopfront. Their current business models are fairly simple, relying primarily on relationships with local pastoralists who sell the cooperative members milk in bulk, which is subsequently re-sold in the refugee camp markets. WaPYDO has implemented the programme, and provides the groups with solar-powered fridges, jugs, and access to a building space where milk can be stored, often close existing markets. All of the registered members are female and more than 90 per cent are refugees. The model has so far created stable, albeit modest, livelihoods for 103 refugees and ten host community members.

We met with the Buramino cooperative next to the market. One of the women explained to us how the cooperative emerged:

> No one established us, we already were a cooperative [with chairwoman, etc.] when they [WaPYDO] came to make us a cooperative. After WaPYDO came to us, they gave us trainings, some refrigerators, some jugs to carry the milk, they also gave us a place in the new market [opened in Buramino in May 2018 with IKEA Foundation funding].

However, they faced challenges when they were encouraged to relocate to the new market: 'It was not suitable for us, so we moved back to the old market. After we went there, no one came to us to buy our milk, so we had no income... because no one goes there... There are still three women there; the other fourteen work in the old market'. One of the success stories, though, has been collective saving. The group has saved collectively, and invested in a shop, now owned by the cooperative, from which one of the members sells. Nearly all of the members have their own retail shop and so 'that place is a wholesaler; if we need something we get it from that shop. We use the money to buy new things.'

There is some variation in the model across the camps. In Hilaweyn, the chairwomen suggested that their cooperative is busier than others: 'In Melkadida I believe they work in shifts of four women per day. Here [in Hilaweyn], all twenty-three members are selling milk every day in different spots around the market area.' The Hilaweyn cooperative reports that they make about 40–50 ETB (around $1) profit from selling 10 litres of camel milk. The WaPYDO livelihood officer in Bokolmayo reports a similar profit for 5 litres of goat milk: assuming that a milk seller sells 35 litres of milk a day, leading to a daily profit of 150–200 ETB ($3–4), minus cooperative contributions, this ultimately results in an individual's income in the Hilaweyn cooperative of approximately 50–70 ETB ($1–$1.40) per day of work. The cooperative pays one-third of profits directly to members as dividend, and the remaining two-thirds are saved.

In Kobe, cooperative members decided that their collective savings should be used to create a social security net, enabling members to take up to three months of supported maternity leave. The fund provides household inputs to members in need and can offer a maternity pay-out of 500–1,000 ETB ($10–20). One cooperative member in Kobe said: 'I gave birth before joining the cooperative and it was very hard. I was only just surviving.' Her colleague, a younger woman contrasted her experience with the support of the maternity fund: 'without the cooperative, I would have been hungry.' The cooperative chairwoman in Hilaweyn said: 'I was jobless before; the cooperative changed my life. Now I am in a powerful position.' Other interviewees reflected that the cooperative functions as a social security network, and that the money they earn creates stability and opportunity in their lives. In different ways, the cooperatives have therefore integrated particular forms of social insurance mechanisms into the cooperatives.

Alongside these three cooperative models are two additional forms of related business groups. The first is for slaughterhouses. Following a UNHCR participatory assessment in 2016, there was a recognition that livestock were often being slaughtered in unhygienic conditions. It was decided that slaughtering practices could be improved while creating a livelihoods opportunity. WaPYDO built slaughterhouses for each of the camps, provided the necessary facilities, such as washrooms, meat hooks, and transportation caskets. It invited applications to join the business group, and offered technical and managerial guidance to members. In 2017, three slaughterhouses generated over 500,000 ETB ($10,250) in income slaughtering 8,572 sheep and goats, 100 cattle, and 220 camels in Bokolmanyo, Kobe, and Melkadida camps. In Melkadida, for example, the slaughterhouse opened in 2016. It offers a facility where animals can be checked, taken to the bleeding room, carved, and transported. It is effectively a one-stop shop for hygienically transforming an animal into a meat product. Forty-three cooperative members work in four different shifts groups. They charge a fee depending on the animal; for example, it is 30 ETB per goat, and they make a total of 9,000 ETB/month ($185) in revenue based on slaughtering an average of thirty-six animals per day.

The other is the CAHWs business groups, which have been established with the support of WaPYDO in all five camps. They have trained individuals with basic veterinary and livestock inspection skills as a means to reduce spread of illness and disease, and to improve the overall hygiene standards across the livestock value chain. Their main task is to inspect and treat live animals in and around the camp brought for slaughter. In 2018, 5,549 households benefitted from CAHWs services. CAHWs have also supported animal vaccination campaigns.

CAHWs operate their own shops, constructed by WaPYDO, which provide animal hygiene (e.g. removal of dead animals), sanitation (e.g. waste collection), and veterinary (e.g. vaccination) services, which are paid for by either the government or NGOs. Ibrahim Ali Hassan, head of CAHWs, for the Bokolmanyo slaughterhouse explained how CAHWs are also integrated into the slaughterhouse process:

> Inside the slaughterhouse we have four rooms; in the first room I am the one standing in the front of the gate checking the health of the animal. When an animal is not healthy, I make a sign on the animal and call the owner (meatseller). The owner has to keep the animal until it is healthy; I treat the animal with medicine at the owner's home. The owner must pay for the costs of both the medicine and veterinary work. Normally it takes 3–4 days until the animal can be slaughtered. The total cost for such a treatment is on average 40–50 ETB [around $1].

Although the slaughterhouses and CAHWs operate on a relatively small scale, the programmes illustrate how public goods integral to a particular value chain can be delivered in ways that support additional income-generating opportunities. Overall, job-creation activities within the livestock value chain have been successful in creating income-generating activities across the entire value chain. They have improved incomes, upgraded public health, diversified food baskets, and expanded livestock markets. Some of the reasons identified by cooperative members and NGOs for success include that a single local implementing partner (WaPYDO) has managed the entire project; that value-chain inputs are relatively low-maintenance and low-tech; and that livestock management is socio-culturally familiar to both refugees and the host community.

Energy and the environment

Climbing the hill that enters the Bokolmanyo camp, the oldest and furthest camp from the border, we visited an energy cooperative. Abdullahi, the chairman, introduced us to its thirteen members, drawn from both the refugee and host communities. All had some previous relevant background and most of the refugees were originally from more educated urban backgrounds. Through the cooperative they have now been trained in basic electrical engineering, mini-grid installation, and solar maintenance. The bulk of their work, Abdullahi tells us, is in maintaining the solar street lighting and solar mini-grids, and in servicing solar home systems, all installed after 2014 as part of the IKEA Foundation grant. After a focus group discussion, Abdullahi walks us over to the Bokolmanyo Health Centre where he shows us the solar generator, which keeps the lights on 24/7. Before the solar installation, babies were frequently delivered using phone torches for lighting, he explains.

The Bokolmanyo cooperative is gradually starting to expand its business beyond servicing the IKEA solar installations, and several of the members aspire to running their own businesses. One refugee member explained what a benefit it is to have host community members in the cooperative, who can travel freely without a movement pass and so make contacts and service contracts outside the camps. Bokolmanyo is the oldest and most advanced of the energy cooperatives but others have emerged in all of the camps, and in early 2018 the first combined meeting of all of the energy cooperatives took place in Melkadida, enabling them to share experiences and build connections.

There is a solar energy cooperative in each of the camps, generally comprising twelve to eighteen members, predominantly male refugees selected by the RCCs on the basis of having some relevant background or technical knowledge. Each cooperative has the same basic business model, relying upon income streams from maintaining externally and predominantly IKEA-funded installations: solar street lamps, solar home systems; eight solar mini-grid installations that serve five public health centres and three commercial arrangements (two in Bokolmanyo, and one in Buramino). The main source of private income comes from the provision of solar charging stations, mainly used by refugees for phone charging. At present, the cooperatives are not profitable enough to purchase all of their own inputs.

While all save a significant proportion of their income—with Kobe said to be putting 40 per cent of profits into their bank account, at the lower end, and Bokolmanyo saving 60 per cent of all profits—the money earned is not yet enough to afford the purchase of new, replacement materials. Kobe, Hilaweyn, and Melkadida in particular are far from capable of being self-reliant, as a majority of their incomes derive from the meagre profits earned through cooperative-run solar charging stations for recharging small electronics. When commercial solar mini-grids are built and operable in Hilaweyn and Melkadida (expected soon), and in Kobe (expected in late

2020), they will join Bokolmanyo and Buramino in being in a better position to increase their savings rate and expand their operations. A cooperative member in Kobe reflected that 'After the mini-grid installation in Kobe, we will be able to reach self-reliance, but before that I don't think it's possible.'

The five cooperatives have varying levels of development and, in turn, profitability. While Buramino and Bokolmanyo earn the most money collectively, members nevertheless take a small sum of money home each month. In Bokolmanyo, for instance, the cooperative earned 15,550 ETB ($320) from mini-grid customers in October 2019, of which 11,800 ETB ($240) was used to pay for new materials purchased in Dollo Ado. A figure of 3,700 ETB ($75) went towards paying transportation costs, and the tiny amount left over was put into their savings account. It is only once they begin to hit the savings target set by the main implementing partner, ReST-CPDA, that larger sums of money will be paid out to cooperative members. Because the cooperatives are not yet offering an income source, most members say that they are working in supplementary jobs, often as daily labourers, in order to better support their families.

Nevertheless, most of the members we spoke to were positive about the experience, highlighting the benefits in terms of training, self-esteem, and were optimistic about future expansion. One Buramino member, for instance, told us '[we are] still in the start-up phase . . . the work that [we] are doing currently is [an investment] for the future.' Another from the same cooperative spoke of his pride on the work: 'I feel that I am encouraged by IKEA and other IPs . . . even my children will tell others that their father has good knowledge and that he is an electrician in the cooperative.' A similar account from Bokolmanyo also accentuated the benefits in terms of self-esteem: 'Anyone who sits without anything to do might feel depressed, but if you have a duty and some activity, you will become happier.' Even in the lowest-performing cooperative, Kobe, a member reported a sense of empowerment, claiming: 'Before I joined the coop, I believed that my family had to depend on food from [monthly] distributions, but after I joined I understood that I can support my family.'

Part of this sense of pride and reinforced self-esteem stems from providing a public good to the wider community. For example, beneficiaries of the solar street lighting told us that they feel safer when they walk at night, which has led to increased social activity after sunset. One Buramino resident told us there has been 'a big change in the community . . . motivating and encouraging us. They say that [the cooperative members] have a good plan.' One of the cooperative members from the same community said 'the small town that you see . . . has come out of the dark. The plots [of land] that we had here were very cheap before the cooperative, but the land prices have increased. If you want to build a shop here it is quite expensive [now].' The energy-related investments have also contributed to greater social cohesion. One Kobe cooperative member explained, 'we are working together [as refugees and hosts] . . . We eat together and drink together, too. If the relationship weren't good, we would have seen a lot of conflict.'

Meanwhile, a parallel energy cooperative is providing opportunities for women. Firewood remains the main household energy source across the camps. However, because it is not available within the camps, it relies upon women travelling long distances into the bush to collect wood, where they are often vulnerable to sexual and gender-based violence. One alternative available within the vicinity of the camps is the prosopis juliflora tree, which is invasive and has an adverse environmental impact unless removed, but which offers a source of household energy. Prosopis cooperatives have therefore been created as a means to simultaneously meet three goals: to reduce negative environmental impacts, to create income-generating activities for women, and to offer protection to women previously exposed to the dangers associated with going into the bush to collect firewood.

One of the biggest potential benefits of the prosopis cooperative model is in terms of protection, reducing some of the risks associated with traditional firewood collection. We spoke to a traditional firewood group in Bokolmanyo with twenty members, who go out into the surrounding bush to collect acacia wood. They told us about their work:

> Whenever we go we get firewood, we go one day and take rest another day, so per month we go to the bush on fifteen days. Whenever we go we take one back of firewood and we sell that back for 30 ETB [less than $1] . . . Except for the firewood we don't get any other income . . . The firewood may stay at the market for three to four days without selling it . . . In the bush there is not enough firewood, we [have to] search [harder] for it . . . We feel back ache, we lack alternative work so that we can buy sugar for our family . . . The people who are in the cooperative are staying inside the camps but for us non-cooperative [collectors], we have to go outside and walk long distances. It is tiring and we bring a small [amount of] firewood which we sell for 30 ETB. [The cooperative members] get rest and they are better [off] than us.

However, from a business perspective, the prosopis projects have been a failure. The business model for the prosopis cooperatives involves sourcing and collecting prosopis, purchasing the raw wood, and then transforming it into charcoal briquettes which can be sold for household use. Cooperatives have been established in each of the five camps, and are comprised predominantly of refugee women who were previously engaged in firewood-collecting activity. There were approximately sixty to eighty refugee and host community members in each of the cooperatives when founded. The model has not proved commercially viable. Soon after creation, there was rapid attrition in the number of active members due to relatively limited income-generating opportunities.

On the supply side, one cooperative reported that due to the lack in availability of prosopis it has completely ceased its activities. Some of the cooperative reported having to travel as far afield as the Kenyan border to source the wood, and suggested that the price had gone up by a factor of ten since the cooperatives began. On the demand side, the market for prosopis-related products has been limited. Some 75 per cent of refugees use firewood as their main fuel source, but NGO staff suggest that prosopis-related charcoal products represent no more than 10 per cent of the household fuel market. The firewood cooperative model therefore revealed an example of an innovative model, with an important potential role in addressing protection issues, but conceived without adequate market linkages.

Microfinance

In a small office in Melkadida, Mohammed, the microfinance coordinator for national NGO, ReST-CPDA's microfinance initiative called Dedebit Microfinance explains the principles behind the IKEA-funded model. The scheme began in 2016 and is the first microfinance programme in Dollo Ado. It works according to Islamic principles, with no interest, and offers both a savings scheme, for any amount upwards of 13 ETB ($0.25), and a loan scheme, both cash and in-kind, with business grants being a major focus.

> The scheme is important because there are no formal banks in the camps, and refugees are not allowed to access formal banking. Even with the opening of Oromia International Bank in Dollo, there won't be much impact on refugees because their criteria are very restrictive—it requires documentation, collateral assets, and interest rates are too high.

The MFI began financial support of UNHCR, using the IKEA Foundation grant, to create a 13 million ETB rotating grant to cover a five-year period, initially in Melkadida before being extended to the others. The initiative was ReST's idea. Mohammed from CPDA explained the model:

> Each saver has a savings card to document inflow and outflow... Accounts and loans are open to all communities... People in cooperatives have a preference for saving their money here, and WaPYDO manages the registration of the cooperatives for this... In terms of the loan programme, applicants have to sign a loan agreement. Loans are issued to an individual, but others need to also participate as guarantor... We dispersed the first loan in November 2017. There is a cap on the amount of the first loan and then those who submit for a second round have to submit a [more developed] business plan.

The model has been accompanied by training in basic financial literacy. A beneficiary, sitting in the office, discussed his experience:

> Initially, we didn't have a business. After we had a loan, we started a business. I own a shop. I was a businessman in Somalia; but wasn't able to start up again until this loan became available. I have been able to pay school fees for private school for English and maths, and others... I've already paid my first cycle loan. I want more loans, and to expand my business to become a rich man; to broaden my portfolio.

One Somali entrepreneur in Melkadida, Muse, explained how he has used the loan to build buy a generator and create a business.

> I took a loan from ReST-CPDA for 22,500 ETB [$460] last year [2018], I received the loan in kind as one diesel generator. It's a very huge generator. [I used it to create] my own workshop—the saw and machines need the electricity. I also linked the generator to different households—they use it for refrigerators and lamps and a garage uses it for welding... Before I received the loan, I did not have a regular income; I worked as a daily labourer sometimes.

The generator is his main business, and it provides him with an income of up to 15,000 ETB ($300) a month, from which he repays the loan at a rate of about 1,900 ETB ($40) a month.

By the end of 2019, a reported 300–600 applicants had sought business loans in each camp, the largest proportion of whom come from the host community, and there had been 525 loans, more than 40 per cent of which have been used to support retail shops, and 13 per cent to support livelihood-related activities. With help from UNHCR and ARRA, the NGO-implementing partner selected applicants based on twelve criteria, with most weight placed on individuals' regular residence in the camps, the cultural and social appropriateness of the business idea within the Somali context, and the willingness to work within groups.

But has the microfinance initiative been sustainable? Unlike some of the other Dollo Ado cooperatives, it has a clear sustainability plan: by charging a 5 per cent mark-up on loan repayments it aims to be able to cover its operating costs from the end of the five-year grant. And just over halfway through the five-year grant, they report having saved enough to cover about 20 per cent of their operating costs for year six. However, the greatest risk to commercial viability is default on loans. Until now, no outright defaults have been reported, but this has been mainly because of the option to restructure loans rather than because of high repayment rates.

The need for macroeconomic investment

It is clear that the IKEA Foundation's investments in livelihood opportunities have made a significant different to the welfare of many of its project beneficiaries as well as the wider community. The approach has pioneered a fundamentally new approach to the design and management of refugee camps, one that aspires to create sustainable economic opportunity rather than long-term dependency. Some of the business models that have been piloted and prototyped such as the whole-value-chain-approach to livestock or the scale of irrigation or the use of cooperatives have never before been applied in a refugee context. Within a remote and arid region, the Foundation has worked effectively to expand markets in agriculture, livestock, and commerce, while also finding more sustainable ways to provide public goods.

However, there are also limitations to what has been achieved, and challenges to scaling and making the approach sustainable, both in Dollo Ado and more widely. Despite what has been achieved, 'Most refugees don't have any means of generating income,' explained an elected refugee representative in Buramino. 'Most refugees in the camp are not working. They are fully reliant on food rations,' highlighted another. Most refugees in the camps depend upon their monthly WFP food basket consisting of 13.5kg cereal, 1.5kg bean/lentils, 0.9 litre oil, 0.15kg salt, and 1kg corn soya beans blend, and have very limited access to the cash economy.

Only 21 per cent of refugee adults report having an income-generating activity. Among the host community 29 per cent of adults have an income-generating activity. For refugees, of those with an income-generating activity, around 28 per cent are self-employed and around 72 per cent are employed in some form. For refugees, by far the most significant source of employment by someone else is as 'incentive workers' for humanitarian NGOs and international organizations or government agencies like ARRA (a total of 61 per cent). For the proximate host communities, a similarly high proportion of those employed work for the government, NGOs, or international organizations, varying between 59 per cent in Buramino and 87 per cent in Bokolmanyo.[9]

Among those with an income-generating activity, incomes are consistently low. The median reported income for people with a job is 800 ETB ($16/month) for refugees in all the camps except Hilaweyn (in which it is 1,000 ETB, $20). Meanwhile, it is 3,000 ETB ($60/month) for nearby hosts around all the camps except Buramino (1,820 ETB, $37) and Bokolmanyo (3,150 ETB, $63). Part of the reason for the strikingly consistent reporting across individuals and camps is that wage rates paid for 'incentive work' is informally 'capped' at around 800 ETB for refugees and 3,000 ETB for locals. Put simply, the bulk of the Dollo Ado economy remains an aid economy, built mainly upon food assistance and employment by humanitarian agencies.

UNHCR, IKEA Foundation, and ARRA have chosen to focus on three main economic pillars—farming, livestock, and retail commerce—in their programmes to support livelihoods. There is certainly evidence to support making these areas of focus, and people are benefitting from the programmes. However, our research reveals that less than 10 per cent of households have adult members engaged in any of those three areas of activity. For agriculture, it is an average of 3 per cent across all the camps. There are both cultural and climatic reasons underlying the low numbers: Somalis tend to avoid agriculture, and the combination of an arid climate and seasonal flooding risks from the river make farming unpredictable. In relation to livestock, Somalis have a pastoral heritage and many keep small animals. An average of around 55 per cent of refugee households have animals. However, these are mostly small animals and for most households, livestock ownership is not viewed as a means of generating a livelihood; it is a savings mechanism or a source of food. Less than 2 per cent of households have commercial livestock as a main income-generating activity. In terms of commercial retail, there is greater potential, reflected in the 28 per cent of people with an income-generating activity being self-employed. But that is still only 5 per cent of the overall adult population and, of them, many are involved in service provision in areas such as transport or manual work, rather than in being shop owners. Despite the creation of the new MFI, one of the biggest reported barriers to entrepreneurship is lack of access to capital. Few refugees have bank accounts, savings schemes, or access to loans. And, most surprisingly within a Somali community, globally renowned for money transfer, an average of only 7 per cent of adult refugees receive any remittances at all.

Refugees' own survival strategies

In practice, most refugees in the five camps are not direct beneficiaries of the IKEA Foundation investments, and the indirect benefits have not yet reached a transformative level for the majority of households. Instead, most refugees' survival strategies rely upon a combination of the cross-border economy with Somalia and the aid economy.

One of the most striking findings of our research was the extent to which Dollo Ado is embedded in the wider regional economy. The cross-border economy with Somalia underpins the livelihood strategies of a significant proportion of both refugees and the host community. Staff of the international community, humanitarian organizations, and local authorities are well aware of this phenomenon. Yet it is rarely publicly recognized, partly because of the traditional nation-state lens through which these organizations undertake their analysis and design programmes, but also because they fear that publicly acknowledging cross-border movements could negatively impact them with detrimental consequences for refugees. Nevertheless, the refugee economy of Dollo Ado cannot be explained without at least some acknowledgement of the transnational and regional nature of the economy.

Informally UNHCR staff have recognized a pattern of oscillation in the number of actual recipients of food rations relative to those registered. For a period of up to two consecutive food rations, heads of household will frequently delegate food collection to another household member but then reappear for the third collection to avoid having their entitlement quashed. Some staff suspect that this is because some refugees with the greatest capacity to work may return to Somalia to work, even within the war economy, before returning to meet bureaucratic requirements.

Many of the businesses across the five camps—retail shops, cafés, restaurants, butcheries, livestock yards—depend upon the cross-border economy, for which Dollo Ado town serves as a commercial hub, connecting the refugee camps with the Somali economy. Ibrahim, for example, runs a retail shop in Melkadida and told us, 'I sell dry food items, soap, beauty goods, spices, cosmetics, batteries, toothpaste, etc. I receive fifteen to twenty customers per day...I buy most of the items from Dollo Ado town from [Ethiopian] traders. I go there once a month.' The livelihood officer of one UNHCR implementing partner, himself an indigenous Somali-Ethiopian, explained the trade networks that intersect in Dollo Ado town:

> From Mogadishu, many electronic items such as mobile phones, televisions, and fridges are imported [to Dollo Ado], since it is cheaper than importing them from Addis. Food items such as rice, pasta, soft drinks, as well as clothing and shoes are coming from Mogadishu...Also, there is a trade of livestock like goats and sheep from Ethiopia to Somalia. Khat is brought from other parts of Ethiopia like Negele and taken to Somalia. Some khat is from Mandera [Kenya].

Refugees visit Dollo Ado town regularly for purposes including business, employment, education, and to meet friends and family. Refugees can access the Hawala system from Dollo Ado town. Refugee shop owners from the camps purchase commodities unavailable in the camps, such as sugar, wheat flour, iron sheets, hardware, construction materials, electronic items, SIM cards, and clothing. They buy these items from Ethiopians in Dollo Ado town and sell them inside the camp. As a senior UNHCR official put it:

> Economic connections with Dollo Ado town keep the camp economies alive...this town has a well-established informal economy. Many items are traded from and to Mogadishu and Mandera, and so many people here rely on the informal economy and benefit from it. This is the lifeline of locals as well as camp residents. Addis is far away, so Dollo Somalia (and Somalia) is a more important market for locals.

Dollo Ado town serves as a gateway between Ethiopia and Somalia. Our research suggests that at least 13 per cent of refugees have travelled to Dollo Ado town at least once in the previous year. And although cross-border movement is officially prohibited by the authorities in the various camps, many refugees in Dollo Ado camps travel regularly to Somalia. According to the International Organization for Migration (IOM), there are about 1,000 movements per day across the border bridge, which represents the only crossing point, and these numbers include both refugees and non-refugees. IOM estimate that refugees constitute about 20 per cent of those crossing, that is, around 200 refugees per day. Their head of office told us:

They move to Somalia and come back to the camp to receive their food rations. So before and after food ration distributions, the movement frequency usually increases. The refugees want to keep their refugee status, but they often go back to Somalia... International borders don't mean much for Somalis in this area.

A staff member from an IOM and UNHCR return helpdesk listed three reasons for refugees to move back and forth: first, to maintain and cultivate land in Somalia based around two main cultivation seasons (October to December, and July to August); second, to support livelihoods activities, including commercial activities; third, for family reasons.

One Somali refugee living with his wife and seven children in Melkadida camp had recently visited Somalia:

In February 2018 [I went] for about 1 month. I went to my hometown Esow [because] my mother was very ill. She is 76 years old... I kept my family here in the camp... I was only given ten days to travel up to Dollo Ado. When I was passing from Dollo Ado to Somalia, no one stopped me. But when returning, I was stopped by Somali officials, and I had to bribe them to let me in.

A female Somali refugee recently travelled back from Kobe camp to her hometown of Baidou in December 2017 and January 2018 to see her ill mother and to attend her brother's funeral:

I went there alone. My neighbours took care of my children. I also told RCC members, who in turn informed an ARRA officer and asked him to provide food rations to my children as usual while I was away... When I came back to the camp, I immediately reported to my zone and block leaders, and they reported my return to the RCC, who passed the report to ARRA.

In some cases, family visits were connected to economic strategies. Some male refugees also had more than one family, either side of the border. For example, one such refugee recently travelled to visit his second wife and check the security of his property in his home village in Somalia:

I have two wives, one with six children who all live in the camp, the other with four children living in Somalia. They live in Gurmay in Bay region. This is my hometown too. I still have my own farmland there... I want to keep my family in Somalia to take care of my plot. This is why I kept them there.

Others visited family in order to borrow money. A widowed refugee visited Baidou for two months between June and August of 2018, explaining: 'I needed to borrow some money from my family. I had to pay debts... [In the camp] I bought clothing for my children and food items like pasta and milk powder on credit from the shops...In total, I had debts of 20,000 ETB [$400].'

Some of our interviewees went to Somalia to access economic opportunities provided by aid agencies supporting internally displaced persons (IDPs). For example, the Kabasa IDP camp, was set up near Dollo, Somalia, in May 2018. Unlike the refugee camps, Kabasa provides cash assistance. A refugee from Hilaweyn camp, described his trip:

> I went to Dollo Somalia for two months between September and October 2018. I only recently came back...I visited Kabasa IDP camp. I wanted to register myself to access cash support in order to assist my family. I learned they give 100 per household...Food rations in Dollo Ado are too small.

Another refugee who went to Kabasa camp explained that there is a trade-off:

> Buramino gives us peace, good education and health facilities, as well as food rations. Kabasa gives people cash support, but there is no peace there. Al-Shabaab is still active in their area. I prefer peace over cash. Many refugees who went there were attracted to the cash programme, but most of them came back [to Ethiopia].

Although there is likely a degree of under-reporting due to the illicit nature of most of the movements, the percentage of Somali refugees who have travelled to Somalia in the last year declines markedly the further away from the border you go (12 per cent Buramino; 6 per cent Hilaweyn; 8 per cent Kobe; 1 per cent Melkadida; less than 1 per cent Bokolmanyo). Furthermore, while Somalis were prepared to report visits back for family or social reasons, very few refugees openly admitted to going back primarily for business or work-related reasons.

Furthermore, some Somali households adopt 'split-family' strategies. Children and the elderly will remain in the camps, where they can receive access to assistance and services such as education. Meanwhile, many of the adult men of working age will either be based in Somalia or divide their time between the camps and Somalia. In that sense, the camps are used as just one part of a household strategy in which the camps offer a set of resources, but so too does ongoing engagement with the economy of south-central Somalia. One striking piece of evidence for this is the demographic profile of our representative sample of refugees who were actually in the camps at the time of the survey. In particular, there was a disproportionately low share of adults in the age groups of 25–30 and 30–35, especially when compared to the demographic profile of the host community. Meanwhile, there was a disproportionately higher number of women than men within the refugee community but not in the host community.

The camps are valued by refugees because they provide a source of social protection. One Somali refugee who lives in Bokolmanyo camp with his wife and ten children, recently went back to Somalia to see his relatives but returned to the camp. He explained his long-term hopes in terms of residency:

> In the long term, I would like to go back [to Somalia]. But now my children are getting education in the camp. Until they finish schooling, I should stay in the camp ... Education in the camp is better than in my hometown in Somalia. In fact, there is no primary and secondary school in my village ... Another reason to stay here is security. For my children, the camp is more peaceful.

An Ethiopian staff member, who since June 2017 has been working on the IOM and UNHCR return helpdesk in Hilaweyn camp, highlighted how refugees try to take advantage of opportunities in the camps:

> Access to education and health facilities is much better in camps than in Somalia. Refugees in the camp benefit from free vocational skill training provided by UNHCR and its IPs. In their home regions in Somalia like Bay and Bakool, educational opportunities are very limited. The country is still unstable in many areas, or under reconstruction in others. Refugees hope that if they get education and vocational skills here, they can utilize them upon their return.

An additional part of refugees' own survival strategies relies upon selling food rations. Some groups of refugee women collectively organize to sell food rations. We interviewed the founder of one of these groups in Hilaweyn camp:

> Many refugees are involved in the sale of WFP food items. Refugees in the camp need cash to buy other items not provided by UNHCR ... I sell rice, porridge, BVT, sorghum, and maize. Taking maize as an example, I buy one kilogram at 12 ETB [$0.25] and sell at 13 ETB [$0.27]. For rice, I buy one kilogram at 15 ETB [$0.31] and sell at 20 ETB [$0.41]. Rice is more popular, so the profit margin is higher.

While the sale of WFP food rations is commonly observed in many other camps, the strategy seems to be particularly prevalent in the Dollo Ado camps because of the lack of alternative income-generating options. Our survey shows that the number of households willing to admit to selling part of their food ration is relatively low: an average of 10 per cent across the camps, with a range of between 4 per cent in Melkadida and 28 per cent in Bokolmanyo. Meanwhile, the median proportion of food rations sold by these households was 43 per cent. However, our qualitative research suggests that there is likely to have been significant under-reporting of food ration sales due to respondents' fear of losing their ration entitlement. The head of WFP in Dollo Ado explained:

> For refugees in Dollo Ado, food rations become a key asset for all refugees. They are entitled to it every month, so refugees see it as a reliable source of income inside the camps...There are also well-established market mechanisms for the food trade here. Once refugees receive their food rations at distribution centres, they sell it to Somali-Ethiopian traders. These traders are aware of the exact dates of food ration distributions in the camps. Many of them are from Dollo Ado town. They sell items to Kenya, Ethiopia, and Somalia.

He told us that, every month, WFP's investment in Dollo Ado camps has a total value of about $11–12 million, including the transportation and indirect costs relating to food delivery. With relatively few livelihood options in the camps, food rations are a key resource for refugees. He further explained: 'Food rations are more than just food. Food rations are also a tool of empowerment, giving an alternative to refugees. This is a key ingredient of the refugee camp economies.'

In Dollo Ado town, there is a particularly well-known wheat processing factory owned by a Somali-Ethiopian host business person. One of his associates gave us an overview of the business model:

> This factory was established in 2014 as a private company. He [the owner] buys wheat from refugees on the day of food distribution. There are no processing factories in the camps, so he takes the wheat to his factory in Dollo and processes it into flour, small pasta. Then he sells it in the refugee camps, among host communities, and in Dollo Somalia and Mandera... It is not easy to get wheat in large quantities in Dollo Ado. Without refugee camps, this business would be hard to run. In Dollo Ado, this factory is the only local provider of flour and pasta; the rest is imported.

Within this business model, the refugee camps appear twice in the supply chain. First, as a source of wheat, and, second, as consumers of the pasta that is produced from it. According to a number of sources, refugee or host community brokers buy up the WFP food rations from refugees, and then sell the wheat flour on to the pasta factory in Dollo Ado. The pasta factory will then distribute pasta to host traders at wholesale prices. They then sell it on at a mark-up to refugee and host brokers operating at the camp level, who in turn retail the pasta back to refugees.

These examples reveal an entrepreneurial and adaptive refugee community, developing survival strategies that often bypass formal organizational responses. But they also highlight two further issues. First, they demonstrate the need for international actors to have a more nuanced understanding of refugees' own economic strategies. For example, how could cross-border economic opportunities be better supported in order to enhance sustainable livelihoods? Or could in-kind food assistance be replaced by alternative, cash-based approaches to assistance. Second, they also highlight that, for the majority, the Dollo Ado economy still fails to deliver adequate income-generating opportunities.

Towards sustainability

A decade has elapsed since the creation of the first Dollo Ado camp, and the camps have passed from the emergency phase to representing a protracted refugee situation. As IKEA Foundation CEO, Per Heggenes, highlights, the next stage is to move towards sustainability. This involves ensuring that initiatives such as the agricultural, livestock, and energy cooperatives can continue without ongoing assistance. However, it must also involve moving Dollo Ado beyond being an economy that is largely based on the circulation of aid money.

The IKEA Foundation has brought the ideas and approach of a private-sector organization. But as a corporate foundation, its engagement has been philanthropic rather than core business led. Encouraging for-profit businesses, whether Ethiopian or global, to invest in Dollo Ado is a more elusive and challenging proposition. With infrastructure, public goods, and a more skilled population, that type of investment may gradually become more realistic over time. But to be viable, the Dollo Ado economy ultimately needs to move beyond an aid-dependent model towards one capable of exporting beyond the Genale Dorya River basin. It will need to produce goods or services that can be sold more widely across the Somali region, or other markets in Ethiopia, and even across borders into Kenya and Somalia. Anecdotally, there are emerging reports that some of Dollo Ado's new agricultural produce is being bought by traders from across the country, and making its way along road networks towards Oromia and Tigray, as well as across the Mandera border into Kenya. But this must be just the start.

The Dollo Ado interventions have mainly taken place on an iterative basis without a clear strategic roadmap at the outset. But what they offer, with hindsight, is a possible blueprint for the future development of refugee economies. There is much that has been positive: the sequencing from emergency assistance to infrastructure to livelihoods, the innovative business models based on cooperatives, the attempts to analyse and identify opportunities across entire value chains, and the successful commercialization of agriculture in a region with significant environmental constraints. UNHCR and the IKEA Foundation have built effective partnerships with local organizations, the host community, and refugees themselves.

Other areas remain weak. The camps urgently need to move from in-kind to cash-based assistance. The potential for digital technology has been hampered by under-investment in telecommunications. Regulatory restrictions on refugees' movement and economic activities inhibit potential opportunities for greater production, consumption, and exchange. Road networks and public transportation between the camps are limited. The nearest university remains over 600km away in Jijiga. Perhaps the biggest thing that has been missing, though, is an evidence base and a guiding conceptual framework for further development.

IKEA's Dollo Ado interventions were conceived more based on dialogue, intuition, and experimentation than on strong research and evidence. And they were implemented without building in adequate baseline data collection. This has resulted in a gap in recognizing and understanding refugees' and host communities' own economic strategies. But, most importantly, it has resulted in a privileging of programme-based microeconomic interventions over and above outlining a long-term macroeconomic vision for the region. Ultimately, the only viable way to move beyond an aid-circulation economy will be to develop such a macroeconomic strategy, and to begin to effectively communicate that strategy, and the IKEA Foundation's success stories so far, to external for-profit investors.

Conclusion

The IKEA Foundation's work in the Dollo Ado camps is unique. It represents the largest private-sector investment in any refugee context in history and has piloted a new approach to refugee camps—one based on self-reliance rather than long-term dependency. Despite facing serious constraints, it has built the foundations of a market-based economy within an arid and isolated region with few natural resources and little obvious comparative advantage. It has done so by sequencing emergency relief, infrastructural development, and creation of livelihoods. Its livelihoods projects have all been conceived to support both refugees and the host community. In the course of its work, the IKEA Foundation has demonstrated that the private sector can work effectively with the United Nations humanitarian system.

Our research shows that the interventions themselves have been a qualified success. From transforming agriculture and livestock farming into commercially viable activities to providing a rotating fund for microfinance, these programmes have generally led to welfare improvements, including higher income levels for beneficiaries, and also expanded opportunities for the wider community. In October 2020, the Foundation received recognition for its work in Dollo Ado at the Financial Times / International Finance Corporation Transformational Business Awards. It collected both the overall 'Excellence in Transformational Business Award' and a 'Special Award: Innovating for the Most Vulnerable and Disadvantaged' based specifically on its programmes to build livelihoods for refugees and the host community in Dollo Ado. Of course, not everything has been perfect, and there are doubts over whether some of the new business models will endure without ongoing external subsidy. But given what Dollo Ado looked like a decade earlier, the advances have been remarkable.

Dollo Ado reveals the potential for market-based development within even the most challenging refugee-hosting regions. It shows that the private sector can play a key role, not just through its funding but also through its ideas, principles, and innovative mindset that it can bring to a refugee context. Nevertheless, the experience also points to limitations. To become sustainable, Dollo Ado needs to shift from being an aid-circulation economy towards being an exporting economy. In order to achieve this, the next step is to a move from microeconomic interventions towards a coherent, and investable macroeconomic plan. The IKEA Foundation's greatest contribution may ultimately be in the learning potential it offers for building future refugee economies, whether in Ethiopia or elsewhere.

PART III

Politics—*what persuades?*

8

The politics of refugee rights

Introduction

Some 85 per cent of refugees live in low- and middle-income countries. The default humanitarian response has generally been refugee camps, in which refugees have limited socio-economic rights, including the right to work and freedom of movement. Many governments do not want to provide such rights because they prefer to encourage refugees to go home, and do not want to allocate scarce resources to non-citizens. But some host countries do let refugees work, even despite hosting large numbers. The most notable examples of countries that give refugees some level of socio-economic freedom are Uganda, Turkey, and Colombia. Meanwhile, the countries with encampment policies that most strongly restrict the right to work include Kenya, Tanzania, and Thailand.[1]

This variation matters because socio-economic rights, including the right to work, are associated with improved welfare outcomes. Our research has shown, for example, that the right to work and freedom of movement for refugees is associated with higher income levels, greater mobility, lower transaction costs for economic activity, and more sustainable sources of employment (see Chapter 5). Being able to work in general is associated not only with better socio-economic outcomes, including income and expenditure, but also improved psychosocial outcomes, relating to its role in providing people with meaning and purpose.[2] The positive psychosocial impact of work has also been identified among refugee populations.[3] Meanwhile, protracted refugee situations in which refugees are usually unable to work are associated with a range of long-term harms.[4]

The regulatory choices of refugee-hosting governments shape the institutional context in which refugees access socio-economic rights and opportunities.[5] And the right to work, alongside other related rights such as freedom of movement, represent an important part of the enabling conditions for refugee self-reliance. It is virtually impossible to imagine refugees being able to meet their socio-economic needs independently of aid, unless they can engage in income-generating activities. In this context, it is crucial to understand the politics that underlies this variation in the right to work, and other related socio-economic rights for refugees. Why do some states give refugees the right to work, while others do not? Explaining variation matters because it offers an opportunity to identify the policy mechanisms through which changes in legislation, policy, and practice can occur.

This research question lies at the intersection of international relations and comparative politics. There is a significant literature on 'international relations and refugees', focusing on, for example, security,[6] as well as international cooperation.[7] There is also a range of work on 'comparative politics and refugees'.[8] However, there is virtually no research on the politics of refugees' socio-economic inclusion, especially in developing countries. What explains variation in the right to work, or access to other socio-economic rights? Political explanations of policy and legislative variation have usually focused on the behaviour of rich countries in areas such as donor governments' financial contributions;[9] resettlement numbers;[10] and asylum admissions policies.[11] However, with few exceptions,[12] political scientists have rarely explained variation in the law, policies, and practices of refugee-hosting states in low- and middle-income countries, even though they host the overwhelming majority of the world's refugees.

Furthermore, there is a complete absence of political science research explaining variation in the law, policies, and practices of such countries relating to socio-economic rights for refugees, such as the right to work. This is despite the extent to which such policies matter for such a large proportion of the world's refugees. And it is despite the centrality of debates relating to refugee self-reliance and socio-economic inclusion within global policy debates. They are, for example, one of the most prominent and widely discussed aspects of the UN Global Compact on Refugees.[13]

In this part of the book, I therefore explore the question of why some states give refugees the right to work while others do not, by looking comparatively at the East African context, in which despite countries hosting refugees of the same nationality there is considerable variation in refugees' socio-economic rights.

One important distinction, though, is between the de jure (in law) and de facto (in practice) right to work. Throughout the proceeding analysis,

I use that distinction in order to be able to recognize the difference between a country allowing refugees to work within national legislation, on the one hand, and tolerating refugees working, on the other. As I show, it is possible to have one without the other. By 'de facto', it should be noted, I do not simply mean that refugees happen to work in the informal sector, but that refugee employment is also actively accepted by political authorities in at least part of the country.

Uganda has offered refugees the de facto right to work virtually since independence, and introduced the de jure right to work in 2006. Ethiopia introduced the de jure right to work for the first time in its 2019 Refugee Proclamation but at the time of writing has not yet implemented it. Kenya has restricted the right to work in its national legislation but since 2014 has de facto begun to expand socio-economic rights in the remote north-western region of Turkana County. Meanwhile, other neighbouring states such as Tanzania continue to restrict the right to work in both law and practice.

For the most part, norms and values play a secondary role to political interests in explaining host countries' willingness to integrate refugees in labour markets. States across the region have generally signed and ratified common international legal instruments. Despite these instruments outlining refugees' socio-economic rights, the host countries show considerable variation in how their national legislation, policies, and practice provide these rights. When we examine the historical emergence of the right to work for refugees across the region, the key turning points are usually related to changes in political incentive structures for key decision-makers, and in particular the conditional access to resources. Usually those resources relate to development assistance which directly benefits host state citizens. For example, as I will explain, the passage of the 2019 Refugee Proclamation in Ethiopia was directly linked to a group of donors offering more than half a billion dollars in conditional development assistance.

Existing work on the international politics of refugee assistance has examined host-country politics through the lens of North–South relations, assuming that donor–host state relations are characterized by asymmetric power relations. Within that context, a number of authors have highlighted the important role of issue-linkage in ensuring that donor–host state bargains are mutually beneficial. For Northern donor states the payoff has generally related to improved migration management, and for Southern host states it has generally related to development assistance.[14]

As I have argued elsewhere, this is a broadly accurate characterization of North–South relations in the international refugee regime.[15] However, what is missing is an account of sub-national politics. Host state government policies, I suggest, are determined by a three-way relationship and set of bargains across global, national, and local levels.

Reflecting this, I outline a theoretical framework relating to what I call the 'bargains of inclusion', within which I explore the political deals that have to hold between global, national, and local levels of governance in order for refugees to be given the right to work, and other related socio-economic rights.

To achieve the right to work for refugees, a bargain has to be struck that is mutually beneficial for donor governments, the central government of the host country, and local political authorities in refugee-hosting areas. Put simply, what matters is not just a payoff for the host government but also a payoff for the local government. In low- and middle-income countries, local politics matters as much for refugees' right to work as national and international politics.[16] By comparatively examining variation in the right to work and its historical emergence across three East African host countries—Uganda, Ethiopia, and Kenya—I use process tracing to offer a granular, qualitative account of how and why the right to work has emerged in each context.

The dependent variable of interest (the outcome I am interested in explaining) is the right to work in relation to two aspects: the de jure right to work (whether it exists in law) and the de facto right to work (whether it exists in practice). I show that, within the case studies, where there is an acceptable payoff at the national level, it leads to the de jure right to work. Where there is an acceptable payoff at the local level, it leads to the de facto right to work.

Given that the research is qualitative, and focuses on a small number of countries in one particular region (East Africa), the aim is to engage in theory-building rather than theory-testing. Nevertheless, the simplified heuristic framework outlined in this chapter is intended to organize comparative analysis and identify patterns that emerge from empirical research. In order to make this argument, this chapter outlines the 'bargain of inclusion' framework and then summarizes its application to the three main case studies.

Self-reliance as a deadlock game

In general, there is relatively limited political science research explaining variation in host-country policies towards refugees. Examining the conditions under which African host countries provide the right to work offers an opportunity to contribute to that literature. In Chapters 9–11 that follow, I provide in-depth qualitative accounts of the emergence of law, policy, and practice relating to refugees' socio-economic rights in three countries. In this chapter, my concern is to offer a simplified framework, one which does not capture every nuance but which synthesizes the main findings within a coherent theoretical framework.

My starting point is that giving refugees the right to work has generally been viewed by host states in developing countries as costly. Although allowing non-citizens the right to work is not necessarily zero-sum, it has historically been perceived to create competition for employment opportunities with citizens of the host country. Many host countries in Africa have long represented the presence of refugees as a 'burden', to be shared by the international community, and as something 'temporary', requiring only provision for basic needs until refugees can return home.[17]

Low- and middle-income countries in fragile neighbourhoods tend to have relatively porous borders and are signatories to international treaties, whether in refugee or human rights law, that prohibit the expulsion of refugees (known as *refoulement*). It is therefore rare that such countries forcibly return refugees to their countries of origin, both because they often lack the capacity to control entry and exit, and because they tend to face international condemnation and opprobrium if they threaten to do so.

The default policy preference of most low- and middle-income countries has become that refugees are hosted in closed camps, with restrictions on their right to work and freedom of movement. This has become the norm in countries as wide-ranging as Sudan, Chad, Tanzania, Botswana, and Rwanda in Africa, and countries such as Thailand, Bangladesh, Jordan, and Iran in Asia. Although international refugee law clearly provides refugees with socio-economic rights, such rights are generally interpreted as being relative to the overall standard of development enjoyed by citizens within the host country.[18] While international condemnation for violations of the principle of *non-refoulement* (forcibly returning people to countries in which they face persecution) is commonplace, host countries rarely face open criticism, much less any form of diplomatic sanction for restricting the socio-economic rights of refugees.

The right to work for refugees, and the provision of related socio-economic rights have become the exception rather than the rule among refugee-hosting countries across the developing world. Change from the default norm of 'restrictive' socio-economic rights to the alternative (but widely perceived as costly) strategy of 'progressive' socio-economic rights has generally required specific and earmarked incentives, including from external actors, in order to make it worthwhile for host state governments.

The international politics of advancing socio-economic rights for refugees is frequently characterized by deadlock. For donor states, it is often viewed as costly and discretionary to provide additional incentives (such as additional development assistance) for host countries to change practice. For host states, it is often viewed as costly and discretionary to provide the right to work. The result is that neither donors nor host states have an incentive to move beyond minimal levels of assistance and minimal levels of rights. This outcome is bad for refugees because it means that long-term encampment ends up as the default option. The impasse between donors and host countries could be illustrated game theoretically.[19]

Structurally, the way out of this game is for the payoffs for self-reliance in a given host country to change. Within the wider international relations literature, one of the ways in which such impasses can be overcome is through 'issue-linkage', that is, adding extra issues of concern (such as development, migration, or trade) to the negotiation, whether by adding them directly to the bargain (tactical linkage) or through changing the perceived causal relationship between two issues (substantive linkage).[20]

Empirically, donor concern with the onward migration of refuges has become the basis on which this kind of impasse has been overcome in recent years. Most of the major donors supporting development-based approaches to refugee assistance—the EU, Denmark, the Netherlands, and the UK, for example—have long been clear that the payoff to them of funding self-reliance relates to a perceived reduction in onward migration.

For example, a 'Vision' paper by Austria during their term of presidency of the European Union in 2018 claimed: 'Improved access to self-reliance can prevent secondary movements...If we can provide adequate assistance and development opportunities to refugees and their surrounding host communities...there is little reason why refugees need to move onwards to Europe.'[21] Indeed, this logic underlies why funding for development-based approaches to protracted displacement—such as through the 4.6 billion euro EU Emergency Trust Fund for stability and addressing root causes of irregular migration and displacement in Africa (EUTF for Africa)—spiked in the immediate aftermath of the so-called European refugee crisis of 2015.[22]

In the context of both donor concern with onward migration from the host state *and* a belief that self-reliance can causally reduce that onward movement, the negotiation then becomes a coordination game relating to 'price': what is the donor's willingness to pay for self-reliance, what is the host state's willingness to accept development aid, and how effectively can they negotiate? Whether or not a price can be agreed is likely to depend on: 1) how highly the host state perceives the cost of self-reliance; 2) how highly the donor state values the resulting reduction in onward migration; and 3) whether the donor state has alternative options for reducing onward migration (e.g. border closure or collaboration with another country).

Logically, the other mechanisms through which the deadlock game might theoretically be overcome include if either donor states or host states started to: 1) inherently value self-reliance for refugees; 2) believe it to be a strong normative obligation; or 3) perceive self-reliance to be a less costly long-term option than encampment.

This intergovernmental analysis of donor–host relations is consistent with existing literature on refugee politics. A number of authors highlight a key role for issue-linkage in facilitating international cooperation between donor states and host states. Furthermore, in most of that literature, the bargains generally involve donor payoffs relating to migration control, and host-country payoffs in terms of development aid. Emanuela Paoletti, for example, demonstrates the important role that issue-linkage has played in Italy's bilateral relationship with Libya on migration.[23] She shows how migration has been used as a bargaining chip by Libya in order to extract concessions relating to development and trade from Italy and the wider EU. Meanwhile Gerasimos Tsourapas uses the concept of 'refugee rentier states' ('rentier' meaning those who monopolize access to a scarce resource as a means of eliciting other resources) to show how Jordan, Lebanon, and Turkey have extracted development and trade concessions particularly from European donors by appealing to the EU's desire to manage onward migration.[24] Indeed, whether at the bilateral or multilateral levels, North–South cooperation on refugees has historically been made possible by perceived payoffs relating to migration for Northern donor states, and perceived payoffs relating to development for Southern host states.[25]

A three-level bargaining model: global, national, and local

However, a purely intergovernmental perspective over-simplifies the politics that relate to refugees' socio-economic rights. It tends to view the host state as a unitary actor. It risks sidelining the important role that sub-national processes and local governments also plays in shaping refugees' access to the right to work and other related socio-economic rights. Particularly in countries with high levels of decentralization, local or regional authorities may exercise high levels of discretion relating to refugees' socio-economic opportunities. This may enable the border regions that host significant numbers of refugees to be either more or less restrictive of socio-economic rights compared to national legislation. Even when the de jure right to work is entirely determined at a central government level, sub-national authorities may exercise significant influence in shaping the de facto right to work and other related socio-economic entitlements.

Most of the literature on inter-state bargaining on refugee policy tends to only look at the nation-state level, and marginalizes the sub-national level. In contrast, the wider international relations literature recognizes a variety of ways in which sub-national politics influences international bargaining.

Robert Putnam's concept of two-level games recognizes that domestic politics and international relations are often inextricably linked in ways that 'state-centric' theories fail to account for.[26] He shows how the scope for committing to bargains at an intergovernmental level is enabled or constrained by a series of domestic-level bargains. Putnam recognized that 'a more adequate account of the domestic-level determinants of foreign policy and international relations must stress politics: parties, social classes, interest groups, legislators, and even public opinion and electorates'.[27] In response, he created the metaphor of the 'two-level game', disaggregating a bargaining process into two stages: 1) bargaining between negotiators leading to tentative agreement (level 1); and 2) separate discussions within each group about whether to ratify the agreement (level 2).[28] He argued that the size of the 'win-sets' available at level 1 'depends upon the distribution of power, preferences and possible coalitions along level 2 constituents'.

A range of literature has built upon these insights to highlight how behaviour at the international level, including the work of international institutions, is frequently shaped by bargains between the central government and the sub-national level. Andrew Moravcsik's work, for example, emphasizes the intra-state political bargains that underpin the EU as an institution or set of institutions.[29] Eric Schickler's work has shown how the US's role in creating post-Second World War multilateral order rested on domestic political bargains.[30] Steve Krasner reveals that even sovereignty itself—the very basis for justifying a state-centric analytical approach—is determined by authority-affecting bargains that leaders of states are and are not willing to enter into in order to achieve particular domestic political ends.[31]

Likewise, whether a given state commits to provide refugees with socio-economic right, is subject to sub-national politics, not least because refugees' right to work is usually enacted at a local level, even if legislation is passed at a central government level. In low- and middle-income countries, most refugee camps and settlements are geographically located in peripheral border locations. Geography therefore necessitates the involvement of sub-national authorities. Of course, many refugees are located in capital cities, but across developing countries, the majority are in camps, settlements, or secondary cities with parallel governance structures.

Local authorities may view the integration of refugees more or less positively than national authorities. As a result, they may play gatekeeping, veto-playing, or subverting roles for the implementation of national policy preferences. They may seek to establish autonomous relationships with international actors as a means to engage in rent-seeking behaviour, even bypassing the central government. They may adopt their own refugee policy frameworks that are either more progressive or more restrictive than those of the national government. The scope of local authorities' autonomous influence over policies relating to refugees' right to work will depend on a variety of factors such as constitutional arrangements, party political alignments between local and national levels, and levels of devolution, for example. Nevertheless, when it comes to refugee rights, sub-national authorities must be regarded as analytically salient actors.

So, what does this mean in an African context? There is a vast literature within political science identifying some of the key characteristic of 'the African state'.[32] Broadly speaking, that literature distinguishes the African state from other regions of the world on the basis of what sovereignty means within the region. It argues that given the legacies of colonialism, many African states are characterized by strong sources of external sovereignty but weak sources of internal sovereignty. In other words, while they are internationally recognized as legitimate, they face a range of challenges to secure domestic recognition.

For some of the most cited authors on the international relations of Africa, central governments' primary goal is 'regime survival' and the only way to achieve this is by sustaining legitimacy from two sources: external and internal. The challenge for many African states within international relations, Christopher Clapham argues, is to simultaneously secure legitimacy from these two sources.[33] These two levels are linked: external recognition matters for resources, which in turn matter as a means to secure support from peripheral regions of the country through patronage and resource distribution. James Milner has shown how Clapham's approach is useful for understanding the politics of asylum in Africa.[34]

Jean-François Bayart and Stephen Ellis build on the approach to describe many Sub-Saharan African states' external relations being characterized by what they describe as 'extraversion': using external recognition of sovereignty as a means to extract resources through aid and trade from international actors, and then redistributing them through patronage networks in order to sustain internal support.[35] Following Bayart and Ellis, in order to sustain the legitimacy needed for regime survival, African states need to engage in both 'extraversion' and what might be called 'intraversion'. They have to secure resources externally but they have to secure authority internally. Applied to the refugee context, adopting progressive refugee policies is instrumentally useful insofar as it contributes to these goals. It enables the regime to attract international resources from donors, which can in turn be (partly) redistributed to the local level in order to secure sub-national authority. This logic has been the basis for Uganda's refugee policy since independence.

The challenge comes from the fact that local authorities in refugee-hosting areas may have their own strategic priorities. If they have sufficient autonomy, they may adopt strategies that are in contradiction to the central government's goals. For example, if local authorities have more restrictive attitudes towards refugees than the central government, they may seek to *block* implementation of refugees' socio-economic rights (e.g. Ethiopia). If, on the other hand, they have more progressive attitudes towards refugees than the central government, they may seek to *bypass* the central government and collaborate directly with international actors (e.g. Kenya).

Figure 8.1 highlights the three broad sets of actors within our framework: donors, central government, and local government. My argument is that any effective bargain to support the right to work for refugees, and other related socio-economic rights, must meet the interests of all three actors. In each case, the negotiating actors can be considered to be elite groups seeking legitimacy vis-à-vis a given constituency, whether electorates, patronage networks, or a combination. Each actor can be conceptualized as having a specific identity, interests, and available tactics.

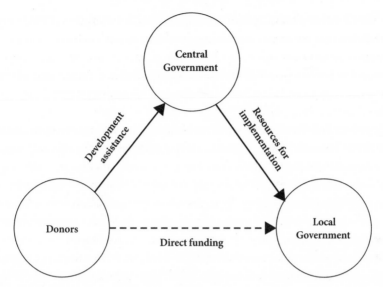

Figure 8.1. Three-level bargaining model: global-, national-, and local-level roles within negotiating the right to work for refugees

First, the *donors* may be bilateral or multilateral aid agencies or government civil servants accountable to elected politicians, who are in turn accountable to an electorate. Donor interests within a refugee policy context may be diverse, and include the goal of ensuring the cost-effective delivery of humanitarian protection, but a key part of it will be to minimize migration externalities, whether by 1) reducing migration or 2) supporting a narrative of migration control, which can offer elected politicians accountability to electorates. Tactically, they can choose how much to fund host governments, whether to place explicit conditions on aid and trade (i.e. 'conditionality'), and whether to work through central governments or directly with local governments.

Second, *central governments* may be elected or unelected politicians at the national level, or the civil servants who represent them. Following the work of Clapham and others, their primary interest might be assumed to be regime survival. Irrespective of whether the state is a substantive democracy or not, maintaining legitimacy requires consent to rule. Central governments will aim to maximize their stay in power. Tactically, refugee policy will be relevant to this goal both because hosting refugees may be perceived as a 'cost' by key constituencies but also because it may provide opportunities for 'extraversion' (accessing resources from donors) and 'intraversion' (distributing resources to improve authority in peripheral regions).

Third, *local governments* may be elected or appointed representatives accountable to local constituencies in refugee-hosting areas. Their interests will be to maximize the economic benefits of refugee presence, including through attracting additional resources, and to minimize any costs associated with presence of refugees, whether relating to identity, security, or the economy. Tactically, local governments may be able to use central governments' desire to attract international resources as a means to extract a share of those resources from the central government. However, depending on the constitutional context, they may also have the option to block central government requests to implement the right to work, or to bypass the central government and collaborate directly with donors.

In order to achieve the effective right to work for refugees, a three-way bargain has to hold across these actors. So, what does an acceptable bargain need to look like in order to achieve the right to work? Most simply, it needs to meet the interests of all three sets of actors. Based on the assumptions above, it seems likely that a bargain will be based on multi-level issue-linkage: on a horizontal level it will involve a bargain that cuts across policy fields, notably migration (the basis for donor interests) and development (the basis for central government and local government interests); on a vertical level, it will need to cut across levels of governance, notably, global, national, and local levels.

At its most crude level, donors have development funds and want cost-efficient humanitarian protection and migration management; local governments want resources and can offer socio-economic inclusion for refugees as a means to cost-effectively deliver humanitarian protection and reduce onward movement; central governments want to stay in power, and can do so by brokering deals across these levels and extracting resources and legitimacy in the process. The strategic interdependence of these goals provides the raw material on which international cooperation is based.

International and regional organizations may have a key role to play in facilitating the emergence of collective action. The UN Refugee Agency (UNHCR), for example, has historically been at its most effective when it has played an active brokerage role in outlining proposals that expand refugee rights while simultaneously meeting the interests of donors, central governments, and local authorities.[36] In the African context, the African Union (AU)[37] and sub-regional organizations such as the Intergovernmental

Authority on Development (IGAD) within the Horn of Africa have some-times also played an important facilitative role in relation to international cooperation on forced displacement. For example, IGAD's 2019 Kampala Declaration on Jobs, Livelihoods, and Self-Reliance for Refugees, Returnees, and Host Communities mediated between the objectives of the UN Global Compact on Refugees and regionally specific priorities and interests.[38]

From the three-level bargaining model follows a series a testable predictions or hypotheses about the structural conditions under which one would expect to observe the right to work for refugees. First, it would be more likely with higher levels of onward refugee migration from the host country to donor countries (*migration*). This is because higher levels of migration would increase the interest of donors and hence the funding they are willing to provide, and the bargaining power of the central government vis-à-vis donors. Second, it would be more likely in the context of higher levels of decentralization in peripheral regions (*decentralization*). This is because greater local-level autonomy is likely to increase the autonomy and bargaining power of local governments vis-à-vis both the central government and donors. Third, it will be more likely in semi-authoritarian regimes (*regime type*). This is because the political costs of creating legislation on the right to work are likely to be lower at central government level with lower levels of electoral accountability. Fourth, it is more likely in contexts in which host communities have shared identities with the refugee population in peripheral regions (*identity*). This is because a perceived common identity is likely to be associated with lower political costs of socio-economic integration. Fifth, it will be more likely in countries with higher levels of corruption (*corruption*). This is because corruption will increase private incentives for rent-seeking at each level. Finally, it also seems likely that signing and ratifying relevant international instruments such as the 1951 Convention on the Status of Refugees will play a role, even though this is not captured within the framework (*law*).

Governments around the world that are well-known for giving large numbers of refugees the right to work, such as Turkey and Colombia, generally have at least several of these characteristics. Furthermore, each of these characteristics can be quantitatively measured. In our preliminary quantitative analysis, Olivier Sterck and I have built a global dataset to explain variation in the de facto and de jure right to work.[39] We invited relevant refugee organizations to code (i.e. assign a score to) the de jure and de facto right to work in the countries in which they have operations, and combined with proxy measures for all of the aforementioned variables as well as other relevant controls such as gross domestic product (GDP)/capita and the total number of refugees. We found evidence that both are positively correlated with being a signatory of the 1951 Convention. But we also find that the de facto right to work is strongly positively correlated with decentralization, adding weight to the suggestion that local government has a particularly important role to play in shaping the de facto right to work for refugees. The dataset, however, is global and includes many high-income countries with relatively few refugees. In order to understand the politics that underpins the right to work in major refugee-hosting countries such as Uganda, Kenya, and Ethiopia, we therefore need to engage in in-depth qualitative research.

Application to East Africa

We focus on three countries in East Africa: Uganda, Kenya, and Ethiopia. Between them, they host more refugees than the whole of Europe and North America combined. They have all gone some way towards providing the right to work to refugees, but with some significant variation.

Uganda has a long-standing commitment to the right to work, which moved from a de facto to a de jure right in 2006. Ethiopia changed its legislation from denying refugees the right to work to offering the right to work in 2019, but at the time of writing that right had not been implemented in practice. Kenya denies refugees the right to work in law, but is gradually moving towards increasing refugees' socio-economic rights in practice in one part of the country—Turkana County. All of these cases deviate from the general practice of almost entirely denying refugees the right to work across most other host countries in East Africa, such as Tanzania and Malawi.

Table 8.1 summarizes the basic findings of my research across the case studies, albeit in simplified form. Uganda has the de jure and de facto right to work. Ethiopia offers the de jure right to work but not the de facto right to work. Kenya has the de facto right to work in part of the country but not the de jure right to work. And Tanzania, for example, has neither the de jure nor the de facto right to work. Based on my empirical research, two conditions seem to explain this variation: 1) a payoff for the central government; 2) a payoff for the local government in refugee-hosting regions. Where both conditions are present (Uganda), the de jure and de facto right to work exists.

Table 8.1. Variation in the right to work for refugees in East Africa

		National Government Payoff	
		Yes	No
Local Government Payoff	Yes	De jure and de facto e.g. Uganda	De facto but not de jure e.g. Kenya
	No	De jure but not de facto e.g. Ethiopia	Neither de jure nor de facto e.g. Tanzania

Where there is a national payoff but no local payoff (Ethiopia), there is the de jure but not de facto right to work. Where there is a local but not a national payoff (Kenya), the de facto right to work exists but there is no de jure right. It is this lop-sided development of socio-economic rights which makes Ethiopia and Kenya such fascinating case studies.

By payoff I mean a direct and earmarked material benefit for either the central or local government. Do they receive a financial transfer which is explicitly dependent upon implementation of the right to work for refugees, which is at a level that is perceived as sufficient for them to provide the right to work to refugees? In Ethiopia, for example, the central government received around $600 million to support its Jobs Compact, part of which required legislative change at the national level. In Kenya, a budget of around $500 million was set out to support the development of the sub-county of Turkana West, between 2018 and 2023, in exchange for a commitment to socio-economically integrate refugees. In Uganda, both the national and local governments in West Nile and the south-west have consistently received payoffs in terms of additional development assistance virtually since independence. These payoffs matter to policy-makers for three potential reasons: they can offer greater opportunities to host-country citizens, can enable government ministers to claim 'success stories' that advance their careers, and can sometimes facilitate patronage and corruption.

Of course, other factors also matter—several of which we have touched upon. And the purpose is not to suggest that only interest-based and material factors matter. Values can and do sometimes play a role, in Africa as in other regions of the world. Across Africa ideas such as *ubuntu* and pan-African solidarity have been frequently invoked to explain hospitality towards refugees.[40] However, elite interests are also a significant part of the story, and the purpose of this framework is to provide a simplified heuristic summary of our main empirical findings. The implication is that the right to work for refugees depends upon ensuring an adequate material payoff to both the central government and the local government within refugee-hosting regions. One without the other will only lead to the partial and lop-sided development of refugees' socio-economic rights. Meanwhile, the absence of material incentives will likely lead to ongoing encampment and the denial of the right to work. To elaborate, I will turn to the case studies.

Uganda has provided the de facto right to work to refugees since before independence in 1962. It committed in principle to develop legislation including this right from the 1970s and finally consolidated the right to work in law in 2008. One reason for Uganda's long-standing support for the socio-economic inclusion of refugees is that it has been relatively low-cost. Its main refugee-hosting regions have had significant amounts of surplus and fairly arable land, and shared a common identity with people crossing from neighbouring countries. Uganda has therefore been able to seek international recognition and reward for something relatively straightforward. There has nevertheless been a political logic underpinning how Uganda has used refu-gee policy as a source of legitimacy and resource extraction. And a striking feature of Uganda's 'progressive' self-reliance model has been that it has consistently been supported by political leaders with illiberal motives.

International donors have been willing to fund and reward Uganda for its tolerant approach to refugees since the 1960s, when the country was already by far the largest recipient of humanitarian and development aid for refugees in Africa. Initially, this international support was linked to Uganda's wider geo-strategic importance during the Cold War. However, by the 1990s, two other motives took centre-stage: managing the onward movement of migration, and seeking more cost-effective approaches to humanitarian protection. These new motives meant even more resources and attention were available to Uganda in exchange for institutionalizing its long-standing approach to refugee self-reliance.

Through successive regimes, the central government has used refugees as an opportunity to extract resources from international donors. International attention has been useful as a source of external legitimacy for consecutive regimes with questionable democratic credentials. While Idi Amin's refugee policies are perhaps best known for his expulsion of the Ugandan Asians, for example, he courted international praise for his creation of new, integrated refugee settlements. Donor funding has also been important as a means to ensure internal authority through the redistribution of resources to peripheral, refugee-hosting regions of the country. This redistribution has been especially important because of the south-west and West Nile regions' strategic importance to successive central governments. Idi Amin and Yoweri Museveni, for example, both lacked support in central Buganda (the historically richest and most powerful sub-kingdom of contemporary Uganda), and so relied heavily upon support from the mainly Rwandan-hosting south-west and the South Sudanese-hosting West Nile region.

During the period when Milton Obote was first prime minister and then president (1962–71), Uganda used the presence of refugees as a means to gain greater development assistance. By the mid-1960s, Uganda hosted nearly a quarter of Africa's refugees but received half of UNHCR's Africa programme budget. As early as 1964, the foreign minister was already being invited to Geneva to speak to the UNHCR Executive Committee about the country's 'self-supporting' approach to refugees, and being used by UNHCR to demonstrate the potential of a development-based approach to refugee assistance.

Idi Amin's (1971–9) regime depended upon the presence of refugees. Lacking support within Buganda and mistrustful of Ugandan elites, he relied upon Rwandans and southern Sudanese exiles as the basis for his military and senior civil service recruitment. It was in fact Amin who was the architect of many of Uganda's now-celebrated refugee settlements, and he did so both because they offered opportunities to nurture loyalty and recruitment and also because he received high international praise—and money—from UNHCR and others for doing so.

Under Obote's second regime (1980–5) he attempted to reassert control within both the south-west and West Nile regions, purging them of Amin loyalists. This desire for control shaped his contribution to the humanitarian infrastructure in those regions. He suspended Amin's tolerance of urban refugees in Kampala and across Uganda's secondary cities like Mbarara and Fort Portal, and redesigned the settlements as spaces of control and surveillance.

When Museveni came to power (1986–), much of his support base mirrored that of Amin. While Amin was a Kakwa with strong links to West Nile, Museveni had a Banyankole background with strong links to the south-west. Amin had worked hard to build his support base in the south-west, and Museveni worked hard to build his support base in West Nile. Both depended upon sustaining the backing of the south-west and West Nile because of their lack of authority in Buganda. If he could not sustain support in West Nile, Museveni's ability to rule would be compromised. For Museveni, the presence of refugees in those regions has offered a means to extract donor funding and redistribute resources to those regions, in a way that has buttressed his authority, and underpinned the patronage networks of key members of his cabinet and military, such as the influential Moses Ali. As international interest in the 'Ugandan model' has grown, Museveni has skilfully packaged and repackaged the country's pre-existing refugee policies for new audiences. From the Self-Reliance Strategy (SRS) of 1996 to 2003, to the Refugee and Host Population Empowerment Strategic Framework (ReHoPE) of 2016 to 2018, to the Comprehensive Refugee Response Framework (CRRF) of 2018 onwards, the international community has been consistently waiting with a new acronym and new sources of funding to support an old model. A key strategic challenge for the central government has been to ensure that it remains the intermediary between the donors and local-level government, through its central 'refugee offices' (usually housed within the Office of the Prime Minister) and that 'direct budget support' is not bypassed by direct international funding for local government.

In Ethiopia, the government had a long-standing encampment policy, with clear restrictions on refugees' right to work and freedom of movement. In 2016, it announced plans to transition to the right to work, and in 2019, its parliament passed a new Refugee Proclamation, ostensibly giving refugees the right to work and other socio-economic rights. Why did this change happen? Ethiopia's volte-face on refugee policy can be explained almost entirely by international conditionality. As part of a deal known as 'the Jobs Compact', the government of Hailemariam Desalegn was offered around $600 million by the UK's Department for International Development (DFID), and the World Bank in the context of the European refugee crisis in order to create 30,000 jobs for refugees within its industrial parks. As part of the deal, Ethiopia committed to change its legislation to let refugees work.

However, it is clear that despite the de jure right to work, there is no immediate prospect of its large-scale implementation in Ethiopia. The Proclamation was widely understood by the government as offering the right to work, incrementally and proportionately to the level of international support for Ethiopia's own national development and industrialization strategy. If the international donor community is willing to support job creation for Ethiopians, the reasoning went, then the government would also allow jobs to be created for refugees. However, even this deal has faced push-back at the local level. For example, in Gambella, with the largest number of South Sudanese refugees, there were strong local protests immediately after the passage of the Proclamation, with local people and the regional government feeling that they were not consulted on a deal brokered in Addis. Even in the Somali region, which generally welcomes Somali refugees, legislative change in Addis was greeted with indifference, amid tension between the central and regional governments.

When Prime Minister Abiy Ahmed came to power in 2018, he was elected on a platform of greater national inclusion than his predecessor's close alignment with the elite in Addis, Oromia, and Tigray. This influenced his approach to the Jobs Compact. For example, reflecting the need to be more even-handed, he changed the sites for the three new industrial parks to be financed by the deal. His alternative selection of the industrial park sites was partly intended to 'buy-off' priority regions in which Abiy needed greater support and credibility. But with that change in approach to ethnic federalism, the government also lost momentum on implementing the right to work for refugees at a sub-national level. Put simply, while Ethiopia's central government sold the de jure right to work to the international community, the lack of buy-in at the local level meant there was little prospect of its wider implementation. Interestingly, by 2020, neither the donor countries' money nor the 30,000 jobs had been delivered, but the new legislation nevertheless sat on the statute books.

In Kenya, the central government has adopted a strict encampment policy for refugees since the early 1990s, denying them the right to work and freedom of movement. It institutionalized this practice within its 2006 Refugee Act. However, since 2014, one particular refugee-hosting region, Turkana County, has adopted a different approach. Despite the legal restriction in the right to work, the practice has started to change from the local level. In that sense, the story is virtually the opposite of Ethiopia; it is one of local change despite impasse at the national level.

Devolution in 2012 gave Kenya's counties greater authority over socio-economic aspects of refugee integration. When Josphat Nanok was elected as governor of Turkana County in 2013, he recognized the opportunity to use those powers. He had spent much of his career as a humanitarian, including working for the World Food Programme (WFP). He recognized the devastating effect on the county's economy when, following peace in South Sudan in 2005, refugees and humanitarian organizations started to leave. In a county in which local Turkana relied on humanitarian agencies for employment and cash flow, he witnessed first-hand how hard-hit Lokichoggio was when WFP finally closed its doors in 2011. He decided instead to make the most of the presence of refugees and agencies in the Kakuma refugee camps as an opportunity for the county's development, and as a vehicle for his own political ambitions.

In November 2014, the governor, UNHCR, and the World Bank convened a roundtable in the county capital, Lodwar. UNHCR needed more land to expand Kakuma but was also keen to avoid creating another camp. Meanwhile, the governor was keen to maximize the return to the county and its citizens in terms of development assistance. After a series of discussions, they committed in 2015 to build the country's first integrated settlement for both refugees and the host community, the Kalobeyei settlement, within which refugees and hosts would share access to services and markets, and refugees could have opportunities for self-reliance. Amid the onset of the European refugee crisis, the EU committed to be the lead funder for the Kalobeyei project through the EUTF for Africa, established primarily to manage irregular migration from Africa. A fifteen-year strategy was created for Kalobeyei called the Kalobeyei Integrated Socio-Economic Development Plan (KISEDP).

The Kalobeyei settlement was opened in 2016. However, by 2018, it was clear that few host-community members were relocating to the new settlement. Reflecting this, the KISEDP was broadened in scope and purpose. Instead of just focusing on the settlement, it was repurposed as a development plan for the entire sub-county of Turkana West, with the aim of directly benefitting refugees and the host community, while supporting their gradual social integration. The KISEDP's first five-year period outlined a proposed budget of $500 million. Over time, the European donor priority has shifted from onward migration to prototyping a more cost-effective model of humanitarian protection. As trust has been built the county has gradually allowed greater socio-economic rights to refugees, such as informally granting refugee entrepreneurs multi-year movement passes to engage in business activities across the county.

Nevertheless, the Turkana County experience has so far had only limited influence at the central government level. Refugee politics in Nairobi are dominated by security concerns and the primary focus is on Kenya's other refugee-hosting region Garissa County, home of the infamous Dadaab camps. In 2019 the government put a new Refugee Bill to parliament, and its focus was primarily on security, with no sign of a change towards providing the right to work or other socio-economic rights at the national level.

Conclusion

In this chapter, I have outlined a simplified heuristic framework for explaining variation in the right to work for refugees in Africa. It is based on in-depth inductive analysis of the three main countries to allow refugees the right to work in East Africa. In that sense, the purpose of the chapter is mainly theory building rather than theory testing. Nevertheless, it offers a means to organize and simplify the more granular comparative analysis that follows.

Uganda has a long history of providing refugee self-reliance, and in unpacking its political history, we reveal that its 'progressive' model has not always been the product of liberal politics. But crucially, it has been underpinned by interdependence between donors, central government, and local government. Meanwhile, Ethiopia and Kenya provide more contemporary stories about the bargains required to create the right to work. In each case, the picture is incomplete without reference to a three-level bargaining model. In Ethiopia, there has been central government buy-in but not local government buy-in, leading to the de jure but not de facto right to work. In Kenya, there has been local government buy-in but not central government buy-in, leading towards the de facto but not the de jure right to work.

The implication is that context matters: a deep understanding of the history and politics of each country is needed in order to understand the politics of refugee rights. Nevertheless, patterns can be derived from comparative analysis. First, the creation of the right to work and regulatory conditions for self-reliance have historically been characterized by deadlock. Second, overcoming the impasse has relied upon interest convergence based on a three-level bargain between donors, central governments, and local governments in refugee-hosting regions. Third, the central and local governments play complementary but different roles in the right to work: central governments usually provide the de jure right to work and local governments the de facto right to work; payoffs are needed at both levels in order to bring substantive and sustainable change in policy and practice.

The explanation I have offered is an interest-based account; not because ideas and values are entirely irrelevant but because material interests make up the bulk of the explanation. One of the most disquieting aspects of the politics and international relations of refugee inclusion is how shaped it is by hard political interests. Refugees are instrumentalized by elites all the way down—from donors, to national governments, to local governments. But recognizing the realpolitik that underlies refugee politics is ultimately crucial if those interests are to be channelled into better outcomes. Over the long run, values may emerge that enable politicians to appreciate refugees' socio-economic rights for their own sake. Stronger norms may emerge that ensure socio-economic rights are understood as an obligation. However, it is primarily interests and power that dominate refugee politics. And if we are to hope for progressive change, those interests, and the conditions under which they converge, need to be understood by academics, policy-makers, and practitioners.

Troubling though this observation may be, and as open as it is to moral hazard, it can also be a source of optimism. We know three things. First, refugees' welfare is shaped by their right to work and other related socio-economic rights. Second, the right to work and socio-economic rights effectively can be bought by the international community. Third, there are strong—and arguably growing—incentives for international donors to finance the creation of those rights and opportunities, albeit related to the perceived causes of onward migration and the creation of more cost-effective models of humanitarian protection. It is for this combination of reasons, and the new opportunities for interest-convergence that they produce, that there has been a gradual rise in host countries' willingness to provide the right to work and self-reliance opportunities for refugees, even in countries like Kenya and Ethiopia, long associated with strict encampment models.

9

Uganda

A political history of refugee self-reliance

Introduction

In 2016, the BBC proclaimed 'Uganda is one of the best places to be a refugee.' In the same year, both United Nations Development Programme (UNDP) and the World Bank published reports describing Uganda's refugee policy as 'progressive'. Indeed, in the immediate aftermath of the so-called European refugee crisis of 2015–16, Uganda received widespread praise as a 'model' refugee host. In contrast to most refugee-hosting countries around the world, it provides refugees with the right to work and significant freedom of movement. It has incorporated these rights within its national legislation, and its rural settlements provide refugees with plots of land to cultivate. By promoting 'self-reliance' for refugees it has been a pioneer in advocating for the socio-economic inclusion of refugees. Many of these policies have been sustained despite Uganda hosting more refugees than any other African country since 2016. And research suggests that many of these policies do make a difference to welfare outcomes for refugees, compared to the encampment policies of neighbouring states.[1]

However, this leads to a hitherto largely unanswered research question: why has Uganda adopted such apparently progressive policies? What, politically, explains the commitment and willingness of the government to provide socio-economic rights to refugees, when so few other host countries in Africa do so? In order to answer this question, this chapter outlines a political history of Uganda's self-reliance model for refugees, examining and explaining continuity and change within the approach from Ugandan independence in 1962 until the present day. The question matters both because it may offer insight into the replicability of the model at a time when the Ugandan approach has become a template for global refugee policy, and because historicizing the politics behind the model offers an opportunity to critically interrogate ahistorical assumptions about the 'progressive' provenance of the policy framework.

There is a significant literature on Ugandan refugee policy, and indeed on the self-reliance model. In particular, numerous authors have called into question whether Uganda's self-reliance model is as successful in promoting positive welfare outcomes for refugees as is often implied by the international community.[2] However, much of this work is mainly contemporary in focus. Meanwhile, although a number of historical works on Uganda touch on refugee policy, few make it their central focus.[3] Consequently, there is gap in the literature in terms of a political history of Ugandan refugee policy, and in particular an account of the evolution and provenance of Uganda's self-reliance model.

In order to address this gap, this chapter draws upon a combination of archival research and semi-structured interviews to provide an episodic history of Uganda's self-reliance policy. The research is based on document analysis of the UN Refugee Agency (UNHCR) archives relating to Uganda between independence in 1962 and 1994, from when UNHCR operates a twenty-five year cut-off. Beyond, 1994, the chapter draws upon informally sourced documents relating to the late 1990s and early 2000s, and interviews with key stakeholder informants involved in particular contemporary and historical periods of Ugandan refugee policy development. Interviews were mainly conducted in Kampala in February 2019, and archival research was mainly undertaken in Geneva in March 2019.

The chapter argues that Uganda's self-reliance policy towards refugees is not a recent creation and has a long history. Discussions that were taking place even in the 1960s were almost identical to discussions that are happening six decades later. Furthermore, many of the key 'progressive' developments have illiberal political origins. For example, the British Empire and Idi Amin played key and neglected roles in the historical development of the Ugandan self-reliance model. Ironically, some of the most apparently 'liberal' policy moves have their origins in the most illiberal leadership and motives. Identifying this matters for historical and political interpretation and also for policy-makers seeking to engage with the Ugandan state on refugee policy.

A common argument in the literature on refugee politics is that semi-authoritarian regimes frequently use refugee and migration policies to extract 'rents' from an international community with either migration or security interests in the region.[4] It is, in other words, a form of what Bayart and Ellis call 'extraversion', whereby states with weak internal legitimacy often depend disproportionately upon external legitimacy and resources.[5] In the Ugandan case, this is part of the story. But an additional and neglected dimension relates to the centrality of sub-national politics, and the important role that refugee policy has played in shaping core–periphery relationships between Kampala and the main refugee-hosting regions.

Specifically, refugee policy in Uganda has served as a means for successive presidents—Obote, Amin, and Museveni—to channel resources into the strategically important hinterlands of West Nile and the south-west, and thereby preserve key patronage networks and sources of authority.[6]

Post-independence: the origins of self-reliance

Remarkably, some aspects of Uganda's current self-reliance model are sixty years old. At independence in 1962, Uganda retained its colonial refugee legislation in the form of the 1960 Uganda Control of Alien Refugees Act, as well as the protectorate's embryonic settlement model. The Nakivale settlement, now Africa's oldest refugee camp and an exemplar of the country's rural settlement model, had already opened in 1958, providing access to plots of arable land to Rwandan Tutsis fleeing conflict and persecution. By retaining a model of tolerance towards self-settled rural refugees, the government inherited the basis of what is today recognized as the country's self-reliance model.

During the 1960s, refugee numbers grew rapidly. Amid colonial liberation wars in Sudan, Congo, and Rwanda, Uganda found itself in a challenging neighbourhood. By 1967, Uganda hosted over 160,000 refugees, nearly a quarter of Africa's total refugee population,[7] and the country accounted for about half of UNHCR's $5 million Africa programme budget.[8] The government nevertheless viewed the presence of refugees as an opportunity.

Uganda's model was celebrated by UNHCR as an exemplar of a development-based approach to refugees, in very similar language to that used six decades later. For example, at UNHCR's 1964 Executive Committee meeting, it convened a 'Discussion of UNHCR's Role in Economic and Social Development Projects'. The meeting 'discussed at length the extent to which UNHCR should participate in...development projects of benefit to refugees and the local population, particularly in Africa', and ways in which UNHCR could collaborate with other UN agencies 'to raise the economic level of these regions for the benefit of refugees and the local population alike'.[9] Uganda's foreign minister was present, and the country was identified as an important illustration of this development-based approach. The meeting showcased projects 'aimed at making the [southern Sudanese] refugees [in West Nile] self-supporting' through the provision of seeds and tools.[10]

By 1968, UNHCR openly praised Uganda for its 'very progressive' approach to allowing refugees to work and move beyond the settlements. Following a meeting between UNHCR and the Ugandan delegation to Geneva, UNHCR noted that, despite restrictions, Uganda was tolerant of 'free-livers', including those living and working in cities:

> [The Ugandan foreign minister]...pointed out that even in the case of refugees who were found to have left the settlement penalties provided by the law were not enforced. Of the 'free-livers' he said quite a large number were working in the Medical Department and some others had found employment as teachers...No permits were required...and refugees were free to obtain employment wherever available. This is indeed a very progressive attitude.[11]

Uganda was increasingly rewarded for this approach, just as it has been ever since. In 1967, it was made only the sixth African state member of UNHCR's Executive Committee.[12] In 1969, UNHCR opened a branch office in Uganda.[13] Uganda was already the highest African recipient of UNHCR coordinated refugee assistance. And throughout the decade, UNHCR increasingly sought development assistance through UNDP in order to support and 'compensate' Uganda for the 'burden' of hosting large numbers of refugees.[14]

The international community's motivation for adopting a development-based approach was not entirely altruistic. Faced with a growing Africa Programme budget that was only 60 per cent funded and had doubled to $10 million between 1967 and 1968, the high commissioner for refugees noted in his address to UNDP:

> Our aim has always been that once refugees have reached the stage of being self-supporting, the settlements which we have helped to establish should be incorporated in a regional development plan carried out under the aegis of the United Nations Development Programme or some other instance concerned with development per se...It is the logical means of ensuring that

refugee programmes go beyond the stage of being alien islands of population and achieve true integration within the scope of plans geared to the well-being of an entire area to the benefit of all its residents. Such a handover is in keeping with the catalytic role of my office.

From a Ugandan Government perspective, the presence of refugees created few costs. Nakivale and Kyangwali in the south-west, opened in 1967, were in sparsely populated areas with an abundance of arable land. Meanwhile, in both West Nile and the south-west, there were strong ethnic similarities between hosts and refugees. Although the government still discussed repatriation as an option, there was an acceptance that local integration was a viable long-term solution. The Ministry of Culture and Community Development (MCCD) was given responsibility for both the refugee portfolio and local development. In 1969, its assistant director for refugees, acknowledged the openness to permanent local integration: 'When they get here they find the life so comfortable that few of them ever dream of going back.'[15]

And promoting the 'self-supporting' agenda conferred two benefits upon the newly independent government. First, it brought development aid to the country in ways that could enhance the Obote Government's legitimacy. Second, this played into a nation-building agenda by bringing resources to peripheral regions of the country. As Obote and his successors would discover, ruling Uganda effectively relied upon maintaining the backing of both the Buganda elite, so strongly privileged by the British, and the tribes in Uganda's other regions. It mattered particularly to Milton Obote, first as prime minister until 1965 and then as president, to channel resources to his political party, the Uganda People's Congress (UPC)'s northern support base. Given its geographical distribution, the refugee portfolio played well within this delicate federal patronage structure, offering opportunities for aid to be channelled through the central government to the north and the south-west.

Idi Amin (1971–9): refugees as allies for political survival

One of the most striking, original insights from my archival research is that key aspects of Uganda's ostensibly 'liberal' self-reliance model were actually created under Idi Amin's tyrannical regime of the 1970s. Amin is generally associated with oppressive refugee policies; he made initial threats to expel all refugees from the country and is well-known for his persecution and expulsion of the Ugandan Asians. However, his refugee policies were more nuanced and ambiguous than the Ugandan Asian story implies.

Amin viewed refugees as an opportunity to strengthen his regime. He sought to control and manage the refugee populations, and he recruited large numbers of soldiers, including at senior rank, from the Sudanese, Rwandan, and Congolese communities. He even created some of the settlements that endure today in West Nile and the south-west, and established a strong working relationship with UNHCR, receiving acclaim for signing the Refugee Convention in 1976. But his ongoing legacy was the politicization of refugees within the country's delicate core–periphery politics.

In January 1971, Amin had been head of the army under Obote. When his president travelled to Singapore for a Commonwealth conference, Amin seized power.[16] Amin purged the Obote-loyalist Lango and Acholi from the army, including through a series of massacres. He recruited people from his own Kakwa tribe to put in their place, and also a significant number of Sudanese, and later Rwandans and Congolese. His recruitment of soldiers from neighbouring countries enabled him to survive several attempted coups, and also shaped his policies towards refugees in Uganda. Put simply, supporting refugees from neighbouring countries was a key part of his strategy for retaining power.

Early in his rule, Amin appeared intolerant of refugees. Early speeches suggested he would expel them all. At a ceremony at which his powerful southern Sudanese ally Moses Ali was sworn in as a minister, Amin suggested he would launch an operation to 'see that all refugees in Uganda go back to their countries as soon as possible and their camps are used by Ugandans who have no homes and those now roaming about in towns without jobs'.[17] Meanwhile, his minister of foreign affairs would occasionally seek to 'clarify' such remarks in order to reassure the international community. In one correspondence with the secretary-general of the OAU, he wrote:

> The policy of the Ugandan Government of providing refuge for people who have been displaced by social upheavals in countries neighbouring to Uganda and elsewhere, has not changed at all. Remarks that my President, General Idi Amin Dada, has made in the recent past relating to this matter have been misrepresented, distorted, and misunderstood.[18]

Certainly, between 1971 and 1975, there were few signs of anything liberal in Amin's refugee policies. He worked collaboratively with the governments of Rwanda and Sudan to encourage refugee repatriation, in order to support his regional allies, President Kayabanda of Rwanda and President Nimeiry of Sudan.[19] Then, most infamously, Amin began to persecute and expel Ugandan Asians from 1975.[20]

However, from 1976, there was a notable—and historically forgotten—shift in Amin's refugee policies, and a striking embrace of what has subsequently become the 'self-reliance model'. With rumbling rebellion and mutiny by predominantly Christian Acholi and Lango, agitating for a return to power of Obote,[21] Amin came to rely increasingly upon Sudanese and Rwandan soldiers to ensure loyalty and professionalism. And he further recognized that working collaboratively with UNHCR could bring much-needed legitimacy and resources, both of which had been dwindling amid criticism of the regime's abusive treatment of Ugandan Asians.

In June 1976, Amin oversaw Uganda's accession to the 1951 Refugee Convention, and created the Determination of Refugee Status Committee. A year later, at a meeting at Cape Town View between Amin and the UNHCR representative to Uganda, UNHCR praised Amin's refugee policies. The *Voice of Uganda* newspaper photographed the representative shaking hands with Amin, and reported that '[The UNHCR representative] said Uganda's contributions to refugee settlement is more than all the African countries put together. He thanked the Ugandan Government under Life President Idi Amin for the most generous contributions not only to refugees there but to those of the other parts of the world.'[22] UNHCR took the opportunity to request that Amin abolish the colonial Refugee Act because of the formal restrictions it placed on free movement.[23]

UNHCR's relationship with Amin was collaborative and pragmatic. In March 1978, for example, UNHCR's representative met with the head of refugees affairs in Kampala, and described Uganda's refugee policy as undergoing 'a phase of consolidation'.[24] In 1979 UNHCR noted that the Amin government had committed to work on a new Refugee Act as requested, and that the right to work and freedom of movement were largely being provided to refugees:

> Refugees do not need work permits except when they are going to work for the Government...Although movement of refugees is restricted by the present Alien Refugee Control Act, in actual fact refugees are free to move in and out of the Settlements. If the journey exceeds a certain period of time and/or distance, permits are issued by the Settlement Commandant.[25]

By that stage, Uganda hosted 130,000 refugees from Rwanda, Sudan, and Zaire. Amin's government worked closely with UNHCR to create and consolidate the rural settlement model on which much of Uganda's contemporary settlement model is based. Settlements established in the 1960s were upgraded with new facilities, and new areas were 'gazetted' as settlements, allowing refugees to live there. UNHCR worked collaboratively with Amin's government to fund infrastructure and services in the settlements, particularly in the south-west of the country,[26] which hosted Rwandan refugees, and to provide basic assistance to southern Sudanese refugees in the then conflict-affected West Nile region. He built new settlements for Zaireans in Ibuga in the west and for Sudanese in Karamoja in the east.

Amin's support for refugees, and his expansion of the settlement model, was not motivated by regard for refugees' welfare per se, but by politics. With very little support from Ugandans in Kampala, he relied upon Rwandans, Sudanese, and Congolese—including refugees—as the basis of his army and his government.

For example, in the south-west, home to several of the settlements that endure today, he benefitted from the backing of both Rwandans and local Banyarwanda, as a means to balance against opposition tribes at the national level. Amin filled his cabinet and military leadership with Banyarwanda.[27] The Banyarwanda within Amin's regime were especially keen to ensure resources flowed into their constituencies, and backing for refugee-hosting areas offered a means to achieve that. Amin encouraged the flow of UNHCR resources to the Rwandan settlements, and allowed Rwandans to live freely in the cities.

His support also related to regional geopolitics. He opposed President Habyarimana's mainly Hutu, post-1973 regime in Rwanda, and viewed support for Rwandan Tutsis in exile as a means to destabilize Rwanda. Meanwhile, he saw his support for Sudanese refugees as a key part of his amicable relationship with Sudanese President Nimeiry, and their joint commitment to fight the destabilizing influence of rebel groups operating on both sides of the Sudan–Uganda border.

The key takeaway from this period is that many of the foundations of Uganda's self-reliance model, far from being recent or liberal creations, were developed under Idi Amin. While refugee policy during the Amin era is inevitably associated with the expulsion of the Ugandan Asians, his reliance upon support in his West Nile heartland, his alliance with Banyarwanda leaders, and his inclusion of significant numbers of Rwandan and Sudanese refugees in the army contributed towards the increasing socio-economic integration of refugees, particularly during the latter period of his rule.

Milton Obote II (1980–5): the settlements as population control

Milton Obote's second period as president was practically the inverse of Amin's insofar as most of Amin's allies were Obote's enemies, and vice versa. And this had significant implications for refugees. However, in common with the Amin era, Obote's regime saw a strengthening of the now-famous Ugandan settlement model. But, far from being a means to enhance the autonomy of refugees, it was used by Obote as a method of population control.

The Uganda–Tanzania War of 1979, in which Obote's Uganda National Liberation Army (UNLA) seized power with Tanzanian support, had long-term implications for refugees and refugee policy. First, it triggered the so-called Ugandan Bush War, in which Amin loyalists in West Nile fought the government and its allies, leading to large-scale internal displacement, and the flight of Ugandan refugees into Sudan. Second, Obote's arrival led to an immediate backlash against both Sudanese in West Nile and Rwandans in the south-west, partly as retribution for their association with the Amin regime. As I will explain, both the new displacement and the backlash mattered because they would reinforce the political importance of refugee policy in the south-west and West Nile once Museveni came to power in the mid-1980s.

In late 1980, revenge killings were carried out in West Nile by Acholi soldiers of the UNLA. The attacks were in retribution for the killing of thousands of Acholi under Amin. In November, the *Guardian* reported 'barely a living person in sight in central and north-west Nile provinces, heaps of rotting bodies…clouds of vultures visible from miles away, and every building from houses to cathedrals burned down'.[28] *The Times* reported 'tribal vengeance carried out by the Ugandan Army and Tanzanian troops after a recent incursion from Sudan by forces loyal to former President Idi Amin…The soldiers had murdered and plundered the West Nile district and had systematically destroyed Arua, the region's capital.'[29]

As a result of the West Nile massacres, hundreds of thousands of Ugandan refugees fled to makeshift camps in southern Sudan or were left internally displaced across West Nile, where they faced food shortages and violence.[30] With government roadblocks, it took time to establish a humanitarian operation across the region. Conflict left widespread damage to buildings, property, and livestock, while farming opportunities were devastated. And there was little government capacity left across the main districts of West Nile.[31]

To compound this, civil war broke out in southern Sudan in 1983, and both Ugandan returnees and Sudanese refugees entered West Nile in need of assistance. The experience of West Nilers seeking sanctuary in Sudan had nurtured solidarity between them and their southern Sudanese hosts, which endured when both groups began to cross back into West Nile. From that point onwards, West Nile would remain an important host to southern Sudanese refugees, and would retain political and strategic importance to Kampala.

Meanwhile, in the south-west, transition to Obote brought a violent backlash in both the cities and the settlements.[32] Tanzanian invasion from the south had already affected the settlements. Refugees were evacuated from the Nakivale and Oruchinga settlements to other nearby settlements.[33] UNHCR noted that '[the] two refugee settlements…were on the verge of complete self-sufficiency…[but] most of the infrastructure that had been built up over the years of integration efforts was destroyed in revengeful action by the invading army.'[34]

Across the south-west, Rwandans were viewed as Amin loyalists, and self-reliance was called into question. UNHCR's representative noted in May 1979 that 'In many parts of the country, xenophobic sentiments are mounting and are taking unfortunate expressions.' In his note to UNHCR headquarters he attached press clippings which claimed 'that Rwandese refugees in Uganda had reached a standard equal or higher than the citizens themselves and that no more help was necessary'.[35]

The backlash was exacerbated by the falling-out between Obote's UNLA and Museveni's National Resistance Army (NRA), who had fought alongside one another to overthrow Amin. The year 1981 saw insurgent attacks by the NRA in Kampala, with Rwandan support. This led Obote to push harder for Rwandan repatriation, which Habyarimana resisted, not wanting the Tutsi refugees to return.[36] The fact that Ankole, where Oruchinga is situated, is Museveni's home territory, meant Obote's army placed even greater restrictions on the Rwandan settlements. From April 1981, senior government ministers publicly requested Rwandans to leave the country or face recriminations, after reporting the seizure of catchments of arms from the settlements.[37]

Prevented by Rwanda from enforcing large-scale repatriation, Obote's government pushed for Uganda's settlement model to be strengthened as a mechanism of population control. Under Amin, the majority of Rwandan refugees in Uganda had been living in secondary cities in the south-west or integrated among the rural host communities, and by 1981, only 35–40 per cent actually lived in the settlements.

Obote used a major international event held in Geneva, the International Conference on Refugees in Africa (ICARA) of 1981, to request funding for seven settlements in the south-west, which hosted 41,000 Rwandans.[38] The requests were for boreholes, roads, vehicles, maize hammer-mills, and health services, for example. The government also asked for subsidy of government officials in both the settlements and government buildings.[39] Around 43 per cent of the requested $2.3 million funding was actually for the settlements; most was for the benefit of the surrounding host communities.[40]

Within a year, the government began rounding up Rwandan refugees and forcing them into the settlements. In September 1982, the Mbarara District Council passed legislation and launched a campaign to forcibly round up all Rwandans from their homes and transfer them to organized settlements.[41] In October, enforcement of the ruling began. UNHCR staff noted, 'Local chiefs and youth wingers of the [government] had ordered the Rwandans out of their homes, in some cases at five or six o'clock in the morning, and many had had their cattle and other property seized and their homes destroyed'. They also received confirmation from a local government administrator that 'his instructions were to expel all Banyarwanda...and if they refused, armed force was to be used to hasten their evacuation.'[42] Special forces subsequently seized property and evicted nearly all Rwandans from Mbarara town, with some fleeing back to Rwanda and others relocating to the settlements.[43]

In November 1982, the chairman of Mbarara District Council explained the motivation for rounding up Rwandans in cities and incorporating them within settlements:

[It is] fitting to make Mbarara a springboard to spark off the spontaneous movement of...the Rwandese refugees into designated settlements for proper and easy administration...Mbarara District did spontaneous...re-grouping Rwandese Refugees back to their settlement Camps for the sake of peace and stability in our District...It is difficult to keep a snake in the bed and feel peaceful in your sleep...For the last twenty years, we have been generous enough to accommodate the Rwandese refugees...not knowing that we were nourishing a viper in our chest until recently we realized they were dangerous criminals, killers, smugglers, and saboteurs...When Amin took over the Government in 1971, Rwandese Refugees were recruited into the National Army...Those who did not join the army deserted their settlement Camps and because they had full confidence in the Amin regime, claimed land, owned estates through dubious names.

Following these events, UNHCR worked pragmatically with the Ugandan Government to establish new settlements to absorb the rounded up—and hitherto largely integrated—Rwandan refugee population. For example, in November 1983 it used Dutch Government money to establish the new Kyaka II refugee settlement, which continues to exist today.[44] The documents outlining the new settlement plans noted its origins in the October 1982 'events' in Mbarara District.[45]

The key legacies from this period are twofold. First, the Ugandan settlements model, already in existence since the colonial era, was scaled up from the early 1980s. This was not a progressive step, but was motivated by the goal of imposing greater control over Rwandan refugees, who could not be repatriated but were perceived as a threat by Obote. Second, from 1983, West Nile emerged as strategically significant within Ugandan politics. Its indelible association as Amin's support base, and as the site of ethnic cleansing under Obote, meant that subsequent heads of state would henceforth need to prioritize the retention of authority within this volatile region. Furthermore, the creation of a large-scale humanitarian operation focused on both returnees and refugees in West Nile offered a renewed opportunity to extract resources from the international community.

Early Museveni (1986–96): self-reliance and patronage

Museveni's allies are comparable to Amin's insofar as he historically lacked support from the Buganda heartland of the country that includes the capital, Kampala, and instead depended upon backing from hinterlands such as the south-west and the West Nile region. Throughout his time as president, he has politically used the presence of refugees in those regions as a means to attract international resources and legitimacy, while also channelling money to the refugee-hosting regions on which he depends for support. To achieve this, Museveni made refugees a development issue.

Upon assuming power in 1986, Museveni lacked support in Buganda, and so relied upon National Resistance Movement (NRM) support from a number of peripheral areas of the country. Few regions were more important than the south-west and West Nile. Support from the former was relatively straightforward; Museveni is from a Banyankole background and has long enjoyed backing from the Rwandan community. Support from the latter was more challenging; Museveni had few personal links to the north. Contested authority in the north had contributed to undermining both Obote and Amin. Furthermore, Museveni faced the prospect of cross-border Sudanese support for rebellion in the north. Ensuring loyalty in the north would be of enduring importance to Museveni. The presence of refugees offered a means to bring patronage and much-needed resources to the region.

In the south-west, Museveni inherited an aggrieved Rwandan population. He immediately tried to improve their predicament by focusing on developing the settlements. Museveni, though, faced a political juggling act. On the one hand, he felt indebted to Rwandans who had supported the NRA and wanted to push for naturalization. On the other, he recognized that many other groups were opposed to their full integration. As a summary note from UNHCR explained:

> The Rwandese refugees, located in eight settlements in the Southwest have prospered or suffered depending on the regime in power...The NRA was supported by the Rwandese during the Bush War and many young males are indeed serving in the army. The President feels he owes these refugees a debt of gratitude and is known to be favourable to naturalization. On the other hand, other ethnic groups in Uganda are not as well-disposed and, indeed, it has only been since February 1989 that the President of Rwanda has been willing to accept the principle of voluntary repatriation.[46]

Museveni initially tried to strike a balance, exploring options for repatriation and naturalization, while also seeking international funding to support 'an integrated approach towards development both in and around the refugee settlements'. He instructed his Ministry of Local Government, which led on refugee affairs, to work closely with UNHCR on a series of development plans, promoting forestry, dairy farming, roads, schools, and infrastructural development in settlements such as Oruchinga and Nakivale, to be funded by European governments.[47]

Museveni worked collaboratively with UNHCR on a coherent plan for durable solutions, and he personally met with the UN deputy high commissioner for refugees, Arthur Dewey, on 18 May 1989.[48] A key part of the plan was to transfer responsibility of the eight settlements back from UNHCR to the government. At the meeting, Dewey lavished praise on Museveni's refugee policies, explaining that 'Uganda, since 1986, has had a demonstrably generous policy towards refugees. This applies not only to the 75,000 Rwandese, most of whom have been resident since the early sixties, but also to 50,000 newly arrived Sudanese.'

But UNHCR also had an ulterior motive for pressing for durable solutions and handover of the settlements. It faced a looming funding crisis, with donor states questioning its ongoing relevance as the Cold War drew to a close. The organization tried to justify the handover by reasoning that Rwandans should, for the most part, no longer be in need of international protection. Instead of being a humanitarian issue, the challenge should, UNHCR argued, be one of national development:

> With regards to the handing over of the administration of the refugee settlements in South West Uganda, I wish to reiterate that this is neither an abrogation of UNHCR's responsibility to refugees now an attempt to burden the Ugandan Government with additional financial responsibilities. The facts are that the Rwandese refugees have been in Uganda for over 25 years and their present needs are of a developmental nature. UNHCR's funding situation at the moment is at a critical stage and the funds available are earmarked for recent influxes. It is difficult to convince donors to provide additional funds to solve problems that are 25 years old. The solution to the problem may be found through funding agencies for national development.[49]

UNHCR pointed to the availability of alternative resources to support an integrated development approach. Suggested funding sources included European Community and UNDP money aimed at trying to 'link refugee aid and development'. Both UNHCR and the Government of Uganda recognized the value of shifting from a humanitarian to a development logic:

> The presence of your Minister of Planning and Economic Development at this meeting reflects your willingness to consider refugee aid as an important component of national development. This, I am pleased to say, support's UNHCR's Executive Committee's Recommendation on the Linking of Refugee Aid with Development during its 39th Session.[50]

For Uganda, a development approach offered an opportunity for money to be channelled directly through Kampala—to the benefit of both Ugandan citizens and government officials. Based on this understanding, a mid-1990 date was agreed for the ceremonial handover of the settlements to the government.

Gradually, the same self-reliance approach was also expanded by Museveni to the north. In West Nile, he faced the challenge of how to reintegrate 320,000 Ugandan returnees, mainly from Sudan, while supporting Sudanese refugees.[51] Much of this involved emergency relief programmes and food assistance, again funded by European donors.[52] In addition to humanitarian aid, however, Museveni increasingly made requests for development-based support for West Nile. In his meeting with Arthur Dewey, he proposed that more assistance go directly to the districts to provide, for example, 'tippers, grinders, a ferry (i.e. capital goods for construction)'.[53]

However, the situation in West Nile was complicated by cross-border conflict. The Sudan People's Liberation Army's (SPLA) war against Khartoum led to 54,000 Sudanese refugees arriving in northern Uganda by 1990. This in turn led to SPLA incursions into the area, rebels seeking sanctuary in refugee camps, and Sudanese bombing of assumed SPLA targets across West Nile. The government and UNHCR therefore made a plan to relocate all Sudanese refugees away from the north.

The plan was to create new settlements and to move from 'care and maintenance' towards a development-based approach, similar to that already applied in the south-west. UNHCR's goal was to phase out humanitarian assistance from 1992 and the quid pro quo for the government was to be the development of marginalized areas of the country that would host the new settlements. New permanent settlements were planned elsewhere in the country such as the Kiryandongo settlement in the remote Masindi District, and interim, transit camp—such as Rhino camp—were established in Adjumani District. UNHCR committed to help raise additional funds for agricultural activity, livelihoods activities, the construction of schools and health facilities, and roads.[54]

In practice, land disputes in Kiryandongo delayed construction of the new settlement.[55] In the meanwhile, the government instead transferred 60,000 Sudanese to the old Kyangwali settlement in the south-west in 1994.[56] The move was seen as a development opportunity by the Hoima District authorities, especially given that at that point only 4,700 Rwandans remained in the settlement, occupying just one-eighth of the available arable land, and the local population was just 12,000. Moving Sudanese refugees to the south-west was greeted as an important development opportunity for a district that was part of Museveni's Banyankole support base.[57]

During 1994, violence in southern Sudan worsened, and the number of refugees arriving in West Nile grew rapidly. By the end of the year, close to 300,000 Sudanese were in Uganda, and most were in West Nile.[58] As numbers rose, it became more important to consider possibilities for self-reliance within the West Nile region.

A significant part of the motivation for settlements in West Nile was to support the SPLA's rear bases in the war against the Sudanese Government. Indeed, the timing of new land allocations for Sudanese refugees across West Nile coincided with the strengthening of NRA alignment with the SPLA and the parallel alignment of the Government of Sudan with the Lord's Resistance Army (LRA) (and the remnants of Obote's UNLA)[59] as a means to destabilize Museveni's regime.[60] Ensuring covert sanctuary and support for the SPLA through offering sanctuary to mainly ethnic Kakwa refugees offered a means to fight against the destabilizing influence of Sudan, the LRA, and the remnants of the Obote regime.[61]

In contrast, the number of Rwandan refugees in Uganda fell dramatically (from 84,000 in February 1994) in the aftermath of the April 1994 Rwandan genocide. Uganda had for decades offered refuge to mainly Tutsi refugees, and the settlements in the south-west were an important source of recruitment for the Rwandan Patriotic Front (RPF) in exile.[62]

Museveni backed numerous RPF plans to overthrow Rwandan President Habyarimana during the early 1990s.[63] In April 1994, following the start of the genocide, the RPF invasion took place and, six months later, the majority of the 1959, 1973, and 1990, predominantly Tutsi, refugees had voluntarily returned to Rwanda. However, a new cohort of Rwandan refugees arrived in their stead: mainly Hutu refugees associated with the Habyarimana regime, some implicated in the genocide, others fearing reprisals from the new regime.[64] The irony was that they would occupy the same settlements in which their Tutsi counterparts had lived for the previous thirty-five years. However, while these refugees inherited the settlement infrastructure of their predecessors, they would not enjoy the same privileged relationship with Museveni's NRM, whose loyalties remained largely with the RPF. Henceforth, Nakivale and the other south-western settlements would no longer just be for Rwandans but, from late 1994, the government began to relocate even Somalis from Kampala to Nakivale.[65]

Late Museveni (1999–): old wine in new bottles

By the late 1990s, West Nile had become strategically important to Museveni. Because it had been Amin's hinterland, Obote had forced most of the native population into exile in southern Sudan from 1979. But when they returned from around 1983 they came back with southern Sudanese refugees, many of whom were also Kakwa, and shared cultural commonalities with the returnees. Museveni worked with the SPLA to ensure southern Sudan did not become a rebel base for his opponents. For pragmatic reasons, Museveni's NRM aligned with the remnants of Amin's support base. For example, General Moses Ali, a southern Sudanese and a member of Amin's cabinet, fought for Museveni's NRA in the Bush Wars. He was rewarded with the role of both deputy prime minister, and—crucially—minister for refugees and disaster relief, allowing him to use the refugee portfolio to bring money into West Nile. This precarious configuration of alliances created an imperative for Museveni to bring resources into West Nile, and the refugee presence offered such an opportunity.

Politically, supporting the integration of refugees in West Nile was not especially challenging. When returnees and refugees came back from Sudan to Uganda they shared a common experience of living side by side in southern Sudan. And, given population scarcity in West Nile, there was a need for people to cultivate the land and build the economy as a means to facilitate state-building in the region.

Developing a written Self-Reliance Strategy (SRS) for West Nile, based on the country's prior experience with Rwandans in the south-west, offered a mutually beneficial opportunity for refugees, hosts, and the Government of Uganda. Meanwhile, with emerging political concern about the 'secondary movement' of refugees to Europe, the SRS could be packaged by UNHCR as a means to also meet European donor concerns relating to both irregular migration and the desire to reduce long-term humanitarian assistance to northern Uganda.

The SRS began in 1999 with a focus on the main refugee-hosting districts in West Nile, home to 56 per cent of the country's Sudanese refugees, who in turn made up 80 per cent of Uganda's 200,000 refugees by the end of the millennium. The strategy was jointly designed by UNHCR and the Office of the Prime Minister (OPM), given responsibility for refugee affairs by Museveni. The SRS had two stated objectives: 'i) to empower refugees and nationals in the area to the extent that they will be able to support themselves;

and (ii) to establish mechanisms that will ensure integration of services for the refugees with those of the nationals.'

The SRS built upon Uganda's historical experience of self-reliance within the settlements. But it also aligned with emerging themes within international refugee policy, such as the 'the humanitarian-to-development gap' and the notion of an exit strategy for international humanitarian assistance.

The basis of the 'deal' was that refugees would be allocated plots of land in designated settlements, for homestead and agricultural purposes. Refugees would be able to access government education, health, and other services on the same basis as nationals. And the government would work towards the long-anticipated new Refugee Bill, which would provide the right to work and freedom of movement. In exchange, UNHCR would mobilize international donors to provide development assistance in support of both the settlements, infrastructure, and public services in ways that were mutually beneficial to refugees and the host community.[66]

One donor government in particular stepped forward to offer support. Denmark provided funding directly to OPM, with limited accountability or oversight. A senior UNHCR staff member at the time explained, 'Uganda came looking for legitimacy from the international community by repackaging something they were already doing', and 'Denmark was the driving force. They were already far to the right.' A senior Danish official involved at the time explained Denmark's role:

> Denmark was a forerunner because we were first in the xenophobia-aid bias. We wanted to solve refugee issues in the region. The Brits tried but we formalised it early. UNHCR smelled the air, so UNHCR saw that there were additional funds to be had. We had to be practical and we had a budget that had to be invested in a short time.

By 2003, UNHCR had developed an initiative called 'Convention Plus', funded by the EU, Denmark, the Netherlands, and the UK, and aimed primarily at using development assistance to countries like Uganda as a means of reducing the secondary movement of refugees to Europe. The key concept was 'Development Assistance for Refugees' (DAR), used to support refugee self-reliance, and Uganda was the international community's proof of concept. Based on the recommendation of the SRS mid-term review, Uganda was adopted as *the* 'DAR pilot of global interest'.[67]

By 2005, though, the international bargain underlying the SRS had largely broken down for a number of reasons. Uganda felt that the international community had failed to provide the promised support, and that DAR and Convention Plus had failed to bring 'additionality' in terms of development resources.[68]

This had a knock-on effect at district level, where the districts did not see the anticipated returns in resources or infrastructure. In Moyo, one of the districts in West Nile, for example, at handover, under-funding and miscommunication meant that UNHCR mistakenly listed schools and boreholes as 'completed' that did not actually exist, contributing to 'a very serious breakdown in trust'.[69]

Nevertheless, in 2006, Uganda finally passed its Refugee Act, formally providing refugees with the right to work and freedom of movement. And, as numbers fell from 200,000 refugees in 2005 to around 75,000 two years later, Uganda continued to provide a manageable number of refugees with access to land within its settlements, access to public services, and the possibility to work in cities, all the time being praised by the international community for doing so. The SRS ticked along as Uganda's default model.

However, from 2015 two things changed. First, refugee numbers in Uganda increased dramatically because of violence in South Sudan and the Democratic Republic of Congo (DRC), reaching a peak of over 1.2 million. Second, Europe faced the 2015–16 'refugee crisis' leading to an upsurge in donor interest in Uganda's model for hosting refugees. These events led to the revival and rebranding of the Ugandan self-reliance model—first under the acronym of ReHoPE (the Refugee and Host Population Empowerment Strategy) in 2015 and then under the acronym of the CRRF (the Comprehensive Refugee Response Framework) in 2019.

ReHoPE, launched in 2015 by Uganda, UNHCR, and the World Bank, was explicitly described as 'a follow-up initiative to the Self-Reliance Strategy'. It promised to bring in an estimated $350 million over five years to support the government's national development plans. For European donors, the initiative was, in the words of one administrator, a way for donors to 'save face on Uganda', showing that there was a sustainable alternative to a mass influx into Europe.[70] Meanwhile, amid the 2016 general elections, Museveni needed to demonstrate that he had a clear-sighted plan for managing the growing influx of refugees.

ReHoPE, though, was short-lived. UNHCR convened a Solidarity Summit for Refugees in Uganda, held in Kampala on 21–2 June 2017. However, it raised only $1.5 million (from India and China) of its $2 billion target.[71] The failure of the summit severely damaged trust between the

United Nations, Kampala, and the host districts.[72] Soon afterwards in early 2018, a massive scandal was announced in which it became clear that the OPM and UNHCR Kampala were riddled with corruption and incompetence. The subsequent UN Office of Internal Oversight Services' audit report showed that UNHCR inappropriately allocated tens of millions of dollars in Uganda in 2017, overpaying for goods and services, awarding major contracts improperly, and failing to avoid fraud, corruption, and waste.[73] Examples of misconduct included a $7.9 million contract for road repairs awarded to a contractor with no experience in road construction.[74]

The events of 2018 were not, however, the first corruption scandal relating to refugee affairs in Uganda. In November 2012, several major donors, including the UK, suspended aid to Uganda amid claims of embezzlement by OPM. Meanwhile, both newspaper reports and UNHCR archives high-light a similar scandal in October 1993, when the Somali Refugee Committee in Kisnenyi, Kampala, made allegations that UNHCR and the government were creating 'ghost refugees' in order to embezzle money; although the UNHCR representative dismissed the claims as 'unfounded and baseless'.[75] The head of a national non-governmental organization (NGO) explained to me that these dynamics of corruption and patronage were a long-standing feature of refugee policy in Uganda. He claimed:

> Money goes to the north and comes back to Kampala. The UN is so intimidated, they allow the government to function as it wants. The international NGOs endorse corruption because they will open a borehole and they will charter a plane for a government official or pay a high per diem and spend $5000 on a Minister for a borehole that costs less than $5000. Money goes back to OPM for 'oversight' or 'budget support', sometimes up to 40 per cent, and you have to have OPM permission to be here…the central government gives small tokens to the north to shut them up, and because Uganda is a key ally of the international community, the UN has given the government the mandate and the power to take their own people hostage.

Nevertheless, the Ugandan model was again repackaged as the CRRF for Uganda. The CRRF essentially offered a means to facilitate development-based responses to refugees in order to enable them to become self-reliant, including through access to labour markets, not just for Uganda but else-where too. In the words of one UNHCR official, 'CRRF is the Uganda model, gone global'.[76] However, rather than providing direct budgetary support through the central government, it instead envisaged direct funding to support the districts.

Despite the track record of corruption and patronage, international donors were willing to continue funding the Ugandan model. Donors were buying a 'success story', Museveni was accessing resources to strengthen his legitimacy in refugee-hosting districts. One donor-country ambassador explained European motivation for backing the model:

> We need a good example…It is really good for the debate. It is good for humanitarians; it is good for xenophobes. The Syrian refugee crisis in Europe required us to need this. We all know how development aid will never mitigate migration. But we maintain the narrative otherwise we have no other narrative…There are many agendas and unholy alliances.[77]

Conclusion

Uganda's refugee policies are frequently viewed as characterized by exceptionalism. However, the basis of Uganda's self-reliance model can be found in the British colonial era, when the rural self-settlement model was first used in Nakivale. Many of the key features of the contemporary model were in place by the 1960s, including the language of 'self-supporting refugees', an acceptance of urban 'free-livers', and the idea of attracting development-based assistance to mutually benefit refugees and the host community. Even at that time, UNHCR praised the Ugandan approach as 'very progressive', rewarding the government with recognition and resources.

Strikingly, given his reputation for oppression and the expulsion of the Ugandan Asians, Idi Amin played an important role in further developing the model. Due to his lack of support from Buganda and his strong alliances in West Nile and the south-west, he relied upon Sudanese and Rwandan refugees in particular as the basis of his army and political entourage. He strengthened the settlement model, and supported the almost full integration of Rwandan refugees in urban areas, even being the Ugandan president who signed the 1951 Convention and committed to create new legislation.

In contrast, when Obote returned to power, he brought repression and backlash against the Sudanese and Rwandan refugee populations because of their close connection to the Amin regime. In retribution for Amin's attacks on the Acholi and Lango tribes in the north, Obote slaughtered people across West Nile, forcing Ugandans and refugees alike to flee into southern Sudan. Meanwhile, the majority of Rwandans living outside of the settlement, were forced back into closed settlements. Nevertheless, Obote's legacy was not to abolish the settlements model but to reinforce it in the south-west as an alternative to urban integration for those Rwandans who could not be repatriated.

Although Museveni has widely been credited with creating Uganda's self-reliance model, he inherited most of its core elements, and there was little original about the SRS, ReHoPE, or the CRRF. In many ways Museveni's key patronage networks resemble those of Amin. With few Bugandan supporters and his tribal heartland in a refugee-hosting area, he, like Amin, relied upon maintaining the backing of local political leaders in West Nile and the south-west. Repeatedly recycling and rebranding the self-reliance model afforded an opportunity to channel resources to key patronage networks, while also enhancing his legitimacy in the eyes of the international community. Furthermore, Museveni frequently recognized the importance of the refugee settlements as a basis for meddling in the domestic politics of neighbouring country rivals.

Overall, the Ugandan self-reliance model for refugees needs to be understood in historical and political context. The right to work and freedom of movement for refugees, although generally beneficial for refugees, have not been provided because of altruism or respect for international legal obligations. Rather, they are the result of a complex alignment of interests across global, national, and local levels. At key junctures, such as the aftermath of the Rwandan genocide or the European refugee crisis, donor governments have wanted to be associated with a refugee 'success', and so they have been prepared to invest in the Ugandan model. Successive Ugandan presidents have used self-reliance as a means to garner legitimacy, resources, and local patronage despite otherwise ambivalent democratic and human rights credentials.

This raises the question of whether the politics that have shaped Ugandan refugee policy are exceptional to the country. Or, alternatively, does the combination of external resource extraction and internal patronage also explain the socio-economic inclusion of refugees in other contexts? Within the region, for example, Ethiopia adopted legislation providing the right to work and freedom of movement for refugees in 2019. Before doing so, the head of its refugee affairs department visited Uganda to learn from the model. Was that move also motivated by a combination of seeking external resources and legitimacy, and the desire of the central government to extend its authority within refugee-hosting hinterlands? Beyond the region, does a similar logic apply to other semi-authoritarian regimes that have shunned camps and embraced the socio-economic inclusion of refugees such as Turkey and Colombia? At the very least, the Ugandan case reveals the ambiguous and complex politics underlying refugee rights.

10

Kenya

How Turkana County turned refugees into an asset

Introduction

Kenya is not known for its progressive refugee policies. Although the nation tolerated the self-settlement of refugees until the late 1980s, the large-scale influx of Somali refugees led to the adoption of an 'encampment' policy, requiring that refugees reside in the Dadaab or Kakuma camps from 1992 onwards. This de facto policy framework was enshrined in legislation through the Kenyan Refugee Act of 2006, which restricts refugees' freedom of movement, and indirectly limits their right to work. At the national level, at least, refugees do not have the right to work or freedom of movement. At a central government level, security concerns relating to Somali refugees have been exacerbated by terrorist attacks in Nairobi, leading to further crackdowns, and even suggestions to close the Dadaab camps and expel all Somali refugees from the country.

In one remote region of Kenya, however, a new approach is emerging. Turkana County, home to the Kakuma refugee camps, has chosen to actively support the socio-economic inclusion of refugees. Despite being one of the poorest regions of Kenya, its approach contrasts markedly with policy in either Garissa County, home to the Dadaab camps, or Nairobi. The county itself is vast, being geographically larger than Switzerland. However, it has few resources, despite recently discovering oil. Its population is mainly comprised of the nomadic, pastoralist Turkana people and its economy is mainly livestock-based. Located in a remote, arid region that borders both South Sudan and Uganda, it has historically hosted large numbers of

254 THE WEALTH OF REFUGEES

refugees but also faced security challenges amid cross-border incursions and cattle rustling.

The Government of Turkana County, however, recognized that refugees, and the presence of international aid organizations, represent a potential benefit rather than a burden for the county. Several members of that government previously worked for humanitarian organizations and witnessed first-hand the devastating economic consequences for the county when South Sudanese refugees went home and international humanitarian organizations closed their offices. As we briefly discussed in Chapter 5, the county and its governor therefore chose to work with the international community to develop an alternative and mutually beneficial approach to hosting refugees.

That alternative vision has become known as the Kalobeyei Integrated Socio-Economic Development Plan (KISEDP), a fifteen-year strategy for the sub-county of Turkana West, where the Kakuma camps are based. It has funding from the European Union and a range of bilateral donors. It is based upon two core elements. First, the new Kalobeyei settlement, built just 3.5km from the Kakuma refugee camps. Unlike the Kakuma camps, it was created as an integrated settlement, intended to be for both refugees and members of the host community. Its goal is to create opportunities for refugees' self-reliance, while also improving socio-economic outcomes for the host community through a range of market-based opportunities. Once particular ideas are piloted in Kalobeyei, the intention is that they could be scaled across Kakuma. The second element is an integrated development plan for the whole of Turkana West. Rather than just focusing on the camps, the KISEDP aims to improve socio-economic outcomes for the entire population of the sub-county. It is an area-based development plan.

The KISEDP approach is unique in making refugees part of the regional development plan for the county. Although it applies only to Turkana West, it is an integrated component of the County Integrated Development Plan (CIDP). Remarkably, the model goes completely against the grain of Kenya's overall refugee policy. There is even some indication that the implementation of the right to work and freedom of movement, although they are central government competences, may gradually be relaxing in Turkana County. For example, under the radar, the county government is giving county-level one-, two-, and three-year movement passes to a small number of refugee entrepreneurs, allowing them to do business in Lodwar and elsewhere. In Nairobi, it is now increasingly understood that Kenya no longer has just one refugee policy but three: one for Dadaab, one for Nairobi, and another for Kakuma. The KISEDP is already being celebrated on a global scale, with the governor of Turkana speaking at events around the world and the KISEDP feted as an exemplar of the UN's flagship refugee response plan, the so-called Global Compact on Refugees, an approach that emphasizes self-reliance and socio-economic inclusion. As one member of the UN Refugee Agency (UNHCR)'s staff put it, 'it has become a model for the rest of the world. It embodies the aims of the Global Compact on Refugees.'[1]

From a political perspective the question is: why has this happened? What has enabled Turkana County to adopt such a radically different approach from the rest of Kenya? The key has been political ownership at the regional level. At a structural level, devolution in Kenya in 2013 gave the counties the authority for nearly all aspects of refugee policy aside from those relating to security and status. At an agentic level, the personality and experiences of the governor himself, Josphat Nanok, have been crucial. He was shaped by his own background as a humanitarian worker and witnessed the devastating effect on the local economy when, following the Comprehensive Peace Agreement in South Sudan, refugees went home, and aid agencies briefly closed down in 2011.

Meanwhile, international resources have been made available to support the KISEDP. Kalobeyei's plans were developed in 2015 and it opened in 2016, in the context of the European refugee crisis. As the EU sought alternative, more sustainable solutions for refugees 'in the region of origin', Kalobeyei fell squarely within the aims and scope of the EU Emergency Trust Fund for Africa (EUTF for Africa), and the settlement's initial design relied upon a 15 million euro grant from the Fund. Managing the onward, secondary migration of refugees was an explicit goal of the EU's backing for Kalobeyei. Over time, the envelope has further expanded, and within the 2018 revised KISEDP, the required budget for full implementation of 'phase 1' of KISEDP (2018–22) was $500 million, much of which it envisaged would go directly through the county's own budget. In addition to traditional donors, the model has gradually brought company CEOs to Kakuma and Kalobeyei, from Vodafone to Safaricom and Morneau Shepell, all signalling opportunity for Turkana County and its political representatives.

What is most remarkable about the Turkana County story is that it is based on local but not national buy-in. It has happened in spite of, rather than because of, national government policy. In that sense, it contrasts markedly with the story of Ethiopia's highly centralized transition towards allowing refugees the right to work and freedom of movement. Rather than coming top-down through the central government, Kenya's transition towards greater socio-economic inclusion is a bottom-up story, in which a local government has built a direct relationship with international actors that largely bypasses the central government. Underlying it all, though, has been a complex and ambiguous set of political interests.

The story of KISEDP

The Kakuma refugee camps were created in 1992 next to Kakuma Town, a Catholic missionary town created in the 1950s in the remote Turkana County, initially for refugees from southern Sudan and Somalia. By 2014, the four Kakuma camps had a population of close to 180,000. Faced with overcrowding, UNHCR needed new land and was exploring options for an additional camp. To access additional land, UNHCR first needed to engage the county government and host community in dialogue because all of the land is regarded as tribal land, commonly shared by the traditionally nomadic, pastoralist Turkana. Furthermore, UNHCR's recently arrived country representative, Raouf Mazou, was reluctant to simply create another camp: 'We wanted to move away from camps. All of the discussion globally had been that camps lead to protracted refugee situations, and we wanted to see if we could do something different.'[2]

UNHCR convened a roundtable in the county capital, Lodwar, on 27 and 28 November 2014 on 'the Integration of Refugees and Host Community Economies'. It was attended by Josphat Nanok, Daniel Nanok (no relation, the member of parliament [MP] for Turkana West), Edwin Ng'etich (acting commissioner for refugee affairs), and representatives from the Turkana County Government, UNHCR, the World Bank, a range of other UN agencies, key donor governments including the EU, the UK, and Switzerland, Professor Rahul Oka of Notre Dame University, and representatives of the refugee and host communities. The roundtable highlighted the protracted nature of the Kakuma camps, lamenting its focus on 'care and maintenance' and the $58 million spent on humanitarian assistance during that year alone.

At the meeting, it was suggested that 'the refugee assistance program, as currently managed, is not financially sustainable, since it is based on the assumption that refugees would receive full assistance for their basic needs until such time as they cease to be refugees'.[3] In his opening comments, the governor pointed out that 'the economic potential of the camp to the undeveloped Turkana County has not been exploited and the host community feels that it has not benefited much'.[4]

The participants in the meeting discussed the available evidence on refugees' developmental impact on the economy of Turkana County. Drawing upon research from the University of Oxford and market assessments conducted by the World Food Programme (WFP), Rahul Oka argued that, contrary to popular assumptions about protracted refugee situations, refugees in Kakuma were not economically homogeneous, technologically illiterate, economically isolated, a burden on host communities, or inherently dependent upon aid. It was strongly emphasized that 'It is inaccurate to portray refugees as poor people who represent an economic burden to the host community. Refugees have some access to capital, thanks to remittances and relief assistance, and bring with them useful skills that could contribute to the economy of the host community.' Representatives of the refugee community told the roundtable participants that 'skilled refugees and refugee entrepreneurs do not need food assistance, but, rather, access to capital, skills training, employment opportunities, and free movement in and out of the refugee camp to conduct business'.[5]

The summary note from the meeting highlights a concern to ensure that the presence of refugees has a positive impact on the host community:

> The skills and assets of refugees have not been used to uplift socio-economic conditions in Turkana West, which is a historically marginalized region... Compared to the refugees, the host community has a higher level of unmet needs. The fact that refugees are better supported has led to a patron-client relationship between the refugees and host community, where the refugees are patrons, and the hosts are the clients. This unequal relationship contributes to the erosion of dignity, to humiliation, and occasional anger amongst the host community, leading to possible conflict and misunderstanding.[6]

The roundtable concluded that there was a need for 'a paradigm shift', transforming refugee programmes into development programmes. As an interim step, UNHCR launched *The Turkana Initiative Aimed at Integrating the Refugee and Host Community Economies*, in partnership with the county government and development partners.[7] The overall objective was to reorient the refugee assistance programme to improve socio-economic conditions for both the refugee and host communities and to reduce dependency on humanitarian aid.

According to one UNHCR staff member, the idea of facilitating greater economic integration between refugees and the host community immediately resonated with Governor Nanok:'he already had it in his mind, and we simply facilitated it'. Here Nanok's own history mattered. Since the early 2000s, Nanok had been a humanitarian worker, initially with non-governmental organizations (NGOs) such as CARE and Oxfam, and then with WFP. He worked for WFP in Lokichoggio, the base for Operation Lifeline Sudan, the international community's multi-agency response to conflict and crisis in southern Sudan. Nanok saw first-hand the contribution that both refugees and humanitarian agencies brought to the regional economy. With the Comprehensive Peace Agreement in Sudan in 2005, however, refugees began to return home, and Operation Lifeline Sudan began to wind down. By 2009, Kakuma's population was so small that it relied upon transfers from Dadaab to justify its continued existence. In 2011, WFP finally closed down its field office in Lokichoggio. Many of Nanok's closest colleagues had similar experiences. The minister of finance and economic planning, Robert Erang Loteleng'o, had previously worked for the International Rescue Committee (IRC), and witnessed the collapse of humanitarian jobs across the region. As the county's trade minister, Jennifer Nawoi Longor, put it '90% of professionals in Turkana must have worked as humanitarians. People who work in the county government worked in NGOs and humanitarian response before…we were all affected by the ghost town of Lokichoggio.'[8] Nanok was keen to ensure that the presence of refugees and humanitarian agencies could leave a positive legacy, even after they leave.

Unsurprisingly, in his opening remarks at the roundtable, Nanok:

> highlighted the need to provide refugee assistance differently to avoid the creation of an artificial and aid-driven economy that will disappear when the refugees return to their countries of origin. Referring to the state of Lokichoggio following the end of Operation Lifeline Sudan (OLS), the Governor urged the roundtable participants to explore ways to avoid the possibility of Kakuma becoming another 'ghost town' when the refugees leave.[9]

At the 2014 roundtable, there was consensus that the next step would need to be data collection. Consequently, the World Bank agreed to undertake an economic and social impact assessment along the lines that it had undertaken in other parts of the world. Its focus would be to explore ways in which the presence of refugees could serve to benefit Turkana's existing CIDP. The World Bank's economist at the meeting, Apurva Sanghi, and Rahul Oka hatched a plan for what would ultimately be published by the World Bank as the 2016 study *"Yes" in My Backyard? The Economics of Refugees and their Social Dynamics in Kakuma, Kenya.*[10] The report would ultimately show the positive economic contribution of refugees to the Turkana economy, and provide a road map for strengthening the benefits.

Discussions continued on the concept of an integrated settlement to address overcrowding. By late 2015, UNHCR was working with the county government on plans for the new Kalobeyei settlement. An initial plan was drawn up and it depicted the idea of refugees living on one side, the host community on the other, and a combination of markets and social services being provided in shared space between the two. UN-HABITAT was brought in to work on the site strategy for what would be Kenya's first planned settlement. Kalobeyei's two key objectives were identified: to offer opportunities for greater interaction between refugees and hosts, and for refugee self-reliance.

The Government of Turkana County allocated some 1500ha of land in Kalobeyei for the new settlement. The aim was that some 30,000 South Sudanese refugees would be relocated from Kakuma during 2016, and that Kalobeyei would eventually host around 60,000 refugees plus up to 20,000 host community members. In order to make this a reality, UNHCR and the county government drafted the first iteration of KISEDP.

And with the European refugee crisis of 2015, political interest from the donors spiked at just the right time. In November 2015, the EU–Africa Migration Summit in Valletta created the new multi-billion euro EUTF for Africa. Support for the KISEDP became one of its early priorities. In April 2016, the EU approved an initial 15 million euros of funding to support the preparatory phase of the KISEDP. Its stated overall objective was 'to create an evidence-based, innovative and sustainable development and protection solution for refugees and host communities...through the establishment of an integrated settlement area, in which refugees and the host community live together peacefully, have access to social services and develop economic ties to build sustainable livelihoods'. The EU established five main performance indicators for its commitment: improved health standards; increased food security and economic wellbeing; increased school enrolment; improved child safety and wellbeing; and increased social cohesion. In outlining its 'intervention logic', the linkage between 'enhancing refugee self-reliance' and 'decreasing the incentives for irregular secondary movements' was explicit:

The intervention logic of this action is that by improving protection, enhancing self-reliance opportunities and integrated service delivery, and building the capacity of local authorities for the delivery of such integrated service delivery, refugees and their host communities will benefit from a safer and more favourable environment, increasing their livelihoods opportunities sustainably, and decreasing the incentives for irregular secondary movements.[11]

Other bilateral donors followed suit, with initial commitments from the United States Agency for International Development (USAID), the UK's Department for International Development (DFID), the Swiss Agency for Development and Cooperation (SDC) Japan, and Germany. Meanwhile, WFP committed to rolling out its electronic cash transfer called Bamba Chakula, operational on a small-scale in Kakuma since 2015, as the basis for assistance delivery in Kalobeyei.

However, progress stalled in 2016. Since late 2013, Kakuma had received a large-scale influx of around 50,000 new South Sudanese refugees. By summer 2016, the Kakuma 4 camp, built mainly to accommodate new arrivals from South Sudan, was overcrowded. With a spike in new arrivals of predominantly female-headed households from the Eastern Equatorial region, the new Kalobeyei settlement needed to be repurposed. Instead of being for transfers from Kakuma, it was used to accommodate new arrivals. And instead of being able to focus on self-reliance, its initial focus was on emergency relief and assistance.

By early 2017, there was doubt that Kalobeyei would ever become the integrated, market-based settlement originally planned. In February, one senior UNHCR staff member based at headquarters explained 'We cannot be judged any longer on whether Kalobeyei achieves self-reliance because the purpose has changed. Because of the influx, it's now just a camp like any other.' Alongside this, UNHCR faced a huge corruption scandal in Kakuma, leading to an investigation and large-scale staff turnover. The county government was also distracted; national elections were scheduled for 2017, and Turkana County was a hotbed of opposition support. For both the international community and the county government, KISEDP was temporarily on the back burner. One UNHCR staff member admitted of this period, 'we were dragging with the KISEDP'.

Nevertheless, infrastructure started to emerge in Kalobeyei. From June 2016, the first new households arrived in the settlement, and boreholes were dug. By the beginning of 2017, the Kalobeyei primary school was constructed, the Food and Agriculture Organization (FAO) and WFP began collaborating on the rollout of kitchen gardens in support of subsistence agriculture, and fifty-six Bamba Chakula traders had been contracted to sell food in exchange for electronically distributed Bamba Chakula, all initially housed in a single tent-based market. From August 2017, work began on permanent shelters, and a vocational training centre was built under the auspices of the Danish Refugee Council.

And there was renewed momentum for the KISEDP created by the launch of *"Yes!" in My Backyard?* in Nairobi in February 2017. One UNHCR staff member recalled that when Nanok arrived, he was surprised by how high-level the event was, with the country director of the World Bank and four or five donor ambassadors present:'Nanok entered and said "wow, this is big". In his statement, he said "Turkana County has only two major resources: its oil and its refugees". He realised then that this could be some-thing special.' On World Refugee Day, in June that year, UNHCR hosted a public debate entitled 'Get to Know Refugees: Their Capabilities and Contribution to the Local Economy' in Nairobi. At the event, Kalobeyei was a focus, and UNHCR staff began to speak confidently once again about 'changing refugee assistance models' in the settlement.[12]

The period from 2016 to 2017 was relabelled as the 'preparatory phase' for KISEDP. And, by 2018, Kalobeyei had infrastructure, had begun to pilot a series of innovative interventions, including Bamba Chakula, kitchen gar-dens, and the world's first cash-for-shelter programme in a refugee camp. It became home to 38,000 refugees and around 2,000 members of the host community. A member of UNHCR's team in Kakuma explained that 'with the mass influx, the Kalobeyei vision was dead ... but with hindsight it was a godsend ... because nobody was transferred from Kakuma. So Kalobeyei doesn't have the Kakuma logic ... they have a different "I can do" logic. If we'd done cash-for-shelter in Kakuma, it wouldn't have worked.' In June 2018, UNHCR's head of communications, Melissa Fleming, came to Kakuma for a TEDx event, and announced on Al Jazeera that:

> There is the old part of Kakuma. And then there is the new part, called Kalobeyei. And that's something we really wanted to highlight here. It repre-sents our new approach that is going global to refugee response. And that is that there are settlements being built that are completely integrated with the local community, and where the local community benefits, where we attract international development assistance as well as private investment.

There was a renewed belief that the original market-based vision for Kalobeyei might just work. And in the year in which UNHCR was due to launch the Global Compact on Refugees, with its emphasis on refugee self-reliance, Kalobeyei represented an important illustration of UNHCR's 'new' model.

By 2018 Kalobeyei symbolized a wider shift towards a market-based approach in Kakuma. The International Finance Corporation (IFC) published its study *Kakuma as a Marketplace*, valuing the overall Kakuma economy at around $56.2 million a year, based on a household expenditure survey and identifying around 4,000 retail shops in Turkana County, of which over half were in the Kakuma camps.[13] With the first TEDx ever in a refugee camp being held in Kakuma and the camp being home to over half the Refugee Olympics Team, Kakuma—and the new Kalobeyei model—began to receive global recognition. And with that, Josphat Nanok too received increasing media coverage for the new model he was credited with supporting. Donors, prospective investors, and politicians began to arrive in Turkana West to learn about the model.

But there remained one significant challenge. Kalobeyei had been conceived as an 'integrated settlement', and yet members of the host community were not moving in. Although Turkana from nearby villages came to the settlement for employment and to use integrated services such as health and education, they preferred to remain in their villages, which supported their usually semi-nomadic lifestyle. By the end of 2018, the number of Turkana living in the settlement was reportedly less than about 200. The idea of a 'hybrid community' was gone. But both the governor and the county government wanted to ensure that the host community benefitted more directly and sustainably from the presence of refugees.

With this in mind, the KISEDP was redrafted and relaunched in both Kakuma and Nairobi in late 2018. Henceforth, KISEDP was no longer just about Kalobeyei, or even Kakuma. It was redesigned as a development plan for the whole of the sub-county of Turkana West. The updated programme was fully aligned with, and referenced in, the new County Integrated Development Plan (CIDP II), with its first phase covering the same period (2018–22). According to UNHCR, the KISEDP strives to be government-led, area-based, community-centred, market-driven, and sustainable. Its overall goal is to create an enabling environment for the people of Turkana West and to invest in people's skills and capabilities. Its four strategic objectives are: to attract private-sector investment to build the local economy; to invest in infrastructure to enhance service delivery; to enhance innovative aid modalities to increase self-reliance; and to improve education to promote market-oriented skills development. It aims to achieve these objectives through three phases: 2018–22, 2023–7, and 2028–30, and it divides into eight components, each with their own objectives, performance indicators, budgets, and flagship projects: health; education; water, sanitation, and hygiene (WASH); protection; spatial, planning and infrastructure; agriculture and livestock; energy; and the private sector and entrepreneurship. The governor of Turkana County is the chairperson of the Steering Committee and the initiative includes forty-four partners.[14]

Although it remains early in the KISEDP process, the degree of collaboration between a regional government and the international humanitarian community is already being heralded as remarkable and unique. It is the first time that an integrated development plan has been jointly created for refugees and the host community with full buy-in from a regional government and UNHCR. In the words of the UNHCR staff member who headed the organization's role in updating KISEDP, 'If anyone wants to learn from this, they have to adapt it to context but the prerequisite is government leadership.' What, therefore, explains the politics that enabled the KISEDP to come into existence within a country better known for its strict encampment policy towards refugees, and what conditions would be required for replication?

County-level politics

In 2012, the Kenyan central government passed the Transition to Devolved Government Act, redistributing significant powers to the County level. Constitutionally, the reforms delegated significant authority for refugee affairs. In the context of Turkana County, decentralization gave Lodwar control over many socio-economic aspects of refugee affairs, including health and education, leaving Nairobi and the Refugee Affairs Secretariat within the Ministry of Interior with authority over issues relating to status and security as identified in the 2006 Refugee Act.

Decentralization laid the foundations for county government leadership on refugee policy. But it still required local leadership—and local political interests—to translate constitutional change into economic opportunity. Josphat Nanok won the 2013 gubernatorial elections and immediately recognized the opportunity provided by both refugees and the new constitutional arrangements. As county trade minister, Jennifer Longor, explained, 'Nanok is the face behind how Turkana operates.' His background enabled him to see the political opportunity in socio-economically integrating refugees. On the one hand, he is from a poor and pastoralist background and able to connect with the sense of alienation experienced by many Turkana. On the other hand, his experience as a humanitarian worker allowed him to identify refugees as a major asset. Longor further explained, 'The governor has a different approach. Other areas feel refugees are a burden. He knows that Turkana is different; Turkana culture has a way of viewing outsiders as a blessing.'

Nanok built important alliances that enabled him to establish independent relationships with the international community without being blocked by Nairobi. In 2017, he was elected as chairperson of the Council of Governors, giving him national recognition and influence, and a seat at the table of Nairobi politics. As one UNHCR staff member put it, 'This has allowed him to meet with President Kenyatta directly, and prevented some of the possible push-back.' Nanok himself is an opposition politician, and a long-standing supporter of Kenyan opposition leader Raila Odinga. Yet, despite this, he has built close connections with Kenyatta's government. Longor explained, 'The "handshake" made a difference. When Raila and Uhuru shook hands after the 2016 election violence, it calmed people down. We developed a more diplomatic way of doing things. There are no conflicts now. It doesn't mean there aren't challenges, but there is diplomatic engagement.'

But it is not just about altruism. For Nanok and his county government, KISEDP represents a political opportunity. One UNHCR staff member suggested, 'ultimately, it's all about power and money', and Nanok, who is due to complete his second term as governor in 2022, is seen as harbouring political ambitions at the national level. In addition to his roles as governor and chairperson of the Council of Governors, he served as deputy leader of the main opposition party, the Orange Democratic Movement (ODM) until June 2019. However, he was ousted from that position by the party's National Executive Council, after declaring his support for Deputy President William Ruto's presidential bid for 2022, which positioned Nanok for a possible role within a Ruto government.

The hoped-for scale of investment in the KISEDP is significant, with an ambitious $500 million targeted from all stakeholders for the first five years of the programme. Even if all of that money does not come through the county budget, at least some of it will. Part of Nanok's reward is that he can justifiably claim to have brought resources to the community. For example, in his role as chairperson of the KISEDP Steering Committee, he has pushed strongly for measurable socio-economic indicators of KISEDP progress. A UNHCR staff member stated, 'We were asked by the government to show what we've done so far under KISEDP. They need the information to make certain statements... The Governor wants data for his statements. There are also rankings in the newspapers on county performance.' Such indicators of progress matter for electoral accountability but they also matter among peers within the Council of Governors. One Kenyan commentator explained, 'There is competition between counties and governors. For example, Kakamega County is now a well-known county for maternal health performance; Governor Nanok wants to be known for making a success of Turkana's refugee policy.'

And the benefits also accrue to particular line ministries—and indeed ministers—within the county government. To take an example, the county Health Ministry stands to benefit significantly from KISEDP because integrated healthcare provision allows the county government to leverage additional resources. As Dr Epem Esekon of the Ministry explained, 'KISEDP has helped us to leverage other resources... If we have funds from the international community in Turkana West, we have more elsewhere.' KISEDP covers fifty-two listed health facilities in Turkana West, of which eight are in Kakuma and Kalobeyei. That frees up resources for the rest of the county.

Furthermore, from November 2019 the Health Ministry has been able to roll out access to the country's private-sector-run and government-subsidized national insurance scheme, the National Hospital Insurance Fund (NHIF), because of KISEDP. Because UNHCR will pay for refugees' NHIF access, this has created a guaranteed market for NHIF to operate in Turkana, where previously the business case was weak. As Esekon put it, 'if we can use NHIS for everyone, refugees and hosts, it becomes a sustainable model; it reduces the overall budget for health'. And KISEDP is changing the way the Ministry delivers health; it is embracing a community health strategy in order to access remote and often nomadic, pastoralist communities. For example, the ministry pays community health volunteers (CHVs) in each village and equips them with smartphones to collect and upload data, and is embracing the use of telemedicine, mobile hospitals, and even cross-border health support. As resources increase, working patterns change, and indicators improve—reflecting positively on individual ministers.

Suggestions have been made that not all of the benefits are legitimate. Corruption and patronage are widespread in Kenya,[15] and Turkana County is no exception. The auditors' report on the county budget for 2017–18 showed that only $144 million was accounted for out of a total tax revenue of

$250 million.[16] The auditors' report expressed concern about why nearly a third of the county's budget is unaccounted for. However, although the national press has made specific allegations relating to Nanok's involvement in corruption and tax evasion, there is no available evidence to substantiate such claims.[17]

Further down the food chain, a major challenge in the County Assembly, and at the community level, has been that for every major investment, every village has wanted their share of the revenue. And this has sometimes even risked scuppering major projects. For example, thirty oil wells have been identified in Turkana South, and Tullow Oil has been given the exclusive right to the reserves for the first five years based on an 80:20 revenue-sharing deal with the government. But despite the huge potential for job creation, agreements have been massively delayed by protests in Lokichar, because of the host community's desire to claim a 5 per cent stake. Another example has been the proposal for the construction of the Tarach Dam, led by the Kenyan Red Cross in collaboration with the county's minister of water and minerals. But because so many actors have wanted a payoff in return for the investment, the idea of a dam had to be downgraded to a series of boreholes. These are just two examples of the ways in which the multiple levels of political entitlement in Turkana County, across national-level MPs, County Assembly representatives, political appointees, and chiefs, creates a complex layering of rent-seeking demands.

National-level politics

Regardless of the underlying politics, the progressive policies adopted in Turkana County are in stark contrast to the reactionary policies of Nairobi. Although a new Refugee Bill has been debated by the parliament for a number of years, the de jure right to work and freedom of movement for refugees across Kenya still seem remote. And yet there are small signs that gradually, from the bottom-up, the KISEDP may be starting to influence refugee policy at the national level.

In 2016, a new Refugee Bill was introduced to the Kenyan parliament as a Private Members' Bill by Agostinho Neto MP. The Bill included a range of progressive reform ideas, including freedom of movement, the right to work, and the possibility for refugees to naturalize after seven years. After significant sensitization and lobbying on behalf of refugee rights, conducted by the Parliamentary Caucus on Human Rights convened by Neto and other MPs such as the late Kenneth Okoth, the Bill passed through its first and second parliamentary readings. However, when it reached the executive level, it was struck down by the president 'because of a lack of consultation'. Indeed constitutionally, parliamentary Bills require consultation at the relevant regional levels, and almost no such consultation had taken place in Garissa County or Turkana County, the major refugee-hosting regions, for example. Moreover, even senior UNHCR staff highlighted that the Bill contained a range of contradictions. For example, as 'it proposed the introduction of the right to work but did not acknowledge that such rights partly exist "within designated areas"... the Bill therefore risked implying that all people in the designated areas have to apply for work permits in order to, for example, undertake incentive work.' In 2017 parliament was dissolved, and with that the Bill was declared 'dead' given that, constitutionally, parliamentary debates on legislation cannot be continued once a parliament has ended and elections taken place.

Within the new parliament, a task force was convened by government to work on bringing a new government Bill to parliament. This time, rather than risk leaving it to private members, the new Bill was proposed by the government and led by the Ministry of the Interior, the home of the Refugee Affairs Secretariat. The new Bill was gazetted in July 2019. Rather than a focus on socio-economic rights and freedoms, this Bill's primary focus was on security issues.

There was no mention of the right to work or freedom of movement. Instead, the Bill's focus was on clarifying the responsibilities of different branches of government for key aspects of refugee management: reception, status determination, control of the 'designated areas', registration and data management, durable solutions, and penalties, for example. The only nod towards a development approach related to two articles focused mainly on ensuring that the host communities could derive benefits from the presence of refugees. Article 34, for example, focused on 'Integration into host communities', albeit that the emphasis is on 'the shared use of social amenities by both the refugees and host communities' (34:1) and 'the handing over of amenities... upon the departure of refugees' (34:3). Article 35 focused on 'Consideration of refugee matters in development plans' and stated that 'the commissioner shall liaise with the national and county governments for the purpose of ensuring that refugee concerns are taken into consideration in the initiation and formulation of sustainable development and environmental plans'.[18]

In that sense, the Bill represented the institutionalization of a Dadaab-focused status quo, and a way for the government to clarify bureaucratic processes relating to the central government's long-standing policy line—that refugee policy 'should carefully manage humanitarian concerns with security concerns'. Furthermore, the Refugee Bill was introduced alongside a new Migration Bill, which aimed at clarifying the process by which all non-citizens, regardless of status, can apply for the right to work.

In the words of one Nairobi-based NGO staff member, 'the legislation is derived almost entirely from a focus on Dadaab; it hardly takes into account what is going on in Kakuma . . . Nairobi refugee discussions focus on Dadaab issues'. In Dadaab, the government's main focus has been on security and repatriation. In 2016, following a series of Al-Shabaab-linked terrorist attacks, the government threatened to immediately close down Dadaab and expel all Somali refugees. Only through effective shuttle diplomacy by UNHCR, the UN secretary-general, and the diplomatic community in Nairobi was this downgraded to a commitment to work gradually towards to 'voluntary repatriation' of Somalis in Dadaab. Alongside this, the government ceased providing Somalis with prima facie recognition, and stopped registering them in Dadaab.

Although Kenya has moved beyond trying to close down Dadaab, the agreement is that Somalis are encouraged to repatriate, but that they must have access to a set of basic conditions upon return including adequate water, health, and education facilities. The January 2019 terrorist attacks in Nairobi have done little to shift the focus from security and repatriation.

Nevertheless, there are some grounds for optimism at the national level. The KISEDP story is beginning to filter through. If progressive legislative change is to happen, it may well come from the bottom-up. As chairperson of the National Council of Governors, Nanok has spoken repeatedly in Nairobi about the KISEDP model. At their April 2019 meeting, Nanok apparently 'sold KISEDP to them'. And in June 2019, the governor of Garissa County, Ali Korane, and several of the county's ministers, travelled to Kakuma to meet Nanok and the UNHCR team. The aim was to learn and to explore the scope for adapting the KISEDP model to Dadaab.

Following the visit, UNHCR's head of field office in Dadaab was tasked with considering how KISEDP might be adapted to the context, with a stronger focus on durable solutions. Furthermore, UNHCR and the county government jointly convened three business association meetings in Garissa County, involving both refugees and members of the host community during

2019. According to one member of the UNHCR team in Kakuma, such an approach was long overdue: 'Garissa has benefitted so much from humanitarian assistance but it has become lazy. It has the lowest percentage of food production in Kenya because it relies upon food aid . . . In a context like this, if refugees leave, you are finished. The level of dependency that has been reached is incredible.' With Korane's visit to Kakuma it appears that Garissa may be starting to listen. Meanwhile, at the Nairobi level, Ruth Kagia, deputy chief of staff to the president and a progressive advocate for refugees within the central government, explained, 'For many in Kenya, the word refugees evoked Dadaab and Dadaab evoked a bad experience. What the UN has done is to focus on Kakuma and partner with a range of actors to make Kakuma a success. It's possible this may gradually change the debate.'[19]

As we saw in Chapter 6, it is certainly too early to proclaim KISEDP a success, and rollout in Dadaab would probably be even more challenging, given the economic and security constraints of the region. But the mere fact that Turkana's experience has led to tentative interest in Garissa County shows the potential for the new model to change the terms of the national political debate.

The international politics

International donors, especially, invested heavily in KISEDP. From an initial 15 million euro commitment by the EU at the inception phase, the budget for the first five years expanded to a total requirement of $500 million. The timeframe for the fifteen-year strategy, running until 2030, demonstrated an unprecedented level of long-term planning.

The initial European impetus was significantly driven by a concern with onward migration. The EU and some of the bilateral donors, including DFID and the Swiss Agency for Development and Cooperation (SDC), had been present at the 2014 Lodwar meeting before the European refugee crisis broke in 2015. Even at that stage, the EU viewed development-based approaches to protracted displacement through a lens of reducing the need for irregular secondary movement to Europe. It had already established a Regional Development and Protection Programme (RDPP), a four-year programme created by eight European donors and the EU. Several of the interested donors were long-time advocates of 'protection in the region of origin' strategies as an alternative to onward migration. At a global level, the

Solutions Alliance had been launched in April of 2014 as a multi-stakeholder network focusing on the relationship between development and solutions to protracted displacement. Key European donors were beginning to view collaboration between UNHCR and the World Bank as a vehicle for reducing the need for secondary migration by refugees.

The European refugee crisis created the funding mechanism for KISEDP. Without the crisis, there would have been no EU Trust Fund relating to irregular migration and displacement in Africa established in Valletta in November 2015. And without the fund, it is unlikely that KISEDP would have got off the ground. The EU's 'intervention logic' behind supporting KISEDP was explicitly linked to 'decreasing the incentives for irregular secondary movements'. Over time, however, as the European refugee crisis dissipated, the link between KISEDP and irregular secondary movement faded. With migrant numbers crossing the Mediterranean in decline, donor motives for backing KISEDP began to change. Furthermore, the empirical relationship between development opportunities in Kakuma and migration to Europe is unclear: although South Sudanese and Somalis have travelled from East Africa to Europe, the numbers passing through Kakuma are likely to be small. Our own research shows that in the period of August 2017 to August 2018, no more than about 2 per cent of recent arrivals moved to a third country, and, of those, the most likely destination was Uganda.[20]

Beyond the European refugee crisis, the donor focus became less on onward migration and more about piloting a new and more sustainable refugee assistance model. KISEDP represented the opportunity to pilot a new way of working that might potentially be scaled elsewhere. Kalobeyei was the first example of an integrated settlement for refugees and hosts that had been designed from scratch. It offered an area-based approach to development within which refugees could benefit from shared markets and public services. And it offered a 'laboratory' for piloting and testing a range of market-based interventions, including cash-based interventions. Above all, KISEDP offered an opportunity for learning and a space for innovation. And UNHCR presented it to donors as an exemplar of the wider Global Compact on Refugees.

Underlying this was the question of whether the new model might offer donors an 'exit option'. Could the KISEDP model facilitate 'the transition from relief to development' and thereby reduce the long-term cost to humanitarian aid budgets? By 2019, major KISEDP donors such as DFID, USAID, and the EU were already asking challenging questions in closed meetings with UN agencies. When could they get out? When would they begin to see the humanitarian aid budget fall? What would be the turning point at which their upfront investment in KISEDP paid dividends? For example, donors were pushing WFP on the viability of introducing means-testing for food aid. If some refugees were being supported to become entrepreneurs, for example, did they really need food assistance? Or could food assistance be reserved for those with the greatest need?

One WFP staff member explained. 'For donors, when they hear "self-reliance", it is synonymous with "exit strategy". They want to know when they can get out. But there is a chicken-and-egg problem. We are asking for even more money upfront because to achieve self-reliance requires that we first build the economy around Kakuma.'[21] Indeed, many donors, including the EU, acknowledge the need for upfront investment in the model to hope to achieve improved sustainability over time. But they are asking the UN agencies for greater clarity in terms of timing and sequencing. The reality is that self-reliance remains remote in Kakuma and Kalobeyei, and it will require major upfront investment to bring in capital for infrastructure and public goods and to develop the preconditions for significant private-sector investment. The question will be whether, with the EU refugee crisis no longer a major political focus, donors are prepared to stay the course and provide the investment needed to yield a more sustainable and potentially scalable model.

Conclusion

Although it remains early in KISEDP's fifteen-year strategy, the plan offers an unprecedented model for refugee assistance. It represents a shift from a humanitarian aid model to an area-based development model. By integrating service delivery for refugees and the host community, and building stronger market-based opportunities for both communities, the approach aims to improve socio-economic outcomes and social cohesion across Turkana West while also facilitating self-reliance for refugees. KISEDP has led to the creation of the new Kalobeyei settlement, as well as an entirely new integrated development model for the sub-county of Turkana West.

For the Government of Turkana County, KISEDP offers a pathway to sustainable development. For refugees, it offers a route to access better services and greater socio-economic opportunity. The model itself is also unprecedented, being based on strong partnership between a local government and the international community. That KISEDP is taking place in Kenya, a country with strict legal limits on refugees' right to work and freedom of movement, makes the story both remarkable and improbable. But what, politically, has made KISEDP possible? How has a sub-national region adopted such a radically different approach to refugees compared to the national government?

If we are to understand the conditions for replication, we also need to understand the politics that has made KISEDP possible. The overall story is unusual insofar as it has unfolded through local political leadership and in spite of the absence of national government buy-in. This is perhaps because of Turkana County's historically peripheral relationship to Nairobi. The Government of Turkana County has been able to pursue an independent relationship with the international community, largely bypassing Nairobi. Devolution in 2012 helped. But, above all, the personality, charisma, and history of the governor, Josphat Nanok, made KISEDP possible. His past life as a humanitarian, his memory of what happened to the Turkana economy when humanitarian agencies packed up and left, and his own political ambitions all coalesced to create an unlikely champion of refugee rights.

But in addition to leadership, KISEDP has also required resources, both for area development and to buy off potential gatekeepers, and its long-term viability will depend upon ongoing donor backing. The European refugee crisis and donors' narrative that development-based responses to protracted displacement could reduce onward migration brought the initial investment. Thereafter, UNHCR's identification of KISEDP as an exemplar of the UN Global Compact on Refugees contributed to a donor willingness to invest in an innovative model offering the potential for learning and replication. However, there are questions about whether donors will stay the course. By 2020, in the midst of the COVID-19 pandemic, UNHCR's Kenya operation was increasingly concerned about a funding shortfall for KISEDP.[22]

Regardless of the long-term outcome of KISEDP, it has seeded an opportunity for refugee self-reliance in one part of a country with an otherwise highly restrictive refugee policy. And there are signs that the model may even be starting to have an influence on thinking in Garissa County and Nairobi. From a political perspective, KISEDP reveals the possibility that progressive change in refugee policy can emerge from the bottom-up, at a sub-national level, even in countries not known for progressive national refugee policies.

11

Ethiopia

Conditionality and the right to work

Introduction

In January 2019, Ethiopia's parliament adopted some of the most progressive refugee legislation in the world. In law, at least, it went from having a strict encampment policy that denies refugees the right to work towards one that ostensibly allows refugees greater freedom of movement and the right to work. Alongside legislative change, a series of other progressive reform measures have been adopted, leading the UN High Commissioner for Refugees to suggest that 'Ethiopia is a shining example of African hospitality'.[1] How and why did this apparent volte-face occur, what are its implications, and what can we learn from it?

Ethiopia's previous Refugee Proclamation (No. 409/2004) allowed the government to 'designate the place and areas in Ethiopia within which recognized refugees...shall live' (Act. 21.2) and provided that 'every refugee shall, in respect to wage earning employment...be entitled to the same restrictions as are conferred or imposed generally by the relevant laws on persons who are not citizens of Ethiopia.'[2] In practice, this meant that, aside from just 23,000 Eritrean refugees with 'Out-of-Camp' status and a handful of other refugees with special needs, the rest of the country's 900,000 refugees were required to reside in one of twenty-six camps in peripheral border locations, and had few socio-economic rights.

In contrast, the updated Refugee Proclamation (No. 1011/2019), passed by the 547-member parliament with just three oppositions and one abstention, sets out a series of socio-economic rights rarely available in refugee-hosting countries. Article 25 provides refugees 'the right to engage in wage earning employment' and 'the right to engage...in agriculture, small and micro-enterprise, handicraft and commerce, and to establish business organizations', while Article 27 provides 'the right to liberty of movement and freedom to choose his residence'.[3] Of course, closer analysis highlights a series of caveats. For example, the right to work is 'in the same circumstance as the most favourable treatment accorded to foreign nationals pursuant to relevant laws' and there are strong indications that the rights, which are subject to a series of implementation directives, will only be rolled out iteratively and based on international investment in job creation that mutually benefits citizens and refugees. Nevertheless, even if full implementation is stalled, the legislative change is significant. Alongside this new legislation, the government also created an internal Strategy Document, which outlines the complementary ambition 'to go from camps to no camps after 10 years.'

This legislative change is the pinnacle of a series of radical reforms to Ethiopia's national refugee policy, which were first signalled to the international community at a refugee conference convened by US President Barack Obama in New York on 20 September 2016. At this Leaders' Summit on Refugees, governments were asked for pledges and Ethiopia's proposals were the stand-out new commitments. A US State Department official commented 'we were surprised, but we approached the Government of Ethiopia, and they said "we are willing to do this, but nobody has ever asked us before"'.[4] The government's 'nine pledges' included work permits for refugees with permanent residence or living in areas permitted for foreign workers, job creation for 30,000 refugees in new industrial park jobs as part of a new Jobs Compact with international donors, expansion of the 'Out-of-Camp' Policy (OCP) to 75,000 refugees, local integration and a pathway to naturalization for the 13,000 refugees present in the country for more than twenty years, land for agricultural irrigation close to refugee camps, improvements to basic and social services, increased education enrolment, and better access to identity and related documentation.[5]

What happened before and after the Leaders' Summit to explain such a radical, and largely unprecedented, change in policy relating to the socioeconomic inclusion of refugees? Understanding the change is historically important in its own right, but also of wider relevance because it offers an opportunity to understand some of the pathways and determinants of progressive change in refugee policy. Although it is only one case, it is the most salient example of rapid and radical policy and legislative change relating to the socio-economic inclusion of refugees. To what extent has change been driven by values, interests, or norms? Is it best explained at the domestic or international levels of analysis?

The most obvious potential explanations for change include: American influence, political reform, Ethiopia's regional role, the values of the country's political leaders, and international norms. However, none of these offers an adequate account, for the following reasons. First, American influence relating to the Leaders' Summit: State Department and White House officials were caught by surprise by the pledges, and they did not engage in sustained lobbying. Second, political reform in Ethiopia: refugee policy reform began prior to the election of 'reformist' Prime Minister Abiy Ahmed in 2018, and came from the office of long-standing Prime Minister Hailemariam Desalegn. Third, Ethiopia's regional role: the government's desire to play the part of a regional hegemon dates back to Meles Zenawi's term as prime minister, and, although embryonic peace and transition arrangements relating to neighbouring states such as Eritrea, Somalia, and South Sudan offered new opportunities, progress on these deals was neither advanced nor unprecedented. Fourth, the values of political leaders: if Ethiopia was simply concerned with the wellbeing of forcibly displaced populations, surely it would also have improved its widely criticized treatment of around 2 million internally displaced persons?[6] Fifth, international norms: Ethiopia's commitments were used to illustrate global normative changes such as the Global Compact on Refugees process but were not driven by them.

The transformation therefore represents an interesting puzzle, which requires deeper exploration. In this chapter, I argue that two related factors—one external and the other internal—shaped the legislative and policy shift. First, the government's desire to attract international assistance and invest-ment. Second, the government's desire to allocate some of those resources to enhance its authority at a sub-national level, including in peripheral refugee-hosting regions. More specifically, the UK, the EU, and the World Bank offered the Government of Ethiopia over $600 million in support of its industrial strategy in return for the provision of 30,000 job opportunities for refugees within its industrial zones as part of a deal known as the Jobs Compact. The funders made legislative change a condition of the deal. This deal in turn gave Ethiopia the opportunity to extend industrial development to regions previously peripheral to the national economy but of political importance in the context of the country's model of ethnic federalism.

Although implementation of the Jobs Compact soon stalled, part of its legacy was the Proclamation. The case demonstrates how international bargains, based on conditionality and issue-linkage, can lead directly to progressive refugee legislation when they empower host-country politicians to achieve domestic political objectives. Methodologically, I use process tracing to show the connection between the Jobs Compact and legislative change, demonstrating counterfactually, that without international investment and its importance to core-periphery politics within Ethiopia, the new Proclamation would not have been passed. The qualitative data within this chapter is based on semi-structured interviews with policy elites conducted mainly in Addis Ababa in March 2019.

Industrial parks and the Jobs Compact

The Ethiopian Jobs Compact was a deal first made public in September 2016. The essence of the bargain was that more than half a billion US dollars was pledged by the UK, the EU, and the World Bank to support the government to create three new industrial parks in exchange for 30,000 jobs in any of the country's more than twenty industrial parks. It emerged when the UK's Department for International Development (DFID) approached the Ethiopian Prime Minister's Office (PMO) about employing refugees in industrial parks, based on similar plans in Jordan.

Industrial parks were already a key pillar of the government's existing industrialization strategy under Prime Minister Hailemariam Desalegn. Ethiopia and its international donors had for over a decade shifted focus from agricultural development to industrialization as a means to achieve export-led growth and job creation. And although the largest international investment for the parks came from China, DFID had supported the parks model since 2013. For example, it had previously invested in the Hawassa industrial park, which specializes in garments and textiles, attracting investment from manufacturers licensed by the PVH Group, which includes brands such as Tommy Hilfiger and Calvin Klein.

In 2015, Europe was gripped by the so-called refugee crisis, where over 1 million asylum seekers, mainly from Syria, had travelled to countries like Germany and Sweden. The combination of public backlash and sympathy contributed to a search for creative solutions. And one such solution was a proposal to support job creation for Syrian refugees in Jordan's eighteen pre-existing industrial zones, as a means to politically facilitate the right to work for Syrians and support Jordan's leap to manufacturing. In early

September 2015, British Prime Minister David Cameron had outlined the basis of a deal with King Abdullah of Jordan, with DFID writing the plans, and bringing the EU and the World Bank on board. It was a model conceived as 'win-win' in terms of Jordan's national development strategy, Europe's immigration management, and refugees' socio-economic rights and opportunities.

Within DFID, the then chief economist, Stefan Dercon, had played a lead role in the conceptual development of the Jordan Compact. That same month, while considering other contexts in which the model might be applied, he approached George Turkington, the head of DFID in Addis Ababa, about the idea of applying the model in Ethiopia. Late that September, Turkington put the idea to Prime Minister Hailemariam Desalegn's senior advisor, Arkebe Oqubay, the former mayor of Addis and the architect of Ethiopia's industrialization strategy.

Oqubay explained, 'The first time DFID raised it, they were not sure we would like it. They knew about Jordan, and they just raised it softly, but we liked it.' From the Ethiopian perspective, it represented an opportunity. Discussions began in September 2015, and both Cameron and Hailemariam Desalegn were briefed on the plans at that stage. As Tadesse Kassa Woldetsadik, a consultant to the Ethiopian Investment Commission (EIC) that played a key role in the discussions, explained, 'It just coincided. From the EIC's perspective, this was just an opportunity to extend the industri-alization agenda.' Indeed, on both sides, there was the prospect of mutual gain based on issue-linkage. For the UK, it was about the link to migration, for Ethiopia it was about development. As Tadesse put it:

> For us, the primary interest is not to accommodate refugees; the key priority for us was the broader agenda of industrialization, job creation, and the expan-sion of industrial parks because we also need investment. From DFID's point of view, it was motivated by migration from the perspective of the UK, and also from Europe; it was a broader political agenda.

For DFID, Ethiopia's industrial strategy was a priority, aligning with UK aid's vision for private-sector-led development. Its previous Hawassa investment was viewed as a success but the migration management agenda provided an additional impetus. Although in 2015 the media focus was on Syria, mixed migration across the central Mediterranean remained a key part of the agenda. DFID recognized that a comprehensive response would also have to involve Africa. Within that context, Ethiopia was recognized as

a country of origin, a transit country, and a source of secondary movement
by refugees. It was widely identified by organizations such as the Mixed
Migration Secretariat as a key node of the smuggling networks that provide
a pathway for refugees and migrants from the Horn of Africa and the Great
Lakes region via Egypt and Libya and into the EU. Jobs and economic
inclusion for refugees, DFID policy-makers reasoned, would offer a better
alternative than using smugglers to cross the Mediterranean.

The EU, the European Investment Bank (EIB), and the World Bank—all
partners on the Jordan Compact—were brought into the discussion by early
2016. Within the Government of Ethiopia, the initiative was institutionalized through collaboration across the Ministry of Finance and Economic
Development (MOFED), EIC, and the Industrial Parks Development
Corporation (IPDC). By June 2016 the parameters of a deal were in place.
The total fund was about $600 million: $50 million would be provided as
grant by the UK to support the training and relocation of refugees into the
parks; EIB committed $250 million in partly concessional loans; the World
Bank offered $250 million, half as grant and half as concessional loans; and
the EU offered $50 million as grant.

All of these funds came with conditions. The World Bank's funding was
based on clear milestones, one of which was the Proclamation itself, which
was a 'key performance indicator' to be delivered by 31 December 2018 in
order to disburse the first tranche of funds without having to go back for
Board approval. The World Bank was able to approve the funding, after its
Board had previously backed the Jordan Compact. And although the Jobs
Compact was a small part of its overall Ethiopia portfolio, Ethiopia's wider
relationship with the Bank and the upcoming 'IDA window' (the process by
which the Bank allocates grants and low-interest loans to poor countries)
offered additional leverage.

As we first saw in Chapter 2, the EU Emergency Trust Fund for Africa
(EUTF for Africa) was a 4.6 billion euro fund launched at the Valletta
Summit at the height of the European migration crisis. The Horn of Africa
and Ethiopia were among its main geographical priorities, and the $50 million
allocated in support of the Jobs Compact represented a fifth of total EUTF
for Africa commitments to the country. The EUTF for Africa could not
create new initiatives; but, Sabrina Bazzanella of the EU Embassy in Addis
explained, 'As the EU, we would not have had the opportunity to support
the Jobs Compact [by ourselves] with the Trust Fund but the World Bank
and DFID were already there, and we had the opportunity to join them.'

The EUTF for Africa's milestones partly replicated those of the World Bank. The 'modalities for implementation', for example, provided direct 'budget support' to the Ministry of Finance in tranches and based on a set of indicators that included the World Bank-coordinated feasibility studies and, significantly, legislative change to allow refugees the right to work.

Indeed, neither the World Bank, nor the EU, nor the EIB would ultimately disburse any of the committed funding until after the Proclamation was passed in 2019.

Tadesse joined the EIC as a consultant in 2015 and was tasked with drafting the overall concept note for the initiative, which was completed by June 2016. The initial agreement was for three new industrial parks creating a total of 100,000 jobs, of which 30 per cent would be earmarked for refugees. The idea of a $500 million investment was benchmarked against the costs of the Hawassa industrial park. The initial plan was that the 30,000 jobs for refugees would be in the three new parks, although it was later agreed that the refugee jobs could be in any of the country's industrial parks.

The initial concept note aimed to select sites close to each of the three main refugee populations: Eritreans in the north, South Sudanese in the west, and Somalis in the south-east. However, the initial selection also reflected criteria such as existing park locations, viability for investment, and—relatedly—the prime minister's political priorities. Under Prime Minister Hailemariam Desalegn, these selection criteria coalesced around privileging the regions underpinning his, and his party's, base: Tigray and Oromia. Reflecting this, the sites initially earmarked were first, Me'kelle (in Tigray), hosting Eritreans; second, Dire Dawa (a chartered city) for Somalis; and, third, either Alage on the border between southern region and Oromia or Hawassa (in Oromia).

Already at that stage, Tadesse notes, legislation was part of this conversation on the Ethiopian side: 'New legislation had to be prepared to allow refugees to get access to work. And this Proclamation revision started jointly and has now been endorsed by the parliament.' One illustration of the early connection between the industrial parks plan and the legislation was Tadesse's own role. Initially recruited as a consultant to the EIC, he soon played a lead role on the drafting committee for the Proclamation.

Plans were in place to publicly launch the initiative in the summer of 2016. David Cameron was due to travel to Ethiopia in July 2016, immediately after the Brexit referendum, and to launch the Jobs Compact in Hawassa. Until that point, the initiative had been kept under wraps due to its political sensitivity at both ends of the bargain. A team from 10 Downing Street and the Cabinet Office had already travelled with the UK's ambassador to Addis, Susanna Moorhead, to Hawassa in June 2016 to make preparations for the launch. The media briefs had been prepared. The planned timing of the launch, after an anticipated Remain success, was strategic. As Arkebe put it:

> The link [to Brexit] was that if the UK was to stay in the EU then an agenda was important on how the government is to manage migration. And the concept was that if the EU is that the best way to stop migration the best way was to ensure that jobs are created in Africa, and that people stay here to benefit from the opportunity.

However, the referendum went against Cameron and he did not remain prime minister long enough to travel to Hawassa.

Nevertheless, preparations continued in late summer 2016. At the international level, the World Bank assumed a lead management role. It established the Economic Opportunities Programme (EOP) in Ethiopia to support jobs for both refugees and hosts. The World Bank also began to hire consultants to work on the details, and updated modalities were agreed, including 'that the 30,000 refugees should not necessarily be located in the three new parks; but that refugees could be employed in any of the parks' and that 'the three new parks can be constructed based on the case of the government'.

At the national level, the EIC took on the lead role and a special unit was established to work closely with donors on implementation. Tadesse explained the work of the unit:

> It was a very risky venture; so we had a whole team of people working on it. The EIC was really leading the process, and we needed to learn from the Jordan process. World Bank staff from Jordan came two or three times. And it did contribute a lot. But the Ethiopian situation is quite unique. So we need to build it our way. We needed to engage the market in discussion and undertake the feasibility studies for the three parks, under the oversight of the prime minister.

Getting ARRA and UNHCR on board

A Steering Committee was set up for the initiative, comprising the MOFED, the Ministry of Labour, the EIC, the IPDC, and, crucially, the

Administration of Refugee and Returnee Affairs (ARRA). This move, in the summer of 2016, was the first time the government's refugee affairs department (ARRA) had been brought on board. ARRA had always been a part of the security and intelligence apparatus of the state, and its attitude to refugees had generally reflected this. However, from 2016, its own position towards the economic inclusion of refugees had begun to soften.

The incoming deputy director (head) of ARRA, Ato Zeynu, who took over the organization in April 2016, became an important champion of the Jobs Compact, nationally and internationally. A member of UNHCR staff in Addis, explained that 'The previous administration of ARRA were blocking our every move [to create economic opportunities for refugees]...In contrast, Zeynu had a humanitarian background having started his career in ARRA in Dima refugee camp.' One non-governmental organization (NGO) staffer in Addis explained 'we could really talk to Zeynu, whereas his predecessor was just scary. You felt the difficulty of where ARRA sat...With Zeynu, you had a partner.' Zeynu travelled in his first year to Uganda to study the self-reliance model, and aspired to create an Ethiopian version. The then head of an international NGO in Addis recalled:

> He'd just come back and was like a kid, he was so enthusiastic. He said 'I've just come back from Uganda and [refugees] are working and [some] have houses bigger than Ugandans. They can do everything a Ugandan can do except vote'. And he said 'we can do this. We can aspire to this'. It was enthusiasm in a culture where you don't see a lot of enthusiasm.

Zeynu also travelled two or three times with UNHCR's representative to Dollo Ado in the Somali region of Ethiopia, where the IKEA Foundation was investing in self-reliance and livelihood opportunities for refugees. The IKEA Foundation's investment of \$100 million in the Dollo Ado camps was the largest private-sector investment ever in a set of refugee camps, and Zeynu chose to work collaboratively with the Foundation's CEO, Per Heggenes. The experience was formative for Zeynu as, according to one observer, it 'allowed [him] to look at the bigger picture...If you can get the donors and private sector to invest in the areas that no-one else is investing in, they can help us do development in these regions, helping people, then leaving a tangible legacy for the countries.' Indeed, the World Bank's lead on refugee affairs in Addis confirmed, 'For ARRA this is a good example of attracting FDI and the private sector...ARRA uses the example with the IKEA Foundation and hails it as a great example of private sector investment.'

Two new 'launch' opportunities loomed on the horizon, both outcomes of the European refugee crisis. On 19 September, the UN General Assembly would hold a High-Level Meeting on Refugees and Migration, and on 20 September, US President Obama would host a Leaders' Summit on Refugees. The former would focus on multilateral commitments and launched the UN Global Compact on Refugees process; the latter on specific pledges by states.

On 19 September, Theresa May used her first policy statement as the UK's new prime minister to announce the Ethiopian Jobs Compact at the General Assembly. On 20 September, the Ethiopian Government took the world by surprise by announcing what subsequently became known as the '9 Pledges'. As Elizabeth Campbell, who worked on compiling pledges for Obama's Leaders' Summit explained: 'The Ethiopian pledges were the stand-out commitments of the Summit.'[7] The pledges themselves had been drafted by Ato Zeynu and his ARRA colleagues with input and suggestions from UNHCR. But the political support on which they were based came from the PMO and was an outcome of the Jobs Compact negotiations.

While the Obama Administration took some of the initial plaudits for the announcement, in practice they had little influence on the '9 Pledges' announcement. The US Government did not provide direct budget support to the Ethiopian Government and had little leverage. As Tadesse explained, '[the agreement] as at an advanced stage by September 2016 . . . the conference simply provided the opportunity to announce plans that were already underway'.

Practical challenges and a new prime minister

In early 2017, Ethiopia was rewarded for the pledges with growing private-sector interest. In March, a delegation travelled to the Group of Eight (G8) summit in Berlin. The model was showcased as relevant to the Group of Twenty (G20) Compact with Africa and the Marshall Plan for Africa. At the G8 summit, the delegation met with Sir Paul Collier, Merkel's advisor on Africa and one of the original creators of the idea of creating employment opportunities for refugees in special economic zones. Other opportunities followed and both the PMO and the EIC pitched the inclusion of refugees within industrial parks at the Investment Forum in London in March 2017, as well as events elsewhere in Europe.

But there were still practical challenges relating to the Jobs Compact. A McKinsey-led feasibility study was commissioned by DFID and overseen by the Ethiopian Government. The McKinsey team looked at three contexts: Alage for South Sudanese, Me'kelle for Eritreans, and Dire Dawa for Somalis. The studies raised doubts about the chosen locations, and Alage in particular was reviewed as too remote and lacking in infrastructure to sustainably host an industrial park.

When Abiy took over as prime minister in April 2018, priorities changed. Coming to power with a mandate to more equitably distribute power and resources beyond Tigray and Oromia, he reconsidered the proposed locations for the three new textile-focused parks. His alternative choices were Semera (in Afar), Aysha (in Somali Region but near Dire Dawa), and Asosa (in Benshangi). As Arkebe explained, 'it was because of the "equitable growth agenda". It was a political decision, but an important decision we had to make.' Tadesse agrees: 'the new PM came in and he had a different set of industrial parks ... because they are the only regions that have no industrial parks and have been lobbying. The other major regions all have at least one.' Abiy's electoral platform of offering more equitable distribution of opportunities, however, created challenges because, while the new areas served the political agenda, it was not clear that they offered the best infrastructural context to attract investment in manufacturing. Even though feasibility studies had already been conducted in the previous government's chosen locations, the new locations were prioritized in order to redistribute opportunity. Abiy was riding a wave of global support, and donors accepted the change. The politics of ethnic federalism trumped economic logic.

Other practical issues awaited the industrial parks plan. The parks were distant from the refugee camps, and most refugees coming from Somalia and South Sudan had no background of working in factories. Most were pastoralists and so, even if some were theoretically willing to work, there was concern that their low manufacturing productivity might risk companies prioritizing other workers. Furthermore, distance meant investment would be needed to provide housing, otherwise low-wage workers would be spending 30–50 per cent of their wages on accommodation. DFID tried to solve this by allocating its $50 million contribution primarily for a combination of training and housing. Nevertheless, a significant and unavoidable concern, particularly among human rights and humanitarian organizations, was that wages would be well below even Ethiopia's median wage. And having not been consulted early in the process, NGOs in Addis were sceptical. The country representative of one international NGO explained 'We really had to battle our way into it...It wasn't an inclusive process and it wasn't especially well coordinated.'

The major donors were slow to disburse funds. Based on McKinsey's feasibility studies, the World Bank Board approved assistance in its June 2018 meeting. But to make that loan effective, it had to be endorsed by the Ethiopian parliament, which was in recess between June and September. With everything approved, the final hurdle for World Bank funding was the passage of the Proclamation in 2019. But other donors dragged their feet, and by 2019 it was unclear whether any of the pledged EU money would actually be disbursed. One government official explained: 'On disbursement, I am optimistic on the World Bank funding because they have done this before, they have experience on Bole Lemi and Kilinto industrial parks. My big concern is on the EIB and EU side. On the DFID grant I am not much concerned that will be OK'. And without disbursement, the government was not prepared to earmark jobs for refugees. The same government official explained, 'we will implement after the release of the funds; without that we are not going to do that. Otherwise, jobs for refugees with be prioritized over Ethiopians, and this is a very politically sensitive issue.' One Addis based development consultant explained, 'The industrial parks are a red herring...the World Bank targets are pitiful, over the next four years it only requires about 1000 work permits for refugees, and only 30,000 at the end of the process.' Indeed, by 2020, relatively little of the $600 million had actually been delivered and none of the 30,000 jobs for refugees were in place.

However, regardless of whether the Jobs Compact is ultimately implemented, its real legacy was the Proclamation. And despite his scepticism about the Compact, the same consultant recognizes the link to the Proclamation: 'The main influence was the $600m; no doubt about that.' Indeed, nearly all Addis-based commentators agree that it was the Jobs Compact which enabled the Proclamation to come into existence. Without the incentive structure created by a more than half billion dollar carrot, the new legislation would not have emerged. As one government representative said: 'The triggering point was Jobs Compact. Without this, this issue would not have been raised...and we would not have had the discussion about the Proclamation. An inducement has come from the Jobs Compact'. The Jobs Compact, agreed under Hailemariam Desalegn, had opened up the political space for legislative change. And much of the drafting process was handed over to UNHCR. As a senior member of staff at UNHCR put it: 'We worked with the government to help them write it out. We pushed the government to put it on paper; in Ethiopia this is not always a priority.' Between them, UNHCR's protection team in Addis and the government consultant, Tadesse, wrote large sections of the Proclamation.

Sustainability and ethnic federalism

The Proclamation, however, has limitations. Despite setting out the right to work and freedom of movement, it contains caveats within the text and is also subject to interpretation. For example, it says that refugees will be given 'the same labour rights as foreign nationals' and so may require specific work permits. It also reiterates that ARRA can require refugees to reside in the 'designated areas', implying that the 'Out-of-Camp' status will continue to be available only to a limited number of refugees. Indeed, the government's own understanding of the Proclamation is that it will gradually offer the right to work and freedom of movement, insofar as Ethiopia is supported through 'international responsibility-sharing'. One government representative clarified:

> The key point is this Proclamation is not saying that one million refugees can work all over the country. This has a political dimension; we have to give priority to local Ethiopians. So this will allow us to recruit the 30,000. Once we get additional resources, the number will be increased.

Another government representative recognized the ambiguity: 'The drafting is quite open ... it gives huge leeway. But we have to be very clear on where we stand. Are we adopting this Uganda-style model or is it a quota-based system with progressive measures tied to international funding? It's not quite clear.' Despite, these limitations, the government has worked on a parallel Strategy Document relating to the Proclamation, and drafted by ARRA, which sets out the aim to go from camps to no camps after ten years.

There is therefore recognition that the socio-economic rights within the Proclamation will be implemented gradually, and the timeframe will be partly dependent upon international funding. However, a further source of ambiguity relating to implementation stems from the Abiy government's relationship to the Proclamation. There is widespread consensus that the refugee issue is less of a priority for Abiy than it was for his predecessor. Abiy came to power on a reformist platform, intent on building peace

across the region, enhancing political freedoms within Ethiopia, and offering greater representation to historically marginalized regions of Ethiopia.

In this context, Abiy's priorities lay elsewhere, including in engaging
Ethiopia's unemployed and politically active youth, ensuring peace with
Eritrea, enhancing Ethiopia's global reputation, and—most relevantly—
managing Ethiopia's delicate ethnic federal balance in a way that would give
him the greatest prospects for success in the scheduled 2021 elections. As
one Addis-based commentator explained,

> We're dealing with a very different government today than before…the gov-
> ernment has changed and the political climate has changed…the activists have
> come back. The opposition has come back…That is creating delays. There is
> not necessarily the same level of focus [relating to refugees] as there was.

Another UN staff member within a different organization in Addis stated,
'The Prime Minister agrees to everything but does not follow through.
There are lot of promises but no follow-up on anything…He's a bit like a
visionary CEO without a COO.'[8]

But insofar as there remained a commitment to support the socio-economic
inclusion of refugees, it was viewed through the lens of ethnic federalism.
Despite a rhetorical concern with greater inclusivity, one UN commentator
explained, 'The PM is only really concerned about Amhara, Oromos, and
Tigrayans' (who make up 67 per cent of the country's population between
them). And Abiy tried to realign the balance across the three regions: 'he has
reduced the power of Tigrayans, and increased that of Amharas and Oromos.
A lot of Tigrayans are not happy with him.' Indeed, Abiy's redesignation of
the proposed sites for the new Jobs Compact industrial parks was a reflection of this, with Me'kelle, the Tigrayan capital, losing its position as one of
the designated beneficiary states within the plan.

Hailemariam Desalegn had led a centralized and technocratic process to
commit to the wide-ranging reforms to refugee law and policy. However,
regional governments and sub-regional governments felt inadequately
consulted. And, for Abiy, whose popularity was based partly on the language
of regional inclusion, this represented a particular challenge.

In Gambella, the Proclamation created the strongest and most violent
backlash. In the words of one NGO commentator, 'the politics of the
Gambella region is the politics of refugees'. This is because of the delicate
demographic balance between Nuer and Anouack, and the Anouack
people's fear that the influx of South Sudanese refugees tips the region's

balance of power away from them and towards the Nuer. And while Gambella hosts nearly 200,000 refugees, its own population of around 500,000 is rarely the focus of national development plans. The same NGO representative explained, 'There was a lack of consultation with the regions on the Proclamation but it passed because it was under the table, and there were more important political concerns, such as relations with the EU and other bilateral donors.' In the immediate aftermath of the Proclamation passing through parliament, violent protests were seen on the streets of Gambella.[9]

When UNHCR's Comprehensive Refugee Response Framework (CRRF)—a development plan for refugees and the host communities—was launched in Gambella in support of the '9 Pledges', it was not well received. One observer explained, 'The CRRF is a swearword in Gambella... we needed to sell the process better from day one, to offer benefits at the sub-national level. But that did not happen. ARRA and UNHCR drove the process in a very technocratic way.' One NGO representative who attended the launch of the CRRF in Gambella in 2018 recalled:

> During the CRRF launch in Gambella, UNHCR mobilised refugees and hosts in a room, and flew people in from Addis who spoke at them in English. Everyone from the host community stood up and said in Anouack, 'are you here to tell us the refugees are going home?' Zeynu responded with a spiel and was like a colonial master, talking down to them...

In the Somali region, by contrast, 'refugees are a non-issue' in the words of one UNHCR staff member. Nearly all refugees are Somali and the majority of the host community identify as ethnic Somali. Jijiga, the regional capital, has hosted Somali refugees since the early 1990s. The presence of refugees is generally perceived to bring economic benefits. For example, in Jijiga there is interdependence between host community members who often register businesses and refugees who bring capital from Mogadishu or Baidoa, for example.

The region has faced political challenges, notably in its relationship with the central government. There is an ongoing internal armed conflict between historically favoured Oromia and the Somali region. The region has also been historically marginalized by the central government, but with attempts to impose control from the centre as a means to avert secession. In the words of a UN staff member: 'They had a regional president that was tolerated because in terms of governance, it was infringing all the basic standards, in terms of human rights, peace; but in terms of allegiance to the Central Government, he ticked the boxes.' Occasionally, the central government has tried to assert authority in the region. For example, in August 2018, violence broke out in the Somali region, and particularly in Jijiga, when the central government tried to impose its own leadership structure on the region.

Indeed, as with the CRRF launch in Gambella, a roll-out meeting also took place in Jijiga in 2018. However, an international NGO representative in attendance explained how little consultation took place with the regional authorities:

> We really had to battle our way into it…it wasn't an inclusive process and it wasn't especially well coordinated…ARRA and UNHCR were stimulating some kind of conversation, based on no background. There was no high-level representation from the Somali region. The representative for the region actually changed three times during the course of the ceremony…It was almost as though UNHCR and ARRA were doing it for themselves.

In Tigray, there was more at stake for the central government. One of Prime Minister Abiy's most important political commitments was the 2018 peace agreement with Eritrea. And for Tigray, on the Eritrean border and home to the largest proportion of Eritrean refugees, a lot was at stake. For Tigray, the presence of refugees was seen as a boon. Cultural and familial links meant Eritreans were not seen as a threat, and their economic contribution has generally been perceived as positive. A member of staff in the Danish Refugee Council in Tigray explained:

> Addis expects the repatriation of Eritreans as part of the deal. But there are local level concerns about the economic cost of return. Tigray is very welcoming. For example, I spoke to a pharmacist who was very worried about return; he explained that Eritreans are the only ones that buy brand drugs from him; everyone else buys generic drugs.

Tigray had long been privileged by the Ethiopian central government. But for Abiy, there was a growing need to transfer influence from Tigrayans towards Amharas and Oromos in order to consolidate power. Furthermore, the priority for Abiy's international reputation was peace with Eritrea rather than the cost of repatriation to the Tigrayan economy. Indeed, Abiy also backtracked on Hailemariam Desalegn's commitment for one of the Jobs Compact industrial parks to be in the regional capital. As one UN staff member put it, 'a lot of Tigrayans are not happy with him'.

In summary, the process relating to the Proclamation was centralized and technocratic. It emerged because the process offered a direct payoff to the PMO and because it offered a role to key parts of the government bureaucracy such as ARRA. But the commitments were based on scant consultation with the regions that actually host most of Ethiopia's refugees. Although the violent backlash in Gambella was unique, it was indicative of a lack of buy-in across the host regions.

Once Abiy became prime minister in 2018, his priorities lay elsewhere: peace with Eritrea, economic and political reform, and increased foreign direct investment. In order to meet these wider priorities, he first needed to reprivilege traditionally more marginalized regions as a means to get wider buy-in. Momentum on the implementation of the Proclamation, Jobs Compact, and CRRF slowed. And the Jobs Compact became seen as a means through which to reallocate economic opportunities towards historically marginalized regions through, for example, redesignating the location of the proposed new industrial parks.

Conclusion

In January 2019, Ethiopia passed some of the most progressive refugee legislation anywhere in the world. It ostensibly shifted from a Kenyan-style encampment policy towards a Ugandan-style self-reliance policy, giving refugees the right to work and freedom of movement. And it did so entirely because of international conditionality. Legislative change was bought by international donors in exchange for more than half a billion US dollars worth of contribution towards Ethiopia's national development strategy.

By committing to build three new industrial parks with the potential to create 100,000 new jobs, donors bought a quota for up to 30,000 refugees to work in any of the country's industrial parks. And with it came a recognition that the deal would require legislative change in order to be implemented. The Jobs Compact provided a politically palatable basis on which the Ethiopian Government could mobilize domestic political commitment for policy change, and predominantly European donors could mobilize additional finance.

In practice, the implementation of the Jobs Compact has been thwarted by practical challenges. But its legacy is political, and, in its absence, there would not have been new legislation. The rollout of the legislation is intended to be incremental. Against the backdrop of massive unemployment among citizens, Ethiopia cannot countenance new jobs for refugees without further international investment. But legislative change has at least institutionalized a commitment to gradually and progressively offer refugees access to socio-economic rights.

In many ways, this is a 'bargain' that is only half complete. The legislation exists, but the implementation of socio-economic rights does not. De jure change has come from a deal between the international community and Ethiopia's central government. However, de facto change will only come with a deal between the central government and the regions that actually host refugees: Tigray, Gambella, and the Somali region. Prime Minister Abiy's decision to change the chosen locations of the new industrial parks is a step towards recognizing that to be sustainable, refugee policy must create opportunities at a sub-national level. Implementation of the legislative promise will only come if two conditions are met: further international investment in Ethiopia's national development strategy linked to refugee rights, and the earmarking of those opportunities for the refugee-hosting regions.

PART IV

Policy—*what next?*

12

Building borderland economies

Introduction

International actors have become de facto 'governors' of economies in refugee camps and settlements. In refugee settings, the rules that shape work, production, consumption, exchange, borrowing, and lending often exist in parallel to those that apply to the wider population. Some of these rules are determined by the national government, but other rule-making tasks and key choices end up being delegated to UN agencies and their implementing partners. For example, while refugees' rights to work, own property, and open a bank account, or their duties to pay taxes or register businesses are usually determined at governmental level, other functions such as subsidizing particular forms of business activity, providing sources of social security, capping salaries for particular kinds of work, allocating land, promoting business investment, and in some case even creating parallel currencies (e.g. Bamba Chakula in Kenya) may lie with international actors—the donors that fund and approve policies and programmes, and the agencies that implement them. Put simply, the UN and its partners play a key—but hitherto largely implicit—role in economic governance. Yet, compared to most authorities managing large populations of a comparable size, they seldom appoint dedicated staff or committees whose job it is to focus on building and implementing an economic, fiscal, and investment strategy on behalf of the community.

The language of 'self-reliance'—alongside related terms such as livelihoods, resilience, and the humanitarian–development nexus—has tended to serve as a placeholder for the international humanitarian community's work on all issues relating to the economic governance of refugee communities. The rather anaemic language reflects a historic desire by humanitarian actors not to trespass on the authority of either host governments or development organizations, such as the World Bank. But the concept of self-reliance does not do justice to the range of economic activities and related governance functions that take place—or should take place—within a refugee community. Furthermore, our case studies on Kalobeyei and Dollo Ado reveal the limitations of self-reliance. For as long as remote refugee-hosting regions simply circulate aid money, they will struggle to grow and self-reliance, whether at an individual, household, or community level, will remain an unrealistic goal for the majority of refugees. The Kalobeyei and Dollo Ado 'experiments' have enabled us to examine the extent to which it is possible to design camps and settlements to support self-reliance. And yet, in both cases, the key finding is that in remote border areas at least, self-reliance will hit a ceiling unless it is accompanied by significant external investment and macroeconomic growth within the region.

Camps and cities represent two distinctively different types of refugee economy. In cities, complex economies are more likely to precede the presence of refugees. Urban areas provide large local markets; the agglomeration of firms and people provide dense labour markets and enable economies of scale to be achieved in the provision of capital-intensive infrastructure and public goods. Enabling refugees to thrive in cities is mainly a question of integration and socio-economic inclusion within pre-existing structures. The urban challenge is to break down access barriers to education, health services, employment, financial services, and community participation. In specific areas in which these are weak or strained by a large number of refugees, it may also be a question of augmenting these services for both refugees and the host community and thereby also improving social cohesion. Our research in capital cities such as Addis Ababa, Kampala, and Nairobi shows that refugees tend to have comparatively better opportunities (in terms of income and employment) in cities than in camps within the same countries, but that they are generally worse off than the proximate host community due mainly to facing access barriers to full socio-economic participation.

Building refugee economies in remote, refugee-hosting areas is a different kind of challenge. In many cases, it is analogous to building a city from scratch in regions that were not the country's first choice for urban development and in which the creation of permanent infrastructure for refugees may be politically discouraged. There are few pre-existing guides for how to do this. How can you take a geographically remote, environmentally inhospitable, and economically underdeveloped region and turn it into a place of shared opportunity where refugees and the local population can thrive? Of course, context will matter, shaping comparative advantage and political feasibility. But, drawing upon what we have learned from our East African case studies, what, if any, more general lessons can we derive, whether for Turkana County in Kenya, the Somali region of Ethiopia, the Isingiro district in Uganda, or elsewhere?

There is surprisingly little literature on how to build remote border economies. However, three broad literatures stand out. The 'Remote Economies' literature is relevant; however, it tends to focus on the Australian outback, Alaska, and the Scottish Highlands rather than developing countries. Meanwhile, the 'Local Economic Development' literature emerged in South Africa during the 1990s, and identifies a sequenced approach to building the economies of generally marginalized rural communities by building infrastructure, marketing locations to external investors through incentives and effective communication, and building endogenous capacity through promoting entrepreneurship and business development. Finally, there is some work on 'Border Economies', which tries to identify neglected opportunities from the bi-national, transnational, and regional circulation of goods, services, and people.

In this chapter, I outline a conceptual framework for thinking about how to build remote economies in refugee-hosting regions. I describe the approach as 'last-mile globalization'. It is derived from a combination of our research in East Africa and engagement with the wider literature.

Limitations of 'self-reliance'

Self-reliance has become the default policy solution of the global refugee regime. It dominates the UN's Global Compact on Refugees and was the main focus of the inaugural Global Refugee Forum in 2019. Its importance stems from the reality that less than 5 per cent of refugees receive a 'durable solution' of being able to go home, receive a pathway to naturalization in a host country, or being resettled in any given year. That means that the median refugee will have to wait more than ten years for an end to their limbo. Indefinite dependency on aid is neither desirable nor sustainable. Self-reliance is capable of garnering international political consensus because it appeals to Northern states' desire to reduce onward migration and cut long-term aid budgets, and because it appeals to Southern states' desire to attract development assistance. It is also intuitively attractive from an advocacy perspective because it promises to help people to help themselves, restoring dignity and purpose, while achieving these wider political goals.

However, is self-reliance a realistic goal in practice? As discussed earlier, the UN Refugee Agency (UNHCR) definition of self-reliance has three core elements—'meet basic needs', 'independently of aid', 'at individual, household, and community levels'. Self-reliance is criticized as a term in the literature for being imprecise—it has rarely been effectively measured; for being economistic—it tends not to account for political self-governance; and for being disingenuous—it is often deployed to serve wider political interests. It is also important to recognize that this is a concept that has emerged exclusively from within the refugee regime— it has become humanitarian organizations like UNHCR's somewhat bland way of talking about development and the economy without transgressing on areas outside of their organizational mandate and perceived competence.

Nevertheless, despite its limitations, self-reliance arguably represents one of the most plausible means to achieve sustainability in terms of ensuring large numbers of refugees can access rights and live in dignity and with purpose. But, as currently conceived, the threshold for self-reliance is extremely difficult to achieve. Most refugees in camps are nowhere near being able to meet their basic needs independently of aid. Is that because the threshold is too high? Is it even the right threshold for assessing welfare outcomes for refugees? Or is it because the wrong policies are being adopted, or that there is an inadequate conceptual framework for facilitating self-reliance outcomes?

In our research in Uganda, we demonstrated the advantages of the country's self-reliance approach for refugees. In particular, the right to work and freedom of movement for refugees is associated with higher income levels, greater mobility, lower transaction costs for economic activity, and more sustainable sources of employment. Put simply, giving refugees basic socio-economic rights improves outcomes—for them and often also for the host community. But, even in Uganda, a huge proportion of refugees, even in the better and most established settlements like Nakivale, are unable to meet their basic needs independently of aid. And some of the policies branded as integral to self-reliance like allocating plots of agricultural land only provide benefits to some members of the community. In Nakivale, as we saw earlier in the book, only 17 per cent of post-2012-arrival Congolese refugees—the nationality group with the greatest overall access to plots—even had access to a plot of land for cultivation.

In Kalobeyei we were able to explore the prospects for self-reliance in a camp especially designed to facilitate self-reliance. And yet two years after arriving in Kalobeyei, South Sudanese refugees there were generally no better off than recently arrived South Sudanese refugees in the nearby Kakuma refugee camps. Moreover, we found that self-reliance levels in Kalobeyei were extremely low; only 2 per cent of South Sudanese refugees perceived themselves to be independent of aid and only 6 per cent had an income-generating activity.

Dollo Ado similarly offered an opportunity to learn about the prospects for designing refugee camps to support self-reliance. However, unlike Kalobeyei, its model was predominantly private-sector- rather than donor-government-led. And while Kalobeyei's main focus was on piloting forms of cash-based assistance in place of in-kind assistance and significant support for the emergence of food retail businesses, Dollo Ado's model focused on piloting a range of innovative livelihoods programmes, notably through the creation of cooperatives relating to agriculture, livestock, and energy, and the implementation of a microfinance programme to promote retail commerce. In contrast, there have been no systematic attempts to commercialize agriculture or livestock, or to finance entrepreneurship in Kalobeyei. Dollo Ado's far greater emphasis on job creation may partly explain why a higher proportion of refugees in Dollo Ado—21 per cent—than Kalobeyei have an independent income-generating activity.

Nevertheless, even Dollo Ado reveals the limitations of self-reliance. Less than 10 per cent of adults are employed in the three main areas of international investment agriculture, livestock, and commercial retail. And the average income for those with work is around $1 per day. Most refugees are almost exclusively dependent upon aid. Even those who have employment largely do so because of the aid economy, either working as non-governmental organization (NGO) 'incentive workers' or in cooperatives that are subsidized by international assistance.

And, relative to most camps, Nakivale, Kalobeyei, and Dollo Ado are the success stories. They have piloted new and innovative models of refugee self-reliance. They have some important achievements. They highlight the potential for a different model of design for refugee camps and settlements. But, in each case, most refugees are not yet close to achieving the threshold to meet UNHCR's definition of self-reliance. The main reason is simple: they have continued to circulate aid money rather than building productive capacity. Each context has pioneered important microeconomic interventions. In Nakivale it has been access to land; in Kalobeyei it has been cash-based assistance; in Dollo Ado it has been commercial agriculture and livestock alongside support for entrepreneurship. Each of these microeconomic interventions have been a qualified success on their own terms, and improved welfare outcomes for both refugees and hosts. And in the case of Kalobeyei and Dollo Ado there is every indication that they will continue to reap gradual rewards in terms of progress.

But the challenge has been that each of these remote regions has lacked the ability to develop productive capacity and begin to export goods and services beyond the host region to other parts of the country or internationally. Until refugee-hosting regions can move from being aid-circulation economies to being productive export economies, there will be limitations on the extent to which they can fulfil the aspiration of self-reliance.

In order to promote sustainable refugee economies, we therefore need to change the lens from a purely microeconomic perspective towards macroeconomic plans for host regions. We need to move beyond just using the language of the humanitarian community—self-reliance, livelihoods, and resilience—to describe refugee economies, and instead think strategically about economic governance and regional development writ large. How can we transform the entire economy of remote refugee-hosting regions at a scale that can support sustainable sanctuary? And what roles and responsibilities does it imply for humanitarian and development organizations?

Remote economies and 'last-mile globalization'

So how can sustainable economies be built in refugee-hosting regions in ways that benefit both refugees and the host community? Our starting point is the recognition that building refugee economies in regions that host camps and settlements is part of a much broader question of how we can build remote border economies in developing countries. And yet there is a lack of literature relating to this question. Much of the economics literature on remote economies relates to regions of the developed world. The economics of remote regions in the developing world is under-researched. Nevertheless, the question of how we achieve sustainable development in refugee-hosting regions such as Dollo Ado, Turkana County in Kenya, or the border regions of Uganda remains under-theorized. Until now, there has been no global road map relating to how to build sustainable economies in remote refugee-hosting border areas. Initiatives to economically integrate refugees in remote regions have therefore usually been characterized by learning-by-doing, iteratively and reactively adapting to challenges, rather than being based on a clear strategy and vision from the outset.

The challenge goes beyond the refugee context. The world has never designed effective ways of bringing the benefits of economic development to the most remote and impoverished regions. And yet these are the regions that many refugees end up in because they are close to national borders. It is a challenge that I describe as 'last-mile globalization'—how can the benefits of global economic integration be made available to the most remote communities, often despite geographical, environmental, cultural, and political barriers?

The term 'last mile' was first used in telecommunications to refer to the final leg of telecommunications networks. It was then adapted to the context of supply chain management and transportation planning to describe the movement of people and goods from a transportation hub to a final destination. The 'last-mile problem' emerged because the last leg of the supply chain was recognized as generally the least efficient, comprising up to 28 per cent of the total cost to move goods.[1] The phrase 'last mile' has more recently been appropriated by the global health community to highlight the gap in healthcare outcomes for people living in remote rural contexts. Worldwide, more than a billion people lack access to healthcare due to distance, and the organization Last Mile Health emerged to support the recruitment, training, and management of community health workers as a solution to this 'last-mile' problem in public health.[2]

And yet, within international development, the last-mile problem affects areas that go beyond the health sector. Access to electricity, internet connectivity, education, and roads, for example, statistically nosedive in remote rural locations, when compared even to cities in the same countries. The energy, connectivity, and income 'gaps', for example, are especially pronounced in remote African regions.[3] Many such regions also suffer from disproportionately weak governance.[4] Paradoxically, while needs may be great, the marginal cost of closing gaps is likely to be high due to remoteness, political incentives for investment are likely to be low unless a region is of strategic importance to the government, and private-sector investment is likely to be deterred by the absence of basic infrastructure and public goods.

The global discourse on 'inclusive globalization'—present everywhere from Davos to the UN General Assembly—has highlighted the unequally distributed benefits of globalization. However, it has tended to focus on the Global North, identifying ways in which those who feel 'left behind' by the advantages of trade and immigration, for example, can share in their benefits. The discussion has focused on blue-collar workers, often turning to populist nationalism as a result of alienation by factors such as the collapse of labour-intensive manufacturing, and the loss of jobs due to automation and offshoring. However, an equally important dimension of inclusive globalization relates to ensuring that the benefits of globalization are also available to remote, marginalized communities in the Global South, including the border regions that host a significant proportion of the world's refugees.

There is relatively limited theory on remote economies in the developing world. The 'Remote Economies' literature identifies a number of features of such economies: small population and limited labour force; small local markets providing limited goods and services; weak connections to external markets and high transportation costs; high dependency on primary sectors and first stage processing. Yet a significant proportion of the remote econ-omies literature focuses on rich-world contexts like the Scottish Highlands and islands, Alaska, and the Australian outback.[5]

Until recently, it has been much rarer to focus on remote economies in developing countries,[6] and even less common to identify policy solutions. And while developing countries share some common features with other remote economies, for example being affected by the consequences of urbanization and economic agglomeration, remote economies in Africa, for instance, also have a range of distinctive features such as low population density; lack of spatial connectivity; inadequate infrastructure; weak integration across eco-nomic sectors; high fertility rates; a predominance of the informal economy; low integration into external markets and limited domestic markets; inad-equate protection of property rights; and weak governance.[7]

One of the first serious pieces of research on remote rural areas (RRAs) in international development emerged from a study undertaken by the Overseas Development Institute (ODI) some two decades ago.[8] The study identified that people living in RRAs account for a substantial proportion of the world's chronically poor. This, they argued, was because of spatial pov-erty traps. Low levels of geographical capital (the physical, social, and human capital of an area) lead to a cycle of one household's poverty reinforcing another's. Those who are able to engage in onward migration tend to leave, and those who are left behind tend to be 'residual populations' with lower levels of human and social capital. They show how a series of additional factors reinforce these spatial poverty traps, including insecurity, weak governance, irrelevance to national politics, and corruption and rent-seeking within local politics. The study, while stopping short of prescribing solutions, points to the need to ensure that political and governance barriers to RRA development are addressed as a precondition for effective livelihoods development.

During the 1990s, a literature emerged that romanticized the idea that localized, 'bottom-up' solutions could emerge in such regions. The so-called Local Economic Development (LED) and Local and Regional Economic Development (LRED) literatures argued that locally based responses offered a means to address the challenges posed by globalization in remote developing-country economies.[9] They proposed a sequenced approach to remote-area development. First, market locations to external investors and create incentive structures for investment such as tax breaks, improved public services, and infrastructure. Second, build local capacity through support for entrepreneurship, small business development, and education. Third, focus on sectoral development in key areas of comparative advantage, including through enhanced public–private collaboration. While the logic of sequencing is a helpful starting point, the approach was criticized for assuming that small-scale 'project-led' interventions aimed at poverty reduction could be adequate for driving economic development in remote Sub-Saharan African economies.[10]

The concept of remote area development has only recently re-emerged. Based on an APEC-funded study, Emmanuel San Andres explains that 'there is no universal definition for remoteness, but generally a remote area lacks connectivity whether due to geographic distance, terrain or travel time'.[11] He argues that despite variation, such regions often have a variety of features that include: limited physical infrastructure, poor access to services, limited economic opportunities, lack of human capital, and governance challenges. In terms of solutions, he proposes that such economies need to develop infrastructure, enhance internet and telecommunications access, diversify income-generating activities, and encourage foreign direct investment including through considering options such as special economic zones (SEZs) and public–private partnerships.[12] Meanwhile, although there is some literature on 'border economies', which describes how borders offer opportunities for arbitrage, illicit transboundary activity, and a range of business activities, it generally provides few insights into how to economically develop remote border economies.[13]

Two key observations follow. First, there has been an absence of academic and policy research on remote economies in general. Second, where this work has emerged it has been disconnected from debates on development-based approaches to refugee-hosting areas. Drawing upon the insights of our research in East Africa therefore offers an opportunity to fill an important gap in thinking in terms of how to build refugee economies in remote refugee-hosting regions.

Sustainable refugee economies

So what are the preconditions for building sustainable economies in refugee-hosting regions? How can economic opportunity be created that mutually benefits both refugees and the host communities? Clearly context matters but there nevertheless appear to be a series of factors that are crucial for sustainable development in remote border regions. Identifying those conditions offers a means to begin to outline a framework or road map for how governments, businesses, and international organizations can more systematically plan their interventions in remote refugee-hosting regions. Until now, the few attempts that have been made to build economies in refugee-hosting regions have largely been ad hoc experiments. Dollo Ado, Kakuma, and Nakivale represent idiosyncratic attempts to create integrated refugee economies. Each has unfolded in the absence of a clear blueprint for how to build refugee economies; they have been iterative and based at least as much on intuition as evidence.

With the benefit of hindsight, we are now able to distil lessons from across contexts. Extrapolating from the successes and failures of Dollo Ado, Kakuma, and Nakivale offers a starting point for considering what a 'sustainable refugee economies framework' might look like. What are the conditions that need to be met in order to create sustainable economies in refugee-hosting regions? Five elements stand out: 1) political will; 2) infrastructure; 3) comparative advantage; 4) socio-cultural applicability; and 5) external inputs. These factors are illustrated in Figure 12.1. They are not necessarily intended to be a sequential road map but rather to outline the

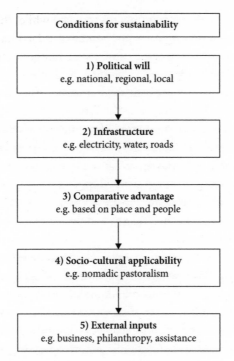

Figure 12.1. Sustainable Refugee Economies Framework

preconditions that need to be met in order for a remote refugee-hosting region to gradually move from simply being an aid economy to being a sustainable economic system capable of supporting self-reliance for refugees and the host community.

Political will

Politics matters. A prerequisite for building refugee economies is political buy-in from the host-country government. There needs to be commitment at both national and local levels, from both formal and informal sources of political authority. As the earlier chapters of this book demonstrate, national-level commitment is especially important for securing legal rights for refugees but local-level commitment is important for the implementation of rights and freedoms. In countries with high levels of political decentral-ization, local governments have particular discretion to determine whether and how refugees are included in local development strategies.

Political will is crucial for building refugee economies for several reasons. First, politics shapes the regulatory environment. Refugees will be far better able to contribute economically if they have the right to work and other basic socio-economic rights such as mobility and property rights. They may still be economically productive in the absence of such rights, but their activities are likely to be confined to the informal sector, and informality in turn creates higher transaction costs and sources of market inefficiency. Indeed, refugees can be a potential boon because they can increase the size of a region's economically active population. They can engage in production, consumption, exchange, entrepreneurship, borrowing, and lending, for example. But all of these activities are subject to public regulation: can refugees work, register businesses, move freely between markets, or open bank accounts, for example?

Second, politics also influences investment risk. If governments signal a commitment to socio-economic integration for refugees, the private sector is likely to perceive investment risk differently. Business commitment to capital investment or job creation in a refugee-hosting region is more likely in the context of predictable and stable government support. Indeed, many remote border regions are inherently perceived as high-risk investment contexts because of proximity to insecurity, weak governance, and limited infrastructure. The fact that they host refugees, however, presents an opportunity to the host government. But to realize this opportunity requires a signalling of a willingness by the government to build a credible development strategy for the region, to include refugees within those plans, and to create an auspicious business environment through good governance in terms of security, the rule of law, the enforcement of contracts, anti-corruption policies, and investment in infrastructure.

Third, it also matters for the provision of public goods. Even if externally funded, political will is a key aspect of the effective delivery of education, health, policing, infrastructure, and macroeconomic management, for example. There needs to be commitment to effective delivery and to extending access to refugee communities. A common challenge in remote regions is that they may be of low political relevance to central governments, or characterized by high levels of corruption and rent-seeking, undermining effective delivery. The relationship between central and local government— referred to as 'subsidiarity'—may be especially important in shaping these dynamics.[14] Is the central government's approach to a remote region predatory, extractive, or supportive? The degree of decentralization within a particular country will shape how much authority is delegated to the sub-national level, and determine which actors are the most salient for effective public goods delivery.

Host governments and societies have lots to gain from economically including refugees within development strategies for remote border regions. Refugees bring greater international attention, additional labour, and expanded markets. But when it comes to refugees and migration, economic rationality and political decision-making do not always align. Political will cannot be taken for granted. It is not a given, and even once attained it is not fixed over time. It is the result of changes in power, interests, and ideas. And if governments are to prioritize the economic development of remote regions, and the inclusion of refugees within regional development plans, then there have to be incentives for influential groups and individuals to engage, including through perceived benefits to their communities, constituencies, and patronage networks. Expanding the scope for political will requires political analysis to identify and map out political authority structures, recognizing key veto players and social influencers. It requires patient relationship-building to establish trust, and resources in order to create and change incentive structures.

One of the historical challenges within the international refugee system has been that the UN humanitarian agencies that govern refugee issues tend to see themselves as 'non-political'. For example, UNHCR's statute defines its work as being of a 'non-political character'. And although this clause was created in the 1950s mainly with the intention of avoiding politicization in the context of East–West rivalry during the Cold War, it has often diminished the importance of political analysis and political engagement as essential for improving refugees' entitlements and capabilities. Although the daily work of UNHCR staff is mired in diplomacy and work with governments, it has few dedicated resources for systematic political engagement. Historically, UNHCR has often been politically effective because of the talents of specific, charismatic individuals, but such skills have rarely been systematically nurtured within organizations that work with refugees. Nevertheless, if the political foundations for building refugee economies are to be created, effective political brokerage is essential.

Our research underscores the importance of political buy-in as a sine qua non for building sustainable refugee economies. In Dollo Ado, there was support from federal, national, and local actors, especially from 2016. Support came with a combination of domestic political change and the influence of external actors. At the federal level, the government of Prime Minister Hailemariam Desalegn gradually recognized the national development opportunity offered by the presence of refugees. The UK Government, the EU, and the World Bank offered around $600 million towards the construction of three new industrial parks in exchange for progress towards the economic integration of refugees. Hailemariam recognized the possibility to leverage the socio-economic integration of refugees as a means to elicit support for Ethiopia's own industrialization strategy. From 2018, incoming Prime Minister Abiy Ahmed sustained Hailemariam's commitment to the 2019 Refugee Proclamation because he too recognized it as a means to derive international legitimacy and resources. With high levels of decentralization under ethnic federalism, the regional and local levels also mattered. A change in UNHCR leadership in both Addis Ababa and Dollo Ado helped to translate national opportunities into positive commitments at the local level. The national representative, Clementine Nkweta-Salami recruited George Woode as head of sub-office for Dollo Ado, and he worked effectively with local representatives—the regional government in Jijiga, the Woreda in Dollo, informal authorities such as the regional Somali king and the representative of the government refugee agency (Administration of Refugee and Returnee Affairs, or ARRA)—in order to build trust. Woode is widely credited with enabling local political actors to better understand the benefits that the presence of refugees could bring for the local host community, given support for basic socio-economic opportunities.

In Kakuma, the support of the Turkana County Government has been central to designing a regional development plan built around the presence of refugees. In particular, the Turkana County governor, Josphat Nanok, played a central role in the creation of the Kalobeyei Integrated Socio-Economic Development Plan (KISEDP), effectively an integrated development plan for the sub-county of Turkana West, which hosts the Kakuma camps. Nanok and his county government were positively predisposed towards including refugees in regional development planning because of their own personal experience of seeing the economic cost to the host community when refugees go home. They understood that refugees represent a resource for the region, and a means to attract investment. Nevertheless, this supportive inclination was nurtured by UNHCR's senior leaders. As in Ethiopia, individuals mattered. The organization's country representative, Raouf Mazou, and the head of sub-office between 2017 and 2019, Sukru Cansizoglu, worked closely with Nanok to create mutual trust and a shared vision for the development of Turkana West. KISEDP was jointly created by UNHCR and the local government. For Nanok and his county government colleagues, there were a variety of incentives: benefits to the local population, political credit for a job well done, and, according to some informants, personal financial gain. The regional development plan had only grudging support from the central government under Uhuru Kenyatta. However, given high levels of decentralization, this did not represent a major impediment for the development plan, other than insofar as certain key capacities, such as granting refugees the right to work and freedom of movement, formally rest with the central government.

In Nakivale, political support for an integrated development approach has been long-standing. Nakivale is Africa's oldest refugee settlement, and it is among Uganda's most prosperous rural refugee communities. The model of allowing refugees to work and move freely has been present more or less continuously since the settlement's creation in 1958, and has enjoyed support from both the central government and local authorities in the Isingiro district, the Ankole sub-region, and the western region. For the Isingiro district local government, and its chairperson, the priorities are agricultural production, schools, and infrastructure, and the presence of both refugees and the international community in its two refugee settlements—Nakivale and Oruchinga—contributes to channelling international resources into the district, whether directly (as is the case through UNHCR's recent Comprehensive Refuge Response Plan) or via the Office of the Prime Minister (OPM) at central government level. Historical solidarity between the local Banyankole population and Rwandan and Congolese refugees has made socio-economic integration politically acceptable. Meanwhile, President Museveni's own Banyankole origins and personal investment in sustaining refugee self-reliance as a source of international legitimacy and resource extraction have facilitated a long-standing commitment to maintain a settlement model based on the partial socio-economic integration of refugees. In Nakivale, as elsewhere in Uganda, UNHCR has had a very minor direct role to play in shaping this underlying political will, other than working to sustain a steady flow of external resources that can create development opportunities for the host community, and a range of benefits and incentives to national and local politicians and their patronage networks. The Isingiro District chairman, Kamurali Birungi, was, for instance, arrested in 2018, based on accusations of theft of UNHCR property, and has had a long-running dispute with the members of parliament (MPs) for the

Isingiro constituencies.[15] A particular policy challenge in Uganda, as elsewhere, is how to create strong incentive structures that are not based primarily on corruption and rent-seeking behaviour.

Infrastructure

Physical capital represents all human-made goods that assist in the production process. One aspect of this, often provided as a public good, is infrastructure—the physical systems of a country or region. Type of infrastructure include: transportation (e.g. roads), communications (e.g. digital connectivity), water (e.g. irrigation), energy (e.g. electricity), social infrastructure (e.g. schools and hospitals), and waste and recycling (e.g. sewage). Infrastructure is crucial for economic development but represents a particular challenge for remote, refugee-hosting regions.

There is a long history of economic thought relating to infrastructure. David Aschauer showed the correlation between investment in infrastructure and economic performance in post-war America, demonstrating how it increases the productivity of both labour and that part of the output function not explained by labour or capital (multifactor productivity).[16] Others such as Janet Rives and Michael Heaney showed that these relationships are not just present nationally but also locally.[17] And based on the dominance of these ideas in the 1950s and '60s, governments around the world adopted a variety of models of infrastructure-driven development. From Roosevelt's New Deal and British Neo-Keynesianism, to contemporary Norwegian, Singaporean, and Chinese state-led capitalism, large-scale government investment became orthodox economic governance. And, empirically, investment matters: the African Development Bank (AfDB) claims that over half of Africa's economic growth is explained by investment in infrastructure.

However, there is generally a lack of investment in infrastructure in emerging markets and low-income countries. Around the world, billions of people lack access to electricity, roads, and safe drinking water, for example. This 'infrastructure gap' applies especially to Africa and, above all, in most remote rural regions. It matters not only directly for population welfare—millions are without adequate water and electricity—but also indirectly as a prerequisite for exploiting natural resources and exporting commodities. Without infrastructure, the inability to export beyond the local context will stymie economic growth.

A particular challenge is how to secure finance for infrastructure. Infrastructure requires large capital investment. The public sector often lacks adequate resources and to elicit private-sector capital requires projects to be 'bankable'—that is, to generate revenue over time. In general, social returns often exceed market returns from infrastructure due to positive externalities. And in remote contexts, risk and uncertainty may undermine the bankability of infrastructural projects. This means that public–private partnerships that guarantee future returns to private investment, or concessionary finance are often needed to facilitate infrastructural investment. China's 'One Belt, One Road' policy has provided significant investment to support infrastructural development, but often through unfavourable terms. Meanwhile, Western multilateral development banks such as the World Bank often provide such sources of finance but based on conditions that regions characterized by weak governance are usually unable to meet. In Africa, around 42 per cent of the continent's $84 billion annual infrastructural investment comes from national governments, 24 per cent from China, 24 per cent from other bilateral and multilateral donors, and less than 3 per cent from the private sector.[18]

Nevertheless, one advantage that Africa has is that as an infrastructure development latecomer, it can potentially 'leapfrog' other parts of the world. It can use innovation to create more resource-efficient infrastructure, including through using low-carbon and digital technologies. Rather than replicating the infrastructural pathways of advanced industrial economies, technologies such as renewable energy, broadband connectivity, and sustainable water management techniques may be affordably available, even in remote regions.

In remote refugee-hosting regions, infrastructure is often especially limited. Historically, such regions rarely receive additional infrastructural finance because of hosting refugees. Only recently have the World Bank and other multilateral development banks started to consider concessionary infrastructural finance in support of refugee-hosting regions *qua* refugee-hosting regions.

In Kakuma, there are huge gaps in infrastructure, especially relating to electricity, water, and roads. Kenya Power supplies electricity to the local Kakuma town but its sub-station grid, which is powered by a diesel generator, does not extend to the refugee camps. Only 5 per cent of households in some parts of the camps report having reliable electricity. Solar street lighting has been installed and solar lanterns made available to refugees, but only a minority of homes and businesses can afford their own solar generator. Many homes are without electricity and those that do generally pay a fee to tap into the generator of a community-level entrepreneur. Meanwhile, although a range of multinational solar companies now operate in the camps, they are generally only able to do so because of subsidy from development agencies such as the SNV Netherlands Development Organization. In terms of water, boreholes and pit latrines have been created for the community in some parts of the camps, but only 60 per cent of refugees claim to have reliable access to water, and a particular limitation relates to water for agriculture. Despite a move towards dryland farming, little progress has been made in securing reliable water or irrigation to use the local Lake Turkana for farming. Kakuma's remote geography is exacerbated by inadequate roads, limiting the prospects for entrepreneurs in Kakuma to export what they produce beyond Turkana County. One of the few areas of relative progress, however, has been digital technology, with 69 per cent of refugees having access to the internet through smartphones.

In Dollo Ado, greater progress has been made in relation to electricity and water. Around 24 per cent of refugee households have access to reliable electricity, mainly as a result of solar systems provided to households, solar street lighting, and solar mini-grids provided by the IKEA Foundation through its 7.7 million euro renewable energy programme. Meanwhile, the Foundation's 4.4 million euro investment in 29km of irrigation canals has transformed the possibility for using water from the River Genale for agricultural purposes, creating a command area of 1,000ha of irrigated cropland. However, in other areas, there are significant limitations. The quality of road and transportation networks, even between the five camps and Dollo Ado town, is extremely poor, limiting the scope for importing and exporting commodities to and from the camps. Access to broadband connectivity is significantly worse than in Kakuma, and there are lower levels of smartphone penetration.

In Nakivale, there has been relatively little additional focus on infrastructure in the settlement. However, it benefits from far more auspicious geography than Kakuma and Dollo Ado. Nakivale's inhabitants therefore have many of the same infrastructural opportunities as rural Ugandan citizens. The road network connecting Isingiro District to nearby Mbarara town and on to Kampala is good, enabling refugees to easily establish and participate in supply chains beyond the region. Relatively high levels of seasonal rainfall mean that agriculture is possible even in the absence of complex irrigation systems, while boreholes adequately service drinking water needs. Meanwhile, although electricity is limited, Nakivale is supplied by the national grid and there is also a thriving secondary market in electricity, whether supplied from the grid, generators, or solar systems.

Comparative advantage

Which sectors should a refugee-hosting region prioritize in order to create the greatest economic opportunities? Or, more technically, what is the optimum allocation of resources to promote regional economic growth? What should the right balance be between agriculture, manufacturing, services, or the digital economy? To what extent is a region rich in land, labour, or capital? What types of land, labour, or capital does it have in abundance—for example, land for growing maize or wheat? Only rarely do policy-makers design development plans for refugee-hosting regions that make explicit strategic choices about their 'comparative advantage'. Implicitly, refugee-hosting contexts—from Dollo Ado to Kakuma—make decisions about the sectors that they prioritize. But these choices need to become explicit and strategic, and be based on more systematic value-chain analysis.

A country or region's 'industrial policy' represents the policies and interventions that a government adopts to affect the allocation of resources in favour of particular sectors such as agriculture or manufacturing. As Joseph Stiglitz and colleagues explain, 'Most countries, intentionally or not, pursue an industrial policy in one form or other, which broadly refers to any government decision, regulation, or law that encourages ongoing activity or investment in an industry.'[19] Such policies are generally justified on the grounds of either market failure—for example, incomplete information or externalities—or the role for institutions to anticipate long-term economic trends.[20]

The challenge for industrial policy is to know how to 'pick winners' that align with the available resources and skills of a particular setting. David Ricardo's principle of comparative advantage has long been the foundation for this. The basic logic is that growth is promoted by specialization, and that economies should focus on areas in which they have a relative abundance of physical and human resources. In other words, countries and regions should focus on goods and services that they can produce using fewer resources or at lower opportunity cost than other countries or regions.

Ricardo's basic rule of thumb is that an economy should decide whether to produce something by comparing the opportunity cost of producing a given commodity with the price at which that commodity can be imported or exported. At equilibrium, no commodity would be produced which could be imported at lower cost, and exports are expanded until marginal revenue equals marginal cost.[21] At the level of international trade, the

Heckscher–Ohlin model suggests that a country will benefit from trade by producing commodities that use more of its relatively abundant factors of production (labour or capital), and import commodities that use more of its relatively scarce factors (unless domestic demand is biased towards the latter). Meanwhile, the Lerner–Samuelson theorem adapts this to suggest that a country has a comparative advantage in good X if that country is relatively well endowed with the factors that are used intensively in the production of X.[22]

The principle of comparative advantage has been contested. For example, it has been criticized as overly static, being extended to recognize the role of dynamic comparative advantage: for example, how China's transition from labour intensive to capital intensive—notably agriculture to manufacturing—relied upon creating virtuous circles. Furthermore, others have recognized how institutions can affect comparative advantage by, for example, creating infrastructure and providing public goods such as roads and telecommunications.[23] Consequently, comparative advantage can be understood dynamically, but it nevertheless implies a need for all economies to consider what relative advantages they have, particularly in terms of people and place, and to use this as a basis for considering the balance of agriculture, manufacturing, services, and digital work to invest in.

In practice, for remote refugee-hosting countries this involves identifying potential tradeable goods and services which might be exported beyond the region. These may be linked to the particular place in terms of natural resources or geography—for example, energy, fisheries and aquaculture, or tourism—or to people in terms of particular forms of human capital such as language skills or digital work. It might also be that some regions can fill a particular niche within global value chains; for example, in areas such as first stage processing, value-adding services, or research and development.

Institutions can play a key role in shaping and nurturing comparative advantage over time. National and regional governments, or even international organizations, have a policy toolbox of options available to encourage the development of particular economic sectors and incentivize firms from more advanced economies to relocate. One such tool is SEZs.

An SEZ is simply a geographical area in which particular incentives are provided to businesses to locate within the zone.[24] Such incentives would generally not be available in the rest of the country and might include low taxation, privileged access to services, preferential access to export markets, streamlined customs procedures, or simply the clustering of sector-specific coordination, networks, and innovation. They are generally used to promote economic development, both within the zones through attracting new firms and jobs and facilitating skills and technology transfer, and also outside the zones through their positive impact on the wider economy.

SEZs are diverse and come in many forms, with different names such as free-trade zones, export-processing zones, enterprise zones, and freeports. They have a long history, dating back for example to Gibraltar in 1704 or Singapore in 1819. The size of zones, their incentive packages, and their proximity to markets can vary significantly. As do their reputations in terms of economic success and labour rights.[25] Nevertheless, they have been widely recognized as an important policy instrument for attracting investment and creating employment opportunity in remote regions. The idea of using SEZs to create jobs for both refugees and host communities has been applied in Jordan and Ethiopia, and the initiative has recently been included in the Government of Turkana County's regional development plan.

Identifying potential comparative advantages in remote regions is often challenging. In Kakuma and the surrounding Turkana County, existing commercial possibilities include livestock, oil, and solar power. With creativity and investment, there may be opportunities to scale dryland agriculture, digital work, manufacturing, and even tourism given the region's historical significance as the cradle of humankind. In Dollo Ado and the surrounding region, opportunities similarly include livestock, agriculture, and solar energy. In order to expand other opportunities in the digital economy, it would first require significant investment in human capital and broadband technology. In Nakivale, the main opportunity has historically been in agriculture. However, access to arable land is now largely exhausted due to growth in the refugee population, and given the region's relatively auspicious geography and infrastructure, there may be scope to explore growth in other sectors such as fisheries and aquaculture or digital livelihoods. Across all these sites and others, more systematic value-chain analysis offers a means to identify where potential untapped opportunities may lie.

Socio-cultural applicability

Culture also shapes economies. No single, universally applicable approach to development will work in every context. And this is likely to be especially important in remote, rural locations. Economic anthropology has long recognized that human economic behaviour needs to be understood within its cultural context, working inductively from ethnographic cases rather than deductively from economic models.

Building upon Karl Polanyi's historical recognition that Western market-based economies are historically and culturally contingent,[26] Marshall Sahlins' *Stone Age Economies* distinguished between 'formalist' approaches to economics, which are based on neo-classical economics and assume rational utility maximization, and 'substantivist' approaches that view the economy as embedded in socio-cultural context.[27] For the substantivists, economic life is produced through cultural rules that govern the production and distribution of goods, and such rules play a wider role in maintaining social relations. Building on these ideas, economic anthropologists avoid looking at 'the economy' as an isolated or predefined area of activity, and instead look at it as 'embedded' in social, cultural, legal, and even religious context.[28]

Economic anthropologists have critically explored the 'cultural embeddedness' of a whole range of areas of 'economic' activity, showing how they often transcend and defy dominant neo-classical economic concepts.[29] The themes explored include, for example, exchange and reciprocity,[30] barter and markets,[31] money,[32] production,[33] households and villages,[34] property,[35] consumption,[36] and globalization.[37]

Being aware of the relationship between culture and economic behaviour is especially important in refugee settings, which are, by definition, diverse and multicultural. For example, Somali refugee communities have a range of economic institutions that are central to their livelihood activities. The Hawala system is an informal, trust-based, money-transfer system used by Somali refugees around the world to send remittances. Meanwhile, many Somali refugees are members of *ayutos*, which are informal savings and social insurance groups within which participants contribute a weekly or monthly amount and then take turns for one member or household to use the collective saving for either a major investment or as a form of social security.

The difficulty is that the playbooks of international institutions and the realities of local context are frequently misaligned. James Ferguson's famous ethnography of the World Bank, *The Anti-Politics Machine*, for instance, reveals how a universalistic development lens can sometimes systematically misinterpret people's lived economic experiences, in ways that may lead to perverse outcomes.[38] He shows how, in Lesotho, the World Bank viewed local rural farmers as entirely dependent on livestock activity, even though the largest part of household income came from cross-border economic strategies. This is because the World Bank's state-centric institutional approach was unable to recognize livelihoods that were not earned on the territory of Lesotho but were instead based on cross-border work within the neighbouring South African economy. The World Bank's attempts to commercialize livestock led to repeated failure because for the community, cattle were not a livelihoods opportunity per se, but a savings mechanism imbued with particular cultural significance.

Each of our three main cases highlights examples of systematic institutional misinterpretation of local economic context, leading to perverse outcomes or missed opportunities. Our research in Dollo Ado reveals strikingly similar dynamics to those identified by James Ferguson. In looking for potential livelihood opportunities, the international community has focused on agriculture, livestock, and retail commerce, even though less than 10 per cent of adult refugees are engaged in these areas. And while building these sectors is important, they are based on an analysis that neglects crucial elements of refugees' own economic strategies. In particular, a key part of the refugees' economic activity is based on cross-border strategies across the Somali–Ethiopian border. Goods, services, and people move regularly across the border; shops in the camps are full of commodities procured in Somalia, and many refugees are only present in the camps during food distributions, retaining homes and businesses in their nearby country of origin. And while many individual UN staff are privately aware of these dynamics, they are invisible at an institutional level because the UN's programmes and data function at a nation-state level that cannot take adequate account of the importance of cross-border strategies.

There is a similar institutional gap in understanding how refugees in Dollo Ado use the aid economy. As we saw in Chapter 7, for example, many families sell a significant proportion of their food rations to a local pasta factory, using cash to purchase the commodities that they want—including pasta. The rations are sold at a fraction of the price paid by international aid agencies, leading to significant loss. Furthermore, a proportion of the refugee households collecting rations also have family members who move between the Dollo Ado refugee camps and internally displaced person (IDP) camps on the other side of the Somali border, where cash-based assistance is provided. Again, while individual UN staff are aware of these dynamics, the lived economic strategies of refugees remain largely invisible to the programming of international institutions.

Similar institutional misinterpretations of refugees' economic behaviour can be found in Kakuma. For example, when the international community created the new Kalobeyei settlement, it made a series of assumptions about why both refugees and the host community would choose to relocate there. In contrast to the four Kakuma camps, it would offer greater cash-based assistance, more refugee–host interaction, and access to agricultural opportunity. Nevertheless, people shunned voluntary relocation. The aim of a 'hybrid' community of refugees and Kenyans was quickly thwarted by the local pastoralist Turkana not wishing to leave their existing lands and become sedentarized within the settlements.[39] Meanwhile, even refugees in the four camps refused to move to Kalobeyei, mainly because they valued their pre-existing social networks as a key part of their socio-economic strategies.[40] Put simply, the international community's assumptions about the economic rationale for refugee and host community willingness to relocate overemphasized market-based incentives and underemphasized the socio-cultural context of household decision-making. The result has been that Kalobeyei has been almost exclusively populated by recently arriving refugees.

In Nakivale, as with Uganda as a whole, the implicit assumption of the self-reliance model is that in rural areas, most refugees work in agriculture. The settlements model is premised upon the idea that, rather than receiving long-term food assistance, refugees are given a plot of land to cultivate for subsistence and sale. However, contrary to other settlements, Nakivale has a sizeable Somali population, and in contrast to Congolese and South Sudanese refugees, the Somalis—who are mainly from urban backgrounds—generally do not engage in subsistence agriculture. In Nakivale, around 40 per cent of Congolese refugee households have access to a plot of land but practically no Somalis have a plot of land, because they either decline the plot or sub-let it, generally preferring to engage in retail commerce. While livelihoods programmes in the settlement have gradually diversified, the predominant focus continues to be on agriculture.

Creating sustainable refugee economies therefore relies upon starting with an understanding of how economic life interacts with culture. In the language of anthropology, it requires an 'emic' (within-community) understanding of economic life, in addition to an 'etic' (external) understanding of development economics. If the assumptions and models of international institutions are based on a misrepresentation of the actual economic behaviour, preferences, and decision-making of refugees and the host community then interventions may lead to unintended negative consequences or simply to the neglect of potential opportunities. One way to ensure that interventions and strategies are adequately socio-culturally embedded is to insist that all evidence and data collection are based on a mixed methods approach that uses participatory, ethnographic, and qualitative methods, as well as more traditional quantitative research methods.

External inputs

Identifying comparative advantages is a necessary but insufficient condition for creating sustainable refugee economies. It also requires investment, whether from business, philanthropy, concessionary finance, or international assistance. The potentially most important, and yet least forthcoming, of these is business. However, in order to attract international investors or multinational corporations (MNCs), it is necessary to build a clear business case for investment. An appeal to corporate social responsibility (CSR) may open the door, but is unlikely to be adequate by itself. A broader case needs to be made based on return on investment, whether relating to labour, supply chain, market access, or bankable infrastructure projects, for example. And business is generally risk averse when it comes to investing in remote border locations in developing countries.[41]

One of the biggest gaps in refugee contexts has been the inability of humanitarian organizations to adequately make and frame the 'business case' for investing in refugee-hosting regions. Discussions have too often focused on philanthropy and CSR rather than profit. And they have geographically emphasized business engagement with refugees and asylum seekers in Europe and the US, rather than in the developing countries that host the majority of the world's refugees. Nevertheless, the business case for investing in contexts like Dollo Ado, Kakuma, and Nakivale can and should be better made. Foundations linked to companies such as the IKEA Foundation, Mastercard Foundation, Vodafone Foundation, Tent Foundation, Hilton Foundation, and Lego Foundation have been an important entry point for many corporations to get refugee camps onto the agendas of large MNCs. However, a significant gap in the international refugee system has been the inability of any international organization, whether UNHCR or the World Bank, for example, to fully embrace the role of broker between the humanitarian and business worlds. How can a business case for investing in refugee economies best be made? And how can there be complementarity and coherence across different types of external input such as business, corporate philanthropy, multilateral development bank concessionary finance, and international assistance?

In reality, most job creation in remote refugee contexts currently comes from small and medium-sized enterprises (SMEs), whether owned by refugees or by the host community. A key part of building the business sector is therefore to train and support community entrepreneurs. By expanding local entrepreneurship capacity, this may in turn contribute to market growth and make the economy more investable than it otherwise would be. In 2019, the University of Oxford collaborated with the World Economic Forum and UNHCR to provide an Executive Leadership and Entrepreneurship Programme to thirty refugees and host-community business people in Kakuma. The course focused on delivering key elements of the Business Model Canvas—which covers topics such as value proposition, customers, finance, and revenue streams—and adapting it specifically to refugee camp contexts.[42] The nine-day intensive course and twelve-week mentorship programme was provided by young CEOs and executives from across Africa and around the world. Our Oxford-based team designed the intervention as a randomized control trial, assessing the impact against a comparable control group. We found that, after six months, although there was not as yet a statistically significant impact on income, the training had increased confidence and led to changes in business practices. This evidence complements our other research in Kakuma, which shows that business training leads to increased revenues and profits by changing business practices in areas such as book-keeping, market research, and price comparison.[43]

Indeed, building human capital and local entrepreneurship offer one important means to gradually make a remote economy more investable. However, the ability to attract external inputs, especially based on a for-profit business case, in turn depends upon all of the other elements of the Sustainable Refugee Economies Framework. And achieving this relies upon having a clear and coherent road map based on these factors, and a compelling way to articulate it to business, donors, and multilateral development banks. Table 12.1 summarizes the extent to which the five elements of the framework have been present in the three refugee-hosting border regions on which we have focused in this chapter and throughout the book.

Table 12.1. Sustainable Refugee Economies Framework applied to Dollo Ado, Kakuma, and Nakivale

	Dollo Ado	Kakuma	Nakivale
1) Political Will	Buy-in from federal, national, and local actors	Buy-in from local government, but limited support from national government, resulting in restrictions on work and mobility rights	Supportive national and local government
2) Infrastructure	Expansion of infrastructure but still gaps especially relating to roads and internet connectivity	Lack of electricity, roads, and water	Moderately good access to roads, electricity, water, and internet
3) Comparative Advantage	Few comparative advantages but focus on agriculture, livestock, and retail commerce. But weak market linkages	Few comparative advantages identified and built upon. Potential in livestock, solar energy, and digital work	Few comparative advantages but agriculture and retail commerce
4) Socio-Cultural Applicability	Attempts to understand cultural context but 'blind spots' in relation to the cross-border economy and the political economy of food assistance	Attempts to include local Turkana people in economic opportunities, including through protecting traditional activities	Livelihood opportunities adapted to suit both refugees and host community, especially in agriculture
5) External Inputs	Most inputs have been from humanitarian assistance and philanthropic investments	Most inputs from humanitarian assistance	Most inputs from humanitarian assistance, but some limited private-sector investment (e.g. in telecommunications)

Conclusion

Building refugee economies is not easy. In urban contexts, it is more about inclusion in existing socio-economic structures. In the remote border regions that host camps and settlements, however, such structures may not exist. International humanitarian organizations have become the de facto governors of refugee economies in many such regions, and yet there has, until now, been no clear road map for how to build sustainable economies in remote refugee-hosting regions. Even beyond the refugee context, the literature on remote economies is relatively limited.

The Sustainable Refugee Economies Framework highlights five key areas that need to be addressed in order to create socio-economic opportunities for refugees and host communities in remote border regions: political will, infrastructure, comparative advantage, socio-cultural applicability, and external inputs. Derived both deductively from theory and inductively from our East African case studies, the framework serves as both a diagnostic and prescriptive tool for considering how to build refugee economies elsewhere in the world.

My aim is not that this framework should become the final word on how to build economies in refugee-hosting regions, but that it can serve as a starting point for the more systematic and evidence-based design of economic policies towards refugees. For too long, the anaemic, programmatic language of 'self-reliance' and 'livelihoods' has detracted from serious consideration of what it takes—politically and economically—in order to build economies. This is the long-overdue conversation that needs to happen if we are to enable refugees to thrive in exile.

13

Beyond Africa
The Syrian and Venezuelan refugee crises

There are refugees and displaced people in practically every region of the world. However, the causes, consequences, and responses to displacement vary across regions. Major refugee-hosting countries—such as Turkey, Lebanon, Iran, Pakistan, Germany, Chad, Thailand, and Bangladesh—each have very different economies, political systems, and legal and policy frameworks relating to refugee rights. Some are predominantly agricultural, some manufacturing, and others service sector economies. Some are substantive democracies and others have semi-authoritarian governments. Some have signed international or regional agreements on refugee rights, while others have not. In some, refugees have the right to work, and in others they do not. In some, refugees mainly live in cities, and in others they mainly live in camps. There is huge variation, and context matters.

The Sustainable Refugee Economies Framework that I outlined in Chapter 12 represents the theory, but what about the practice? How does what we can learn from East Africa apply to other refugee-hosting countries around the world? Over the last few years, I have been invited to advise other governments on their responses to large-scale refugee crises. Often, they have had an interest in learning from our research in Africa, and exploring whether any of the insights might be adapted to a different regional context.

How can societies turn the presence of large numbers of refugees from a burden into a development opportunity? Under what conditions can the skills, talents, and aspirations of refugees be harnessed to support economic transformation in remote border regions? What types of wider insights and lessons can be learned from seemingly progressive examples like the Ugandan model?

During the twenty-first century, the two numerically largest refugee emergencies have been the Syrian and Venezuelan crises. In 2015, I worked with the Government of Jordan to explore options for integrating Syrian refugees into the labour market. In 2019, I travelled to Colombia to reflect on ways to transform the presence of Venezuelan refugees into a national development opportunity. In neither case could I claim to have any regionally specific expertise. However, I learned a lot from the conversations, the policies that subsequently emerged, and from their impact, which I reflect upon here.

Colombia and the Venezuelan refugee crisis

Since 2015, Venezuela has been characterized by political and economic mismanagement under President Nicolás Maduro. The government has armed up to half a million people as pro-government militia contributing to one of the highest murder rates in the world. Socio-economic collapse has led to hyperinflation, 90 per cent poverty levels, and an endemic lack of access to food and basic services for everyone except government loyalists. Consequently, from 2017, people started leaving the country in large numbers. By the end of 2019, well over 4 million people—up to 13 per cent of the 30 million population—were 'externally displaced', mainly in neighbouring countries, and there were predictions that that number could double to 8 million by the end of 2020, with nearly half of all Venezuelans claiming that they intend to emigrate.[1]

Venezuelans dispersed across Peru, Ecuador, Brazil, Argentina, and Chile. But no country received more than neighbouring Colombia, which received one-third of all externally displaced Venezuelans. Nearly every country in the region initially adopted generous policies, opening borders and providing temporary access to labour markets and public services. However, by the end of 2018, as numbers rose and public opinion turned against Venezuelans, most governments in the region introduced more restrictive measures. For example, in August 2018, Ecuador introduced border controls and in January 2019, a xenophobic backlash against Venezuelans led to a significant exodus into Colombia, after a Venezuelan murdered his pregnant Ecuadorian girlfriend. Meanwhile, in late 2018, Peru suspended access to work permits amid concern that it was generating a pull factor, and the governor of Brazil's Roraima State appealed to the Supreme Court to close the border until a relocation scheme was in place.

Despite the backlash across the region, Colombia tried to sustain a more generous viewpoint. Its approach was pragmatic. Realizing that it could not stop immigration with its long, porous, and poorly governed border, President Iván Duque chose instead to try to manage it in a way that could maximize the benefits to Colombians. The government adopted a regularization programme, distributing residency cards called *Permiso Especial de Permanencia* (PEP), which offered the right to work and access to public services to Venezuelans, in successive waves. Some PEP distribution waves required Venezuelans to produce passports and others were based simply on census participation. By the end of 2019, about half of the Venezuelans in Colombia were regularized through the scheme.

But the challenge was how to make such a large influx sustainable. Every day in 2019, around 45,000 Venezuelans crossed the border at the Simón Bolívar Bridge in Cúcuta, of whom most would collect food and then cross back, but around 2,000 would stay and 2,000 would try to traverse the country and then enter Ecuador. Those who aspired to remain in Colombia dispersed around the country, with most going to the large cities where the pressure on health and education facilities has been significant, and few additional jobs have been available, whether in the formal or the informal economy. The World Bank estimated a cost to Colombia equivalent to 0.5 per cent of gross domestic product (GDP) per year.[2] In this context, it was unsurprising that public opinion was gradually turning against Colombia's open-door policy. Meanwhile, the government received very little international support—just $300 million in pledges or about twenty-six times less per displaced person than Middle Eastern host countries in the Syrian refugee crisis.[3]

In February 2019, I visited Colombia at the invitation of the Government of Colombia. It wanted to figure out whether the presence of Venezuelans could become a development opportunity for the country. Under what conditions could the large-scale presence of refugees and migrants actually be an economic benefit rather than a burden? The government knew that I was not a regional expert, but wanted to see what lessons could be gleaned from other parts of the world. During the mission, we visited the border regions of La Guajira and Norte de Santander, spent time in Bogotá, and spoke to a wide variety of people, including Venezuelan migrants and their representative organizations, national and local government, non-governmental organizations (NGOs) and international organizations, and business and the private sector.

At the border-crossing point of Cúcuta, where 80 per cent of Venezuelan migrants into enter Colombia, we witnessed thousands of people, many emaciated and exhausted, dragging suitcases and trolleys across the Simón Bolivar Bridge, in the hope of filling them with food and basic supplies unavailable on the other side of the border in the La Parada market square. Nearly 4,000 people a day queued for a meal at the Casa de Paso Divina Providencia's food kitchen, and 4,000 more at the city's other three kitchens. Beyond that, the most basic emergency services were provided by UN agencies and NGOs. The story was similar—but on a much smaller scale—at the Paraguachón border crossing close to the town of Maicao in La Guajira; there was a food kitchen, temporary accommodation for the most vulnerable, and a throng participating in informal economic exchange.

In the cities, where most Venezuelans travel, socio-economic opportunities are scarce. Bogotá had received around 300,000 Venezuelans. But there is limited assistance available beyond access to education, healthcare, and the right to work for those with a PEP. In the city's recently built migration centre, only a handful of beds are available for a maximum of five nights. There I met Esteban, a 3-year-old Venezuelan boy and his parents. They had been in Ecuador but, following the outbreak of xenophobic violence, had been forced to hitch-hike over 1,000km from Quito back to Bogotá. Without regularized status, they were only able to buy and sell lollipops at traffic lights for a few dollars a day, and faced expulsion from the temporary shelter. But the situation was not much better for those with a regular status. Twenty-year-old Carolina and her mother were also at the shelter and, although they had the PEP, they too had few options; 'I was going to go to university in Venezuela, and now that is gone. I used to have a job as a waitress here, but now there is nothing for us. We have no money and nowhere to go; I do not know what will happen.'

The biggest gap was jobs. Colombia has a highly regulated labour market. All job vacancies have to be advertised on a central database. But according to the national public employment agency (SENA), there were only 9,240 listed vacancies in the entire country. At a regional level, just 314 vacancies were available in Norte de Santander in a region in which 40,000 people were registered as looking for work in the previous year, of whom 4,000 were Venezuelans.[4] Put simply, the formal labour market is inadequate. About 40 per cent of Colombia's economy is in the informal or illegal sectors. However, here there is massive pressure; there was a ubiquitous sense amongst Colombians that Venezuelans were undercutting Colombians' informal sector jobs.

In the border regions in particular, the narrative from mayors and local entrepreneurs was one of immense and growing resentment that wages and prices were being undercut. In this context, it was unsurprising that there was growing resentment. In the build-up to local elections in October 2019, there was real concern there might be a backlash in the already economically weak and politically unstable border regions. The head of the chamber of commerce of La Guajira explained: 'There is small-scale smuggling and the influx of products changes supply and prices. It is costing local businesses and causing anger.' One UN staff member even claimed to have received death threats from a local mayor's office in relation to plans to offer cash-based assistance to Venezuelans.

Against this backdrop, was there a way in which the presence of Venezuelans could possibly become a boon for Colombia? At the end of my visit, in my presentations at the Presidential Palace, the US Embassy, the European Commission, to various UN agencies, and in interviews and opinion pieces for the press, I emphasized three main themes which I believed might be worth considering based on my wider research.[5]

First, I suggested that Colombia needed to build a strategic plan in order to transform the mass influx of Venezuelans into a development opportunity for its border regions. There was, I argued, precedent for this. Mexico's Yucatan Peninsula, for instance, had benefitted immensely from the local integration of Guatemalan refugees during the 1990s to build its agricultural economy, receiving European and American aid money as the starting point. Could Colombia identify sources of comparative advantage in host border regions and use the Venezuelan crisis as a hook for assistance and investment in historically marginalized regions? In La Guajira, for example, many of the people we spoke to suggested that opportunities may exist to expand the ecotourism industry, given the presence of the Wayuu indigenous people and the beaches of the Atlantic coast. In Norte de Santander there are potential opportunities to expand ceramics, textiles, and palm oil production, for example. However, it was also clear that as well as simply identifying these sources of comparative advantage, the central government would need to build an effective working relationship with the borderland regions. And the challenge was that these were regions characterized by historical underinvestment, weak governance, and high levels of political risk. These were economies described to me as being 'like the wild west', in which criminal gangs and paramilitaries dominate business and influence politics, and within which trust between the central government and the border regions is extremely weak.

Second, I suggested that Colombia should consider reframing the influx to ensure that the country could benefit from refugee-related assistance. Up until that point, the government had been reluctant to describe the Venezuelans as 'refugees', for fear of creating an open-ended commitment or stretching its already bottlenecked asylum system to breaking point. The government therefore described most Venezuelans as 'migrants' and the UN Refugee Agency (UNHCR) described them as 'externally displaced Venezuelans'. It was true that most Venezuelans did not fit the 1951 Convention definition of a refugee, generally fleeing the economic consequences of the underlying political situations rather than political persecution per se. They were in many ways what I have previously called 'survival migrants' in my earlier writing about situations such as the Zimbabwean crisis of the early 2000s.[6] They were fleeing serious socio-economic deprivations caused by weak governance. However, Latin America also has its own refugee definition—outlined within the 1984 Cartagena Declaration— and most Venezuelans incontrovertibly met that definition in fleeing 'massive violations of human rights or other circumstances which have seriously disturbed public order'. Labelling was not just a question of rights, I suggested, but also of access to international assistance and investment. By refusing to label this a refugee crisis, Colombia risked locking itself out of eligibility for relevant budget lines and international policy processes. Regardless of how Venezuelans were labelled, Colombia needed to make sure it was eligible for refugee-related development funding.

Third, I suggested that Colombia might convene an international solidarity summit in order to attract investment and assistance. At the time of my visit, UNHCR was promoting the concept of 'global solidarity summits' as a means to support host governments around the world. Such summits had a successful historical precedent in Latin America. The International Conference on Refugees in Central America (CIREFCA) of 1989 had provided support for self-reliance and the local integration of hundreds of thousands of displaced Central Americans. It targeted on refugees, internally displaced persons, externally displaced persons, and returnees.

The 1989 conference focused on transforming the integration of refugees and displaced persons into a development opportunity, and it attracted around half a billion dollars of investment, mainly from European governments and the United States. Crucially, the conference was not a one-off pledging summit but a multi-year process that built trust and credibility, and included concrete follow-up mechanisms. It involved leadership by an inter-agency secretariat. CIREFCA is widely acknowledged to be one of the most successful initiatives in the history of the refugee system, facilitating development opportunities for hundreds of thousands of refugees and host-country citizens. Given that UNHCR had revived the concept of multi-stakeholder solidarity summits, might Colombia work with other countries across the region on a Solidarity Summit?

Colombia was able to implement some of these ideas.

First, when the Duque government launched its four-year, $325 billion National Development Plan (NDP) in May 2019, the 1,457-page document hardly mentioned the Venezuela situation, other than as context.[7] Far from integrating Venezuelan refugees and migrants into national development plans, they have remained marginal to it. Meanwhile, the idea of 'mini-development plans' for 'departments' like La Guajira and Norte de Santander has stalled. One of the limiting factors has been the tenuous relationship between the central government and those regions, with the Office of the President ultimately exercising little authority in regions dominated by corruption and armed gangs. In April 2019, Colombia became one of very few middle-income countries to be eligible for World Bank funding based on hosting refugees, and received a grant of £31.5 million through the Global Concessional Financing Facility (GCFF).[8] In return, Colombia agreed to facilitate Venezuelans' access to the labour market and public services. However, the Inter-American Development Bank (IADB) has stalled on providing development funding, partly because its Board is dominated by Central American governments with priorities to the north of the Panama Canal.

Second, there has been some progress in recognizing the situation as a refugee crisis. In May 2019, UNHCR finally published a 'Protection Guidance Note' arguing that most Venezuelans are in need of international protection and should be regarded as refugees.[9] Following this, there has been far greater engagement than previously between UNHCR and the Government of Colombia, with the Office of the President's representative, Felipe Muñoz, attending numerous high-level UNHCR events, including the Global Refugee Forum in December 2019 and working directly with the High Commissioner for Refugees, Filippo Grandi.

Third, in October 2019, the European Commission convened an International Solidarity Summit on the Venezuelan Refugee and Migrant

Crisis in Brussels, in collaboration with UNHCR and the International Organization for Migration (IOM). The event was attended by 120 delegations. It focused on principles of solidarity such as access to asylum, combatting xenophobia, and the need for responsibility-sharing. Explicitly not a pledging conference, it nevertheless led to 120 million euros of additional contributions from EU member states, plus 50 million euros of additional EU funding.[10] These amounts though are relatively small compared to the UN's 2020 Regional Refugee and Migrant Response Plan for Venezuela, which calls for $1.35 billion, $739.2 million of which would go to Colombia. The Government of Colombia has continued discussions with UNHCR and IOM about a possible follow-up conference in the region to be convened at a later date.

Overall, the Government of Colombia has been enthusiastic about a development-based approach. However, progress at the diplomatic level has not always been matched by implementation. The big gap has been the creation of credible development plans for the most affected regions, including the border regions. Little progress has been made in creating such plans for regions like La Guajira and Norte de Santander because of corruption and weak governance in these departments, and a difficult relationship between the departments and the central government. In Colombia, working with the border regions is no easy task.[11] In this context, international assistance has continued to focus on meeting the immediate humanitarian needs of refugees and migrants, rather than facilitating private-sector-led development.

Jordan and the Syrian refugee crisis

The only displacement crisis of the twenty-first century bigger than Venezuela has been Syria, with 12 million of the 21 million population displaced, including around 5.5 million refugees, by the end of 2019. Since large-scale violence and persecution began in 2011, the majority of refugees have travelled to neighbouring middle-income countries such as Turkey, Lebanon, and Jordan. From late 2014, however, with declining humanitarian assistance and increasingly restrictive public policies in all three of those countries, increasing numbers of Syrians began to move onwards, crossing the Aegean Sea to Europe in what became known as the European refugee crisis.

In April 2015, my colleague Paul Collier and I were invited by the Jordanian royal family's think tank, the WANA Institute, to travel to Jordan to advise the government on its response. At that point, Jordan hosted at least 650,000 refugees, and possibly as many as 1 million according to the government, against the backdrop of a population of just 9.5 million. Around 200,000 were in the Za'atari and Azraq refugee camps but the majority were in cities. Initially, Syrians had been welcomed, albeit with severe restrictions on the right to work and strong encouragement to reside in the camps. Gradually, though, security became more of a priority and, with the emergence of Islamic terrorist violence in Syria after September 2014, Jordan began to increase border restrictions.[12] As humanitarian aid waned, the Jordanian Government became increasingly concerned about the security and development challenge it faced.

The WANA Institute was keen to explore with us how Jordan might sustainably integrate Syrian refugees. One of the biggest barriers was that Syrian refugees were not allowed to work, and there was huge political opposition to labour market access. There was high unemployment, particularly among Jordanian graduates, and the country's professional guilds vetoed entry into high-skilled sectors. Even in low-skilled employment, the government privileged Egyptian migrant workers, based on a long-standing bilateral relationship.

And yet one of the preferences expressed by the Syrian refugees we spoke to in Za'atari and Amman was the desire to work—to be active and to be able to support their families. One man in Za'atari explained that his eldest son had recently returned to Syria to fight for ISIS because of a lack of economic opportunity in the camp. Most political pathways to refugee employment were blocked.

After a morning spent in Za'atari, our government minder took us to visit the nearby King Hussein bin Talal Development Area, one of the country's pre-existing special economic zones (SEZs). It was just a fifteen-minute drive from Za'atari, and the government had invested around $100 million in connecting it to the electricity grid and the road network. However, it lacked two things: labour and foreign direct investment. Might allowing refugees to work in the SEZs be a way to address these gaps, and simultaneously benefit Jordan and the refugees?

During our time in Jordan, we brainstormed the idea of allowing refugees to work in Jordan's SEZs at numerous meetings, with international organizations, NGOs, senior government officials, and members of the royal family. The essence of the proposal was that giving refugees access to labour markets could be an opportunity for Jordan. It could generate tariff reductions on exports to Europe, attract concessionary finance from the World Bank, and thereby support Jordan's aspiration to make the leap towards becoming a manufacturing economy. It could also potentially incubate Syrian businesses no longer able to operate in Syria, preparing them and Syrian workers to ultimately be better placed to return home and rebuild their economy and society, we argued.

After initial reluctance to consider any form of Syrian access to labour markets, senior members of the government—including the then minister of planning and international cooperation, Imad Fakhoury, who would ultimately lead the process—agreed that we could draft a white paper, without our names on it, which cabinet could circulate. If it went well, they could take the credit; if it went badly, they could blame us. We wrote the paper, and published a shorter and less technical version in *Foreign Affairs* later that year.[13]

Tragic circumstances made that paper even more relevant than it might otherwise have been. Over the summer of 2015, the numbers of Syrians travelling to Europe skyrocketed. And on 1 September 2015, Britain's major newspapers all published the image of 2-year-old Alan Kurdi, drowned on a beach in Bodrum, on their front covers. The British Prime Minister David Cameron immediately made the Syrian refugee crisis a major priority and in the following week travelled to both Jordan and Lebanon in search of solutions. While in Amman, he met with King Abdullah, who presented the SEZs proposal to him. Upon his return, Cameron asked the chief economist of the Department for International Development (DFID) to develop a British Government proposal.

Thereafter, at a London Pledging Summit in February 2016, the UK Government played a leading role in concluding a deal called the Jordan Compact to support Syrian refugees. Its focus was on enabling refugees to have access to jobs. Under the agreement, Jordan committed to reduce its regulatory barriers on refugees' right to work, cutting the cost of work permits to virtually nothing for most low-skilled work categories in sectors like agriculture, construction, textiles, and manufacturing. In return, donors agreed a more general support package to strengthen Jordan's capacity to host refugees. A key part of the deal related to SEZs. The EU would provide tariff-free access to European markets on condition that businesses in Jordan's SEZs employ a certain proportion of Syrian refugees, produce in any of fifty-two product categories, and that products involve at least 30 per cent value addition in Jordan. In addition, the World Bank would for the first time offer low-interest loans to a middle-income country hosting refugees. The stated objective of the summit was to provide 200,000 work permits for Syrians over three to five years.

So how has the model performed since, and what more general lessons can be learned? On the positive side, it created the qualified right to work for refugees in a country in which it did not previously exist. Within six months, it had led to 45,000 work permits being granted to Syrian refugees, and 166,000 by the end of 2019. Furthermore, some of the SEZs have been able to host and incubate Syrian businesses employing Syrian and Jordanian workers. For example, the Sahab SEZ hosts several Syrian manufacturing firms, which have relocated to Jordan. The Al Fayhaa Company focuses on plastics and rubber, including flexible and hygienic packaging, in its 18,000sq ft factory. Under Syrian management, when I visited in 2017, it employed eighty-two Syrians out of 313 employees, and was exporting to Sweden, Spain, France, and the Netherlands under the Compact, with 40 per cent of its sales to the EU.

However, the Jordan Compact has also faced significant challenges.

First, relatively few refugees actually wanted to work in the SEZs. The main target sector within the SEZs has been garments and textiles because this was one of the few sectors in which Jordan was not worried about competing away Jordanian jobs. International organizations such as UNHCR and the International Labour Organization (ILO) convened numerous jobs fairs and tried to facilitate employment matching, but with limited success. One UNHCR livelihoods officer explained,

> I was expecting people to jump on it but a lot of professional tailors were not interested because they were already doing it in the informal sector. The garment sector was very selective towards women. They only wanted women aged 18–40. Working hours were very long, with production lines running eight–ten hours a day, six days a week, and at minimum wage…We quickly found out that women didn't want these jobs.[14]

There were economic and cultural reasons why women did not take the jobs. First, wages did not meet needs; average earnings of $150 per month in the garment factories did not meet so-called 'survival minimum expenditure baskets' of around $250 per month. Second, gender norms meant that many women did not want to work; they instead wanted jobs for their often under-age boys who were working in the informal sector. Indeed, this could have been foreseen if appropriate socio-economic assessments had been undertaken prior to implementation.

Second, there was limited external investment. For example, even in the garments sector, few multinational companies (MNCs) relocated to the SEZs. Classic Fashion Apparel moved to operate in the Al Hassan Industrial Estate in Irbid, employing Syrian refugees after the Compact, and selling to the likes of Wal-Mart and ASDA. IKEA began placing orders from factories within the SEZs. And a German–Jordanian collaboration emerged to create a renewable energy factory employing Syrians in the Aqaba Economic Zone. But these examples were rare. MNCs were reluctant to place orders with the factories at sufficient levels to scale the SEZ model, especially in an economy with little prior comparative advantage in low-skilled manufacturing and with a GDP growth rate of just 2.5 per cent. And despite numerous pitches at executive-level business events in London and elsewhere, led by the government and supported by the likes of the IKEA Foundation, there was little investment by firms. Ultimately, neither the business case nor the corporate social responsibility (CSR) case was sufficiently compelling to encourage manufacturing investment in Jordan.

Third, most of the work permits did not relate to new jobs in the SEZs but the formalization of existing construction and agricultural work, mainly in urban areas. In that sense, the data on the allocation of work permits cannot be understood as an indicator of new job creation. However, the regularization of informal sector jobs at least has the advantage of reducing refugees' risk of exploitation. In particular, formalization brought a series of labour rights obligations, including the minimum wage, a forty-eight-hour working week, social security, maternity leave, and annual leave. In practice, not all of these rights are adequately enforced, particularly in sectors like construction and agriculture, but formalization has been a step towards greater regulation.

The Jordan model therefore ticked the boxes for political will and infrastructure, but fell short in terms of being based on a compelling comparative advantage, being adequately adapted to cultural context, and receiving adequate external investment.[15]

The experience should not rule out considering a role for SEZs within refugee policy. If well designed and implemented, SEZs may offer a means to incentivize investment and unlock commitment to letting refugees work. Nevertheless, the experience should also serve as a warning in several respects. First, the work has to be attractive to refugees, and this requires greater due diligence in terms of socio-economic assessments, understanding minimum expenditure baskets, and appreciating cultural and gendered interpretation of work. Second, the investment case for business engagement has to be more thoughtfully conceived and tested through pilots and consultations at a board level. Relying on CSR and goodwill towards refugees, even during a major refugee crisis, will not be sufficient. Third, the sectoral focus of SEZs has to relate to areas in which there is a genuine comparative advantage; Jordan was not, with hindsight, a great destination for low-skilled manufacturing.

Ultimately, the Jordan Compact was a political success but an economic failure. On the one hand, it created the right to work for refugees in a country in which it did not previously exist. It represents an entry point on which job creation and entrepreneurship programmes for Syrians have been able to build; this was possible partly because of the commitment of key individuals such as the minister for planning and international cooperation, Imad Fakhoury, who saw the presence of refugees as an opportunity for national development. On the other hand, however, the economics of building a manufacturing base in Jordan simply did not work. Investors did not recognize the opportunity, even given trade concessions and infrastructural investment.

Conclusion

From my brief experiences of working outside of the African context, it has been clear that context matters. There is great value in comparing experiences, and learning from 'best practices' across regions. But ultimately, insights from one region need to be filtered through an in-depth understanding of regional and national context. In my visits to Colombia and Jordan, I was only able to contribute an external perspective, based on research, rather than in-depth, context-specific knowledge. It became clear that there were unique challenges and opportunities for building refugee economies in each of the countries. However, there were also some similarities and it was possible to derive relevant insights from other contexts.

In Jordan, formal labour markets were heavily regulated, with significant labour protections for members of guilds and specific groups of migrant workers such as Egyptian migrant workers. Meanwhile, the economic opportunity for creating new jobs was extremely limited by low economic growth rates, the closure of borders with its fragile neighbours, and the country's lack of obvious sources of economic comparative advantage.

Furthermore, while the government's priority was to create economic opportunity and contain Syrian refugees outside major urban areas, the majority of refugees chose to live in cities rather than the country's two main camps.

In Colombia, the constraints were in some ways similar. The country has a very large informal sector, making up around 40 per cent of all employment, which accounts for most low-skilled labour and self-employment. Colombian citizens were extremely worried about Venezuelans competing for informal work opportunities. Meanwhile, on a political level, although the country's larger cities were generally able to absorb Venezuelans into the informal economy, the historically strained relationship between the central government and the border regions made it politically challenging to create a Venezuelan influx-specific development strategy for those regions.

Both countries therefore presented three common challenges. First, refugees were mainly in cities rather than rural or border regions. Second, there were few formal labour market opportunities available to refugees. Third, although the governments were focused significantly on remote border regions, those regions lacked obvious sources of comparative advantage.

The two cases reinforce just how hard it is to build refugee economies in practice. Even given two proactive governments receptive to the idea of seeing refugees as a development opportunity, translating this into a coherent development strategy has been fraught with difficulty. Economically, it has not been obvious that there are particular sectors that could absorb large numbers of refugee workers in the formal economy. Politically, while both countries have been pioneering in opening their labour markets to refugees, they have faced a backlash for doing so. Finally, though, even beyond the economics and politics, there has been a policy process to navigate.

Both countries had well-respected individuals leading their refugee policy process: Felipe Muñoz in Colombia and Imad Fakhoury in Jordan. Yet in order to build refugee economies, they have faced four main policy tasks: to build a development strategy that meets national interests and benefits refugees; to attract international investment; to retain domestic political support; and to ensure effective implementation. Jordan was successful in creating a mechanism to attract international investment, but struggled with implementation. In Colombia, it is too early to judge progress.[16]

If there is an overall lesson, it is that building refugee economies is both a necessary and a difficult policy challenge.

14

Refugees, COVID-19, and future trends

Introduction

From January 2020, the coronavirus pandemic spread rapidly from China to over 200 countries around the world. The initial impact was on public health in Group of Twenty (G20) countries. But thereafter attention quickly shifted towards the impact on developing countries. The pandemic's greatest impact will ultimately be on the global poor. And that impact will arise not primarily from the direct impact of the virus, but the indirect impact of lockdown measures on economies. The pandemic has prompted the onset of the greatest economic recession since the Great Depression of the 1930s, leading to negative economic growth rates in many already-poor countries, and contributing to the collapse of international trade, foreign direct investment, development assistance, government tax revenues, and remittance flows, all crucial for sustaining the lives and livelihoods of the world's poorest people.

On a global scale, within a few months of the crisis, an estimated 1.6 billion informal sector jobs were at risk,[1] 130 million additional people had been plunged into food insecurity, and 25 per cent more people required food assistance. The impact on developing countries has been described as 'the world's first global humanitarian crisis', and a 'triple crisis'—for health, governance, and economies.[2]

Refugees—the overwhelming majority of whom are in these low- and middle-income countries—were particularly affected from the start of the crisis. This is partly because they risk being excluded from or discriminated against in governments' social protection measures. In cities, from Kampala to Nairobi, refugees were explicitly excluded from initial government food distributions amid COVID-19 lockdowns from April 2020. In camps, humanitarian assistance capacity was hard hit by international staff withdrawals, the suspension of non-governmental organization (NGO) missions, and severe budget restrictions.

The long-term impact on refugees will be even more profound. The legacy of COVID-19 will shape the drivers of forced displacement and the ways in which governments respond to displaced people. Economic depression will exacerbate all of the main drivers of displacement: conflict, authoritarianism, and state fragility. It will also further aggravate the sources of political polarization that have undermined the willingness of rich countries to admit migrants and asylum seekers on to their territory. And some of the backlash against non-citizens will extend to developing countries. So how should the international refugee system respond and adapt? And are the ideas presented throughout this book still relevant to the present context?

The purpose of this chapter is not to accurately predict future trends. It is to provide a structured way of thinking about forced displacement scenarios by drawing upon the best research in social science. How will global recession impact on the causes, consequences, and responses to forced migration? What does existing social science tell us about likely scenarios? I explore the extent to which the analysis provided throughout this book remains relevant to those scenarios. Unsurprisingly, I suggest that they have more relevance than ever: refugees have key economic contributions to make to the post-COVID world, and we need more than ever to recognize those contributions.

COVID-19 is likely to serve as an accelerator and multiplier of pre-existing trends in the global political economy. For example, it may amplify the types of political polarization revealed by Brexit, the election of Donald Trump, and rising populist nationalism. It will exacerbate structural unemployment in ways that were already evident amid the offshoring and automation of manufacturing. It will further challenge public support for all aspects of globalization. It will accelerate the rise of China, as the country to emerge most rapidly from the pandemic. And these trends may also contribute to rising unilateralism and declining commitment to multilateralism. The refugee system is deeply embedded within, and affected by, these transformations in the global political economy. The already adverse implications of these trends for refugee protection are likely to intensify.

The crisis reinforces that we live in what this book has described as 'an age of displacement'. The paradox of rising numbers and declining political support is likely to become even more stark.

This creates an urgency to find sustainable responses. Here, the main ideas developed by this book have a role to play. Economically, empowering refugees to become contributors within their host societies offers a means to reduce humanitarian costs and to maintain the backing of host communities. Politically, there is even more imperative to ensure that donor governments continue to support host countries based on enlightened self-interest. Underlying this will be the need to recognize the interdependence between refugee protection in the Global South and consequences for the North.

Upfront investment will be needed by rich countries in order to mitigate the longer-term risk that developing countries turn their backs on refugees, with serious implications for human rights, security, and onward migration. The tasks of building 'refugee economies' and facilitating 'bargains of inclusion' are more vital than ever. However, the challenge is also greater than before. Western publics will need to be persuaded to maintain international development aid. Developing countries will need persuading to keep their doors open to refugees, let alone to offer greater socio-economic rights. Relying on an appeal to altruism is unlikely to be enough. It will take bargains that meet the interests of donors, hosts, and refugees.

One of the keys to sustainability, I argue in this chapter, will be to unlock the 'wealth of refugees'—their skills, talents, and aspirations—and ensure that they can play an active role in contributing economically, socially, and culturally to receiving countries. Within a post-COVID-19 world of scarcity and precarity, refugees themselves have an important role to play in economic recovery, the provision of social protection, and the emergence of progressive narratives that highlight the contributions of refugees. It is more important than ever to shift the paradigm away from 'refugees as a burden' towards that of 'refugees as a benefit', and to do so in a way that is strategic and politically engaged.

Increased forced displacement

Scenario-building is rife with difficulties, and there are no certainties about what future levels of displacement will look like. Nevertheless, we know generally what the main drivers of displacement are around the world: authoritarianism, conflict, and fragile states. And there is strong evidence that suggests a global economic depression will have a significant adverse impact on all three.

First, authoritarianism. When Hannah Arendt wrote the *Origins of Totalitarianism*, she envisaged that the main cause of refugee movements would be political systems that prohibit all forms of political opposition and require absolute obedience to the state, such as Nazism and Stalinism.[3] Indeed, the 1951 Convention on the Status of Refugees' focus on people fleeing 'persecution' is a product of this era, in which despotic regimes targeted individuals on the basis of race, religion, nationality, membership of a social group, or political opinion. Certainly, the number of authoritarian regimes in the international system grew, notably with the global expansion of the Cold War until the mid-1970s. Since then, however, and broadly speaking, the share of democracies around the world has been on an upward trend and now sits close to its post-Second World War record—at 58 per cent of countries.[4] With that, authoritarianism gradually become a relatively less prevalent driver of displacement.[5]

However, there has been a gradually increasing concern about rising authoritarianism of a different kind to the totalitarian regimes that Arendt was concerned about. Although only 13 per cent of countries are regarded as autocracies, around 28 per cent are a mixture of democracy and authoritarianism.[6] Indeed, there has been a growth in what might be described as 'competitive authoritarian' regimes, which maintain elections, but impose restrictions on the free and fair nature of those elections or impose restrictions on the media or judiciary, for example.[7] Andrea Kendall-Taylor and her colleagues show how many of these regimes emerge from within democracies and most are led by individual populist rulers. Examples include Russia under Vladimir Putin, Venezuela under Nicolás Maduro, the Philippines under Rodrigo Duterte, Hungary under Viktor Orbán, Brazil under Jair Bolsonaro, and Turkey under Recep Tayyip Erdoğan.[8] Within such regimes, elections may be retained for legitimacy but represent a form of theatre, with freedoms eroded among political opponents.[9]

The economic depression created by COVID-19 risks exacerbating this trend. Indeed, there is historical evidence that economic recessions contribute to what political scientists call 'democratic reversals' among relatively recent democracies. For example, Milan Svolik shows how a $1,200 increase in gross domestic product (GDP)/capita increases the likelihood of democratic consolidation from 20 per cent to 80 per cent.[10] The causal mechanisms through which economic downturn leads to democratic reversals are not well established, but appear to relate to reduced GDP growth being correlated with rising popular support and the greater concentration of scarce resources in the hands of the regime.

Under COVID-19, beginning with the Chinese Government's stringent lockdown rules, we saw governments across the world suspend a range of civil liberties using security-based justifications. In some countries, civil liberties have been suspended in ways that some human rights campaigners regard to be disproportionate and opportunistic. In March 2020, Hungary's Viktor Orbán passed emergency legislation allowing him to rule by decree until the COVID-19 crisis is over. In Kenya, police brutality was highlighted in the context of enforcing social distancing measures. India implemented a complete twenty-one-day lockdown with only four hours' notice, leaving millions without food, and providing police with an excuse to target the country's Muslim minorities. In the US, the Department of Justice asked Congress for the power to detain both citizens and non-citizens indefinitely without trial. Meanwhile, governments from Thailand to Tanzania have detained journalists and doctors for criticizing the governments' response.[11]

Second, conflict. Like authoritarianism, the long-term trend on conflict has been downwards. Battle-related deaths from inter-state and internal armed conflict declined significantly between the end of the Cold War and the early 2000s.[12] Meanwhile, although the overall number of conflicts increased after the end of the Cold War, the types of conflict shifted from inter-state to intra-state and from major to minor levels of intensity.[13] The exception to this trend came from 2014 when the Syrian crisis contributed to a significant spike in conflict-related deaths. Trends in displacement and refugee numbers have broadly tracked trends in battle-related deaths.[14]

There is evidence that serious economic shocks increase the likelihood of conflict. At a general level, there is research on the economic drivers of conflict, demonstrating the relationship between development indicators and internal armed conflict.[15] In an influential study, economics professor Ted Miguel and his colleagues examine the effects of economic shocks on civil conflict in Sub-Saharan Africa. They find that a negative growth shock of 5 percentage points increases the likelihood of conflict by 0.5 percentage points the following year.[16] Conversely, Paul Collier estimates that if the GDP growth rate increases by 1 percentage point from the mean within their sample, the risks of conflict decline by 0.6 per cent.[17] Other researchers explore specific mechanisms underlying the relationships between economic shocks and conflict. For example, Thorsten Janus and Daniel Riera-Crichton show that every 1 per cent decline in the terms of trade increases the risk of civil war onset by about 0.5 per cent.[18] Oeindrila Dube and Juan Vargas show how declining commodity prices for primary products such as coffee and oil increased levels of internal armed conflict in Colombia during the 1990s.[19]

The size and scale of the economic depression emerging from the COVID-19 response suggest there will be a massive impact on variables such as GDP/capita, the terms of trade, commodity prices, state capacity, and public services such as education across low- and middle-income countries, all of which been identified as factors that are important for explaining conflict.[20] And the social science literature predicts where we might see such conflicts. Paul Collier and Anke Hoeffler's research on the economics of conflict predicts that the most at-risk countries are likely to have characteristics such as primary commodities as a high proportion of their exports, geographically dispersed populations, a history of previous civil conflict, low education levels, and have one large and dominant ethnic group (the logic being that a dominant group is more likely to try to oppress minority groups, than if there are several equal-sized groups).[21]

With COVID-19 there is already an indication that even the early stages of the crisis are having an impact on conflict dynamics. With global media focused almost exclusively on the health impact of the pandemic, many conflicts have fallen off the radar of international scrutiny. For example, in April 2020 alone, around 200,000 people were displaced in the Ituri region of the Democratic Republic of Congo, as the minority ethnic Lendu militias attacked the majority Hema population.[22] This escalating conflict barely registered in the global media.

The UN secretary-general's 2020 call for a global ceasefire was respected in some parts of the world. For example, in Yemen, conflict between the Saudi-led military coalition and Yemen's Houthi was suspended as a result of COVID-19. But elsewhere, governments and armed groups took advantage of weakened international capacity to scrutinize and monitor conflict. One of the biggest risk factors has been the diversion of international military and peace-making capacity. And unsurprisingly, the biggest escalations of violence in 2020 were in countries with well-resourced non-state armed actors such as Libya, Iraq, Somalia, and Mali, where Islamic armed groups from Daesh to Al-Shabaab became resurgent amid the diminished Western military presence.

Third, fragile states. The concept of 'fragile and failed states' is often criticized for its lack of specificity.[23] It is an umbrella category that describes a variety of different types of countries. It includes countries characterized by weak state capacity or legitimacy that are unable to meet their citizens' most fundamental rights. Unlike functioning states, they may lack a monopoly on the use of coercive violence within their own territory, giving rise to generalized violence. Over time, state fragility has become the most significant driver of forced displacement and refugee movements. A growing majority of refugees are no longer fleeing individualized persecution by a government that is 'out to get them'—instead they are fleeing the breakdown of law and order or serious socio-economic rights deprivations. In many cases, it is the absence of a strong state that motivates people to flee.

In Africa and Latin America, regional treaties have updated the legal definition of a 'refugee' to include people fleeing 'serious disturbances to public order' or 'generalized violence'. In Europe, most courts and bureaucracies have reinterpreted the 1951 Convention to protect people fleeing war and armed conflict. However, there remain huge inconsistencies in whether and to what extent people fleeing serious socio-economic rights deprivations in fragile and failed states like Iraq, Afghanistan, and the Democratic Republic of Congo receive refugee status.[24]

The COVID-19-induced global depression will have a significant negative impact on fragile states. They already have larger informal economies, greater numbers of food-insecure people, reduced fiscal capacity, inadequate social protection, and weaker health systems.[25] They will be more vulnerable to a range of COVID-19-related changes. Across Africa in general, more than 10 per cent of people were driven into extreme poverty by the first month of the COVID-19 crisis alone.[26] Fewer than 18 per cent of Africans have access to social protection,[27] and this is likely to be even fewer in fragile states. Declining remittances and international development assistance will undermine economic opportunity and push more people into poverty. These dynamics may in turn force people to seek employment through non-state armed actors, such as gangs and rebel groups.

Accurately predicting the numbers of newly displaced people that will result from the legacy of COVID-19 is impossible. However, we understand the factors that have historically led to forced displacement—authoritarianism, conflict, and state fragility. Existing social scientific research shows that economic shocks are likely to exacerbate each of these drivers of displacement. Although a variety of policy interventions can be adopted to mitigate these impacts, it is highly probable that we will see a significant increase in the numbers of people forcibly displaced over the next decade, as a result of the fallout from global economic depression.

Table 14.1 summarizes the way in which the pandemic-induced global recession is likely to affect the causes, consequences, and responses to forced

Table 14.1: The impact of global recession on the causes, consequences, and responses to forced displacement

Causes	Consequences	Responses
Conflict e.g. Miguel et al., 2004[a]: a 5% negative economic shock leads to a 0.5% increase in likelihood of conflict in Africa	**Employment** e.g. Dempster et al., 2020[b]: 60% of forced migrants work in sectors highly impacted by COVID-19, compared to 41% of hosts	**Public Attitudes** e.g. Isaksen, 2019[c]: attitudes to immigration in Europe are positively correlated with GDP growth and employment levels
Authoritarianism e.g. Svolik, 2008[d]: a $1,200 increase in GDP/capita increases the likelihood of democratic consolidation from 20% to 80%	**Assistance** e.g. Dabla-Norris et al., 2010[e]: aid flows contract sharply during donor economic downturns	**Travel** e.g. Fix et al., 2009[f]: the 2008 global recession led to a proliferation in government restrictions on immigration
Fragile States e.g. Carment et al., 2008[g]: GDP/capital statistically significant and negatively correlated with indicators of state fragility	**Remittances** e.g. World Bank, 2020[h]: remittances to low- and middle-income countries predicted to fall 19.7% due to COVID-19	**Human Rights** e.g. the Council of Europe, 2013[i]: austerity measures reduce governments' willingness and ability to uphold human rights
⬇	⬇	⬇
Rising Numbers	**Increasing Needs**	**Declining Will**

Sources: [a] Miguel, E., Satyanath, S., & Sergenti, E. (2004), Economic shocks and civil conflict: an instrumental variables approach. *Journal of Political Economy, 112*(4), 725–53;

[b] Dempster, H. et al (2020), *Labor Market Impacts of COVID-19 on Forced Migrants* (Washington DC: Center for Global Development);

[c] Isaksen, J. V. (2019), The impact of the financial crisis on European attitudes toward immigration. *Comparative Migration Studies, 7*(1), 24;

[d] Svolik, M. (2008), Authoritarian reversals and democratic consolidation. *American Political Science Review, 102*(2), 53–68;

e Dabla-Norris, E., Minoiu, C., & Zanna, L.-P. (2010), Business cycle fluctuations, large shocks, and development aid: new evidence, IMF Working Papers 10/240 (Washington DC: International Monetary Fund);

f Fix, M., Papademetriou, D. G., Batalova, J., Terrazas, A., Lin, S. Y. Y., & Mittelstadt, M. (2009), *Migration and the Global Recession* (Washington DC: Migration Policy Institute);

g Carment, D., Samy, Y., & Prest, S. (2008), State fragility and implications for aid allocation: an empirical analysis. *Conflict Management and Peace Science*, 25(4), 349–73;

h World Bank (2020), How the World Bank is helping countries with Covid-19, Factsheet (Washington DC: World Bank), https://www.worldbank.org/en/news/factsheet/2020/02/11/how-the-world-bank-group-is-helping-countries-with-covid-19-coronavirus

i Council of Europe (2013), Austerity measures across Europe have undermined human rights (Belgium: Council of Europe), https://www.coe.int/en/web/commissioner/-/austerity-measures-across-europe-have-undermined-human-rights

displacement. It highlights the relationship between economic recession, on the one hand, and the three main drivers of displacement (conflict, authoritarianism, and fragile states), the three main sources of support for displaced people (employment, assistance, and remittances), and three of the main behaviours that shape governments' responses to refugees (public attitudes, travel, and human rights) on the other. In each case, it features examples of social science research that shed light on the relationship between these variables and global recession.

The impact on refugees

Benoît Decerf and colleagues estimate the total number of years of life likely to be lost due to COVID-19 globally.[28] They show that the pandemic has had very different effects on rich and poor countries. For countries with ageing populations and low levels of poverty, the biggest impact is on health, through deaths due to the virus. For countries with younger populations and higher initial poverty levels, the biggest impact is on the economy, through deaths related to other causes. Most refugees are in poor countries and they tend to be young and poor. Reflecting this, the greatest effect of COVID-19 on refugees is likely to result from the global economic recession.

Refugees in low- and middle-income countries tend to already be affected by multidimensional poverty. They face interlinked deprivations across areas such as health, education, and living standards. Sabina Alkire and her colleagues at the Oxford Poverty and Human Development Initiative show how people who begin from positions of multidimensional poverty are at greater risk in terms of COVID-19.[29] They show that the more pre-existing deprivations people have, the more at risk they are. Deprivations relating to water, nutrition, and cooking fuel predict vulnerability to the virus; other deprivations may predict vulnerability to the economic fallout. As we showed in Chapter 3, even compared to host communities, refugees in our focus countries have generally even greater levels of initial socio-economic deprivation.

Furthermore, existing social science research suggests that three of the most important sources of income and support for refugees are all likely to be significantly affected by a global recession.

First, refugee employment is likely to be affected. Refugees are more likely to be in high-risk employment sectors or in the informal sector than host communities. The Center for Global Development, for example, showed that across Turkey, Uganda, Colombia, Jordan, Lebanon, Peru, Ethiopia, and Iraq, 60 per cent of forced migrants work in sectors predicted to be highly impacted by COVID-19—food services, trade, manufacturing, and business—compared to 41 per cent of hosts. Furthermore, in some of these countries, employed forced migrants were twice as likely as hosts to work in the informal sector.[30] The International Labour Organization (ILO) similarly showed how Syrian refugees in Jordan have been dispropor-tionately vulnerable to the economic consequences of the pandemic, and that there were increasing signs of competition between refugees and hosts for labour market opportunities.[31] And, just as we saw in Chapter 3, a reduction refugee employment and consumption are a crucial part of what underpins positive host community attitudes towards refugees.

Second, humanitarian assistance may be hard hit. Of course, there is no inevitability that COVID-19 will lead to a cut in international development and humanitarian assistance. Ngaire Woods, for example, has called for a global response that mirrors the multilateral cooperation of the post-Second World War era. She writes optimistically: 'After COVID-19 there is a risk that the world could be yet more divided, conflictual, and nationalistic. But an alternative scenario is within reach. In this scenario, collective action within communities and, where necessary, internationally, will make a more rapid and peaceful exit from the crisis possible.'[32] In many ways, the juxta-position of these scenarios for the future of multilateralism mirrors the debate between realism and idealism within international relations during the first half of the twentieth century.[33] In calling for solidarity and collect-ive action, Woods contrasts the failures of post-First World War cooperation with the success of post-Second World War multilateralism. The latter is certainly a scenario to advocate and hope for.

However, evidence from previous recessions reveals how aid levels are linked to GDP/capita growth rates. In an International Monetary Fund (IMF) working paper following the 2008 financial crisis, Era Dabla-Norris and colleagues examined the impact of economic recessions on bilateral and multilateral development assistance between 1970 and 2005. They found that bilateral aid flows are on average procyclical with respect to business cycles in donor and recipient countries. Most soberingly, aid outlays contract sharply during severe donor economic downturns, and this effect is magnified by higher public debt levels of the type that have emerged since 2020.[34]

Indeed, the immediate signs following the outbreak of COVID-19 are mixed. In terms of development assistance, the World Bank Group committed up to $160 billion to address the immediate health, economic, and social shocks faced by developing countries, including over $50 billion of grants and concessional loans.[35] However, the prospects for humanitarian assistance through the UN were less sanguine. Throughout 2020, the UN updated its humanitarian appeals to reflect growing needs. By May 2020, the UN estimated a cost of $90 billion to address the humanitarian impacts of COVID-19's socio-economic consequences, but had received about 13 per cent of its $28 billion pre-coronavirus humanitarian appeal, with few signs of significant new bilateral or multilateral commitments.[36]

Third, remittances will fall. The World Bank estimates that remittances to low- and middle-income countries will drop by 19.7 per cent due to COVID-19, as wages and employment levels fall for migrant workers.[37] In Sub-Saharan Africa, the predicted fall is 23 per cent, which will have a particularly significant impact on refugee communities, who frequently rely in remittances as a source of both income and investment in, for example, businesses and education. In our research we found, for example, that 43 per cent of Somalis in Nairobi receive remittances that work out at an average of around $2,300 per year—more than the GDP/capita of Kenya.

Reduced willingness to provide asylum

Over recent years, there has been a growing backlash against asylum and immigration amid rising populism and nationalism in Europe and the

United States. One of the biggest political divides across Western democracies in recent years has been globalization. David Goodhart described the schism as between the 'Anywheres' and the 'Somewheres'—people who have a liberal, cosmopolitan identity and tend to support globalization, versus people who are attached to a particular place or community and tend to be concerned about the impact of globalization on the economy, culture, and security.[38] Although the distinction has been criticized as an over-simplification,[39] its focus on attitudes towards globalization reveals an important aspect of the divisions present in Brexit, the 2016 US presidential elections, and the rise of nationalist political parties across Europe.[40]

Across Europe and the United States, immigration rose dramatically in its political salience following the 2015–16 refugee crisis.[41] Public attitudes polarized around immigration, and the issue became a rallying call for the Far Right.[42] And yet underlying this was a paradox. Across Western countries, the people with the strongest anti-immigration attitudes or the greatest likelihood to support anti-immigration parties tended to live in the regions with the lowest numbers of immigrants. This applied to the political geography of Brexit-voting areas, US presidential election voting districts, and support for Germany's Alternative für Deutschland.

The regions with the greatest support for anti-immigration parties tended to have in common that they historically had a concentration of labour-intensive manufacturing industries, that had been eroded through offshoring and automation. From the American rustbelt to Saxony in East Germany and the British north-east, the regions with the strongest levels of support for anti-immigration parties and policies lived in regions with few immigrants but structurally damaged economies in the aftermath of dein-dustrialization. In contrast, regions with more positive attitudes to immigration tended to have higher numbers of immigrants, but economies characterized by a greater proportion of jobs in sectors linked to technology and innovation.

Much of the immigration debate in Europe was not actually about immigrants—even less so refugees. Underlying it was the transformation in the global economy. But immigration became a useful proxy issue around which opportunistic politicians could mobilize people who felt either left behind or threatened by structural economic transformation. It was far easier for politicians in Europe to blame immigration than it was to articulate to their electorates the complexities of the global economy, and to be transparent about what was already an inherently 'bad news' story for predominantly white, working-class men.

The global economic depression following COVID-19 will exacerbate these underlying causes of anti-immigration sentiment in Europe. It will lead to a significant increase in unemployment in Europe, the collapse of businesses, and declining standards of living. The greatest impact by far will be on the poorest and already most alienated members of society. It is not inevitable that this will translate into anti-immigration sentiment. There are conceivably ways to create positive public narratives around migration even in times of economic downturn.

But history tells us that major recessions often lead to a backlash against immigration. In the United States, a spate of restrictive legislation began with the Emergency Quota Act in 1921, in the context of the 1920-1 depression. In the UK, openness to immigration in the aftermath of the Second World War came to a halt with the Commonwealth Immigration Act of 1962, as GDP growth declined from 6 per cent to less than 2 per cent in the preceding two years. Germany suspended its *Gastarbeiter* scheme in 1973 amid the onset of the 1973-5 oil-shock-induced recession. In the aftermath of the 2008 financial crisis, countries adopted a range of policies to restrict immigration and, amid rising unemployment, Spain, the Czech Republic, and Japan even paid migrants to go home.[43] Joachim Vogt Isaksen provides evidence from time series data across twenty-five European countries that public attitudes become less positive towards immigration during economic crises.[44] Related work describes a variety of potential mechanisms, including drawing upon 'scapegoat theory' and showing effects on competition for scarce resources such as jobs, housing, and public services.[45]

Within the first months of the COVID-19 outbreak, more than 200 countries imposed unprecedented restrictions on migration. Entire immigration systems were suspended, including refugee resettlement and asylum. In the EU, for example, nearly all governments effectively suspended processing new asylum applications. Elsewhere, the United States, Mexico, and Canada all suspended access to asylum, imposing blanket deportation on new arrivals, and 'push-backs' of asylum seekers took place in Greece, Malta, and Italy, for example. The practice of *refoulement* (returning people to a country in which they face a well-founded fear of persecution), became normalized virtually overnight. Other countries have imposed greater internal mobility and encampment restrictions on refugees. These limitations were justified on the grounds of preventing transmission of the virus.

One important litmus test will be the extent to which these control measures remain in place once the pandemic abates. Many commentators suggested that the pandemic represented a thinly veiled pretext for some leaders to implement a long held preference for restrictive migration policies.[46] Meghan Benton of the Migration Policy Institute argued that the sequencing to reliberalize mobility after COVID-19 will see states prioritize particular forms of mobility, based on short-term economic interests.[47] And forms of migration—such as asylum—that lack public support, may be subject to prohibitively high barriers such as 'immunity passports' and participation in contact-tracing apps, which may not be available to people who arrive through irregular channels. Benton suggests that in this new world, a key fault line of global inequality will be between 'movers' and 'non-movers' (similar to Zygmunt Bauman's famous distinction between 'tourists' and 'vagabonds'),[48] with the rich and privileged able to resume travel, and the poorest and most marginalized excluded.

However, the impact on the willingness to provide asylum is unlikely to be restricted to rich countries. Faced with rising unemployment, declining tax revenues, and cuts in public services, the low- and middle-income countries that host most refugees will also come under pressure to privilege citizens over non-citizens in the allocation of scarce resources. Existing research shows that one of the main historical reasons why such states have restricted refugees' socio-economic rights, for example, is that they are concerned about resource competition between citizens and refugees.[49]

The search for sustainable solutions

Global economic depression will therefore exacerbate the paradox of rising numbers but declining political will. Reconciling this paradox requires that we identify sustainable solutions—approaches that ensure refugees receive access to their human rights and can live dignified and meaningful lives, but approaches which can also function effectively at scale.

Neither open migration nor mass resettlement will be available to large numbers of refugees. Advocating for spontaneous arrival asylum and resettlement remains important—they serve crucial and irreplaceable protection roles, and they symbolically demonstrate rich countries' commitment to share responsibility for hosting the world's refugees. But they will not be a politically or geographically realistic option for most refugees.

The only realistic option for most refugees will be to create sustainable protection in the countries that immediately neighbour areas of conflict and crisis. In cities, this involves including refugees with existing socio-economic systems. In remote border regions, it involves moving beyond traditional refugee camps to create thriving communities that can benefit both refugees and host communities. But, as this book has revealed, even these tasks are economically and politically challenging—and they risk being hijacked by those with vested interests.

Building refugee economies will become ever more important. The global economic depression means that refugees and proximate host communities will face severe impacts on their livelihoods as informal sector work disappears, commodity prices tumble, and NGOs take on fewer staff. Nevertheless, as international aid budgets decline, opportunities for self-reliance will become even more crucial. Aid organizations will need to focus more than ever on bridging the humanitarian–development gap, ensuring that resilience, livelihoods, and self-reliance remain on the agenda. However, they will need to take seriously this book's argument that self-reliance will be unattainable in any meaningful sense unless it is accompanied by both socio-economic rights for refugees and by macroeconomic transformation in remote refugee-hosting regions.

But how can the humanitarian–development divide be bridged in a resource-constrained world? It requires two things: first, to make the argument that upfront investment is the only means to reduce longer-term costs, and, second, to include a role not only for public actors but also for a range of private actors. The task of building refugee economies will require innovative financing mechanisms and incentives for business engagement.

For example, how could financial disclosures—additional information attached to a company's financial statements—be used to highlight and incentivize greater engagement by companies whose work connects to refugee communities?[50] In the climate change arena, the Task Force on Climate-Related Disclosures (TFCD) has created a mechanism for companies to declare how their work impacts on climate change.[51] Could this concept be applied to forced displacement, so that companies that work near to refugee camps, in sectors from energy to infrastructure, reveal the positive externalities of their work—whether through employment, supply chain, or infrastructure, for example? As with climate change, the value to companies would be to attract equity or debt finance from impact investors, incentivizing greater positive contributions within refugee-hosting regions.

Alternatively, how might forms of blended finance, in which grant funding is used to attract greater levels of private capital, be applied to refugee contexts?[52] At its most simple level this may be about subsidizing private investment: the Dutch NGO, SNV Netherlands Organization, subsidizes solar electricity companies in Kakuma.[53] At a more complex level, it may involve creating new financial markets to underwrite risk and offer a return to private social impact. The International Committee of the Red Cross's (ICRC's) humanitarian impact bonds offer a relevant example. The model is based on a payment-by-results system in which 'social investors' (e.g. the Munich Re insurance group) provide upfront investment for a programme, and then 'outcome funders' (e.g. governments) pay the ICRC according to the results achieved.[54]

Governments have a vital role to play. But creating bargains that ensure host countries of first asylum give rights to refugees will be even more politically complex. There will be no guarantees that an appeal to altruism will bring donor money or host-country commitment. In a resource-constrained world, international cooperation will rely primarily upon interest convergence. How can donor and host-country interests be simultaneously met through the creation of sustainable opportunities for both refugees and host communities?

Amid rising debt across the G20, there is an inevitability that bilateral and multilateral aid budgets will fall. A strong and persuasive case will need to made to rich governments and their electorates for why development and humanitarian aid should continue to be prioritized. In part that case can draw upon the sentiment of solidarity evoked during the COVID-19 pandemic. But it will also need to be a case based upon enlightened self-interest. A failure to invest in meeting humanitarian needs in poor countries may lead to greater long-run costs—in terms of insecurity, violence, and mass migration. Early evidence suggests that human smuggling networks were thriving amid COVID-19, charging higher fees and opening new routes, such as from West Africa to the Canary Islands.[55] The case needs to be made that rich countries must collectively invest in global public goods, including refugee protection.

But refugee-hosting countries will also need persuading, not just to provide socio-economic rights, but even to open their borders or to refrain from mass deportations. Early in the COVID-19 crisis, Ethiopia continued to pursue the socio-economic integration of refugees through its so-called 'Out-of-Camp' Policy (OCP). However, as the economic impact reaches host-country citizens, the willingness to allow refugees to move and work may stall. There is a danger that host countries return to old-fashioned encampment policies for refugees, outsourcing responsibility to increasingly impoverished international organizations.

Brokering new bargains of inclusion, between Northern donors and Southern hosts will become an essential task for multilateral organizations. They will have to involve recognizing Northern interests in immigration control and Southern interests in development, but also ensuring that refugee rights are the ultimate goal.

Beyond intergovernmental bargains, there will be an even greater role for non-state actors. UNHCR's Global Compact on Refugees emphasizes a 'whole-of-society' approach to refugee protection. Indeed, with diminishing state capacity, a whole range of other actors will have contributions to make. New forms of solidarity that have emerged in the context of COVID-19 have the potential to become important vehicles for refugee inclusion. First, mayors and municipal authorities have increasingly emerged as among the most progressive and inclusive voices when it comes to refugee rights. This is reflected in initiatives such as the Global Mayoral Forum, through which progressive mayors from New York to Gaziantep have committed to integrate refugees.[56] Second, trade unions have sometimes become vocal advocates for refugee inclusion, in ways that have the potential to overcome barriers between native workers and displaced people.[57] Third, communities might become sponsors of private resettlement, following Canada's now famous model of allowing private citizens to fund and support refugee resettlement to the country.[58] And the digital revolution accelerated by COVID-19 arguably offers many more ways for private citizens and communities to engage in transnational solidarity, from crowdfunding to campaigning.[59]

However, perhaps the greatest untapped contribution comes from refugees themselves. Recognizing and building upon the skills, talents, and aspirations of refugees represents the best available means to reduce the perceived cost of refugee hosting, to augment the perceived benefits, and to transform narratives. Part of that is about supporting the economic contribution of refugees, discussed throughout this book. But the contribution of refugees should not be reduced to their economic productivity. It is economic, social, and cultural. The COVID-19 crisis has also revealed the previously neglected importance of refugee-led social protection; the role that refugees can play as providers of assistance and protection to other refugees and to members of the host community, whether through refugee-led organizations (RLOs) or informal networks.

The World Humanitarian Summit (WHS) in 2016 placed a strong emphasis on 'localization', recognizing and supporting 'crisis-affected people' as important first responders to crisis. The resulting Grand Bargain committed states to channel 25 per cent of humanitarian funding to 'national and local actors'. But this promise has never been realized in practice. In the refugee context, there has been a gradual shift towards recognizing refugees' contributions to protection. The inaugural UN Global Refugee Forum in 2019 invited participation by RLOs, such as the Global Refugee-Led Network (GRN). However, as a recent book that I published with Kate Pincock and Evan Easton-Calabria shows, in practice, RLOs have rarely received international recognition or funding.[60] This is despite often providing highly valued services to the community in areas from vocational training to psychosocial support.

However, during COVID-19, RLOs found themselves on the front line of the humanitarian response. The Ugandan context illustrates this well. In camps, UN and NGO capacity has been hit by the suspension of international travel, and RLOs have filled gaps. In the Nakivale settlement in the south-west of Uganda, the Wakati Foundation (meaning 'passing of time' in Swahili) has been sewing masks and distributing them to the community. Its founder, Alex Mango, set up the organization in 2013. It employs refugees to work on small-scale building projects, while providing training and employment to up to 250 refugees per year on an annual budget of around $75,000. Faced with the crisis, it has adapted, employing refugees to produce colourful face masks while also raising awareness among the community.[61]

Many of the most acute early challenges posed by COVID-19 were in urban areas, where international assistance is limited. In Kampala, for example, in April 2020, many refugees faced severe food shortages because of the lockdown as the government publicly announced on national television that 'refugees should be in the camps' and that 'non-nationals will not get food aid' except in refugee camps. Again, RLOs filled key gaps.

Hope for Children and Women Victims of Violence (HOCW), for example, founded by Congolese refugee, Bolingo Ntahira, ordinarily supports around 1,300 refugees a year through vocational training, psychosocial support, and English lessons. During the COVID-19 crisis, it distributed food and soap to refugees and Ugandans in the Ndejje area of Kampala, with hundreds of beneficiaries. Similarly, Young African Refugees for Integral Development (YARID), an award-winning organization, distributed baskets of flour, soap, beans, sugar, and cooking oil to the most vulnerable in the community. It identified recipients through community networks, and delivered food on *bodaboda* (motorcycle taxi) where needed, and reached hundreds of households.[62]

The UNHCR is willing, in principle, to work with RLOs. But funding for such organizations is virtually non-existent. This is partly because donor governments place unrealistic compliance standards on grant-making. Bilateral development agencies are especially concerned about the fiduciary risks of funding small-scale grassroots organizations of any kind, mainly because of accountability to taxpayers and electorates, but also concerns about resource diversion relating to corruption or terrorism. Meanwhile, many host governments insist that UNHCR privilege national NGOs as official 'implementing partners'. For example, in Kampala, UNHCR has had just one implementing partner for over two decades, the national NGO InterAid, despite a litany of complaints from refugees. And so RLOs usually remain out in the cold, dependent upon modest sources of funding that come from their refugee members, transnational networks, or crowdfunding.[63] Many such organizations do not yet have the capacity to deliver assistance at scale, but at least some have the potential to do so given the right support.

In a world of growing needs and declining resources, localization offers significant promise. It provides a potential way to enhance the effectiveness, efficiency, and legitimacy of aid. But it requires new mechanisms for humanitarian funding that can mitigate donor risk, build RLO capacity, and provide robust monitoring and accountability. At the global level, refugees are beginning to coordinate. The GRN created a Refugee Participation Pledge, signed by numerous states including Canada, Australia, Denmark, and the Netherlands, and the Open Society Foundations were among the first funders to mobilize resources in support of RLOs in the context of COVID-19. This indicates the potential that the crisis offers for gradually creating more inclusive and participatory forms of humanitarian governance.

With governments and international organizations increasingly struggling to deliver aid at scale, focusing on the role of refugees themselves offers an untapped opportunity for lasting transformation in humanitarian governance. The starting point for that system should surely be to ask: how can refugees participate and contribute? It is not that the 'international community' should immediately abandon refugees to 'self-reliance', 'self-protection', or 'self-governance', but that it should find ways to partner with refugees in order to build more effective, efficient, and legitimate forms of localized response.

Conclusion

It is impossible to accurately predict future forced displacement trends. There are simply too many uncertain variables. However, it is possible to build scenarios based on understanding the factors that influence the drivers of displacement and responses to displacement. And existing social science can indicate how these factors may be influenced by particular forms of shock, such as a major global depression.

The COVID-19 pandemic that struck the world in 2020 will have a lasting legacy for refugees and forced displacement. The main impact will stem not from the health consequences of the virus but the economic consequences of lockdown. Global economic depression will have its most devastating long-term impact in developing countries, many of which are either countries of origin or receiving countries for refugees.

We know from existing research that recessions and serious economic shocks have a negative impact on key drivers of displacement, such as authoritarianism, conflict, and state fragility. We also know that they reduce countries' willingness to accept migrants in general, and asylum seekers in particular. These trends will simply accentuate the age of displacement in which we already lived; more people will flee for their lives, and states' willingness to integrate them will lessen.

How this will play out is not a foregone conclusion. It is subject to political choice. Progressive leadership, alternative narratives, and new forms of transnational solidarity offer ways to mitigate some of these trends. However, the basic structural dilemma will remain the same: how to provide protection to refugees, at scale, faced with ever-greater economic and political constraints.

The grounds for optimism comes from being able to think creatively about ways to do more with less; to create sustainable sanctuaries in the countries that neighbour conflict and crisis. This is a model that will place considerable onus on supporting the capacity and agency of refugees as contributors. In cities, it will rely upon integration into existing social and economic systems. In rural areas, it will rely upon designing new forms of settlement and community that simultaneously serve refugees and host communities. The research in this book has provided evidence-based insights into what such sustainable sanctuary could look like—as well as the economic and political conditions for their emergence.

The legacy of COVID-19 makes those same challenges more urgent than ever. It also makes them even harder to overcome, because it erodes the capacity of states—both donor and host states—to protect and assist refugees. These governments need to be persuaded that supporting refugees is not only a moral imperative, but also necessary out of enlightened self-interest, as a means to mitigate long-term threats to security. In the language of this book, new bargains of inclusion will be needed in order to build viable refugee economies. But states will also need support from an expanded coalition of actors, including businesses, communities, transnational networks, mayors, trade unions, and, most importantly, refugees themselves.

15

Conclusion

My aim in writing this book has been to use research to offer practical and evidence-based solutions for refugees. I have focused mainly on three African countries to explore what their experience of hosting more refugees than the EU combined can teach the world. I have explored three related questions. *Ethically*, what is right? *Economically*, what works for achieving what is right? *Politically*, how do we get powerful actors to do what works for achieving what is right?

My motivation for writing the book is to improve outcomes for refugees. But my ideas are far from utopian. This is because my starting point is that in order to have impact, research needs to be politically engaged. It has to begin with a realistic set of assumptions about the boundaries of what is possible but balance those with a sense of hope about how those constraints might be gradually overcome.

The premise of the book is that we live in an age of displacement: numbers are rising but the political willingness to protect refugees is declining. Trends such as climate change, the economic legacy of COVID-19, and fragile states underlie the former; factors such as populist nationalism, rising structural unemployment, and waning support for multilateralism underpin the latter. These contradictory trends create an urgent need to find sustainable solutions for refugees in a rapidly changing world. Refugees need to be able to receive access to their human rights and to live dignified and purposeful lives. But we need to find a way to do this which can function at scale, and which governments and their citizens will be willing to provide.

Revisiting the argument

I began with ethics, grounding the analysis in a political realist tradition of framing normative goals based on balancing criticality with feasibility.

In an age of displacement, I argued that three normative criteria underlie sustainability: rights, politics, and scale. Put simply, sustainability requires finding refugee policies that can ensure refugee rights, retain local, national, and international political support, and be viable at scale and over time. Attaining all of these imperatives simultaneously is a practical and empirical challenge.

States have obligations towards refugees, and all states should engage in responsibility-sharing to support refugees, but three archetypal mechanisms stand out for allocating primary responsibility for any particular group of refugees which I describe as: free choice, equitable quotas, and neighbouring countries. I suggested that each one has a role to play and that all these mechanisms can and should exist in parallel. However, in order to simultaneously meet our normative criteria, development-based approaches in neighbouring countries offer the most viable route for the overwhelming majority of the world's refugees, who flee fragile and conflict-affected countries in developing regions of the world.

But traditional models for protecting the 85 per cent of refugees in low- and middle-income countries have rarely enabled them to live dignified and purposeful lives. Camps have denied people socio-economic freedoms; cities have often denied people assistance while leaving them excluded from full socio-economic participation. Building sustainable protection requires a rethink of traditional approaches to refugee assistance in both camps and cities. The only way to achieve that is to move beyond a purely humanitarian approach, and to also adopt a development-based approach to support the capabilities of refugees; to build on their skills, talents, and aspirations. The imperative is, put simply, to help refugees to help themselves, and to support their host communities.

However, this approach—usually framed by humanitarian policy-makers as 'self-reliance'—has proved historically elusive and has too often been applied disingenuously by governments. The elusiveness of self-reliance has partly been because policy-makers have lacked an adequate understanding of the economic and political conditions that make refugee self-reliance possible. And, so, achieving sustainable refugee policies becomes an empirical challenge: to build an evidence base relating to the economic and political conditions that make them possible, and to render visible the reasons why there is so often a disjuncture between the rhetoric and reality of refugee self-reliance. Hence, I turned to three countries in East Africa to see what insights they could offer.

In terms of economics, I drew upon our original Refugee Economies Dataset, covering over 16,000 refugees and host-community members in camps and cities to explore three themes closely related to sustainability: welfare outcomes, social cohesion, and mobility. In each of these areas, we found compelling evidence that creating socio-economic rights and opportunities for refugees are crucial for achieving sustainability. Giving refugees the right and opportunity to work, for example, seems likely to make refugees better off, improve relations with the host community, and reduce the aspiration to engage in onward migration outside of Africa.

Among the most interesting findings were, first, that refugees are systematically worse off than host-community members everywhere except Kakuma, but that there is considerable variation in welfare outcomes among refugees; second, that refugee incomes and other related welfare outcomes are shaped by socio-economic entitlements and opportunities such as employment, education, and living in a country that provides the right to work; third, that host communities' perceptions of refugees are strongly influenced by their perceived economic contribution; fourth, that onward migration to rich countries appears very small but aspiring to migrate internationally may be negatively correlated with development indicators such as asset levels, while actually migrating abroad may be negatively correlated with having remunerated employment.

These findings contribute to a range of academic debates such as explaining welfare outcomes for refugees, exploring the determinants of host community attitudes towards refugees, and reassessing the applicability of the so-called 'migration hump' relationship to refugee populations. However, more importantly, they provide clear evidence to policy-makers that investing in socio-economic rights and opportunities for refugees offers a pathway for simultaneously meeting all of the requirements for sustainability. Put simply, development-based approaches can work—for refugees, host communities, and the wider world.

In order to explore more specifically what kinds of interventions are likely to be most effective, I examined three 'innovative' examples of attempts to support the socio-economic inclusion of refugees: the Ugandan self-reliance model, the designed Kalobeyei settlement in Kenya, and the private-sector-funded Dollo Ado camps in Ethiopia. What could these three models, each of which aspire to go beyond traditional approaches to refugee camps, teach us about the design of functioning refugee economies?

From Uganda's self-reliance model, we learn that the right to work and freedom of movement for refugees is associated with greater mobility, lower transaction costs for economic activity, higher incomes, and more sustainable sources of employment when compared with Kenya. For example, the Ugandan model is associated with 16 per cent higher income levels when controlling for other variables.

From Kalobeyei, we learn how challenging it is to design new refugee settlements with the intention of supporting self-reliance. Based on a 'natural experiment' of comparing outcomes for recently arrived South Sudanese refugees in the 'old' Kakuma camps versus the 'new' Kalobeyei settlement, we found that indicators for self-reliance across both contexts were similarly poor. For example, less than 2 per cent of South Sudanese refugees in Kalobeyei perceived themselves to be independent of aid, and just 6 per cent had an income-generating activity two years after the opening of the settlement. The new model is a step in the right direction but has not yet delivered on its promise.

From Dollo Ado, we learn that the private sector can play an important role in building refugee economies. Over a seven-year period the IKEA Foundation invested around $100 million in the camps with a focus on economic development and livelihood opportunities, notably through a new 'cooperatives model' creating employment and entrepreneurship opportunities for refugees and the host community. Using a range of impact evaluation methods, we found that many of these cooperatives, including agricultural and livestock cooperatives, and a microfinance scheme, have improved welfare outcomes and enhanced social cohesion between refugees and the host community. However, we also learn that there are limitations to this form of philanthropic investment. Only 21 per cent of adult refugees and 29 per cent of hosts had an income-generating activity, linkages between the cooperatives and markets remained weak, and most people remained dependent upon the aid-circulation and informal cross-border economies.

Between them, the three cases tell us that implementing an effective self-reliance model for refugees—based on the right and opportunity to work—can lead to better outcomes for refugees, when compared to the absence of these opportunities. However, they also reveal quite how difficult it is to create refugee self-reliance in practice, especially in the remote border regions where most refugee camps and settlements are located.

Both Kalobeyei and Dollo Ado point to the need to move beyond a purely microeconomic focus to engage with wider macroeconomic questions. Until the entire economy of a border region expands—through investment in public goods, infrastructure, and human resources, for example—refugees and the proximate host communities alike will remain dependent upon the market-based circulation of a finite amount of humanitarian aid. The step-change required to achieve self-reliance is to create sufficient productive capacity such that remote refugee-hosting regions can actually export goods and services regionally, nationally, and internationally.

If a pre-condition for self-reliance is the right and opportunity to work, then it depends upon host countries adopting and implementing legislation that gives refugees basic socio-economic entitlements. But behind that lies politics. In terms of politics, I therefore explored what the three countries can tell us about the conditions under which host countries are willing to grant refugees the right to work and other related socio-economic rights. Uganda has allowed refugees the right to work since independence; Kenya has restricted refugees' socio-economic rights since the early 1990s but implemented those restrictions differently in different parts of the country; Ethiopia adopted legislation in 2019 allowing refugees the right to work but has yet to fully implement that legislation. In each case the reasons for providing or denying the right to work are complex, historically contingent, and context specific. Nevertheless, there is a broad—if admittedly reductionist—pattern that underlies the variation.

Generally speaking, host governments have given refugees the right to work when they have received a payoff for doing so, usually in terms of international development assistance that benefits citizens or strengthens politicians' power, legitimacy, and access to patronage. When the central government benefits directly from international payoff, they adopt the de jure right to work. When local governments benefit from an international payoff they adopt the de facto right to work. Uganda provides the de jure and de facto right to work; Kenya provides the de facto right to work in Turkana County but no de jure right to work; Ethiopia provides the de jure right to work but no de facto right to work. Meanwhile, Tanzania, for example, denies refugees both the de jure and the de facto right to work.

Uganda has been widely praised for its progressive refugee policies. However, a striking feature of Uganda's 'progressive' self-reliance model is that it has emerged from paradoxically illiberal sources and for illiberal motives. Indeed, archival research reveals that Idi Amin was in fact one of the main historical architects of Uganda's self-reliance model. Successive

Ugandan Governments have used refugee policy as a source of legitimacy and resource extraction. Donor funding has also been important as a means to ensure internal authority through the redistribution of resources to peripheral, refugee-hosting regions of the country. This redistribution has been especially important because of the south-west and West Nile regions' strategic importance to successive central governments. Idi Amin and Yoweri Museveni, for example, both lacked support in central Buganda, and so relied heavily upon support from the mainly Rwandan-hosting south-west and the South Sudanese-hosting West Nile region.

In Ethiopia, donor money was the trigger for persuading the government to adopt new legislation giving refugees the right to work and other socio-economic rights. The legislation was, quite simply, part of a deal known as the Jobs Compact, in which the government was offered around $600 million towards its national industrialization strategy in exchange for creating 30,000 jobs for refugees within its industrial parks and changing its legislation to enable this. However, there is no immediate prospect of its large-scale implementation in Ethiopia, especially amid push-back at the local level.

In Kenya, the central government has adopted a strict encampment policy for refugees since the early 1990s. However, since 2014, one particular refugee-hosting region, Turkana County, has adopted a different approach after Kenya's counties were devolved greater authority over the socio-economic aspects of refugee integration. Turkana County's governor recognized the opportunity to use those powers to bring international resources to the county. He was willing to adopt a fifteen-year strategy called the Kalobeyei Integrated Socio-Economic Development Plan (KISEDP), which initially proposed the Kalobeyei settlement model and then expanded to create an integrated development model for the entire sub-country in which Kakuma and Kalobeyei are based. Donors—notably including the EU—supported the new model, and KISEDP's first five-year period seeks a proposed budget of $500 million, a large proportion of which is intended to support the county government.

And in the background, there has also been murky and sometimes disingenuous donor politics. Donor funding has been available to provide these payoffs not primarily because of an altruistic concern with refugee protection per se, but because of the goals of reducing long-term humanitarian aid budgets and onward migratory movements to Europe and the rich world.

The implications are twofold. First, the politics of refugee rights are messy and ambivalent; they involve a series of linked interests only tangentially related to refugee assistance. Second, though, if countries are to adopt the right to work for refugees, policy-makers need to understand and engage with those politics. In order to achieve the right to work for refugees, a bargain has to be struck that is mutually beneficial for donor governments, the central government of the host country, and local political authorities in refugee-hosting areas. Interestingly, what matters is not just a payoff for the host government but also a payoff for the local government. In low- and middle-income countries, local politics matters as much for refugees' right to work as national and international politics. Particularly in decentralized states—like Kenya, Ethiopia, and Uganda—international actors need to establish sub-national political relationships.

Finally, in terms of policy, I outlined what all of this means in terms of creating a road map for sustainable refugee economies, and the very different challenges for creating socio-economic opportunity for refugees in cities compared to remote border regions. In urban contexts, the challenge is about inclusion in existing socio-economic structures. In remote border regions, it is about building economies.

Implications for academic research

Refugee and Forced Migration Studies has gradually expanded as an inter-disciplinary area of study over the last half-century. It has evolved from its early advocacy roots to be a space of serious social scientific enquiry. In terms of disciplines, it has grown from a predominant focus on anthropology and law to gradually include political science and economics. In terms of methods, it has expanded from single case studies towards comparative methods, and from almost exclusively qualitative research towards greater use of quantitative methods including surveys and experimental methods. In terms of theory, forced migration theory has gone from deliberation about how to delineate the line between 'forced' and 'voluntary' migration towards examining how the study of forced displacement can contribute to debates across the social sciences, relating to concepts such as identity, networks, norms, space, power, and institutions.

The book's academic approach can be characterized as having three particular features.

First, *interdisciplinarity*. Given the starting point of attempting to engage with a series of real-world issues, rigid disciplinary boundaries made no sense as a basis for researching a complex set of global challenges. And, so, while the thematic focus has been on refugees' socio-economic lives and contributions, the research has engaged with ideas from across the full spectrum of social science.

Second, *methodological pluralism*. The research has drawn upon a wide range of first-hand data collection methods. It draws upon an original multi-country panel dataset on the economic lives of refugees, covering camps and cities, and refugees and host communities. However, this is also complemented by a range of other methods including qualitative methods from semi-structured interviews to focus group discussions, archival research, and impact evaluation methods including quasi-experimental methods. The research with refugee communities also used participatory methods including recruiting and training refugees and host community members as research assistants.

Third, *political engagement*. It has tried to be relevant to practice by balancing criticality with feasibility. In particular, it began with a series of normative foundations, first making explicit a series of assumptions about what is desirable and what is realistic, and then trying to use economics to identify what works to achieve those goals, and political science to identify what needs to happen to persuade powerful actors to do what works to achieve those goals.

This approach has been possible because I have been able to undertake research at a scale that is rare within Refugee and Forced Migration Studies. It has relied upon significant funding and being able to assemble a diverse and talented interdisciplinary research team. Nevertheless, these three characteristics have been important for being able to get insights that transcend particular contexts, triangulate across methods and sources, and have strategic implications for the future of the global refugee system.

Although my primary goal has been to contribute to policy and practice, the book's findings have a series of implications for academic debates. It offers the basis for a research agenda on the 'political economy' of refugee assistance—one that moves beyond purely descriptive, normative, or interpretive accounts that are common to academic work on refugees, and towards explanatory social science. The book's specific theoretical contribution can be thought of as explaining social behaviour relating to refugees at three main levels: sociological, political, and economic.

Sociologically, the research engages with several important debates within the Migration Studies literature, which have on the whole rarely been applied to refugees or explored in an African context. For example, by exploring the determinants of refugees' residency, mobility, and migration choices, the research critically engages with the well-established 'migration hump' relationship, which suggests that as income levels increase up to a certain threshold, the demand to emigrate increases.[1] This relationship has often been presumed to also apply to refugees in first countries of asylum. However, our preliminary findings from Nairobi and the Kakuma refugee camps suggest that the migration hump relationship may not apply in the same way to refugees' aspirations or choices relating to onward migration. Instead, development indicators such as 'having a job' and 'asset levels' appear to be negatively correlated with the aspiration to migrate beyond the region of origin.

Furthermore, our research is among the first to apply the wider literature on host-community attitudes towards immigrants to refugees.[2] In particular, it examines how inter-group interaction affects host community attitudes towards refugees, but takes the analysis beyond an exclusively European context.[3] Our findings suggest that host-community attitudes are especially shaped by perceptions of economic contribution, reinforcing Kirk Bansak and colleagues' findings for Europe.[4] Furthermore, economic interactions may influence these perceptions. However, within a given host community, there may be different perspectives: hosts with interactions relating to consumption and employment may have more positive perceptions; hosts whose interactions relate to competition over scarce resources such as land may have more negative perceptions. Across all three countries, host-community perceptions of refugees' contributions were more positive in refugee camp contexts than cities.

Politically, the book contributes to existing theory on the international politics of refugee assistance. In particular, it contributes to work that examines interaction and bargaining between Northern 'donor' states and Southern 'host' states. Gerasimos Tsourapas, in particular, has characterized many major refugee-hosting countries as 'rentier states', seeking to extract resources from international donors.[5] Meanwhile, others have recognized that donor–host relations are frequently characterized by 'issue-linkage', within which payoffs are made within other policy fields—improved migration management for the North and development assistance for the South.[6]

Without contradicting this work, I extend it by including an account of sub-national politics. In low- and middle-income countries, local politics matters as much for refugee rights to work as national and international politics.[7] I therefore show the need to conceptualize the international politics of refugee assistance as a multi-level bargaining process that involves global, national, and local actors. This, I suggest, is especially important in countries like Ethiopia, Kenya, and Uganda, which have high levels of decentralization, and in which local political actors have the authority to make important decisions that affect refugees' lives. The in-depth historical case studies reveal how the politics of refugee rights has been inextricably connected to patronage networks at both local and national levels. This in turn engages with wider research on the international relations of Sub-Saharan Africa,[8] revealing how East African states engage with donor governments and international organizations within the refugee context.[9]

Economically, the book also contributes to the rapidly growing literature on refugees within economics, and more specifically within development economics. It identifies what is conceptually distinctive about the economic lives of refugees, compared with, for example citizens or other migrants. Drawing upon ideas from New Institutional Economics and Identity Economics,[10] it suggests that institutions and identity may conceptually distinguish refugees from other groups, and provides an empirical basis for these claims. This premise of difference, and our mixed-methods approach, opens up the opportunity to observe and try to understand what is particular about 'the economic lives of refugees' in the way that, for example, Abhijit Banerjee and Esther Duflo examine 'the economic lives of the poor' as behaviourally distinctive.[11]

Furthermore, one of the unique features of our work is the breadth and depth of our first-hand research. In particular, our panel dataset, based on over 16,000 survey respondents, provides the opportunity to examine a broader range of questions than the existing literature on the economics of refugees, which has a predominant focus on the impact of refugees on host countries.[12] For example, through the Refugee Economies Dataset we are able to systematically explore the determinants of variation in welfare outcomes, such as income, expenditure, assets, consumption, subjective wellbeing, physical and mental health, and food security for refugees and the host communities. The next step is to be able to take the insights that emerge from our descriptive statistics and regression analysis, and to undertake randomized controlled trials that test the propositions and hypotheses generated by our survey data.

Implications for policy and practice

Against the backdrop of an age of displacement, the world needs a clear-sighted strategic vision for how to ensure that all refugees receive access to their human rights and can live dignified and purposeful lives. To achieve that, though, refugee policies need to be sustainable. They need to be viable for large and growing numbers of people. All countries around the world can and should admit refugees onto their territory. But the majority of refugees should be supported in the countries that immediately neighbour the country of origin. The key to making refugee assistance sustainable is to unlock the potential contribution of refugees themselves.

Refugees have capabilities as well as vulnerabilities. Collectively, they have the potential to be economic contributors to their host societies. This, however, is not inevitable. It relies upon host countries and the wider international community adopting policies and practices that give refugees socio-economic entitlements and opportunities. These include the right to work, job creation, and support for entrepreneurship in refugee-hosting regions. Creating socio-economic opportunities for displaced populations is associated with better outcomes for refugees, host communities, and the wider world.

Rethinking self-reliance

This is not a new idea, but the way in which it has historically been pursued has been partly wrong-headed. The concept of refugee 'self-reliance' has been used to highlight the potential for refugees—as individuals, households, and communities—to live independently of humanitarian aid. And while the idea of supporting refugees' autonomy, access to opportunity, and even self-governance are desirable goals, self-reliance has too often been pursued in disingenuous ways. The concept has served as a means for donor countries to contain refugees in the South, for host states to elicit resources that support patronage, and for international organizations to ensure ongoing relevance. Perhaps even more importantly, our research reveals that self-reliance is very difficult to achieve in practice. And while self-reliance does not have to be a binary—some autonomy is better than none—the stated goal of 'independence from aid' has been elusive. In practice, few refugees even in the contexts most celebrated as examples of 'self-reliance' achieve independence from aid.

However, these limitations are not a reason to reject the concept; they are a reason to understand what is not working and then implement it better. One of the biggest problems is that self-reliance has been seen as a programmatic goal that can be achieved by humanitarian aid organizations drawing upon the toolbox of international development assistance. But it requires much more than that. Self-reliance has to be situated within what might be crudely described as 'big economics' and 'big politics'. On the one hand, it relies upon building entire economies such that remote border regions can begin to export goods and services rather than simply circulate aid money. In other words, it is as much about macroeconomic issues as microeconomics. On the other, it also relies upon understanding the wider power relations and interests that shape government regulation towards refugees. Self-reliance is not viable unless refugees enjoy the right to work and other related socio-economic rights. But host governments' refugee policy choices connect to politics in areas that include other priorities, such as security and national development.

Creating the conditions to enable displaced populations to flourish and contribute to national economies is therefore a task that has to go far beyond the mandate of humanitarian organizations. It requires engaging senior politicians, business leaders, and investors, not only on the basis of altruism but by enabling them to see how their interests are served by supporting the entitlements and capabilities of refugees and other displaced populations. This in turn requires a recalibration in the role that humanitarian organizations play in supporting refugees. Their role should not just be to deliver programmes but to engage in the type of high-level political and economic analysis, and engagement, that help to achieve 'bargains of inclusion' and build 'refugee economies'. Put simply, there can be no refugee self-reliance without a seismic advance in the refugee system's ability to engage with economics and politics.

Understanding urban and rural contexts

Economically empowering refugees requires different policies in cities compared to camps. In urban areas, complex economic systems already exist. The challenge is one of economic inclusion; how can refugees be supported to access entitlements and opportunities on the same basis as citizens? Denied assistance, affected by discrimination, and faced with restrictions on the right to work, register businesses, and own property, refugees in cities are systematically worse off than nearby citizens. They also face more negative host-community perceptions than refugees in camps because of a more pervasive sense that they create competition for resources. In some cities, refugees of particular nationalities enjoy the support of host communities of the same ethnicity; this is the case in the 'Somali' neighbourhoods of Eastleigh in Nairobi, Kisenyi in Kampala, and Bole Michael in Addis Ababa, for example. But nationality groups without these sources of ethnic solidarity, such as Congolese refugees in Nairobi and Kampala, are more likely to struggle. The policy challenge is to break down sources of socio-economic exclusion, enhance access to public services, and ensure area-based assistance models that target the entire—refugee, host, and migrant—population of refugee-hosting neighbourhoods.

Urbanization, though, is not a panacea for refugee protection. In Africa, only a small minority of registered refugees live in urban areas. Chapter 3 showed that, although refugees in cities earn more, own more, and work more, they are not necessarily happier, healthier, or better fed than those who live in rural areas. And many host governments, including those in Ethiopia, Kenya, and Uganda, are unwilling to accept all refugees moving to cities. Furthermore, our research reveals some surprising advantages to rural settlement. Host communities in rural areas across our focus countries tend to have more positive perceptions of refugees than those in cities. This appears to be because those in remote rural communities recognize that the presence of refugees and aid organizations brings much-needed economic opportunities that would not otherwise be available. And, far from all refugees preferring to live in cities, our research also shows that, in Kenya, for example, between survey waves, a small number of refugees chose to move back from the city to the camps, while others chose to divide families between camps and cities as part of so-called 'split family strategies'. Put simply, the future of sustainable refugee assistance need not be exclusively urban.

However, we need to reimagine what rural refugee settlement looks like. In such contexts, the challenge is to build entire economies in remote border locations, sometimes from scratch. The camps and settlements discussed in this book—Nakivale, Kakuma, and Dollo Ado—all benefit from a myriad of humanitarian programmes designed to support self-reliance. But, to different degrees, they are all in geographically remote and economically marginalized regions. Even where refugees have been supported with 'livelihoods' or 'market-based' programmes, the underlying challenge has been that these are aid economies. There is very little money in circulation that does not come through international humanitarian assistance. Kakuma and Dollo Ado in particular lack wider market linkages. Until the economies of Turkana County and the Somali region of Ethiopia can build productive capacity and become capable of exporting goods and services beyond the region, there will be a ceiling on socio-economic opportunity for refugees and the host community. This is why a road map is needed, along the lines of that provided in Chapter 12, for how to build remote economies in refugee-hosting regions.

Most refugee camps are highly problematic because they deny refugees socio-economic rights—especially the right to work and freedom of movement. However, there is no reason why settlements for refugees and the host community could not be redesigned in more humane and sustainable ways. The old rural settlements in Uganda and new camp designs in Kalobeyei and Dollo Ado have been far from perfect. But they offer a starting point for learning. All reveal the potential for agricultural programmes, if appropriately designed, to be a basis for sustainable livelihoods. Kalobeyei tells us about some of the conditions under which various forms of cash-based intervention can be effective. Dollo Ado offers insights into a novel cooperative model for refugee and host-community vocational training and job creation. But to be truly effective, rural settlements will have to go beyond circulating aid money and build productive capacity.

The exact balance between urban and rural settlement options for refugees will vary across different regions. In contexts such as the Middle East or Latin America, with higher levels of urbanization, the balance is likely to be towards socio-economic inclusion in cities. In Africa and parts of Asia, the weighting is likely to remain towards rural settlement. Regardless of the balance in different regions, the existing model for refugee camps needs to change. Sustainable sanctuary can be effectively designed within the remote border regions of host countries in ways that bring significant benefits to the host community.

Ensuring participatory governance

Across our cases, when things have gone wrong, it has frequently been because policy-makers did not spend enough time actually talking to refugees. Examples abound of how institutional interventions have sometimes been misaligned with refugees' own behaviour and lived experiences.[13] Five illustrations of such 'blind spots' stand out. First, *cross-border livelihoods*: in Dollo Ado, humanitarian programmes were designed from a state-centric perspective, rendering invisible the centrality of Somali refugees' cross-border livelihood strategies.[14] Second, *social networks*: when Kalobeyei was designed, it was originally intended that its new residents would relocate from Kakuma, but organizations were surprised when few were willing to move because of the value they placed on their existing social networks in Kakuma.[15] Third, *credit and debt*: when organizations rolled out unrestricted cash assistance in Kalobeyei they expected it to lead to greater consumer choice, but organizations learned that refugees often ended up tethered to one retailer due to pre-existing debts.[16] Fourth, *economic culture*: in the Ugandan settlements, the distribution of plots of land is viewed as central to the self-reliance model, and yet some nationality groups, notably Somalis, decline to undertake any agricultural activity in the settlements.[17] Fifth, *refugee-led protection*: across all of our contexts, refugees claimed that a crucial source of social protection comes from within the community, and yet formal humanitarian governance systematically marginalizes refugee-led protection.

These types of distortion might be avoided with a better quality of dialogue between international organizations and refugees, and by greater refugee participation within the governance of refugee settlements. Self-reliance is often conceived in narrowly economic ways, but also needs to include a focus on social and political autonomy. One of the moral justifications for the external governance of refugee camps is that, during the emergency phase, it is necessary to meet life-saving needs. But, over time, the validity of that assumption erodes. Refugee camps and settlements become de facto communities, and greater levels of self-governance become appropriate.

Some of the anecdotally most integrated refugee camps around the world have forms of self-governance in place; examples include the Sahrawi refugee camps in Algeria,[18] the Palestinian camps in the Middle East,[19] and the Burmese camps in Thailand.[20] Of course, these examples are partly self-governed because they have been partly run by political organizations 'in exile' (the Polisario Front, the Palestinian Authority, and the Karen National Liberation Army, respectively), and the viability of this depends on the diversity of a settlement's population and the group's relationship with the host government. However, self-governance can also operate on a spectrum from meaningful consultation, to representation within decision-making bodies, to the delivery of public services. Even within the East African context, where refugees' political participation is usually limited by law, refugee-led organizations already play a key role in providing a source of social protection across refugee communities, despite a lack of external funding and recognition.[21] Many offer services valued by the community and have the potential to take on a greater role, particularly within a reimagined refugee settlement model.

Navigating the future

Climate change and the economic legacy of COVID-19 are among the most pressing global challenges faced by the world today: both have profound implications for forced displacement. In particular, they will lead to a significant increase in the scale of displacement around the world, in part because they will each exacerbate existing sources of poverty and weak governance. It seems probable that over the next decades, the current figure of around 75 million forcibly displaced people around the world will multiply significantly, and many of these people may seek to cross international borders. In the short term, amid global recession, the willingness of publics and politicians to share scarce resources with distant strangers will be tested to breaking point. Meanwhile, rich and poor countries alike will question their capacity to admit refugees onto their territories. With rising structural unemployment exacerbated by recession, automation, and offshoring there may well be a significant global backlash against migration and mobility in general.

For everyone who cares about refugee protection, denial is not an option. The challenges of a rapidly changing world need to be understood. We may face a world of growing conflict, authoritarianism, and state fragility. Global recession and rising xenophobia will threaten tolerance towards refugees and migrants, and multilateral cooperation will struggle to reinvent itself. The refugee system will have to adapt to these wider transformations in the international political economy.

But adapting to the new reality does not preclude trying to change it for the better. The balance that needs to be struck is to be realistic while also being hopeful enough to identify opportunities to transcend those constraints. Public narratives can be changed, and a key part of that will involve encouraging publics to recognize both the moral obligations we all have to protect refugees *and* the economic, social, and cultural contributions they bring to our societies.

In the next decades, delivering effective refugee protection will be one of humanity's most important tasks. It will require both principle and pragmatism.

Endnotes

CHAPTER I

1. This is the highest number of displaced people since records began. For the latest statistics, see UNHCR (2020), *Global Trends in 2019* (Geneva: UNHCR).
2. For analysis of the relationship between asylum and liberal democratic values see, for example, Gibney, M. (2004), *The Ethics and Politics of Asylum: Liberal Democracy and the Response to Refugees* (Cambridge: Cambridge University Press).
3. According to UNHCR, in 2018, the three countries hosted 2,490,129 refugees, compared with 2,329,351 for all the European Union countries and 427,350 for the United States and Canada combined. See UNHCR (2019), *Global Trends in 2018* (Geneva: UNHCR). By April 2020, the combined total hosted by Ethiopia, Kenya, and Uganda had risen to 2,680,250 refugees between them. See UNHCR (2020), Global focus, available at: http://reporting.unhcr.org/ehagi
4. UNHCR (2019), *Global Trends in 2018* (Geneva: UNHCR).
5. The overall trend in the 'secondary movement' of refugees from first countries of asylum to rich countries is challenging to quantify. However, one indicator is the number of spontaneous arrival asylum seekers arriving in rich countries from other regions of the world. This number fluctuates based on a range of factors. But the overall trend in Europe and the United States, for example, appears to be increasing.
6. Chaulia, S. S. (2003), The politics of refugee hosting in Tanzania: from open door to unsustainability, insecurity and receding receptivity. *Journal of Refugee Studies*, *16*(2), 147–66; Milner, J. (2014), Can global refugee policy leverage durable solutions? Lessons from Tanzania's naturalization of Burundian refugees. *Journal of Refugee Studies*, *27*(4), 553–73.
7. Reuveny, R. (2007), Climate change-induced migration and violent conflict. *Political Geography*, *26*(6), 656–73; Biermann, F., & Boas, I. (2010), Preparing for a warmer world: towards a global governance system to protect climate refugees. *Global Environmental Politics*, *10*(1), 60–88.
8. Debates on the relationship between climate change and displacement are complex and contested. For critical analysis, see, for example: Bettini, G. (2013), Climate barbarians at the gate? A critique of apocalyptic narratives on 'climate refugees'. *Geoforum*, *45*, 63–72; Nicholson, C. T. (2014), Climate change and the politics of causal reasoning: the case of climate change and migration. *The Geographical Journal*, *180*(2), 151–60; Morrissey, J. (2012), Rethinking the 'debate

on environmental refugees': from 'maximalists and minimalists' to 'proponents and critics'. *Journal of Political Ecology*, *19*(1), 36–49.

9. For my take on this relationship, see Betts, A. (2013), *Survival Migration: Failed Governance and the Crisis of Displacement* (Ithaca, NY: Cornell University Press).

10. Restrepo, D., Sutton, T., & Martinez, J. (2019), *Getting Migration in the Americas Right: A National Interest-Driven Approach* (Washington, DC: Center for American Progress).

10. World Bank (2017), *Sahel Refugees: The Human Face of a Regional Crisis* (Washington, DC: World Bank).

11. Dennison, J., & Geddes, A. (2019), A rising tide? The salience of immigration and the rise of anti-immigration political parties in Western Europe. *The Political Quarterly*, *90*(1), 107–16.

12. Grande, E., Schwarzbözl, T., & Fatke, M. (2019), Politicizing immigration in Western Europe. *Journal of European Public Policy*, *26*(10), 1444–63.

13. Goodwin, M., & Milazzo, C. (2017), Taking back control? Investigating the role of immigration in the 2016 vote for Brexit. *The British Journal of Politics and International Relations*, *19*(3), 450–64.

14. Hansen, M. A., & Olsen, J. (2019), Flesh of the same flesh: a study of voters for the alternative for Germany (AfD) in the 2017 federal election. *German Politics*, *28*(1), 1–19.

15. Givens, T. E. (2020), Immigration, race and the radical right: politics and policy from colonialism to Brexit. *JCMS: Journal of Common Market Studies*, *58*(3), 514–26.

16. The relationship between factors such as deindustrialization and the geographical distribution of attitudes to immigration are under-researched but I explore them in a TEDx Oxford talk from 2019 entitled, 'It's not about migration, it's about economic transformation'.

17. Public attitudes to immigration are complex and diverse. But electorates in rich countries generally support restrictions such as the deportation of illegal immigrants, and offer conditional support for immigration. See, for example, Pew Global Research's Global Attitudes Survey, available at: https://www.pewresearch.org/global/2019/03/14/around-the-world-more-say-immigrants-are-a-strength-than-a-burden

18. See, for example, Hargrave, K., Pantuliano, S., & Idris, A. (2016), *Closing Borders: The Ripple Effects of Australian and European Refugee Policy. Case Studies from Indonesia, Kenya, and Jordan* (London: ODI).

19. Oliver Bakewell makes the case for 'policy irrelevant' forced migration research. Bakewell, O. (2008), Research beyond the categories: the importance of policy irrelevant research into forced migration. *Journal of Refugee Studies*, *21*(4), 432–53. Elena Fiddian-Qasmiyeh similarly reflects upon the importance of critical research in Refugee and Forced Migration Studies. Fiddian-Qasmiyeh, E. (2020), Introduction: refuge in a moving world. Refugee and migrant journeys across disciplines, in Fiddian-Qasmiyeh, E. (ed), *Refuge in a Moving World: Tracing Refugee and Migrant Journeys across Disciplines* (London: UCL Press).

20. Robert Cox distinguishes between 'problem-solving theory', which aims to make existing institutions more effective in addressing practical challenges, and 'critical theory', which critiques the underlying structures of power that underpin prevailing institutions. In my view, both have a valuable and complementary role to play in Refugee and Forced Migration Studies. See: Cox, R. W. (1996), *Approaches to World Order* (Cambridge: Cambridge: University Press), 89–90.

21. John Rawls makes the case for non-ideal moral theory, in order to take into account empirical features of the human condition such as scarcity and limited altruism. Rawls, J. (1999), *The Law of Peoples: With 'The Idea of Public Reason Revisited'* (Cambridge, MA: Harvard University Press), 22. The approach contrasts with Cohen's timeless and 'fact-free' view of justice as the basis for 'ideal-theory'. Cohen, G. A. (2009), *Rescuing Justice and Equality* (Cambridge, MA: Harvard University Press). Much of the subsequent debate is about how much factual input should be part of normative political theory.

22. See, for example, Steve Krasner's analysis of the relationship between norms and interests in international relations. Krasner, S. D. (1999), *Sovereignty: Organized Hypocrisy* (Princeton, NJ: Princeton University Press).

23. UNHCR (2006), *The Handbook for Self-Reliance* (Geneva: UNHCR).

24. One might think of four schools of thought for politically engaged scholarship: realists, idealists, activists, and innovators. The *realists* hold power, interests, and ideas broadly constant; they try to identify the opportunities for interest convergence to achieve ethically desirable goals. The *idealists* assume that power, interests, and ideas can be changed; they engage in critiquing power while building an alternative and better normative vision. The *activists* seek to identify mechanisms for how power, interests, and ideas can be changed in order to reshape the boundaries of the possible. The *innovators* seek to identify the practical solutions that can reconfigure power, interests, and ideas; they seek to reimagine the 'good society'. None of these positions is mutually exclusive, all can and should be compatible, and they probably coexist to different degrees in everyone engaged in thinking critically about forced migration.

25. Refugee camps have a long history, but became more widely used from the 1980s as opportunities for integrated, rural self-settlement in Africa, for example, were reduced, and UNHCR shifted its focus towards a 'care and maintenance' approach. The use of refugee camps by humanitarian agencies also varies from region to region. Nevertheless, as a broad characterization, refugee camps remain the dominant contemporary mode of aid delivery for refugees, reflected in the concentration of humanitarian funding. For a nuanced account of the historical evolution of refugee assistance, see Gatrell, P. (2015), *The Making of the Modern Refugee* (Oxford: Oxford University Press).

26. The US Committee for Refugees and Immigrants (2005), *Warehousing Refugees: A Denial of Rights, a Denial of Humanity* (Washington, DC: USCRI).

27. Loescher, G., Milner, J., Newman, E., & Troeller, G. (2008), *Protracted Refugee Situations: Political, Human Rights and Security Implications* (Tokyo: United Nations University Press).

28. Easton-Calabria, E. E. (2015), From bottom-up to top-down: the 'pre-history' of refugee livelihoods assistance from 1919 to 1979. *Journal of Refugee Studies*, *28*(3), 412–36; Skran, C. M. (2011), *Refugees in Inter-war Europe* (Oxford: Oxford University Press).

29. Gorman, R. F. (ed.) (1993), *Refugee Aid and Development: Theory and Practice* (New York: Greenwood Press).

30. For in-depth analysis of these policy processes, see Betts, A. (2009), *Protection by Persuasion: International Cooperation in the Refugee Regime* (Ithaca, NY: Cornell University Press).

31. Betts, A., Bloom, L., Kaplan, J. D., & Omata, N. (2017), *Refugee Economies: Forced Displacement and Development* (Oxford: Oxford University Press), 13–39.

32. Hovil, L. (2018), Uganda's refugee policies: the history, the politics, the way forward (International Refugee Rights Initiative), available at: https://reliefweb.int/sites/reliefweb.int/files/resources/IRRI-Uganda-policy-paper-October-2018-Paper.pdf; Kaiser, T. (2005), Participating in development? Refugee protection, politics and developmental approaches to refugee management in Uganda. *Third World Quarterly*, *26*(2), 351–67.

33. For critical perspectives on self-reliance, see, for example, Easton-Calabria, E., & Omata, N. (2018), Panacea for the refugee crisis? Rethinking the promotion of 'self-reliance' for refugees. *Third World Quarterly*, *39*(8), 1458–74; Krause, U., & Schmidt, H. (2020), Refugees as actors? Critical reflections on global refugee policies on self-reliance and resilience. *Journal of Refugee Studies*, *33*(1), 22–41; Fiddian-Qasmiyeh, E. (2015), *South-South Educational Migration, Humanitarianism, and Development: Views from the Caribbean, North Africa and the Middle East* (Abingdon: Routledge).

34. For an example of early quantitative research within Refugee Studies, see, for example: Salehyan, I., & Gleditsch, K. S. (2006), Refugees and the spread of civil war. *International Organization*, *60*(2), 335–66.

35. According to UNHCR, in 2020, 16 per cent of Kenya's 494,645 registered refugee population live in urban areas, while 5.7 per cent of refugees in Uganda live in Kampala, and 3.6 per cent of refugees in Ethiopia live in Addis Ababa. UNHCR (2020), Global focus, available at: http://reporting.unhcr.org/ehagi

CHAPTER 2

1. Erdal, M., Carling, J., Horst, C., & Talleraas, C. (2018), Defining sustainable migration, PRIO Paper.

2. Betts, A., & Collier, P. (2018), Sustainable migration framework. EMN Working Paper No. 1.

3. Mushaben, J. M. (2017), Wir schaffen das! Angela Merkel and the European refugee crisis. *German Politics*, *26*(4), 516–33; Smeets, S., & Beach, D. (2020), When success is an orphan: informal institutional governance and the EU–Turkey deal. *West European Politics*, *43*(1), 129–58.

4. For a broader historical account of the sources of backlash against globalization, see, Williamson, J. G. (1998), Globalization, labor markets and policy backlash in the past. *Journal of Economic Perspectives*, *12*(4), 51–72.

5. For a compelling comparative analysis of the rise of populism in Europe and North America after 2016, see: Norris, P., & Inglehart, R. (2019), *Cultural Backlash: Trump, Brexit, and Authoritarian Populism* (Cambridge: Cambridge University Press).

6. See, for example: Içduygu, A., & Nimer, M. (2020), The politics of return: exploring the future of Syrian refugees in Jordan, Lebanon and Turkey. *Third World Quarterly*, *41*(3), 415–33; Tsourapas, G. (2019), The Syrian refugee crisis and foreign policy decision-making in Jordan, Lebanon, and Turkey. *Journal of Global Security Studies*, *4*(4), 464–81.

7. *The Economist* (2019), Darkness falls: millions of refugees from Venezuela are straining neighbours' hospitality, 12 September, available at: https://www.economist.com/the-americas/2019/09/12/millions-of-refugees-from-venezuela-are-straining-neighbours-hospitality

8. For an account of how refugee policy has changed in Denmark and Scandinavia over time, see, for example, Brochmann, G., & Hagelund, A. (2012), *Immigration Policy and the Scandinavian Welfare State 1945–2010* (London: Palgrave Macmillan); Rytter, M. (2018), Made in Denmark: refugees, integration and the self-dependent society. *Anthropology Today*, *34*(3), 12–14; Gammeltoft-Hansen, T. (2017), The ugly duckling: Denmark anti-refugee policies and Europe's return to unilateralism. *Danish Foreign Policy Yearbook* (Copenhagen: Dansk Udenrigspolitisk Institut), 99–125.

9. Brankamp, H., & Daley, P. (2020), Laborers, migrants, refugees: managing belonging, bodies, and mobility in (post) colonial Kenya and Tanzania. *Migration and Society*, *3*(1), 113–29.

10. Young, J. G. (2017), Making America 1920 again? Nativism and US immigration, past and present. *Journal on Migration and Human Security*, *5*(1), 217–35.

11. See, for example, Martin, P. L. (1991), *The Unfinished Story: Turkish Labour Migration to Western Europe: with Special Reference to the Federal Republic of Germany* (Geneva: International Labour Organization).

12 We will revisit these questions about the determinants of social cohesion, 'native' (i.e. host-citizen) attitudes to refugees, and inter-group perception in more detail in Chapter 3. However, for an excellent summary article that reviews the political science literature on 'native' attitudes to immigration, see: Hainmueller, J., & Hopkins, D. J. (2014), Public attitudes toward immigration. *Annual Review of Political Science*, *17*, 225–49.

13. Rawls, J. (1999), *The Law of Peoples: With 'The Idea of Public Reason Revisited'* (Cambridge, MA: Harvard University Press), 13.

14. Sen, A. K. (2009), *The Idea of Justice* (Cambridge, MA: Harvard University Press), 58.

15. Gibney, M. J. (2004), *The Ethics and Politics of Asylum: Liberal Democracy and the Response to Refugees* (Cambridge: Cambridge University Press), 25–6.

16. Stemplowska, Z., & Swift, A. (2012), 'Ideal and non-ideal theory', in Estlund, D. (ed.), *The Oxford Handbook of Political Philosophy* (Oxford: Oxford University Press), 373–89.

17. Williams, B. A. O. (2005), *In the Beginning Was the Deed: Realism and Moralism in Political Argument* (Princeton, NJ: Princeton University Press).

18. This is a question that political theorists have wrestled with, not least in relation to immigration. Joseph Carens, for example, has highlighted the challenge for 'non-ideal' accounts to determine how much of the real world should be part of a normative account. He suggests that the amount of 'is' that needs to be part of an 'ought' argument depends on the particular aims of one's theory. Carens, J. H. (1996), Migration, politics, and ethics: realistic and idealistic approaches to the ethics of migration. *International Migration Review, 30*(1), 156–70; Carens, J. (2013), *The Ethics of Immigration* (Oxford: Oxford University Press).

19. For an argument on how non-ideal theory can contribute to progressive social change, see the work of Lea Ypi; for example, Ypi, L. (2010), On the confusion between ideal and non-ideal in recent debates on global justice. *Political Studies, 58*(3), 536–55.

20. World Bank (2018), *Groundswell: Preparing for Internal Climate Migration* (Washington, DC: World Bank).

21. On the relationship between public attitudes and refugee resettlement, see, for example, Esses, V. M., Hamilton, L. K., & Gaucher, D. (2017), The global refugee crisis: empirical evidence and policy implications for improving public attitudes and facilitating refugee resettlement. *Social Issues and Policy Review, 11*(1), 78–123; Yigit, I. H., & Tatch, A. (2017), Syrian refugees and Americans: perceptions, attitudes and insights. *American Journal of Qualitative Research, 1*(1), 13–31. For a critical take on the politics of refugee resettlement, see: Garnier, A., Jubilut, L. L., & Sandvik, K. B. (eds.) (2018), *Refugee Resettlement: Power, Politics, and Humanitarian Governance* (Oxford: Berghahn Books).

22. See, for example: Dancygier, R. M., & Donnelly, M. J. (2013), Sectoral economies, economic contexts, and attitudes toward immigration. *The Journal of Politics, 75*(1), 17–35; Pardos-Prado, S., & Xena, C. (2019), Skill specificity and attitudes toward immigration. *American Journal of Political Science, 63*(2), 286–304; Cavallaro, M., & Zanetti, M. A. (2020), Divided we stand: attitudes, social classes, and voting for the radical right after the Great Recession in Europe. *Ethnic and Racial Studies, 43*(2), 313–32; Isaksen, J. V. (2019), The impact of the financial crisis on European attitudes toward immigration. *Comparative Migration Studies, 7*(1), 1–20.

23. Arendt, H. (1951), *The Origins of Totalitarianism* (San Francisco: Houghton Mifflin Harcourt), 297–8. See also Benhabib, S. (2004), *The Rights of Others: Aliens, Residents, and Citizens* (Cambridge: Cambridge University Press).

24. The idea of 'basic rights' has been developed by Henry Shue, and applied to the refugee context by Andrew Shacknove: Shacknove, A. E. (1985), Who is a refugee? *Ethics, 95*(2), 274–84; Shue, H. (2020), *Basic Rights: Subsistence, Affluence, and US Foreign Policy* (Princeton, NJ: Princeton University Press; Beitz, C. R., & Goodin, R. E. (eds.) (2009), *Global Basic Rights* (Oxford: Oxford University Press).

25. Morgenthau, H. J., Thompson, K. W., & Clinton, W. D. (1948), *Politics among Nations: The Struggle for Power and Peace* (New York: McGraw-Hill/Irwin).

26. These elements of 'persecution' and 'alienage' are the two criteria that underlie Shacknove's (1985) understanding of who, ethically, we should regard as a refugee: Shacknove, A. E. (1985), Who is a refugee? *Ethics, 95*(2), 274–84.

27. On 'duties of rescue' see, for example, Durieux, J. F. (2016), The duty to rescue refugees. *International Journal of Refugee Law, 28*(4), 637–55, or Betts, A., & Collier, P. (2017), *Refuge: Transforming a Broken Refugee System* (London: Penguin Allen Lane).

28. One way to ground this is from an International Society view of international political theory, which Emma Haddad applies to ground a legitimacy-based view of states' obligations towards refugees: Haddad, E. (2008), *The Refugee in International Society: Between Sovereigns* (Cambridge: Cambridge University Press).

29. This view of 'asylum' as being linked to a need for citizenship is most clearly outlined by Price, M. E. (2009), *Rethinking Asylum: History, Purpose, and Limits* (Cambridge: Cambridge University Press).

30. Rebecca Buxton has argued in her doctoral research at the University of Oxford that political 'membership' is an obligation owed to all refugees, in addition to simply humanitarian protection. However, the challenge is to consider how 'thick' or 'thin' political membership can or should be relative to citizenship, especially for those who do not require an alternative long-term pathway to citizenship, and the role that time plays in changing entitlements and obligations relating to membership.

31. David Owen argues that we should distinguish between 'asylum' (for those fleeing a permanent severance of the state–citizen relationship as a result of persecution), 'sanctuary' (for those fleeing generalized violence), and 'refuge' (for those fleeing a crisis such as a natural disaster). He suggests that the remedies and obligations of the international community vary depending upon these different contexts and drivers of displacement. See: Owen, D. (2019), *What Do We Owe to Refugees?* (Bristol: Polity).

32. International political theory is relatively silent on the ethics of international cooperation. However, it offers a means through which states can collectively fulfil ethical obligations in ways that a more efficient, and hence reduce the costs of meeting moral obligations, as well as a constitutive role in shaping norms and values across states. See, for example, Hurrell, A. (2002), Norms and ethics in international relations, in Carlsnaes, W., Risse, T., & Simmons, B. (eds), *Handbook of International Relations* (London: Sage), 137–54, or Frost, M., &

Mervyn, F. (1996), *Ethics in International Relations: A Constitutive Theory* (Cambridge: Cambridge University Press).

33. For a discussion of the ethics of proximity and geography relating to refugees, see Gibney, M. J. (2004), *The Ethics and Politics of Asylum: Liberal Democracy and the Response to Refugees* (Cambridge: Cambridge University Press), 25–6, 240.

34. Singer, P., & Singer, R. (1988), The ethics of refugee policy, in Gibney, M. (ed), *Open Borders? Closed Societies? The Ethical and Political Issues* (New York: Greenwood Press), 111–30.

35. Gibney, M. J. (2004), *The Ethics and Politics of Asylum: Liberal Democracy and the Response to Refugees* (Cambridge: Cambridge University Press), 25–6, 63.

36. Mushaben, J. M. (2017), Wir schaffen das! Angela Merkel and the European refugee crisis. *German Politics*, *26*(4), 516–33.

37. *New York Times* (2017), Bild apologises for false article on sexual assaults in Frankfurt by migrants, 16 February, available at: https://www.nytimes.com/2017/02/16/world/europe/bild-fake-story.html

38. For a critique of the EU–Turkey deal and an overview of its origins, see: Lehner, R. (2019), The EU–Turkey 'deal': legal challenges and pitfalls. *International Migration*, *57*(2), 176–85.

39. *The Guardian* (2017), What the stunning success of AfD Means for Germany and Europe, 24 September, available at: https://www.theguardian.com/commentisfree/2017/sep/24/germany-elections-afd-europe-immigration-merkel-radical-right

40. *Financial Times* (2017), Merkel admits she would turn back the clock on refugee policy, 19 September, available at: https://www.ft.com/content/11150514-7e78-11e6-8e50-8ec15fb462f4

41. Eurobarometer (2018), TNS opinion and social: Brussels. GESIS data archive, available at: https://www.gesis.org/eurobarometer-data-service/search-data-access/data-access

42. For commentary on this, see the work of James Dennison; for example, Dennison, J. (2020), How issue salience explains the rise of the populist right in Western Europe. *International Journal of Public Opinion Research*, *32*(3), 397–420; Dennison, J. (2019), A review of public issue salience: concepts, determinants and effects on voting. *Political Studies Review*, *17*(4), 436–46; Dennison, J. (2019), *Impact of Public Attitudes to Migration on the Political Environment in the Euro-Mediterranean Region–First Chapter* (Florence: European University Institute).

43. For an overview of the European response to asylum and immigration policy in the aftermath of 2015, see, for example, Collett, E., & Le Coz, C. (2018), *After the Storm: Learning from the EU Response to the Migration Crisis* (Washington, DC: Migration Policy Institute).

44. The European Commission (2020), *New Pact on Migration and Asylum* (Brussels: European Commission), available at: https://ec.europa.eu/info/strategy/priorities-2019-2024/promoting-our-european-way-life/new-pact-migration-and-asylum_en

45. Congressional Research Service (2019), *Immigration: Recent Apprehension Trends at the US South-Western Border* (Washington, DC: Congressional Research Service), available at: https://fas.org/sgp/crs/homesec/R46012.pdf

46. Pierce, S., Bolter, J., & Selee, A. (2018), *US Immigration Policy under Trump: Deep Changes and Lasting Impacts* (Washington, DC: Migration Policy Institute).

47. *Washington Post* (2019), Nearly 1 million migrants arrested along Mexican border in fiscal 2019, most since 2017, 8 October, available at: https://www.washingtonpost.com/immigration/nearly-1-million-migrants-arrested-along-mexico-border-in-fiscal-2019-most-since-2007/2019/10/08/749413e4-e9d4-11e9-9306-47cb0324fd44_story.html

48. See, for example: Crandall, R. (2019), Exodus from the northern triangle. *Survival, 61*(1), 91–104.

49. The Trump Administration created the Migrant Protection Protocol, which includes a 'Remain in Mexico' policy to process asylum claims in Mexico. This approach to 'offshoring' asylum claims replicates policies previously applied in Australia and attempted by the EU.

50. There is relatively little systematic research showing the relationship between deindustrialization and attitudes to immigration, but patterns can be seen on maps of voting areas across Europe and the United States suggesting a possible correlation between the loss of labour-intensive manufacturing jobs and support for anti-immigration political parties.

51. Gallup (2019), Potential Net Migration Index, available at: https://news.gallup.com/poll/245225/gallup-migration-research-center.aspx

52. Migali, S., & Scipioni, M. (2018), *A Global Analysis of Intentions to Migrate* (Brussels: European Commission).

53. Bahar, D., & Dooley, M. (2019), Venezuela refugee crisis to become the largest and most underfunded in modern history. Blog post, 9 December (Washington, DC: Brookings), available at: https://www.brookings.edu/blog/up-front/2019/12/09/venezuela-refugee-crisis-to-become-the-largest-and-most-underfunded-in-modern-history/

54. Betts, A. (2019), Nowhere to go: how governments in the Americas are bungling the migration crisis. *Foreign Affairs, 98*(6), 122–33.

55. Betts, A. (2019), Nowhere to go: how governments in the Americas are bungling the migration crisis. *Foreign Affairs, 98*(6), 122–33.

56. *The Economist* (2019), Darkness falls: millions of refugees from Venezuela are straining neighbours' hospitality, 12 September, available at: https://www.economist.com/the-americas/2019/09/12/millions-of-refugees-from-venezuela-are-straining-neighbours-hospitality

57. Bennouna, C. (2019), Latin America shuts out desperate Venezuelans but Colombia's border remains open—for now, *The Conversation*, 7 October, available at: https://theconversation.com/latin-america-shuts-out-desperate-venezuelans-but-colombias-border-remains-open-for-now-123307

58. Felipe Muñoz, the Colombian president's advisor on the border regions, presented an overview of this data at a meeting at the University of Oxford on 17 September 2019.

59. El Deeb, S. (2019), In Lebanon, Syrian refugees face new pressure to go home, *Seattle Times*, 19 June, available at: https://www.seattletimes.com/nation-world/nation/in-lebanon-syrian-refugees-face-new-pressure-to-go-home/

60. For analysis of the changing policy responses of Lebanon to refugees, see, for example, Hägerdal, N. (2018), Lebanon's hostility to Syrian refugees. *Middle East Brief*, *116*, 1–8; Chatty, D. (2018), *Syria: The Making and Unmaking of a Refuge State* (Oxford: Oxford University Press).

61. For research on the history of refugee policy in Tanzania, see: Chaulia, S. S. (2003), The politics of refugee hosting in Tanzania: from open door to unsustainability, insecurity and receding receptivity. *Journal of Refugee Studies*, *16*(2), 147–66; Sommers, M. (2001), *Fear in Bongoland: Burundi Refugees in Urban Tanzania* (vol. 8) (Oxford: Berghahn Books); Milner, J. (2014), Can global refugee policy leverage durable solutions? Lessons from Tanzania's naturalization of Burundian refugees. *Journal of Refugee Studies*, *27*(4), 553–73.

62. Betts, A (2018), Don't make African nations borrow money to support refugees, *Foreign Policy*, 21 February, available at: https://foreignpolicy.com/2018/02/21/dont-make-african-nations-borrow-money-to-support-refugees/

63. Lemma, A., Hagen-Zanker, J., Wake, C., Raihan, S, & Eusuf, A. (2018), Strategies for inclusive growth in Cox's Bazar. EDIG Research Report No. 4 (London: ODI and DFID).

64. Lischer, S. K. (2015), *Dangerous Sanctuaries: Refugee Camps, Civil War, and the Dilemmas of Humanitarian Aid* (Ithaca, NY: Cornell University Press); Salehyan, I. (2009), *Rebels without Borders: Transnational Insurgencies in World Politics* (Ithaca, NY: Cornell University Press).

65. See, for example, Human Rights Watch (2019), Bangladesh: clampdown on Rohingya refugees, available at: https://www.hrw.org/news/2019/09/07/bangladesh-clampdown-rohingya-refugees

66. IOM (2008), *Migration and Climate Change* (Geneva: IOM).

67. World Bank (2018), *Groundswell: Preparing for Internal Climate Migration* (Washington, DC: World Bank).

68. Brown, O. (2007), Climate change and forced migration: observations, projections and implications (No. HDOCPA-2007–17). Human Development Report Office (HDRO), United Nations Development Programme (UNDP).

69. Nicholson, C. T. (2014), Climate change and the politics of causal reasoning: the case of climate change and migration. *The Geographical Journal*, *180*(2), 151–60.

70. Betts, A. (2013), *Survival Migration: Failed Governance and the Crisis of Displacement* (Ithaca, NY: Cornell University Press).

71. IOM (2018), *El Salvador: Flow Monitoring Survey on Profile of Humanitarian Needs of Migrants in Transit* (Geneva: IOM), available at: https://www.iom.int/sites/default/files/dtm/dtm-es-r2-survey-31-10-2018-eng_002.pdf

72. Centre for American Progress (2019), *Getting Migration in the Americas Right: A National-Interest Driven Approach* (Washington, DC: Centre for American Progress).

73. UNHCR (2019), Majority fleeing Venezuela in need of international protection, available at: https://www.unhcr.org/uk/news/briefing/2019/5/5ce3bb734/majority-fleeing-venezuela-need-refugee-protection-unhcr.html

74. World Bank (2018), *Migracion Desde Venezuela a Colombia* (Washington, DC: World Bank).

75. For legal analysis on the concept of 'safe third country', see, for example, Gil-Bazo, M. T. (2006), The practice of Mediterranean states in the context of the European Union's justice and home affairs external dimension: the safe third country concept revisited. *International Journal of Refugee Law, 18*(3–4), 571–600. Foster, M. (2008), Responsibility sharing or shifting? 'Safe' third countries and international law. *Refuge: Canada's Journal on Refugees, 25*(2), 64–78.

76. For critical analysis of the Dublin system, see: Schuster, L. (2011), Turning refugees into 'illegal migrants': Afghan asylum seekers in Europe. *Ethnic and Racial Studies, 34*(8), 1392–407; Mouzourakis, M. (2014), We need to talk about Dublin: responsibility under the Dublin system as a blockage to asylum–burden sharing in the European Union. Refugee Studies Centre Working Paper Series No. 105.

77. Oberman, K. (2016), Immigration as a human right, in Fine, S., & Ypi, L. (eds), *Migration in Political Theory: The Ethics of Movement and Membership* (Oxford: Oxford University Press), 32–53.

78. Bertram, C. (2018), *Do States Have the Right to Exclude Immigrants?* (London: John Wiley & Sons).

79. Ypi, L. (2019), Opening plenary lecture at 'Democratizing Displacement' conference, held at the Refugee Studies Centre, University of Oxford, 18–19 March. See also Flikschuh, K., & Ypi, L. (eds.) (2014), *Kant and Colonialism: Historical and Critical Perspectives* (Oxford: Oxford University Press); Ypi, L. (2018), Borders of class: migration and citizenship in the capitalist state. *Ethics & International Affairs, 32*(2), 141–52.

80. Walzer, M. (1983), *Spheres of Justice: A Defence of Pluralism and Equality* (London: Basic Books), 36–61.

81. Miller, D. (2016), Is there a human right to immigrate?, in Fine, S., & Ypi, L. (eds), *Migration in Political Theory: The Ethics of Movement and Membership* (Oxford: Oxford University Press), 11–31; Miller, D. (2005), Immigration: the case for limits, in Cohen, A., & Wellman, C. H. (eds.), *Contemporary Debates in Applied Ethics* (London: Wiley-Blackwell), 193–206.

82. Gibney, M. J. (2004), *The Ethics and Politics of Asylum: Liberal Democracy and the Response to Refugees* (Cambridge: Cambridge University Press), 25–6, 63.

83. Carens, J. (2013), *The Ethics of Immigration* (Oxford: Oxford University Press), 298.

84. See, for example, Betts, A., Sterck, O., Geervliet, R., & MacPherson, C. (2017), *Talent Displaced: The Economic Lives of Syrian Refugees* (London: Deloitte), or Pew (2016), Asylum seeker demography: young and male, available at: https://www.pewresearch.org/global/2016/08/02/4-asylum-seeker-demography-young-and-male/

85. Research by Kirk Bansak and his colleagues shows that European public support for asylum is related to factors that include a proportional and equitable basis for allocating responsibility between states, and the humanitarian needs of the claimants, for example. See: Bansak, K., Hainmueller, J., & Hangartner, D. (2016), How economic, humanitarian, and religious concerns shape European attitudes toward asylum seekers. *Science, 354*(6309), 217–22; Bansak, K., Hainmueller, J., & Hangartner, D. (2017), Europeans support a proportional allocation of asylum seekers. *Nature Human Behaviour, 1*(7), 1–6.

86. James Hathaway and Alexander Neve argue that the refugee system should be based on 'common-but-differentiated responsibility-sharing', whereby all countries contribute but nation-states contribute mainly in the areas in which they have a comparative advantage; for example, in providing money or admitting people onto their territory.

87. The 1951 Convention on the Status of Refugees, Preamble. For commentary, see, for example, Zimmermann, A., Dörschner, J., & Machts, F. (eds.) (2011), *The 1951 Convention Relating to the Status of Refugees and Its 1967 Protocol: A Commentary* (Oxford: Oxford University Press).

88. For discussion for the Global Compact on Refugees, see, for example, Türk, V., & Garlick, M. (2016), From burdens and responsibilities to opportunities: the comprehensive refugee response framework and a global compact on refugees. *International Journal of Refugee Law, 28*(4), 656–78; Betts, A. (2018), The global compact on refugees: towards a theory of change? *International Journal of Refugee Law, 30*(4), 623–6; Hathaway, J. C. (2018), The global cop-out on refugees. *International Journal of Refugee Law, 30*(4), 591–604.

89 Hathaway, J. C., & Neve, R. A. (1997), Making international refugee law relevant again: a proposal for collectivized and solution-oriented protection. *Harvard Human Rights Journal, 10*, 115.

90. Suhrke, A. (1998), Burden-sharing during refugee emergencies: the logic of collective versus national action. *Journal of Refugee Studies, 11*(4), 396–415.

91. Grahl-Madsen, A. (1982), Refugee and refugee law in a world in transition. *Mich. YBI Legal Stud., 3*, 65.

92. Kaul, I., Grungberg, I., & Stern, M. A. (1999), *Global Public Goods: International Cooperation in the 21st Century* (Oxford: Oxford University Press), *450*.

93. Woods, N. (2014), *The Globalizers: The IMF, the World Bank, and Their Borrowers* (Ithaca, NY: Cornell University Press).

94. Sandler, T., & Hartley, K. (1999), *The Political Economy of NATO: Past, Present and into the 21st Century* (Cambridge: Cambridge University Press).

95. Boyle, A. E. (1991), Saving the world-implementation and enforcement of international environmental law through international institutions. *Journal of Environmental Law, 3*, 229; Wolf, A. (2014), *Quotas in International Environmental Agreements* (London: Routledge).

96. Hathaway, J. C. (2018), The global cop-out on refugees. *International Journal of Refugee Law, 30*(4), 591–604.

97. Schuck, P. H. (1997), Refugee burden-sharing: a modest proposal. *Yale Journal of International Law, 22*, 243; Jones, W., & Teytelboym, A. (2018), The local refugee

match: aligning refugees' preferences with the capacities and priorities of localities. *Journal of Refugee Studies, 31*(2), 152–78; Moraga, J., & Rapoport, H. (2014), Tradable immigration quotas. *Journal of Public Economics, 115*, 94–108.

98. Moraga, J., & Rapoport, H. (2015), Tradable refugee-admission quotas and EU asylum policy. *CESifo Economic Studies, 61*(3–4), 638–72.

99. Moraga, J., & Rapoport, H. (2015), Tradable refugee-admission quotas and EU asylum policy. *CESifo Economic Studies, 61*(3–4), 638–72.

100. Anker, D., Fitzpatrick, J., & Shacknove, A. (1998), Crisis and cure: a reply to Hathaway/Neve and Schuck. *Harvard Human Rights Journal, 11*, 295.

101. Anker, D., Fitzpatrick, J., & Shacknove, A. (1998), Crisis and cure: a reply to Hathaway/Neve and Schuck. *Harvard Human Rights Journal, 11*, 295.

102. Kuosmanen, J. (2013), What (if anything) is wrong with trading refugee quotas?. *Res publica, 19*(2), 103–19.

103. Jones, W., & Teytelboym, A. (2017), The international refugee match: a system that respects refugees' preferences and the priorities of states. *Refugee Survey Quarterly, 36*(2), 84–109.

104. Betts, A. (2009), *Protection by Persuasion: International Cooperation in the Refugee Regime* (Ithaca, NY: Cornell University Press).

105. For discussion of the failure of the EU refugee relocation scheme, see: Bauböck, R. (2018), Refugee protection and burden-sharing in the European Union. *JCMS: Journal of Common Market Studies, 56*(1), 141–56; Duszczyk, M., Podgórska, K., & Pszczółkowska, D. (2019), From mandatory to voluntary: impact of V4 on the EU relocation scheme. *European Politics and Society, 21*(4), 470–87; Francisco, I. (2019), Flexible vs mandatory solidarity and the 2015 refugee relocation mechanism (Bachelor's thesis, Leiden University).

106. UNHCR (2014), *Alternatives to Refugee Camps* (Geneva: UNHCR), available at: https://www.unhcr.org/alternatives-to-camps.html

107. Zetter, R. (2019), Theorizing the refugee humanitarian–development nexus: a political-economy analysis. *Journal of Refugee Studies* (available online).

108. For details on the EUTF, see: https://ec.europa.eu/trustfundforafrica/index_en

109. Walzer, M. (1983), *Spheres of Justice: A Defence of Pluralism and Equality* (London: Basic Books), 36–61.

110. Gibney, M. J. (2004), *The Ethics and Politics of Asylum: Liberal Democracy and the Response to Refugees* (Cambridge: Cambridge University Press), 25–6, 63.

111. The phrase 'anchors not walls' was used in a report of the UK Parliamentary Committee on International Development report on protracted displacement in Africa: UK Parliament (2019), Forced displacement in Africa: anchors not walls, available at: https://publications.parliament.uk/pa/cm201719/cmselect/cmintdev/1433/143303.htm

112. See, for example, Turner, L. (2020), 'Refugees can be entrepreneurs too!' Humanitarianism, race, and the marketing of Syrian refugees. *Review of International Studies, 46*(1), 137–55; Morris, J. (2020), Extractive landscapes: the case of the Jordan refugee compact. *Refuge: Canada's Journal on Refugees / Refuge. Revue canadienne sur les réfugiés, 36*(1), 87–96; Easton-Calabria, E. (2020), Warriors of self-reliance: the instrumentalization of Afghan refugees in Pakistan. *Journal*

of Refugee Studies, *33*(1), 143–66; Daley, P. (2013), Rescuing African bodies: celebrities, consumerism and neoliberal humanitarianism. *Review of African Political Economy*, *40*(137), 375–93.

113. Piketty, T. (2014), *Capital in the Twenty-First Century* (Cambridge, MA: Harvard University Press); Saad Filho, A. (2001), *The Value of Marx: Political Economy for Contemporary Capitalism* (Abingdon: Routledge).

114. Appadurai, A. (ed.) (1988), *The Social Life of Things: Commodities in Cultural Perspective* (Cambridge: Cambridge University Press).

115. Sennett, R. (2006), *The Culture of the New Capitalism* (New Haven, CT: Yale University Press); Sandel, M. J. (2000), What money can't buy: the moral limits of markets. *Tanner Lectures on Human Values*, *21*, 87–122; Dufour, D. R. (2008), *The Art of Shrinking Heads: The New Servitude of the Liberated in the Era of Total Capitalism* (Cambridge: Polity).

116. Sen, A. (1999), *Development as Freedom* (Oxford: Oxford University Press).

117. Mill, J. S. (1860), *On Liberty* (London: John W. Parker).

118. For analysis on the relationship between refugee employment and mental health, see for example: Beiser, M., Johnson, P. J., & Turner, R. J. (1993), Unemployment, underemployment and depressive affect among Southeast Asian refugees. *Psychological Medicine*, *23*(3), 731–43. Fleay, C., Hartley, L., & Kenny, M. A. (2013), Refugees and asylum seekers living in the Australian community: the importance of work rights and employment support. *Australian Journal of Social Issues*, *48*(4), 473–93; Blight, K. J., Ekblad, S., Persson, J. O., & Ekberg, J. (2006), Mental health, employment and gender: cross-sectional evidence in a sample of refugees from Bosnia-Herzegovina living in two Swedish regions. *Social Science & Medicine*, *62*(7), 1697–709.

119. Wolpe, H. (1972), Capitalism and cheap labour-power in South Africa: from segregation to apartheid. *Economy and society*, *1*(4), 425–56; Lipton, M. (1986), *Capitalism and Apartheid: South Africa, 1910–1986* (Cape Town: New Africa Books).

120. For a discussion of 'bare life', see Owens, P. (2009), Reclaiming 'bare life'? against Agamben on refugees. *International Relations*, *23*(4), 567–82.

121. Betts, A., & Jones, W. (2016), *Mobilising the Diaspora* (Cambridge: Cambridge University Press).

122. Pincock, K., Betts, A., & Easton-Calabria, E. (2020), *The Global Governed? Refugees as Providers of Protection and Assistance* (Cambridge: Cambridge University Press).

123. Bender, F. (2019), The ethics of refugee self-governance in refugee camps. Paper presented at the 'Democratising Displacement' conference, Refugee Studies Centre, 16–17 March.

124. Chimni, B. S. (1998), The geopolitics of refugee studies: a view from the south. *Journal of Refugee Studies*, *11*(4), 350–74.

125. Zetter, R. (2019), Theorizing the refugee humanitarian–development nexus: a political-economy analysis. *Journal of Refugee Studies* (available online).

CHAPTER 3

1. International Finance Corporation (2018), Kakuma as a marketplace: a consumer and market study of a refugee camp and town in north-west Kenya, Understanding Poverty Report, 3 May (Washington, DC: IFC), available at: https://documents.worldbank.org/en/publication/documents-reports/documentdetail/482761525339883916/kakuma-as-a-marketplace-a-consumer-and-market-study-of-a-refugee-camp-and-town-in-northwest-kenya

2. Turkana County is 68,680km²; Switzerland is 41,285km².

3. *The Guardian* (2017), They call him the millionaire: the refugee who turned his camp into a business empire, 10 May, available at: https://www.theguardian.com/global-development-professionals-network/2017/may/10/millionaire-refugee-mesfin-getahun-kakuma-refugee-camp

4. International Finance Corporation (2018), Kakuma as a marketplace: a consumer and market study of a refugee camp and town in north-west Kenya, Understanding Poverty Report, 3 May (Washington, DC: IFC), available at: https://documents.worldbank.org/en/publication/documents-reports/documentdetail/482761525339883916/kakuma-as-a-marketplace-a-consumer-and-market-study-of-a-refugee-camp-and-town-in-northwest-kenya

5. Carrier, N. C. (2016), *Little Mogadishu: Eastleigh, Nairobi's Global Somali Hub* (Oxford: Oxford University Press).

6. WEF (2016), Could refugees boost entrepreneurship in Germany?, available at: https://www.weforum.org/agenda/2016/02/could-refugees-boost-entrepreneurship-in-germany

7. UNHCR (2020), Syrian entrepreneur finds her niche in Berlin, available at: https://www.unhcr.org/uk/news/stories/2020/2/5e566dd64/syrian-entrepreneur-finds-niche-berlin-catering-hungry-city.html

8. The German Federal Office for Migration and Refugees (BAMF) records employment data for refugees, available at: https://www.bamf.de/EN/Startseite/startseite_node.html

9. Foster, M. (2007), *International Refugee Law and Socio-Economic Rights: Refuge from Deprivation* (Cambridge: Cambridge University Press).

10. Sen, A. (1999), *Development as Freedom* (Oxford: Oxford University Press).

11. Beiser, M. and Hou, F. (2001), Language acquisition, unemployment and depressive disorder among Southeast Asian refugees: a 10-year study. *Social Science & Medicine, 53*(10), 1321–34.

12. Bansak, K., Hainmueller, J., & Hangartner, D. (2016), How economic, humanitarian, and religious concerns shape European attitudes toward asylum seekers. *Science, 354*(6309), 217–22.

13. IRC (2018), Kenya: citizens' perceptions of refugees, available at: https://www.rescue.org/report/kenya-citizens-perceptions-refugees

14. See, for example, Skran, C., & Easton-Calabria, E. (2020), Old concepts making new history: refugee self-reliance, livelihoods and the 'refugee entrepreneur'. *Journal of Refugee Studies, 33*(1), 1–21.

15. Betts, A., Bloom, L., Kaplan, J. D., & Omata, N. (2017), *Refugee Economies: Forced Displacement and Development* (Oxford: Oxford University Press).

16. North, D. C. (1991), Institutions. *Journal of Economic Perspectives, 5*(1), 97–112; Williamson, O. E. (2000), The new institutional economics: taking stock, looking ahead. *Journal of Economic Literature, 38*(3), 595–613.

17. Becker, G. S. (1973), A theory of marriage: part I. *Journal of Political Economy, 81*(4), 813–46; Grossbard-Shechtman, S., & Grossbard-Shechtman, S. (2019), *On the Economics of Marriage* (New York: Routledge).

18. Avio, K. (1998), The economics of prisons. *European Journal of Law and Economics, 6*(2), 143–75.

19. Abramitzky, R. (2009), The effect of redistribution on migration: evidence from the Israeli kibbutz. *Journal of Public Economics, 93*(3–4), 498–511; Putterman, L. (1983), Incentives and the Kibbutz: toward an economics of communal work motivation. *Zeitschrift für Nationalökonomie/Journal of Economics, 43*(2), 157–88.

20. Akerlof, G. A., & Kranton, R. E. (2000), Economics and identity. *The Quarterly Journal of Economics, 115*(3), 715–53; Akerlof, G. A., & Kranton, R. (2010), Identity economics. *The Economists' Voice, 7*(2), 1–3.

21. North, D. C. (1993), Institutions and credible commitment. *Journal of Institutional and Theoretical Economics, 149*(1), 11–23; Bardhan, P. (1989), The new institutional economics and development theory: a brief critical assessment. *World Development, 17*(9), 1389–95; Harriss, J., Hunter, J., & Lewis, C. (1995), *The New Institutional Economics and Third World Development* (London: Routledge); Nabli, M. K., & Nugent, J. B. (1989), The new institutional economics and its applicability to development. *World Development, 17*(9), 1333–47.

22. Hoff, K., & Stiglitz, J. E. (1990), Introduction: imperfect information and rural credit markets. Puzzles and policy perspectives. *The World Bank Economic Review, 4*(3), 235–50; Greenwald, B. C., & Stiglitz, J. E. (1986), Externalities in economies with imperfect information and incomplete markets. *The Quarterly Journal of Economics, 101*(2), 229–64.

23. Meagher, K. (2010), *Identity Economics: Social Networks & the Informal Economy in Nigeria* (London: James Currey).

24. For a notable exception, see Collier, P. (2016). The cultural foundations of economic failure: a conceptual toolkit. *Journal of Economic Behaviour and Organization, 126*, 5–24.

25. Banerjee, A. V., & Duflo, E. (2007), The economic lives of the poor. *Journal of Economic Perspectives, 21*(1), 141–68.

26. Jacobsen, K. (2005), *The Economic Life of Refugees* (Bloomfield, CT: Kumarian Press).

27. Werker, E. (2007), Refugee camp economies. *Journal of Refugee Studies, 20*(3), 461–80.

28. Alix-Garcia, J., & Saah, D. (2010), The effect of refugee inflows on host communities: evidence from Tanzania. *The World Bank Economic Review, 24*(1), 148–70; Maystadt, J. F., & Verwimp, P. (2009), Winners and losers among a refugee-hosting population. ECORE Discussion Paper; Maystadt, J. F., &

Duranton, G. (2019), The development push of refugees: evidence from Tanzania. *Journal of Economic Geography*, *19*(2), 299–334; Taylor, J. E., Filipski, M. J., Alloush, M., Gupta, A., Valdes, R. I. R., & Gonzalez-Estrada, E. (2016), Economic impact of refugees. *Proceedings of the National Academy of Sciences*, *113*(27), 7449–53.

29. Fransen, S., Ruiz, I., & Vargas-Silva, C. (2017), Return migration and economic outcomes in the conflict context. *World Development*, *95*, 196–210; Ruiz, I., & Vargas-Silva, C. (2020), The impacts of refugee repatriation on receiving communities. *Journal of Economic Geography* (available online).

30. Ruiz, I., & Vargas-Silva, C. (2015), The labor market impacts of forced migration. *American Economic Review*, *105*(5), 581–6; Ruiz, I., & Vargas-Silva, C. (2013), The economics of forced migration. *The Journal of Development Studies*, *49*(6), 772–84.

31. Sterck, O., Rodgers, C., Flinder Stierna, M., Siu, J., & Betts, A. (2020), *Cash Transfer Models and Debt in the Kalobeyei Settlement* (Oxford: Refugee Studies Centre); Delius, A., & Sterck, O. (2019), Cash transfers and micro-enterprise performance: evidence from refugee camps in Kenya. CSAE Working Paper.

32. Betts, A., Bloom, L., Kaplan, J. D., & Omata, N. (2017), *Refugee Economies: Forced Displacement and Development* (Oxford: Oxford University Press).

33. Beiser, M., & Hyman, I. (1997), Refugees' time perspective and mental health. *American Journal of Psychiatry*, *154*(7), 996–1002.

34. For work on the economics of time horizons, see, for example, Andreoni, J., & Sprenger, C. (2012), Risk preferences are not time preferences. *American Economic Review*, *102*(7), 3357–76; Lea, S. E., Webley, P., & Walker, C. M. (1995), Psychological factors in consumer debt: money management, economic socialization, and credit use. *Journal of Economic Psychology*, *16*(4), 681–701; Kahn, K., Dercon, S., Pozuelo, J. R., Stein, A., Pettifor, A., & Blakemore, S.-J. (2020), Cash transfers in adolescence: a developmental perspective. *Lancet Child and Adolescent Health*, *4*(3), 177–8.

35. For work that considers how being a 'migrant' influences decision-making and behaviour, see, for example, Gadd, M., Sundquist, J., Johansson, S. E., & Wändell, P. (2005), Do immigrants have an increased prevalence of unhealthy behaviours and risk factors for coronary heart disease? *European Journal of Cardiovascular Prevention & Rehabilitation*, *12*(6), 535–41; Czaika, M. (2015), Migration and economic prospects. *Journal of Ethnic and Migration Studies*, *41*(1), 58–82.

36. See, for example, Betts, A., Sterck, O., & Omata, N. (2018), *Refugee Economies in Kenya* (Oxford: Refugee Studies Centre).

37. Betts, A., Sterck, O., & Omata, N. (2018), *Refugee Economies in Kenya* (Oxford: Refugee Studies Centre).

38. Betts, A., Bloom, L., Kaplan, J. D., & Omata, N. (2017), *Refugee Economies: Forced Displacement and Development* (Oxford: Oxford University Press).

39. UNHCR (2019), *Global Trends in 2018* (Geneva: UNHCR), 14.

40. We aim to publish the full dataset online in 2022 for use by other researchers, practitioners, and policy-makers.

41. UNHCR (2020), *Global Trends in 2019* (Geneva: UNHCR).

42. See, for example, the work of the OCHA Centre for Humanitarian Data, available at: https://centre.humdata.org

43. Mukherjee, S., & Benson, T. (2003), The determinants of poverty in Malawi, 1998. *World Development*, *31*(2), 339–58; Geda, A., De Jong, N., Mwabu, G., & Kimenyi, M. (2001), Determinants of poverty in Kenya: a household level analysis. *ISS Working Paper Series/General Series*, *347*, 1–20; Adeyemi, S. L., Ijaiya, G. T., & Raheem, U. A. (2009), Determinants of poverty in sub-Saharan Africa. *African Research Review*, *3*(2), 162–77.

44. Tschirley, D., & Weber, M. (1994), Food security under extremely adverse conditions: determinants of household income and consumption in rural Mozambique. *World Development*, *22*(2), 159–73; Abafita, J., & Kim, K. R. (2014), Determinants of household food security in rural Ethiopia: an empirical analysis. *Journal of Rural Development/Nongchon-Gyeongje*, *37*(2), 129–57; Muche, M., Endalew, B., & Koricho, T. (2014), Determinants of household food security among southwest Ethiopia rural households. *Asian Journal of Agriculture Research*, *8*(5), 248–58.

45. Murthy, V. N., & Okunade, A. A. (2009), The core determinants of health expenditure in the African context: some econometric evidence for policy. *Health Policy*, *91*(1), 57–62; Akinkugbe, O., & Mohanoe, M. (2009), Public health expenditure as a determinant of health status in Lesotho. *Social Work in Public Health*, *24*(1–2), 131–47.

46. Glewwe, P. (1991), Investigating the determinants of household welfare in Côte d'Ivoire. *Journal of Development Economics*, *35*(2), 307–37; Blaauw, D., & Pretorius, A. (2013), The determinants of subjective well-being in South Africa: an exploratory enquiry. *Journal of Economic and Financial Sciences*, *6*(1), 179–94; Sulemana, I. (2015), An empirical investigation of the relationship between social capital and subjective well-being in Ghana. *Journal of Happiness Studies*, *16*(5), 1299–321.

47. Blume, K., Gustafsson, B., Pedersen, P. J., & Verner, M. (2007), At the lower end of the table: determinants of poverty among immigrants to Denmark and Sweden. *Journal of Ethnic and Migration Studies*, *33*(3), 373–96; Connor, P. (2010), Explaining the refugee gap: economic outcomes of refugees versus other immigrants. *Journal of Refugee Studies*, *23*(3), 377–97.

48. Fazel, M., Reed, R. V., Panter-Brick, C., & Stein, A. (2012), Mental health of displaced and refugee children resettled in high-income countries: risk and protective factors. *The Lancet*, *379*(9812), 266–82; Schweitzer, R., Melville, F., Steel, Z., & Lacherez, P. (2006), Trauma, post-migration living difficulties, and social support as predictors of psychological adjustment in resettled Sudanese refugees. *Australian & New Zealand Journal of Psychiatry*, *40*(2), 179–87; Silove, D., Ventevogel, P., & Rees, S. (2017), The contemporary refugee crisis: an overview of mental health challenges. *World Psychiatry*, *16*(2), 130–9.

49. Hainmueller, J., & Hopkins, D. J. (2014), Public attitudes toward immigration. *Annual Review of Political Science*, *17*, 225–49; Hopkins, D. J. (2010), Politicized

places: explaining where and when immigrants provoke local opposition. *American Political Science Review, 104*(1), 40–60.

50. Hainmueller, J., & Hopkins, D. J. (2014), Public attitudes toward immigration. *Annual Review of Political Science, 17*, 225–49.

51. Mayda, A. M. (2006), Who is against immigration? A cross-country investigation of individual attitudes toward immigrants. *The Review of Economics and Statistics, 88*(3), 510–30.

52. Dustmann, C., & Preston, I. P. (2007), Racial and economic factors in attitudes to immigration. *The BE Journal of Economic Analysis & Policy, 7*(1), 1–41.

53. Hainmueller, J., & Hiscox, M. J. (2007), Educated preferences: explaining attitudes toward immigration in Europe. *International Organization, 61*(2), 399–442.

54. Sniderman, P. M., Hagendoorn, L., & Prior, M. (2004), Predisposing factors and situational triggers: exclusionary reactions to immigrant minorities. *American Political Science Review, 98*(1), 35–49; Ford, R. (2011), Acceptable and unacceptable immigrants: how opposition to immigration in Britain is affected by migrants' region of origin. *Journal of Ethnic and Migration Studies, 37*(7), 1017–37.

55. Hopkins, D. (2010), Politicized places: explaining where and when immigrants provoke local opposition. *American Political Science Review, 104*(1), 40–60; Hainmueller, J., & Hopkins, D. J. (2014), Public attitudes toward immigration. *Annual Review of Political Science, 17*, 225–49.

56. Allport, G. (1954), *The Nature of Prejudice* (Reading, MA: Addison-Wesley).

57. Quillian, L. (1996), Group threat and regional change in attitudes toward African-Americans. *American Journal of Sociology, 102*(3), 816–60.

58. Hopkins, D. (2010), Politicized places: explaining where and when immigrants provoke local opposition. *American Political Science Review, 104*(1), 40–60.

59. Steinmayr, A. (2016), Exposure to refugees and voting for the far-right: (unexpected) results from Austria. SSRN Working Paper.

60. Dustmann, C., Vasiljeva, K., & Piil, A. (n.d.), Refugee migration and electoral outcomes. CReAM Discussion Paper Series CPD 19/16.

61. Dinas, E., Matakos, K., Xefteris, D., & Hangartner, D. (2019), Waking up the golden dawn: does exposure to the refugee crisis increase support for extreme-right parties? *Political Analysis, 27*(2), 244–54.

62. Sanghi, A., Onder, H., & Vemuru, V. (2016), *'Yes' in My Backyard: The Economics of Refugees and Their Social Dynamics in Kakuma, Kenya* (Washington, DC: World Bank).

63. For literature on the economics of migration decision-making, see: Stark, O., & Bloom, D. E. (1985), The new economics of labor migration. *The American Economic Review, 75*(2), 173–8; Dustmann, C. (1999), Temporary migration, human capital, and language fluency of migrants. *Scandinavian Journal of Economics, 101*(2), 297–314; Borjas, G. J. (2014), *Immigration Economics* (Cambridge, MA: Harvard University Press); Taylor, E. J. (1999), The new economics of labour migration and the role of remittances in the migration process. *International Migration, 37*(1), 63–88.

64. Crawley, H., & Hagen-Zanker, J. (2019), Deciding where to go: policies, people and perceptions shaping destination preferences. *International Migration, 57*(1),

20–35; Carling, J., & Talleraas, C. (2016), *Root Causes and Drivers of Migration* (Oslo: Peace Research Institute Oslo—PRIO).

65. De Haas, H. (2017), Myths of migration: much of what we think we know is wrong. *Spiegel Online*, 21 March, available at: http://heindehaas.blogspot.com/2017/03/myths-of-migration-much-of-what-we.html

66. Clemens, M. A. (2014), Does development reduce migration? CGD Working Paper No. 359.

67. De Haas, H. (2007), Turning the tide? Why development will not stop migration. *Development and Change*, *38*(5), 819–41; Czaika, M. (2015), Migration and economic prospects. *Journal of Ethnic and Migration Studies*, *41*(1), 58–82; Martin, P. L. (1993), *Trade and Migration: NAFTA and Agriculture* (Washington, DC: Institute for International Economics).

68. Clemens, M. A. (2014), Does development reduce migration? CGD Working Paper No. 359.

69. For some of the analysis that considers that refugee decision-making relating to migration may deviate from standard migration and development accounts, see, for example: Naudé, W. (2010), The determinants of migration from Sub-Saharan African countries. *Journal of African Economies*, *19*(3), 330–56; Dustmann, C., Fasani, F., Frattini, T., Minale, L., & Schönberg, U. (2017), On the economics and politics of refugee migration. *Economic Policy*, *32*(91), 497–550; Ruhe, C., Martin-Shields, C., & Groß, L. M. (2020), The asylum hump: why country income level predicts new asylum seekers, but not new refugees. *Journal of Refugee Studies* (available online).

70. For examples of research that examine migration decision-making on the basis of post-hoc interviews, see, for example: Robinson, V., & Segrott, J. (2002), *Understanding the Decision-Making of Asylum Seekers* (vol. 12) (London: Home Office); Crawley, H. (2010), *Chance or Choice? Understanding why Asylum Seekers Come to the UK* (London: Refugee Council); Crawley, H., Duvell, F., Jones, K., & Skleparis, D. (2016), Understanding the dynamics of migration to Greece and the EU: drivers, decisions and destinations. MEDMIG Research Brief No. 2, available at: http://www.medmig.info/wp-content/uploads/2017/02/research-brief-02-Understanding-the-dynamics-of-migration-to-Greece-and-the-EU.pdf and Hagen-Zanker, J., & Mallett, R. (2016), Journeys to Europe: the role of policy in migrant decision-making. *ODI Insights*, available at: https://www.odi.org/publications/10317-journeys-europe-role-policy-migrant-decision-making

71. Hein de Haas has highlighted this 'receiving-country bias' in migration research. See, for example, De Haas, H. (2011), The determinants of international migration: conceptualizing policy, origin and destination effects. International Migration Institute Working Paper No. 32.

72. Our team's analysis of the data on migration, mobility, and residency is ongoing, and more research is needed to make definitive claims about the relationship between refugee migration and development.

CHAPTER 4

1. Urbanization in Africa is 43 per cent compared to 55 per cent globally.
2. Data taken from UNHCR website for 2020, available at: https://www.unhcr. org/ke/figures-at-a-glance
3. UNHCR (2019), *Global Trends in 2018* (Geneva: UNHCR).
4. See the literature on urban refugees, for example: Jacobsen, K. (2006), Refugees and asylum seekers in urban areas: a livelihoods perspective. *Journal of Refugee Studies*, *19*(3), 273–86; Grabska, K. (2006), Marginalization in urban spaces of the global south: urban refugees in Cairo. *Journal of Refugee Studies*, *19*(3), 287–307; Campbell, E. H. (2006), Urban refugees in Nairobi: problems of protection, mechanisms of survival, and possibilities for integration. *Journal of Refugee Studies*, *19*(3), 396–413; Pavanello, S., Elhawary, S., & Pantuliano, S. (2010), *Hidden and Exposed: Urban Refugees in Nairobi, Kenya* (London: Overseas Development Institute); Landau, L. B. (2014), Urban refugees and IDPs, in Loescher, G. et al. (eds.), *The Oxford Handbook of Refugee and Forced Migration Studies* (Oxford: Oxford University Press).
5. The data and analysis in this section are derived from Betts, A., Fryszer, L., Omata, N., & Sterck, O. (2019), *Refugee Economies in Addis Ababa: Towards Sustainable Opportunities for Urban Communities?* (Oxford: Refugee Studies Centre).
6. Shortly before our research in Addis, Cardiff University and the Danish Refugee Council collaborated on a pioneering study on urban refugee economies in Addis Ababa. See: Brown, A., Mackie, P., Dickenson, K., & Gebre-Egziabher, T. (2018), *Urban Refugee Economies: Addis Ababa, Ethiopia* (London: International Institute for Environment and Development).
7. Carrier, N. C. (2016), *Little Mogadishu: Eastleigh, Nairobi's Global Somali Hub* (Oxford: Oxford University Press).
8. Interviews and data discussed in this section, are drawn partly from Betts, A., Sterck, O., & Omata, N. (2018), *Refugee Economies in Kenya* (Oxford: Refugee Studies Centre).
9. This data is derived from UNHCR, available at: https://www.unhcr.org/ke/ wp-content/uploads/sites/2/2020/05/Kenya-Infographics-30-April-2020–1.pdf
10. This analysis is developed in Betts, A., Bloom, L., Kaplan, J. D., & Omata, N. (2017), *Refugee Economies: Forced Displacement and Development* (Oxford: Oxford University Press).
11. For thoughtful ideas and best practice on urban refugee policy, see, for example, the work of Urban Refugees, founded by Sonia Ben Ali, available at: http:// www.urban-refugees.org

CHAPTER 5

1. BBC (2016), Uganda: 'one of the best places to be a refugee', 16 May, available at: https://www.bbc.co.uk/news/36286472
2. *New York Times* (2018), A new deal for refugees, 21 August, available at: https:// www.nytimes.com/2018/08/21/opinion/refugee-camps-integration.html

Washington Post (2019), Uganda treats refugees better than the United States, 5 July, available at: https://www.washingtonpost.com/opinions/uganda-treats-refugees-better-than-the-united-states-does/2019/07/03/1a246300-9c27-11e9-83e3-45fded8e8d2e_story.html and the *Economist* (2016), Why Uganda is a model for dealing with refugees, 26 October, available at: https://www.economist.com/the-economist-explains/2016/10/25/why-uganda-is-a-model-for-dealing-with-refugees

3. IRRI (2018), *Uganda's Refugee Policies: The History, The Politics, The Way Forward* (Kampala: IRRI); Hovil, L. (2018), The need for a more honest discussion of Uganda's model refugee policies, *Refugees Deeply*, 22 October, available at: https://www.newsdeeply.com/refugees/community/2018/10/22/we-need-a-more-honest-discussion-of-ugandas-model-refugee-policies

4. *Economist* (2018), Refugees need not be a burden if they are allowed to work, 21 August, available at: https://www.economist.com/international/2018/04/21/refugees-need-not-be-a-burden-if-they-are-allowed-to-work

5. The data in this chapter were first published as Betts, A., Chaara, I., Omata, N., & Sterck, O. (2018), *Refugee Economies in Uganda* (Oxford: Refugee Studies Centre), and are based on the contributions of the co-authors to that work.

6. Betts, A., Sterck, O., & Omata, N. (2018), *Refugee Economies in Kenya* (Oxford: Refugee Studies Centre).

7. Betts, A., Sterck, O., & Omata, N. (2018), *Refugee Economies in Kenya* (Oxford: Refugee Studies Centre), 8–10.

8. The Ugandan Refugee Act of 2006 became operational in 2009.

9. For critical analysis of the Ugandan Refugee Act, see Refugee Law Project (2006), *Critique of the Ugandan Refugee Act (2006)* (Kampala: RLP), available at: https://www.refugeelawproject.org/files/legal_resources/Refugees ActRLPCritique.pdf

10. Milner, J. (2009), *Refugees, the State and the Politics of Asylum in Africa* (London: Palgrave Macmillan), 107.

11. The Kenyan Refugee Act (2006), available at: http://kenyalaw.org/kl/fileadmin/pdfdownloads/Acts/RefugeeAct_No13of2006.pdf

12. The Kenyan Refugee Bill (2019), available at: http://www.parliament.go.ke/sites/default/files/2020–05/Refugees%20Bill%2C%202019_compressed%20%281%29_0.pdf

13. The World Bank's International Comparison Program (IPC) tracks annual PPP conversion rates. For example, in 2018, these were 0.49 for Kenya and 0.32 for Uganda (benchmarked against the USA=1). For a strong data visualization of these conversion rates, see https://ourworldindata.org/what-are-ppps. It should also be noted that there are a range of critiques of using PPP for both macroeconomic and microeconomic income comparisons in international development. See, for example, Deaton, A., & Dupriez, O. (2011). Purchasing power parity exchange rates for the global poor. *American Economic Journal: Applied Economics*, 3(2), 137–66.

14. In 2019, the World Bank estimated GDP/capita at PPP of \$4522 in Kenya and \$2284 in Uganda. See: https://data.worldbank.org/indicator/NY.GDP.PCAP.PP.CD

15. All of these figures were calculated by applying PPP exchange rates to reported incomes in the local currency in 2018.

16. For regression table, see Betts, A., Chaara, I., Omata, N., & Sterck, O. (2019), *Refugee Economies in Uganda* (Oxford: Refugee Studies Centre), 39–41.

17. At least at a 90% confidence level.

18. Although the overall weighted average for the camps is reduced greatly to 24 per cent by the 13 per cent unemployment rate among South Sudanese refugees.

19. For Somalis, the comparison is 40 per cent for Kakuma and 5 per cent for Nakivale.

20. This is a direct quote from an anonymous refugee leader. However, given that there is only one UNHCR urban implementing partner, the claim is substantiated by paragraph 17 of UN Internal Audit Division (2018), 'Audit of the Operations in Uganda for the Office of the United Nations High Commissioner for Refugees', OIOS Report No. 2018/097, available at https://oios.un.org/audit-reports

21. Pincock, K., Betts, A., & Easton-Calabria, E. (2020), *The Global Governed? Refugees as Providers of Protection and Assistance* (Cambridge: Cambridge University Press).

CHAPTER 6

1. For existing research on the Kakuma refugee camps, see, for example: Jansen, B. J. (2018), *Kakuma Refugee Camp: Humanitarian Urbanism in Kenya's Accidental City* (London: Zed Books); Jansen, B. J. (2008), Between vulnerability and assertiveness: negotiating resettlement in Kakuma refugee camp, Kenya. *African Affairs*, *107*(429), 569–87; Montclos, M. A. P. D., & Kagwanja, P. M. (2000), Refugee camps or cities? The socio-economic dynamics of the Dadaab and Kakuma camps in northern Kenya. *Journal of Refugee Studies*, *13*(2), 205–22; Alix-Garcia, J., Walker, S., Bartlett, A., Onder, H., & Sanghi, A. (2018), Do refugee camps help or hurt hosts? The case of Kakuma, Kenya. *Journal of Development Economics*, *130*, 66–83; Brankamp, H. (2020), Refugees in uniform: community policing as a technology of government in Kakuma refugee camp, Kenya. *Journal of Eastern African Studies*, *14*(2), 270–90.

2. Details of the Kalobeyei Integrated Socio-Economic Development Plan (KISEDP) are available at: https://www.unhcr.org/ke/wp-content/uploads/sites/2/2018/12/KISEDP_Kalobeyei-Integrated-Socio-Econ-Dev-Programme.pdf

3. The UNHCR Head of Communications said on Al Jazeera in July 2018, 'There is the old part of Kakuma. And then there is the new part, called Kalobeyei. And that's something we really wanted to highlight here. It represents our new approach that is going global to refugee response. And that is that there are settlements being built that are completely integrated with the local community, and where the local community benefits, where we attract international development assistance as well as private investment.'

4. Our research team has subsequently evaluated the impact of the first rollout of unrestricted cash assistance in Kalobeyei. See: Sterck, O., Rodgers, C., Siu, J., Flinder Stierna, M., & Betts, A. (2020), *Cash Transfer Models and Debt in the Kalobeyei Settlement* (Oxford: Refugee Studies Centre).

5. Under a training programme led by the NGO InZone, refugee athletes meet for coaching sessions almost every morning in Kalobeyei.

6. For more on natural experiments, see Dunning, T. (2012), *Natural Experiments in the Social Sciences: A Design-Based Approach* (Cambridge: Cambridge University Press).

7. See in particular: Betts, A., Omata, N., & Sterck, O. (2020), The Kalobeyei settlement: a self-reliance model for refugees? *Journal of Refugee Studies*, *33*(1), 189–223.

8. Others, notably the NGOs RefugePoint and Women's Refugee Commission, have collaborated on trying to develop indicators for self-reliance. See, for example, Beversluis, D., Schoeller-Diaz, D., Anderson, M., Anderson, N., Slaughter, A., & Patel, R. B. (2017), Developing and validating the refugee integration scale in Nairobi, Kenya. *Journal of Refugee Studies*, *30*(1), 106–32; and Leeson, K., Bhandari, P. B., Myers, A., & Buscher, D. (2020), Measuring the self-reliance of refugees. *Journal of Refugee Studies*, *33*(1), 86–106. Our indicators attempt to build on and improve that work, but with a focus on a conceptually grounded definition of 'self-reliance' that can be used for empirical research and retrospective evaluation.

9. Betts, A., Omata, N., & Sterck, O. (2020), The Kalobeyei settlement: a self-reliance model for refugees? *Journal of Refugee Studies*, *33*(1), 189–223.

10. UNHCR (2005), *The Self-Reliance Handbook* (Geneva: UNHCR).

11. See, for example, Leeson, K., Bhandari, P., Myers, A., & Buscher, D. (2020), Measuring the self-reliance of refugees. *Journal of Refugee Studies*, *33*(1): 86–106.

12. Betts, A., Fryszer, L., Omata, N., & Sterck, O. (2019), *Refugee Economies in Addis Ababa: Towards Sustainable Opportunities for Urban Communities?* (Oxford: Refugee Studies Centre).

13. For a review of the literature on the impact of particular types of cash programme in development and humanitarian contexts, see, for example: Bastagli, F., Hagen-Zanker, J., Harman, L., Barca, V., Sturge, G., Schmidt, T., and Pellerano, L. (2016), *Cash Transfers: What Does the Evidence Say? A Rigorous Review of Programme Impact and the Role of Design and Implementation Features* (London: Overseas Development Institute).

14. The research in this section draws upon a series of working papers and articles published by the Refugee Economies Programme. These include: Sterck, O., Rodgers, C., Siu, J., Flinder Stierna, M., & Betts, A. (2020), *Cash Transfer Models and Debt in the Kalobeyei Settlement* (Oxford: Refugee Studies Centre); Betts, A. Delius, A., Rodgers, C. Sterck, O., & Flinder Stierna, M. (2019), *Doing Business in Kakuma: Refugees, Entrepreneurship, and the Food Market* (Oxford: Refugee Studies Centre); MacPherson, C., & Sterck, O. (2019), Humanitarian versus development aid for refugees: evidence from a regression discontinuity

design. CSAE Working Paper No. WPS/2019-15; Delius, A., & Sterck, O. (2020), Cash transfer and micro-enterprise performance: quasi-xperimental evidence from Kenya. SSRN Working Paper.

15. MacPherson, C., & Sterck, O. (2019), Humanitarian versus development aid for refugees: evidence from a regression discontinuity design. CSAE Working Paper WPS/2019-15.

16. MacPherson, C., & Sterck, O. (2019), Humanitarian versus development aid for refugees: evidence from a regression discontinuity design. CSAE Working Paper No. WPS/2019-15, 29-30.

17. Betts, A. Delius, A., Rodgers, C. Sterck, O., & Flinder Stierna, M. (2019), *Doing Business in Kakuma: Refugees, Entrepreneurship, and the Food Market* (Oxford: Refugee Studies Centre); Delius, A., & Sterck, O. (2020), Cash transfer and micro-enterprise performance: quasi-experimental evidence from Kenya. SSRN Working Paper.

18. At the time of our research, there were 190 contracted Bamba Chakula shops in Kakuma and 45 in Kalobeyei, out of a total of 890 food retail shops in Kakuma and 195 in Kalobeyei. We estimated the total value of the food industry across the four camps and settlements based on responses to our business survey, triangulated with additional information provided by international humanitarian organizations.

19. Sterck, O., Rodgers, C., Siu, J., Flinder Stierna, M., & Betts, A. (2020), *Cash Transfer Models and Debt in the Kalobeyei Settlement* (Oxford: Refugee Studies Centre), 12-14.

20. These percentages are calculated without control variables. Calculations that include control variables suggest and even greater percentage point increase in alcohol and tobacco consumption: 7.6 percentage points increase for alcohol instead of 4 percentage points without control variable, and 3.7 percentage points increase for tobacco instead of 2 percentage points without control variables. See Siu, J., Sterck, O., & Rodgers, C. (forthcoming), *The Freedom to Choose: Theory and Quasi-Experimental Evidence on Cash Transfer Restrictions.*

21. Sterck, O., Rodgers, C., Siu, J., Flinder Stierna, M., & Betts, A. (2020), *Cash Transfer Models and Debt in the Kalobeyei Settlement* (Oxford: Refugee Studies Centre), 30.

22. Comment made at public roundtable held at Amnesty International, Nairobi, 6 August 2019.

CHAPTER 7

1. The IKEA Foundation is an independent charitable foundation that owns INGKA Holding (via the INGKA Foundation), which owns and operates 90 per cent of the IKEA stores worldwide. These two entities, however, have separate governance arrangements and the company has no influence on Foundation grant making. However, the Foundation and the company often work together on common issues such as climate change and refugees, sometimes based on the Foundation laying the groundwork for subsequent company involvement.

2. The underlying research for this chapter relates to two published reports: Betts, A., Bradenbrink, R., Greenland, J., Omata, N., & Sterck, O. (2019), *Refugee Economies in Dollo Ado: Development Opportunities in a Border Region of Ethiopia* (Oxford: Refugee Studies Centre); Betts, A., Marden, A., Bredenbrink, R., & Kaufmann, J. (2020), *Building Refugee Economies: An Evaluation of the IKEA Foundation's Programmes in Dollo Ado* (Oxford: Refugee Studies Centre).

3. E-mail correspondence with Per Heggenes, 27 September 2020.

4. Currency conversions in this chapter are based on $1 = 50 ETB, based on the October 2020 exchange rate.

5. Betts, A., Marden, A., Bredenbrink, R., & Kaufmann, J. (2020), *Building Refugee Economies: An Evaluation of the IKEA Foundation's Programmes in Dollo Ado* (Oxford: Refugee Studies Centre), 51–70.

6. Betts, A., Marden, A., Bredenbrink, R., & Kaufmann, J. (2020), *Building Refugee Economies: An Evaluation of the IKEA Foundation's Programmes in Dollo Ado* (Oxford: Refugee Studies Centre), 68.

7. Betts, A., Bradenbrink, R., Greenland, J., Omata, N., & Sterck, O. (2019), *Refugee Economies in Dollo Ado: Development Opportunities in a Border Region of Ethiopia* (Oxford: Refugee Studies Centre).

8. Betts, A., Marden, A., Bredenbrink, R., & Kaufmann, J. (2020), *Building Refugee Economies: An Evaluation of the IKEA Foundation's Programmes in Dollo Ado* (Oxford: Refugee Studies Centre), 85–94.

9. Betts, A., Bradenbrink, R., Greenland, J., Omata, N., & Sterck, O. (2019), *Refugee Economies in Dollo Ado: Development Opportunities in a Border Region of Ethiopia* (Oxford: Refugee Studies Centre).

CHAPTER 8

1. Zetter, R., & Ruaudel, H. (2016), Refugees' right to work and access to labor markets: an assessment. KNOMAD Working Paper.

2. Evidence of the positive relationship between employment and psychosocial wellbeing can be found in, for example: McKee-Ryan, F., Song, Z., Wanberg, C. R., & Kinicki, A. J. (2005), Psychological and physical well-being during unemployment: a meta-analytic study. *Journal of Applied Psychology, 90*(1), 53–76; Aycan, Z., & Berry, J. W. (1996), Impact of employment-related experiences on immigrants' psychological well-being and adaptation to Canada. *Canadian Journal of Behavioural Science, 28*(3), 240; Goldsmith, A. H., Veum, J. R., & Darity Jr, W. (1997), The impact of psychological and human capital on wages. *Economic Inquiry, 35*(4), 815–29; Witte, H. D. (1999), Job insecurity and psychological well-being: review of the literature and exploration of some unresolved issues. *European Journal of Work and Organizational Psychology, 8*(2), 155–77; Arnold, K. A., Turner, N., Barling, J., Kelloway, E. K., & McKee, M. C. (2007), Transformational leadership and psychological well-being: the mediating role of meaningful work. *Journal of Occupational Health Psychology, 12*(3), 193.

3. Evidence of the relationship between employment and refugees' psychosocial wellbeing can be found in, for example: Beiser, M., Johnson, P. J., & Turner, R. J. (1993), Unemployment, underemployment and depressive affect among Southeast Asian refugees. *Psychological Medicine*, *23*(3), 731–43; Ryan, D., Dooley, B., & Benson, C. (2008), Theoretical perspectives on post-migration adaptation and psychological well-being among refugees: towards a resource-based model. *Journal of Refugee Studies*, *21*(1), 1–18; Warfa, N., Curtis, S., Watters, C., Carswell, K., Ingleby, D., & Bhui, K. (2012), Migration experiences, employment status and psychological distress among Somali immigrants: a mixed-method international study. *BMC Public Health*, *12*(1), 749.

4. For the harmful effects of protracted refugee situations, see: Harrell-Bond, B. E. (1986), *Imposing Aid: Emergency Assistance to Refugees* (Oxford: Oxford University Press); Loescher, G., & Milner, J. H. (2005), Protracted refugee situations: domestic and international security implications. Adelphi Working Paper No. 375; Crisp, J. (2003), No solution in sight: the problem of protracted refugee situations in Africa. UNHCR Working Paper.

5. Jacobsen, K. (2005), *The Economic Life of Refugees* (Bloomfield, CT: Kumarian Press); Werker, E. (2007), Refugee camp economies. *Journal of Refugee Studies*, *20*(3), 461–80.

6. For work on refugees and security, see: Greenhill, K. M. (2010), *Weapons of Mass Migration: Forced Displacement, Coercion, and Foreign Policy* (Ithaca, NY: Cornell University Press); Lischer, S. K. (2005), *Dangerous Sanctuaries: Refugee Camps, Civil War, and the Dilemmas of Humanitarian Aid* (Ithaca, NY: Cornell University Press); Salehyan, I. (2008), The externalities of civil strife: refugees as a source of international conflict. *American Journal of Political Science*, *52*(4), 787–801; Hammerstad, A. (2014), *The Rise and Decline of a Global Security Actor: UNHCR, Refugee Protection, and Security* (Oxford: Oxford University Press).

7. For work on refugees and international cooperation, see: Loescher, G. (2001), *The UNHCR and World Politics: A Perilous Path* (Oxford: Oxford University Press); Orchard, P. (2014), *A Right to Flee* (Cambridge: Cambridge University Press); Haddad, E. (2008), *The Refugee in International Society: Between Sovereigns* (Cambridge: Cambridge University Press).

8. For comparative politics literature on refugees, see: FitzGerald, D. S. (2019), *Refuge Beyond Reach: How Rich Democracies Repel Asylum Seekers* (Oxford: Oxford University Press); Hamlin, R. (2014), *Let Me Be a Refugee: Administrative Justice and the Politics of Asylum in the United States, Canada, and Australia* (Oxford: Oxford University Press); Milner, J. (2009), *Refugees, the State and the Politics of Asylum in Africa* (Basingstoke: Palgrave Macmillan).

9. The so-called 'burden-sharing' literature has focused particularly on what explains states' willingness to contribute financially to the work of the global refugee regime. See, for example: Thielemann, E. R. (2003), Between interests and norms: explaining burden-sharing in the European Union. *Journal of Refugee Studies*, *16*(3), 253–73; Roper, S. D., & Barria, L. A. (2010), Burden sharing in the funding of the UNHCR: refugee protection as an impure public good'. *Journal*

of Conflict Resolution, *54*(4), 616–37; Suhrke, A. (1998), Burden-sharing during refugee emergencies: the logic of collective versus national action. *Journal of Refugee Studies*, *11*(4), 396–415.

10. There is strikingly little research on the politics of refugee resettlement. A notable exception is Garnier, A., Jubilut, L. L., & Sandvik, K. B. (eds). (2018), *Refugee Resettlement: Power, Politics, and Humanitarian Governance* (Oxford: Berghahn Books).

11. For research explaining variation in states' admissions policies, see, for example: Ivarsflaten, E. (2005), Threatened by diversity: why restrictive asylum and immigration policies appeal to Western Europeans. *Journal of Elections, Public Opinion & Parties*, *15*(1), 21–45; Zaun, N. (2018), States as gatekeepers in EU asylum politics: explaining the non-adoption of a refugee quota system. *JCMS: Journal of Common Market Studies*, *56*(1), 44–62; Steele, L. G., & Abdelaaty, L. (2019), Ethnic diversity and attitudes towards refugees. *Journal of Ethnic and Migration Studies*, *45*(11), 1833–56; Hatton, T. J. (2016), Refugees, asylum seekers, and policy in OECD countries. *American Economic Review*, *106*(5), 441–5.

12. See, for example, Tsourapas, G. (2019), *The Politics of Egyptian Migration to Libya* (Cambridge: Cambridge University Press); Milner, J. (2009), *Refugees, the State and the Politics of Asylum in Africa* (Basingstoke: Palgrave Macmillan); Abdelaaty, L. (2021), *Discrimination and Delegation: Explaining State Responses to Refugees* (New York: Oxford University Press).

13. Türk, V., & Garlick, M. (2016), From burdens and responsibilities to opportunities: the comprehensive refugee response framework and a global compact on refugees. *International Journal of Refugee Law*, *28*(4), 656–78.

14. For work on the role of issue-linkage in the politics of refugees and migration, see: Paoletti, E. (2010), *The Migration of Power and North–South Inequalities: The Case of Italy and Libya* (Basingstoke: Palgrave Macmillan); Betts, A. (2009), *Protection by Persuasion: International Cooperation in the Refugee Regime* (Ithaca, NY: Cornell University Press); Tsourapas, G. (2017), Migration diplomacy in the Global South: cooperation, coercion and issue-linkage in Gaddafi's Libya. *Third World Quarterly*, *38*(10), 2367–85.

15. I argue that although 'North' and 'South' are problematic oversimplifications, they offer a useful heuristic framework for capturing donor–host interaction with the history of the refugee regime. See Betts, A. (2009), *Protection by Persuasion: International Cooperation in the Refugee Regime* (Ithaca, NY: Cornell University Press).

16. For research on the local politics of forced displacement, see: Schmidt, A. (2014), Status determination and recognition, in Betts, A., & Orchard, P. (eds.), *Implementation and World Politics: How International Norms Change Practice* (Oxford: Oxford University Press), 248–68; Orchard, P. (2014), Implementing a global internally displaced persons protection regime, in Betts, A., & Orchard, P. (eds.), *Implementation and World Politics: How International Norms Change Practice* (Oxford: Oxford University Press), 105–23.

17. Milner, J. (2009), *Refugees, the State and the Politics of Asylum in Africa* (Basingstoke: Palgrave Macmillan).

18. Foster, M. (2007), *International Refugee Law and Socio-Economic Rights: Refuge from Deprivation* (Cambridge: Cambridge University Press), 156.

19. Whether the impasse was best represented by a Deadlock Game, Prisoner's Dilemma, or Rambo Game would depend on assumptions about the preferences of the two actors. Suhrke, A. (1998), Burden-sharing during refugee emergencies: the logic of collective versus national action. *Journal of Refugee Studies*, 11(4), 396–415, uses Prisoner's Dilemma to capture the tendency towards free-riding and sub-optimal provision of refugee protection within the international refugee regime; Betts, A. (2009), *Protection by Persuasion: International Cooperation in the Refugee Regime* (Ithaca, NY: Cornell University Press) uses a Rambo (or Suasion Game) to capture the power asymmetry between 'Northern' donors and 'Southern' hosts. A Deadlock Game assumes instead that there is under-provision because it serves the interests of both actors within the game.

20. For international relations research on the role of issue-linkage in international cooperation, see: Haas, E. B. (1980), Why collaborate? Issue-linkage and international regimes. *World Politics*, 32(3), 357–405; Odell, J. S. (2009), Breaking deadlocks in international institutional negotiations: the WTO, Seattle, and Doha. *International Studies Quarterly*, 53(2), 273–99; Davis, C. L. (2004), International institutions and issue-linkage: building support for agricultural trade liberalization. *American Political Science Review*, 98(1), 153–69.

21. Austria (2018), Vision paper: creating a better protection system for a globalised world. Paper presented at the EMN Austria Meeting, Vienna, 4 October.

22. For analysis of the European Union Trust Fund for Africa (EUTF), see: Zanker, F. (2019), Managing or restricting movement? Diverging approaches of African and European migration governance. *Comparative Migration Studies*, 7(1), 1–18.

23. Paoletti, E. (2010), *The Migration of Power and North–South Inequalities: The Case of Italy and Libya* (Basingstoke: Palgrave Macmillan).

24. Tsourapas, G. (2019), *The Politics of Egyptian Migration to Libya* (Cambridge: Cambridge University Press).

25. Betts, A. (2009), *Protection by Persuasion: International Cooperation in the Refugee Regime* (Ithaca, NY: Cornell University Press).

26. Putnam, R. D. (1988), Diplomacy and domestic politics: the logic of two-level games. *International Organization*, 42(1), 427–60.

27. Putnam, R. D. (1988), Diplomacy and domestic politics: the logic of two-level games. *International Organization*, 42(1), 432.

28. Putnam, R. D. (1988), Diplomacy and domestic politics: the logic of two-level games. *International Organization*, 42(1), 436.

29. Moravcsik, A. (2013), *The Choice for Europe: Social Purpose and State Power from Messina to Maastricht* (Abingdon: Routledge).

30. Schickler, E. (2016), *Racial Realignment: The Transformation of American Liberalism, 1932–1965* (Princeton, NJ: Princeton University Press).

31. Krasner, S. (1999), *Sovereignty: Organized Hypocrisy* (Princeton, NJ: Princeton University Press).

32. The 'African state' is reductivist as an account of the complexity and diversity of African politics. However, it has been widely used to identify some common analytical features of post-colonial states in Sub-Saharan Africa. See: Herbst, J. (2014), *States and Power in Africa: Comparative Lessons in Authority and Control* (Princeton, NJ: Princeton University Press); Clapham, C. (1996), *Africa and the International System: The Politics of State Survival* (Cambridge: Cambridge University Press); Jackson, R. (1991), *Quasi-States: Sovereignty, International Relations and the Third World* (Cambridge: Cambridge University Press).

33. Clapham, C. (1996), *Africa and the International System: The Politics of State Survival* (Cambridge: Cambridge University Press).

34. Milner, J. (2009), *Refugees, the State and the Politics of Asylum in Africa* (Basingstoke: Palgrave Macmillan).

35. Bayart, J. F., & Ellis, S. (2000), Africa in the world: a history of extraversion. *African Affairs, 99*(395), 217–67.

36. See, for example, Betts, A. (2009), *Protection by Persuasion: International Cooperation in the Refugee Regime* (Ithaca, NY: Cornell University Press).

37. In 2019, for example, the AU organized a series of events to celebrate and commemorate its role in relation to forced displacement, including in relation to the 1969 Organisation of African Union (OAU) Refugee Convention and the 2009 AU Convention on Internally Displaced Persons.

38. For an overview of IGAD's role in relation to forced displacement, see for example: Hopkins, G. and Buffoni, L. (2019), The IGAD Kampala Declaration on jobs, livelihoods, and self-reliance: from declaration to reality. *Palgrave Communications,* 157, available at https://doi.org/10.1057/s41599-019-0370-2

39. At the time of writing, this research is at a preliminary stage, and is in draft form as Betts, A. and Sterck, O. (2020), Bargains of inclusion: why some states give refugees the right to work. Draft paper.

40. Mhalanga, J. (2020), Refugee protection in the era of complex migratory flows: a reflection on ubuntu and social work practice. *African Journal of Social Work, 10*(1):41-5.

CHAPTER 9

1. Betts, A., Chaara, I., Omata, N., & Sterck, O. (2018), *Refugee Economies in Uganda* (Oxford: Refugee Studies Centre).

2. For research on the strengths and limitations of Uganda's approach to refugee assistance, see: Kaiser, T. (2005), Participating in development? Refugee protection, politics and developmental approaches to refugee management in Uganda. *Third World Quarterly, 26*(2), 351–67; Kaiser, T. (2006), Between a camp and a hard place: rights, livelihood and experiences of the local settlement system for

long-term refugees in Uganda. *The Journal of Modern African Studies, 4,* 597–621; Dryden-Peterson, S., & Hovil, L. (2004), A remaining hope for durable solutions: local integration of refugees and their hosts in the case of Uganda. *Refuge: Canada's Journal on Refugees, 22*(1), 26–38; Merkx, J. (2000), Refugee identities and relief in an African borderland: a study of Northern Uganda and Southern Sudan. *Refugee Survey Quarterly, 21*(1), 113–46; Hovil, L. (2007), Self-settled refugees in Uganda: an alternative approach to displacement? *Journal of Refugee Studies, 20*(4), 599–62.

3. See, for example: Dolan, C. (2009), *Social Torture: The Case of Northern Uganda, 1986–2006* (Oxford: Berghahn Books); Nabuguzi, E. (1993), Peasant response to economic crisis in Uganda: rice farmers in Busoga. *Review of African Political Economy, 20*(56), 53–67; Karugire, S. R. (2010), *A Political History of Uganda* (Kampala: Fountain Publishers).

4. The work of Gerasimos Tsourapas is especially instructive on the role of 'rentier states' in refugee politics. See, for example: Tsourapas, G. (2019), The Syrian refugee crisis and foreign policy decision-making in Jordan, Lebanon, and Turkey. *Journal of Global Security Studies, 4*(4), 464–81; Tsourapas, G. (2018), *The Politics of Migration in Modern Egypt: Strategies for Regime Survival in Autocracies* (Cambridge: Cambridge University Press).

5. Bayart, J. F., & Ellis, S. (2000), Africa in the world: a history of extraversion. *African Affairs, 99*(395), 217–67.

6. For research on Ugandan politics, see, for example: Green, E. (2008), Decentralisation and conflict in Uganda. *Conflict, Security & Development, 8*(4), 427–50; Green, E. (2010), Patronage, district creation, and reform in Uganda. *Studies in Comparative International Development, 45*(1), 83–103; Tangri, R., & Mwenda, A. M. (2003), Military corruption & Ugandan politics since the late 1990s. *Review of African Political Economy, 98,* 539–52; Oloka-Onyango, J., & and Barya, J. J. (1997), Civil society and the political economy of foreign aid in Uganda. *Democratization, 4*(2), 113–38.

7. UNHCR Archives (1968), Triumph for Uganda's refugee policy, *The People,* 26 September.

8. UNHCR Archives (1967), 10C/Box 4/ARC 2B4, HC welcomes Uganda as 31st member of Excom, Background Paper for President's Meeting with HC, Prince Sadruddin Aga Khan, 8 November.

9. UNHCR Archives (1964), 10c Box-4 ARC 2B4, 12th session of ExCom, 22–30 October (Rome).

10. UNHCR Archives (1964), 10c Box-4 ARC 2B4, 12th session of ExCom, 22–30 October (Rome).

11. UNHCR Archives (1968), 11/1/Box 324 (21/UGA/RWA), A meeting with the Uganda delegates to the executive committee, 28 October.

12. UNHCR Archives (1967), 10C/Box 4/ARC 2B4, HC welcomes Uganda as 31st member of Excom, Background Paper for President's Meeting with HC, Prince Sadruddin Aga Khan, 8 November.

13. UNHCR Archives (1969), 11/1/Box 76, Agreement between the government of the Republic of Uganda and UNHCR concerning the establishment of a branch office of UNHCR in Uganda, 7 February.

14. UNHCR Archives (1967), 10C/Box 4/ARC 2B4, HC welcomes Uganda as 31st member of Excom, Background Paper for President's Meeting with HC, Prince Sadruddin Aga Khan, 8 November.

15. UNHCR Archives (1969), 11/1/Box 76, Agreement between the government of the Republic of Uganda and UNHCR concerning the establishment of a branch office of UNHCR in Uganda, 7 February.

16. UNHCR Archives (1971), Uganda army faction ousts President Obote, *Washington Post*, 26 January.

17. UNHCR Archives (1973), Fonds 11/2 Box 203, Amin says refugees must leave Uganda, *Daily Nation*, 21 June.

18. UNHCR Archives (1972), HC Aga Khan letter to Minister of Foreign Affairs, Wanume Kibedi, 20 August.

19. UNHCR Archives (1972), HC Aga Khan letter to Minister of Foreign Affairs, Wanume Kibedi, 20 August.

20. UNHCR Archives (1975), Situation of Ugandans of mixed racial background, R. Seeger (Regional Protection Officer to the Rep, Kenya), 15 April.

21. UNHCR Archives (1977), Amin acknowledges mutiny in his army, *NY Times*, 24 February.

22. *Voice of Uganda* (1977), (Rep to HC): UNHCR rep and Amin meet at Cape Town View, 30 June.

23. *Voice of Uganda* (1977), (Rep to HC): UNHCR rep and Amin meet at Cape Town View, 30 June.

24. UNHCR Archives (1978), Report on a meeting with officials from the Ministry of Culture and Community Development, 7 March.

25. UNHCR Archives (1979), Uganda Report on UNHCR Activities 1979.

26. UNHCR Archives (1978), Report on a meeting with officials from the Ministry of Culture and Community Development, 7 March.

27. For example, he appointed Justus Byagagire and Raphael Nshekanablo to Ministerial positions, and John Bunyenyezi to a military leadership position. Nigaahe (2017), Kigezi ethnicity, 19 May, available at: https://medium.com/@nigaahe/kigezi-ethnicity-280ec99aec1c

28. UNHCR Archives (1980), *Guardian*, 26 November.

29. UNHCR Archives (1980), *The Times*, 9 December.

30. UNHCR Archives (1983), 11/3 Series 2 Box-730, Guy Prim (RBA) to Paul Shears (Oxfam), 22 February.

31. UNHCR Archives (1983–4), 11:3 Series 2 Box 333, 110, UGA—Programming Uganda (vol. 13), Submission for funding of the special programme for the relief and rehabilitation of returnees and the reconstruction of public infrastructure in the West Nile Province of Uganda—1983.

32. UNHCR Archives (1979), Mission to Kyaka, Kahunge, and Rwamwanja, From Lundgren to HC, 6/3; UNHCR Archives (1979), 100.UGA.RWA.624.UGA,

Meetings on the security situation of refugees in Uganda living in the area of the Tanzanian/Ugandan border, 22 February.

33. UNHCR Archives (1979), 100.UGA.RWA.624.UGA, Meetings on the security situation of refugees in Uganda living in the area of the Tanzanian/Ugandan border, 22 February.

34. UNHCR Archives (1981), Note for the file: Rwandese in Uganda, Michael Moller, 26 March.

35. UNHCR Archives (1979), 100, UGA-RWA—79/AP/UGA/ED/1, M. H. Lundgren to HC, Re: statement by Rwandese Refugee Student Association, 5 July.

36. UNHCR Archives (1981), 11/2/Box 205, T. M. Unwin (Rep) to R. Kalberger (RBA), Meeting with Min Muwanga, 6 May.

37. The Report on the Visit of the Hon. Patrick Mwondha, Deputy Min of Local Administration, to Bundibugyo District (prepared by Peter Matovu, UNHCR Snr Counselling Officer), 15 April 1981.

38. Across seven settlements, hosting around 41,000 of Uganda's 113,000 refugees—Oruchinga (11,000), Nakivale (16,000), Ibuga (4,500), Kyaka (5000), Rwamwanja (4,320), Kyangwali (6,100), and Kahunge (7,050)—Uganda submitted requests totalling $144,000. In addition, much larger requests were submitted to 'support the government's comprehensive rehabilitation and development programme' and address 'wear and tear, deterioration by war, and economic collapse since 1971'. These requests included 'repair of boreholes for provision of water to enable integration of refugees' for $971,000 and 'infrastructure support around settlement, especially roads' for $1.3 million.

39. UNHCR Archives, Discussion with Amis Bireke-Kaggwa, D-Dir, Refugees MCCD (T. M. Unwin—Rep).

40. UNHCR Archives, Discussion with Amis Bireke-Kaggwa, D-Dir, Refugees MCCD (T. M. Unwin—Rep).

41. UNHCR Archives (1982–3), Fonds 11: 2 Box 333 110, UGA Programming Uganda (vol. 11).

42. UNHCR Archives (1982), Mission to Mbarara District, 21–2 October, Patrick de Sousa, Amdin, Programme Officer, 26 October.

43. Those Banyarwanda forced to flee included the family of the Speaker of the National Assembly, Francis Butagira and the Bishop of Ankole, Bishop Shalita. *Uganda Pilot* (1982), Habyarimana appeals for aid, 21 October.

44. UNHCR Archives (1983), 28/11/83: Netherlands to UNHCR, UNHCR: Establishment of Kyaka II Settlement in Uganda.

45. UNHCR Archives (1983), 28/11/83: Netherlands to UNHCR, UNHCR: Establishment of Kyaka II Settlement in Uganda.

46. UNHCR Archives (1989), Chipman (RBA) to Kpenou (RBA) 'DHC's Mission to Uganda, 18–19 May.

47. UNHCR Archives (1987), the areas Deforestation of land in and around Oruchinga and Nakivale (UNHCR Study 1987 w/local government and Swedish funding).

48. UNHCR Archives (1989), DHC visits Uganda: DS for Rwandese; plans for West Nile Chipman (RBA) to Kpenou (RBA) 'DHC's Mission to Uganda, 18–19 May.

49. UNHCR Archives (1989), Fonds 11/3 ARC-2F3, Mr W. Young Rep to Arthur Dewey, DHC, on meeting with Museveni, 6 June.

50. UNHCR Archives (1989), Fonds 11/3 ARC-2F3, Mr W. Young Rep to Arthur Dewey, DHC, on meeting with Museveni, 6 June.

51. UNHCR Archives (1989), DHC visits Uganda, Chipman (RBA) to Kpenou (RBA), DHC's mission to Uganda, Detailed briefing notes, 18–19 May.

52. UNHCR Archives (1986), 768.ITA, 13 September.

53. UNHCR Archives (1989), DHC visits Uganda, Chipman (RBA) to Kpenou (RBA), DHC's mission to Uganda, Detailed briefing notes, 18–19 May; Dewey meeting with Museveni, 18 May.

54. UNHCR Archives (1990), Phelps (RBA) to Chipman (Head RBA), Relocation of 54,000 Sudanese refugees currently in N. Uganda, Purpose: Adjumani-Pakelle Area/examine security situation, 14 March.

55. UNHCR Archives (1991), Farah to Head Desk RBA, Note to the file: mission to southwestern Uganda, Mission: 21–3 November 1991, Purpose: monitor situation at Rwanda/Zairean borders, 4 December.

56. UNHCR Archives (1994), 11/3 001.UGA, A. S. Farah (Rep) to P. Meijer, Desk RBO, Transfer of Koboko caseload: Kyangwali mission report, 24 January.

57. UNHCR Archives (1994), 11/3 001.UGA, A. S. Farah (Rep) to P. Meijer, Desk RBO, Transfer of Koboko caseload: Kyangwali mission report, 24 January.

58. 148,000 refugees were in Pakelle; 94,000 in Koboko; 11,000 in Ifake; 3,100 in Palorinya; and 5,000 in Rhino Camp.

59. UNHCR Archives (1994), Uganda–Sudan relations: long history of hostility, New Vision, 22 August.

60. UNHCR Archives (1994), Sitrep, August.

61. UNHCR Archives (1994), New Vision, 2 September.

62. UNHCR Archives (1990), Weekly Topic: Rwandese refugee army overruns garrisons, 12 October.

63. UNHCR Archives (1991), New Vision, Rwanda alleges attack, 3 October.

64. UNHCR Archives (1994), 0.25 UGA, Sitrep, September.

65. UNHCR Archives (1994), 0.25 UGA, Sitrep, 25 November to 2 December.

66. UNHCR (2003), *Self-Reliance Strategy Mid-Term Review* (Geneva: UNHCR).

67. UNHCR (2003), *Self-Reliance Strategy Mid-Term Review* (Geneva: UNHCR).

68. Interviews with UNHCR staff involved in the policy process, Geneva, March 2019.

69. Interviews, Kampala, February 2019.

70. Interviews, Kampala, February 2019.

71. Interviews, Kampala, February 2019.

72. Interviews, Kampala, February 2019.

73. UN Internal Audit Division (2018), 'Audit of the Operations in Uganda for the Office of the United Nations High Commissioner for Refugees', OIOS Report No. 2018/097, available at https://oios.un.org/audit-reports.

74. This example is detailed in paragraph 67 of the OIOS report.

75. UNHCR Archives (1993), Refugees fight UNHCR over 'Museveni money', *The Monitor*, 15 October.
76. Interviews, Kampala, February 2019.
77. Interviews, Kampala, February 2019.

CHAPTER 10

1. Interviews in this chapter were conducted in Kakuma refugee camp, Nairobi, and Lodwar, Kenya, in July and August 2019.
2. Turkana County Roundtable on the integration of refugee and host community economies, co-organized by UNHCR and the World Bank on 26–8 November 2014, in Lodwar, Turkana County, Meeting Note.
3. Turkana County Roundtable on the integration of refugee and host community economies, co-organized by UNHCR and the World Bank on 26–8 November 2014, in Lodwar, Turkana County, Meeting Note.
4. Turkana County Roundtable on the integration of refugee and host community economies, co-organized by UNHCR and the World Bank on 26–8 November 2014, in Lodwar, Turkana County, Meeting Note.
5. Turkana County Roundtable on the integration of refugee and host community economies, co-organized by UNHCR and the World Bank on 26–8 November 2014, in Lodwar, Turkana County, Meeting Note.
6. Turkana County Roundtable on the integration of refugee and host community economies, co-organized by UNHCR and the World Bank on 26–8 November 2014, in Lodwar, Turkana County, Meeting Note.
7. Turkana initiative: Kalobeyei Integrated Socio-Economic Development Programme (KISEDP), Concept Note, 2014.
8. Interviews conducted on Lodwar, Turkana County, July and August 2019.
9. Turkana County Roundtable on the integration of refugee and host community economies, co-organized by UNHCR and the World Bank on 26–8 November 2014, in Lodwar, Turkana County, Meeting Note.
10. World Bank (2017), *'Yes in My Backyard?': The Economics of Refugees and Their Social Dynamics in Kakuma, Kenya* (Washington, DC: World Bank Group).
11. EU (2016), *Regional Development and Protection Programme in Kenya: Support to the Kalobeyei Development Programme* (Brussels: European Commission), available at: https://ec.europa.eu/trustfundforafrica/region/horn-africa/kenya/regional-development-and-protection-programme-kenya-support-kalobeyei_en
12. Get to know refugees: their capabilities and contribution to the local economy, Nairobi, Meeting Note, 21 June 2017.
13. International Finance Corporation (2018), *Kakuma as a Marketplace: A Consumer and Market Study of a Refugee Camp and Town in Northwest Kenya* (Washington, DC: International Finance Corporation).
14. The fully revised KISEDP strategy document is available at: https://www.unhcr.org/ke/wp-content/uploads/sites/2/2018/12/KISEDP_Kalobeyei-Integrated-Socio-Econ-Dev-Programme.pdf

15. Transparency International (2019), Corruption perceptions index, available at: https://www.transparency.org/en/cpi#

16. The auditors' reports are in the public domain, available at: https://www.turkana.go.ke/index.php/documents/turkana-ce-audit-report-2017_18-pdf/

17. In September 2019, Kenya's *Citizen Weekly* included Nanok in a list of ten country governors allegedly accused by the Kenyan Revenue Authority of corruption and tax evasion. *Citizen Weekly* (2019), Revealed: 10 governors in tax evasion probe, 3 September, available at https://weeklycitizen.co.ke/revealed-10-governors-in-tax-evasion-probe

18. Kenya Refugee Bill (2019), available at: http://www.parliament.go.ke/sites/default/files/2020-05/Refugees%20Bill%2C%202019_compressed%20%281%29_0.pdf

19. Statement to forum on: Development-based approaches to refugee assistance, Nairobi, 4 August 2018.

20. In collaboration with the World Food Programme, we collected data in two waves from recently arrived South Sudanese refugees in both Kakuma and Kalobeyei, and conducted follow-up attrition surveys to identify the reasons why people who could not be found during the second wave had left. See: Betts, A., Omata, N., Rodgers, C., Sterck, O., & Flinder Stierna, M (2019), *The Kalobeyei Model: Towards Self-Reliance for Refugees* (Oxford: Refugee Studies Centre).

21. Comment made during public roundtable discussion, Rift Valley Institute, Nairobi, 6 August 2019.

22. Information based on private correspondence with UNHCR staff.

CHAPTER II

1. The UN High Commissioner for Refugees, Filippo Grandi, made this statement on 20 June 2017 during a visit to Ethiopia to mark World Refugee Day.

2. Refugee Proclamation (No. 409/2004).

3. Refugee Proclamation (No. 1011/2019).

4. Campbell, E. (2017), The US Leaders' Summit on Refugees: outcomes and lessons learned, delivered at 'Beyond Crisis: Rethinking Refugee Studies', Keble College, Oxford, 16–17 March.

5. For an overview of the '9 Pledges', see: UNHCR (2018), *Comprehensive Refugee Response Framework (CRRF) Ethiopia—Briefing Note* (Addis Ababa: UNHCR), available at: https://data2.unhcr.org/en/documents/download/65916

6. The number of IDPs in Ethiopia peaked at around 3 million in 2018 and subsequently fell to around 2 million in 2019, including people displaced by both conflict and disaster. Several human rights reports have drawn attention to the poor treatment of IDPs both by non-state armed actors and the government. See, for example, US State Department (2018), 'Ethiopia Country Reports on Human Rights Practices' (Washington DC: US State

Department), pp. 20–21. Available at: https://www.state.gov/wp-content/ uploads/2019/03/Ethiopia-2018.pdf

7. Campbell, E. (2017), The US Leaders' Summit on Refugees: outcomes and lessons learned, delivered at 'Beyond Crisis: Rethinking Refugee Studies', Keble College, Oxford, 16–17 March.

8. This interview was conducted with a senior member of UN staff in Addis Ababa in March 2019. At the time Abiy was perceived in a very positive light by the international community. He would go on to be awarded the Nobel Peace Prize later that year. In was only by late 2020, with conflict in Tigray, that Abiy began to overtly obstruct requests by the international community.

9. See, for example: https://ethsat.com/2019/01/ethiopia-refugee-law-faces-backlash/

CHAPTER 12

1. For discussion of the 'last mile' in humanitarianism, see Balcik, B., Beamon, B. M., & Smilowitz, K. (2008), Last-mile distribution in humanitarian relief. *Journal of Intelligent Transportation Systems, 12*(2), 51–63.

2. See Last Mile Health, available at: https://lastmilehealth.org

3. Vemeru, V. et al. (2020), *From Isolation to Integration: The Borderlands of the Horn of Africa* (Washington, DC: World Bank), available at: http://documents.world-bank.org/curated/en/167291585597407280/The-Borderlands-of-the-Horn-of-Africa.

4. Bird, K., Hulme, D., Moore, K., & Shepherd, A. (2002), Chronic poverty and remote rural areas. ODI Working Paper No. 13.

5. Copus, A. K., & Crabtree, J. R. (1996), Indicators of socio-economic sustainability: an application to remote rural Scotland. *Journal of Rural Studies, 12*(1), 41–54; Altman, J., Buchanan, G., & Larsen, L. (2007), *The Environmental Significance of the Indigenous Estate: Natural Resource Management as Economic Development in Remote Australia* (Canberra: Centre for Aboriginal Economic Policy Research (CAEPR), The Australian National University); Goldsmith, S. (1990), Understanding Alaska's remote rural economy, *Population, 2000*, 411–94.

6. Kitchen, H., & Slack, E. (2006), Providing public services in remote area'. In Bird, R., & Vaillancourt, F. (eds), *Perspectives on Fiscal Federalism* (Washington, DC: World Bank), 123–39.

7. Rodríguez-Pose, A., & Tijmstra, S. (2005), *Local Economic Development as an Alternative Approach to Economic Development in Sub-Saharan Africa.* A report for the World Bank (London: LSE), available at: http://knowledge.uclga.org/IMG/pdf/ledn_sub-saharan_africa.pdf

8. Bird, K., Hulme, D., Moore, K., & Shepherd, A. (2002), Chronic poverty and remote rural areas. ODI Working Paper No. 13.

9. Patterson, C. (2008), Country report: local economic development in South Africa. Prepared for the GTZ strengthening local governance programme's

LED component in South Africa, available at: http://knowledge.uclga.org/ IMG/pdf/country_report_led_in_south_africa.pdf

10. Rodríguez-Pose, A., & Tijmstra, S. (2005), *Local Economic Development as an Alternative Approach to Economic Development in Sub-Saharan Africa.* A report for the World Bank (London: LSE), available at: http://knowledge.uclga.org/ IMG/pdf/ledn_sub-saharan_africa.pdf

11. San Andres, E. (2019), *Unlocking the Economies Potential of Remote Areas* (Singapore: APEC), available at: https://www.apec.org.au/remote-areas-development

12. APEC (2018), *Development and Integration of Remote Areas in the APEC Region* (Singapore: APEC), available at: https://www.apec.org/Publications/2018/11/ Development-and-Integration-of-Remote-Areas-in-the-APEC-Region

13. Andersson, R. (2014), *Illegality, Inc.: Clandestine Migration and the Business of Bordering Europe* (Oakland, CA: University of California Press).

14. Michalopoulos, S., & Papaioannou, E. (2013), Pre-colonial ethnic institutions and contemporary African development. *Econometrica, 81*(1), 113–52.

15. He has denied these charges, and suggested they were fabricated by his election rivals.

16. Aschauer, D. A. (1989), Is public expenditure productive? *Journal of Monetary Economics, 23*(2), 177–200.

17. Rives, J. M., & Heaney, M. T. (1995), Infrastructure and local economic development. *Journal of Regional Analysis and Policy, 25*(1), 58–73.

18. For research on China in Africa, see Oqubay, A., & Lin, J. Y. (eds.) (2019), *China–Africa and an Economic Transformation* (Oxford: Oxford University Press); Taylor, I. (2007), *China and Africa: Engagement and Compromise* (Abingdon: Routledge); Rotberg, R. I. (ed.) (2009), *China into Africa: Trade, Aid, and Influence* (Washington, DC: Brookings Institution Press).

19. Stiglitz, J., Lin, J. Yifu, & Monga, C. (2013), The rejuvenation of industrial policy: policy research. World Bank Working Paper No. 6628.

20. Williamson, O. E. (2000), The new institutional economics: taking stock, looking ahead. *Journal of Economic Literature, 38*(3), 595–613.

21. Chenery, H. B. (1961), Comparative advantage and development policy. *The American Economic Review, 51*(1), 19.

22. Goldin, I. (1990), Comparative advantage: theory and application to developing country agriculture. OECD Development Centre Working Paper No. 16.

23. Yeaple, S. R., & Golub, S. S. (2007), International productivity differences, infrastructure, and comparative advantage. *Review of International Economics, 15*(2), 223–42; Chatterjee, A. (2017), Endogenous comparative advantage, gains from trade and symmetry-breaking. *Journal of International Economics, 109*, 102–15.

24. Wong, M. D., & Buba, J. (2017), *Special Economic Zones: An Operational Review of Their Impacts* (Washington, DC: World Bank Group), 12.

25. Wong, M. D., & Buba, J. (2017), *Special Economic Zones: An Operational Review of Their Impacts* (Washington, DC: World Bank Group), 12.

26. Polanyi, K. (1944), *The Great Transformation* (Boston, MA: Beacon Press).

27. Sahlins, M. (1972), *Stone Age Economics* (New York: de Gruyter).

28. Gudeman, S. (2001), *The Anthropology of Economy: Community, Market, and Culture* (Oxford: Blackwell); Wilk, R., & Cloggett, L. (2018), *Economies and Cultures: Foundations of Economic Anthropology* (New York: Routledge); Plattner, S. (1989), *Economic Anthropology* (Stanford, CA: Stanford University Press).

29. Hann, C. (2017), The Anthropocene and anthropology: micro and macro perspectives. *European Journal of Social Theory, 20*(1), 183–96.

30. Mauss, M. (1990), *The Gift: The Form and Reason for Exchange in Archaic Societies* (London: Routledge); Malinowski, B. (1922), *Argonauts of the Western Pacific* (London: Routledge).

31. Geertz, C. (1979), Suq: the bazaar economy in Sefrou, in Rosen, L. (ed.), *Meaning and Order in Contemporary Morocco: Three Essays in Cultural Analysis* (Cambridge: Cambridge University Press), 123–314.

32. Bohannan, P. (1959), The impact of money on an African subsistence economy. *The Journal of Economic History, 19*(4), 491–503; Dalton, G. (1965), Primitive money. *American Anthropologist, 67*(1), 44–65.

33. Wilk, R. R. (2019), *The Household Economy: Reconsidering the Domestic Mode of Production* (London: Routledge).

34. Scott, J. (1976), *The Moral Economy of the Peasant: Rebellion and Subsistence in Southeast Asia* (New Haven, CT: Yale University Press); Gudeman, S., Gutierrez, A. R., & Rivera, A. (1990), *Conversations in Colombia: The Domestic Economy in Life and Text* (Cambridge: Cambridge University Press).

35. Strathern, M. (1999), *Property, Substance, and Effect: Anthropological Essays on Persons and Things* (London: Athlone Press).

36. Appadurai, A. (1986), *The Social Life of Things: Commodities in Cultural Perspective* (Cambridge: Cambridge University Press).

37. Ferguson, J. (1990), *The Anti-Politics Machine: 'Development', Depoliticization and Bureaucratic Power in Lesotho* (Minneapolis, MN: University of Minnesota Press).

38. Ferguson, J. (1990), *The Anti-Politics Machine: 'Development', Depoliticization and Bureaucratic Power in Lesotho* (Minneapolis, MN: University of Minnesota Press).

39. Rodgers, C. (2020), The 'host' label: forming and transforming a community identity at the Kakuma refugee camp. *Journal of Refugee Studies.*

40. Betts, A., Omata, N., & Sterck, O. (2020), Self-reliance and social networks: explaining refugees' reluctance to relocate from Kakuma to Kalobeyei. *Journal of Refugee Studies, 33*(1), 62–85.

41. Winters, L. A., & Martins, P. M. (2004), *Beautiful but Costly: Business Costs in Small Remote Economies* (London: Commonwealth Secretariat).

42. The 'business canvas model' has become the basis for business start-up training around the world. See for example, the work of Alexander Osterwalder: Osterwalder, A., Pigneur, Y., Smith, A., & Etiemble, F. (2020), *The Invincible Company: How to Constantly Reinvent Your Organization with Inspiration from the World's Best Business Models* (London: John Wiley & Sons).

43. Betts, A., & Delius, A. (2020), An impact evaluation of the World Economic Forum's Executive Leadership and Entrepreneurship Programme in Kakuma Refugee Camp (unpublished paper).

CHAPTER 13

1. OAS (2019), Report of the OAS Working Group to address the regional crisis caused by Venezuela's migrant and refugee flows, available at: http://www.oas.org/documents/eng/press/OAS-Report-to-Address-the-regional-crisis-caused-by-Venezuelas-migrant.pdf

2. World Bank (2018), Migracion desde Venezuela a Colombia: Impactos y estrategia de respuesta en el corto y mediano plazo, (Washington, DC: World Bank).

3. Data presented by Felipe Muñoz (2019), Advisor to the president of Colombia on the Venezuelan border situation, at meeting at Brasenose College, Oxford, 17th September.

4. Data provided by the national public employment agency (SENA) office in Cucuta.

5. These points are summarized in Betts, A. (2019), *Venezuela's Survival Migration as a Development Opportunity—Mission Report* (Oxford: Refugee Studies Centre), available at: https://www.rsc.ox.ac.uk/files/files-1/research-in-brief-12-venezuelan-survival-migration.pdf Betts, A. (2019), Why Venezuelan migrants need to be recognised as refugees, *New Humanitarian*, 27 February, available at: https://www.thenewhumanitarian.org/opinion/2019/02/27/why-venezuelan-migrants-need-be-regarded-refugees

6. Betts, A. (2013), *Survival Migration: Failed Governance and the Crisis of Displacement* (Ithaca, NY: Cornell University Press).

7. Colombia Reports (2019), Duque launches four-year development plan, 28 May, available at: https://colombiareports.com/colombias-president-duque-launches-4-year-development-plan/

8. Global Concessional Finance Facility (2019), Colombia eligible for GCFF support for inflows of Venezuelan national and host communities, available at: https://globalcff.org/colombia-eligible-for-global-concessional-financing-facility-support-for-inflows-of-venezuelan-nationals-and-hosting-communities/

9. UNHCR (2019), *Guidance Note on International Protection Considerations for Venezuelans* (Geneva: UNHCR), available at: https://data2.unhcr.org/en/documents/details/69883

10. EU External Action (2019), International Solidarity Conference on the Venezuelan Refugee and Migrant Crisis, available at: https://eeas.europa.eu/headquarters/headquarters-homepage/68374/international-solidarity-conference-venezuelan-refugee-and-migrant-crisis_en

11. For background on the politics of the Colombia borderlands, see: Idler, A. (2019), *Borderland Battles: Violence, Crime, and Governance at the Edges of Colombia's War* (Oxford: Oxford University Press).

12. Betts, A., Ali, A., & Memisoglu, F. (2017), *The Local Politics of the Syrian Refugee Crisis: Exploring Responses in Turkey, Lebanon, and Jordan* (Oxford: Refugee Studies Centre).

13. Betts, A., & Collier, P. (2015), Help refugees help themselves: let displaced Syrians join the labor market, *Foreign Affairs*, November/December.
14. Interviews with UNHCR Staff, Geneva, December 2019.
15. For critiques of the Jordan Compact, see, for example: Lenner, K., & Turner, L. (2018), Making refugees work? The politics of integrating Syrian refugees into the labor market in Jordan. *Middle East Critique*, *28*(1), 65–95; Barbelet, V., Hagen-Zanker, J., & Mansour-Ille, D. (2018), *The Jordan Compact: Lessons Learnt and Implications for Future Refugee Compacts* (London: ODI).
16. One indication of further progress came on 7th February 2021 when President Duque announced that all Venezuelans in Colombia would be granted legal status.

CHAPTER 14

1. ILO (2020), *Protecting Migrant Workers During the COVID-19 Pandemic, Policy Brief* (Geneva: ILO).
2. DFID (2020), International assistance approach to COVID-19 in fragile states and humanitarian emergencies. Background paper for DFID roundtable, Thursday, 7 May.
3. Arendt, H. (1951), *The Origins of Totalitarianism* (Orlando, FL: A Harvest Book).
4. Pew (2019), Despite Global Concerns About Democracy, More than Half of Countries are Democratic (Washington, DC: Pew), available at: https://www.pewresearch.org/fact-tank/2019/05/14/more-than-half-of-countries-are-democratic/
5. Fransen, S., & de Haas, H. (2019), *The Volume and Geography of Forced Migration* (Washington, DC: International Migration Institute).
6. Pew (2019), Despite Global Concerns About Democracy, More than Half of Countries are Democratic (Washington, DC: Pew), available at: https://www.pewresearch.org/fact-tank/2019/05/14/more-than-half-of-countries-are-democratic/
7. Levitsky, S., & Way, L.A. (2002), Elections without democracy: the rise of competitive authoritarianism. *Journal of Democracy*, *13*(2), 51–65; Ottaway, M. (2013), *Democracy Challenged: The Rise of Semi-Authoritarianism* (Washington, DC: Carnegie Endowment).
8. Kendall-Taylor, A., Lindstaedt, N., & Frantz, E. (2019), *Democracies and Authoritarian Regimes* (Oxford: Oxford University Press).
9. Wolf, M. (2019), The rise of populist authoritarians. *Financial Times*, 22 January, available at: https://www.ft.com/content/4faf6c4e-1d84-11e9-b2f7-97e4dbd3580d
10. Svolik, M. (2008), Authoritarian reversals and democratic consolidation. *American Political Science Review*, *102*(2), 53–68; Svolik, M. W. (2012), *The Politics of Authoritarian Rule* (Cambridge: Cambridge University Press; Fuller, C. R. (2017), Cooperative authoritarians and regime stability. *New Global Studies*, *11*(1), 1–28.

11. Roth, K. (2020), How authoritarians are exploiting the COVID-19 crisis to grab power, available at: https://www.hrw.org/news/2020/04/04/how-authoritarians-are-exploiting-covid-19-crisis-grab-power

12. Pettersson, T., Högbladh, S., & Öberg, M. (2019), Organized violence, 1989–2018 and peace agreements. *Journal of Peace Research*, *56*(4), 589–603.

13. Pettersson, T., Högbladh, S., & Öberg, M. (2019), Organized violence, 1989–2018 and peace agreements. *Journal of Peace Research*, *56*(4), 589–603.

14. Fransen, S., & de Haas, H. (2019), *The Volume and Geography of Forced Migration* (Washington, DC: International Migration Institute).

15. On the relationship between economic shocks and internal armed conflict, see, for example: Chassang, S., & Miquel, G. P. (2009), Economic shocks and civil war. *Quarterly Journal of Political Science*, *4*(3), 211–28; Kim, N., & Conceição, P. (2010), The economic crisis, violent conflict, and human development. *International Journal of Peace Studies*, *15*(1), 29–43; Collier, P. (2003), *Breaking the Conflict Trap: Civil War and Development Policy* (Washington, DC: World Bank); Collier, P., & Hoeffler, A. (2005), Resource rents, governance, and conflict. *Journal of Conflict Resolution*, *49*(4), 625–33; Stewart, F., & Fitzgerald, V. (2001), *War and Underdevelopment: Country Experiences* (vol. 2) (Oxford: Oxford University Press).

16. Miguel, E., Satyanath, S., & Sergenti, E. (2004), Economic shocks and civil conflict: an instrumental variables approach. *Journal of Political Economy*, *112*(4), 725–53.

17. Collier, P., Hoeffler, A., & Rohner, D. (2009), Beyond greed and grievance: feasibility and civil war. *Oxford Economic Papers*, *61*(1), 1–27.

18. Janus, T., & Riera-Crichton, D. (2015), Economic shocks, civil war and ethnicity. *Journal of Development Economics*, *115*, 32–44.

19. Dube, O., & Vargas, J. F. (2013), Commodity price shocks and civil conflict: evidence from Colombia. *The Review of Economic Studies*, *80*(4), 1384–421.

20. Fearon, J. D., & Laitin, D. D. (2003), Ethnicity, insurgency, and civil war. *American Political Science Review*, *97*(1), 75–90.

21. Collier, P., & Hoeffler, A. (1998), On the economic causes of civil war. *Oxford Economic Papers*, *50*, 563–73.

22. The New Humanitarian (2020), Rebel splits and failed peace talks drive new violence in Congo's Ituri, 17 May, available at: https://www.thenewhumanitarian.org/feature/2020/05/05/Ituri-Congo-Hema-Lendu-CODECO-demobilisation

23. For a critique of the concept of 'fragile and failed states' see, for example, Call, C. T. (2008), The fallacy of 'the fragile state'. *Third World Quarterly*, *29*(8): 1491–507.

24. Betts, A. (2013), *Survival Migration: Failed Governance and the Crisis of Displacement* (Ithaca, NY: Cornell University Press), 10–28.

25. Teachout, M., & Zipfel, C. (2020), *The Economic Impact of COVID-19 Lockdowns in Sub-Saharan Africa* (London: International Growth Centre).

26. Carment, D., Samy, Y., & Prest, S. (2008), State fragility and implications for aid allocation: an empirical analysis. *Conflict Management and Peace Science, 25*(4), 349–73.

27. ILO (2017), *World Social Protection Report, 2017–19* (Geneva: ILO).

28. Decerf, B., Ferreira, F. H., Mahler, D. G., & Sterck, O. (2020), Lives and livelihoods: development research. World Bank Working Paper.

29. Alkire, S., Dirksen, J., Nogales, R., & Oldiges, C. (2020), Multidimensional poverty and COVID-19 risk factors: a rapid overview of interlinked deprivations across 5.7 billion people. OPHI Briefing No. 53.

30. Dempster, H. et al. (2020), *Labor Market Impacts of COVID-19 on Forced Migrants* (Washington, DC: Center for Global Development).

31. ILO (2020), *Facing Double Crises: Rapid Assessment of the Impact of COVID-19 on Vulnerable Workers in Jordan* (Geneva: ILO).

32. Woods, N. (2020), Global governance: planning for the world after COVID-19, in World Economic Forum (ed.), *Challenges and Opportunities in the Post-COVID-19 World* (Geneva: WEF), 8–11, available at: http://www3.weforum.org/docs/WEF_Challenges_and_Opportunities_Post_COVID_19.pdf

33. See, for example, Angell, N. (1933), *The Great Illusion* (London: William Heinemann); and Carr, E. H. (1939) *The Twenty Years' Crisis* (London: Palgrave Macmillan).

34. Dabla-Norris, E., Minoiu, C., & Zanna, L.-P. (2010), Business cycle fluctuations, large shocks, and development aid: new evidence. IMF Working Papers No. 10/240.

35. World Bank (2020), How the World Bank is helping countries with Covid-19 (Washington, DC: World Bank), https://www.worldbank.org/en/news/factsheet/2020/02/11/how-the-world-bank-group-is-helping-countries-with-covid-19-coronavirus

36. OCHA (2020), Consolidated Covid-19 related humanitarian appeal, available at: https://fts.unocha.org/appeals/952/summary

37. World Bank (2020), World Bank predicts sharpest decline in remittances in recent history (Washington, DC: World Bank), available at: https://www.worldbank.org/en/news/press-release/2020/04/22/world-bank-predicts-sharpest-decline-of-remittances-in-recent-history

38. Goodhart, D. (2017), *The Road to Somewhere: The Populist Revolt and the Future of Politics* (London: C. Hurst & Co.).

39. Bloomfield, J. (2017), *Dangerous Road to Divisive Places*, Open Democracy, available at: https://www.opendemocracy.net/en/opendemocracyuk/dangerous-road-to-divisive-places

40. Norris, P., & Inglehart, R. (2019), *Cultural Backlash: Trump, Brexit, and Authoritarian Populism* (Cambridge: Cambridge University Press).

41. Dennison, J., & Geddes, A. (2019), A rising tide? The salience of immigration and the rise of anti-immigration political parties in Western Europe. *The Political Quarterly, 90*(1), 107–16.

42. Blinder, S., & Allen, W. L. (2016), Constructing immigrants: portrayals of migrant groups in British national newspapers, 2010–2012. *International Migration Review*, *50*(1), 3–40; Stockemer, D. Niemann. A, Unger, D., & Speyer, J. (2019), The 'refugee crisis', immigration attitudes, and Euroscepticism. *International Migration Review* (available online).

43. For analysis of the relationship between the 2008–9 global recession and migration, see, for example: Fix, M., Papademetriou, D. G., Batalova, J., Terrazas, A., Lin, S. Y. Y., & Mittelstadt, M. (2009), *Migration and the Global Recession* (Washington, DC: Migration Policy Institute); Rogers, A., Anderson, B., & Clark, N. (2009), *Recession, Vulnerable Workers and Immigration* (Oxford: COMPAS).

44. For analysis of the relationship between recession and attitudes to immigration, see, for example: Isaksen, J. V. (2019), The impact of the financial crisis on European attitudes toward immigration. *Comparative Migration Studies*, *7*(1), 24; see also: Dancygier, R., & Donnelly, M. (2014), Attitudes toward immigration in good times and bad, in Bermeo, N., & Bartels, L (eds.), *Mass Politics in Tough Times: Opinions, Votes, and Protest in the Great Recession* (Oxford: Oxford University Press).

45. Savelkoul, M., Gesthuizen, M., & Scheepers, P. (2011), Explaining relationships between ethnic diversity and informal social capital across European countries and regions: tests of constrict, conflict and contact theory. *Social Science Research*, *40*(4), 1091–107.

46. Reidy, E. (2020), The COVID-19 excuse? How migration policies are hardening around the globe. *The New Humanitarian*, available at: https://www.thenewhumanitarian.org/analysis/2020/04/17/coronavirus-global-migration-policies-exploited

47. Benton, M. (2020), *The Rocky Road to a Mobile World after COVID-19* (Washington, DC: Migration Policy Institute), available at: https://www.migrationpolicy.org/news/rocky-road-mobile-world-after-covid-19

48. Bauman, Z. (1998), *Globalization: The Human Consequences* (New York: Columbia University Press).

49. Jacobsen, K. (2002), Livelihoods in conflict: the pursuit of livelihoods by refugees and the impact on the human security of host communities. *International Migration*, *40*(5), 95–123.

50. Peloza, J. (2009), The challenge of measuring financial impacts from investments in corporate social performance. *Journal of Management*, *35*(6), 1518–41; Reverte, C. (2012), The impact of better corporate social responsibility disclosure on the cost of equity capital. *Corporate Social Responsibility and Environmental Management*, *19*(5), 253–72.

51. For an overview of the role of financial disclosures in the climate change context, see: Stanny, E., & Ely, K. (2008), Corporate environmental disclosures about the effects of climate change. *Corporate Social Responsibility and Environmental Management*, *15*(6), 338–48; Carney, M. (2015), Breaking the tragedy of the horizon–climate change and financial stability. Speech given at

Lloyd's of London, 29 September, available at: https://www.bankofengland.co.uk/speech/2015/breaking-the-tragedy-of-the-horizon-climate-change-and-financial-stability

52. Willitts-King, B., Bryant, J., & Spencer, A. (2019), *Valuing Local Resources in Humanitarian Crises* (London: Overseas Development Institute).

53. Patel, L., Razzaq, F., & Sosis, K. (2019), Assessing the potential for off-grid power interventions in Turkana County with a focus on the communities around Kakuma and Kalobeyei. Energy 4 Impact, available at: https://www.energy4impact.org/assessing-potential-grid-power-interventions-turkana-county-0

54. ICRC (2017), The world's first 'Humanitarian Impact Bond' launched to transform financing of aid in conflict-hit countries, available at: https://www.icrc.org/en/document/worlds-first-humanitarian-impact-bond-launched-transform-financing-aid-conflict-hit

55. UNHCR-IOM (2020), *COVID-19 and Mixed Population Movements: Emerging Dynamics, Risks, and Opportunities* (Geneva: UNHCR-IOM).

56. Betts, A., Memisoglu, F., & Ali, A. (2020), What difference do mayors make? The role of municipal authorities in Turkey and Lebanon's response to Syrian refugees. *Journal of Refugee Studies* (available online).

57. Erdoğdu, S. (2018), Syrian refugees in Turkey and trade union responses. *Globalizations*, 15(6), 838–53.

58. Kumin, J. (2015), *Welcoming Engagement: How Private Sponsorship Can Strengthen Refugee Resettlement in the European Union* (Brussels: Migration Policy Institute Europe).

59. Hall, N. (2019), Norm contestation in the digital era: campaigning for refugee rights. *International Affairs*, 95(3), 575–95.

60. Pincock, K., Betts, A., & Easton-Calabria, E. (2020), *The Global Governed? Refugees as Providers of Protection and Assistance* (Cambridge: Cambridge University Press).

61. Betts, A., Easton-Calabria, E., & Pincock, K. (2020), Why refugees are as an asset in the fight against COVID-19, *The Conversation*, available at: https://theconversation.com/why-refugees-are-an-asset-in-the-fight-against-coronavirus-136099

62. Betts, A., Easton-Calabria, E., & Pincock, K. (2020), Why refugees are as an asset in the fight against COVID-19, *The Conversation*, available at: https://theconversation.com/why-refugees-are-an-asset-in-the-fight-against-coronavirus-136099

63. Pincock, K., Betts, A., & Easton-Calabria, E. (2020), *The Global Governed? Refugees as Providers of Protection and Assistance* (Cambridge: Cambridge University Press).

CHAPTER 15

1. Clemens, M. A. (2014), Does development reduce migration? CGD Working Paper No. 359; De Haas, H. (2007), Turning the tide? Why development will not stop migration. *Development and Change*, 38(5), 819–41.

2. Hainmueller, J., & Hopkins, D. J. (2014), Public attitudes toward immigration. *Annual Review of Political Science, 17,* 225–49.

3. Dinas, E., Matakos, K., Xefteris, D., & Hangartner, D. (2019), Waking up the golden dawn: does exposure to the refugee crisis increase support for extreme-right parties? *Political Analysis, 27*(2), 244–54.

4. Bansak, K., Hainmueller, J., & Hangartner, D. (2016), How economic, humanitarian, and religious concerns shape European attitudes toward asylum seekers. *Science, 354*(6309), 217–22.

5. Tsourapas, G. (2019), The Syrian refugee crisis and foreign policy decision-making in Jordan, Lebanon, and Turkey. *Journal of Global Security Studies, 4*(4), 464–81.

6. Betts, A. (2009), *Protection by Persuasion: International Cooperation in the Refugee Regime* (Ithaca, NY: Cornell University Press); Paoletti, E. (2010), *The Migration of Power and North–South Inequalities: The Case of Italy and Libya* (Basingstoke: Palgrave Macmillan).

7. Schmidt, A. (2014), Status determination and recognition, in Betts, A., & Orchard, P. (eds.), *Implementation and World Politics: How International Norms Change Practice* (Oxford: Oxford University Press), 248–68; Orchard, P. (2014), Implementing a global internally displaced persons protection regime, in Betts, A., & Orchard, P. (eds.), *Implementation and World Politics: How International Norms Change Practice* (Oxford: Oxford University Press), 105–23.

8. Clapham, C. (1996), *Africa and the International System: The Politics of State Survival* (Cambridge: Cambridge University Press).

9. Milner, J. (2009), *Refugees, the State and the Politics of Asylum in Africa* (London: Palgrave Macmillan).

10. Williamson, O. E. (2000), The new institutional economics: taking stock, looking ahead. *Journal of Economic Literature, 38*(3), 595–613; Akerlof, G. A., & Kranton, R. (2010), Identity economics. *The Economists' Voice, 7*(2), 1–3.

11. Banerjee, A. V., & Duflo, E. (2007), The economic lives of the poor. *Journal of Economic Perspectives, 21*(1), 141–68.

12. Alix-Garcia, J., & Saah, D. (2010), The effect of refugee inflows on host communities: evidence from Tanzania. *The World Bank Economic Review, 24*(1), 148–70; Maystadt, J. F., & Verwimp, P. (2009), Winners and losers among a refugee-hosting population. ECORE Discussion Paper; Sanghi, A., Onder, H., & Vemuru, V. (2016), *'Yes' in My Backyard: The Economics of Refugees and Their Social Dynamics in Kakuma, Kenya* (Washington, DC: World Bank).

13. Ferguson, J. (1990), *The Anti-Politics Machine: 'Development', Depoliticization and Bureaucratic Power in Lesotho* (Minneapolis, MN: University of Minnesota Press).

14. Betts, A., Bradenbrink, R., Greenland, J., Omata, N., & Sterck, O. (2019), *Refugee Economies in Dollo Ado: Development Opportunities in a Border Region of Ethiopia* (Oxford: Refugee Studies Centre).

15. Betts, A., Omata, N., & Sterck, O. (2020), Self-reliance and social networks: explaining refugees' reluctance to relocate from Kakuma to Kalobeyei. *Journal of Refugee Studies, 33*(1), 62–85.

16. Sterck, O., Rodgers, C., Flinder Stierna, M., Siu, J., & Betts, A. (2020), *Cash Transfer Models and Debt in the Kalobeyei Settlement* (Oxford: Refugee Studies Centre).

17. Betts, A., Chaara, I., Omata, N., & Sterck, O. (2018), *Refugee Economies in Uganda* (Oxford: Refugee Studies Centre).

18. Fiddian-Qasmiyeh, E. (2014), *The Ideal Refugees: Gender, Islam, and the Sahrawi Politics of Survival* (Syracuse, NY: Syracuse University Press).

19. Chatty, D. (2010), *Displacement and Dispossession in the Modern Middle East* (Cambridge: Cambridge University Press).

20. McConnachie, K. (2014), *Governing Refugees: Justice, Order and Legal Pluralism* (Abingdon: Routledge).

21. Pincock, K., Betts, A., & Easton-Calabria, E. (2020), *The Global Governed? Refugees as Providers of Protection and Assistance* (Cambridge: Cambridge University Press).

Index

For the benefit of digital users, indexed terms that span two pages (e.g., 52–53) may, on occasion, appear on only one of those pages.